The Deaths of Others

THE DEATHS OF OTHERS
The Fate of Civilians in America's Wars

John Tirman

OXFORD
UNIVERSITY PRESS

OXFORD
UNIVERSITY PRESS

Oxford University Press, Inc., publishes works that further
Oxford University's objective of excellence
in research, scholarship, and education.

Oxford   New York
Auckland   Cape Town   Dar es Salaam   Hong Kong   Karachi
Kuala Lumpur   Madrid   Melbourne   Mexico City   Nairobi
New Delhi   Shanghai   Taipei   Toronto

With offices in
Argentina   Austria   Brazil   Chile   Czech Republic   France   Greece
Guatemala   Hungary   Italy   Japan   Poland   Portugal   Singapore
South Korea   Switzerland   Thailand   Turkey   Ukraine   Vietnam

Published by Oxford University Press, Inc.
198 Madison Avenue, New York, NY 10016

www.oup.com

Oxford is a registered trademark of Oxford University Press

Library of Congress Cataloging-in-Publication Data
Tirman, John.
The deaths of others : the fate of civilians in America's wars / John Tirman.
   p.   cm.
Includes bibliographical references.
ISBN 978-0-19-538121-4 (hbk. : acid-free paper) 1. United States—History, Military—20th century.
2. United States—History, Military—21st century. 3. United States—Military policy.
4. Civilians in war. 5. Battle casualties. 6. War and society—United States.
7. Militarism—United States. 8. United States—Foreign public opinion. I. Title.
E840.4.T57   2011
355.00973—dc22   2010046707

1 3 5 7 9 8 6 4 2

Printed in the United States of America
on acid-free paper

For Coco

CONTENTS

The Deaths of Others

Introduction

Death and Remembrance in American Wars

A friend and I were walking across the National Mall in Washington, D.C., one day in the spring of 2009 and happened upon the Korean War Memorial, which I had never seen closely. It commemorates the Americans who died protecting South Korea from an invasion by North Korea; some three million people died in the three-year war, more than 30,000 of them U.S. soldiers. The memorial was striking in design, with its platoon of bronze-cast soldiers, frozen in time, making its way through the mud and cold, and the eerie photographic images on an adjacent marble wall. But one thing was missing—any mention of the Korean people. Even the South Korean forces were lumped together with all the countries that served under the UN command. We then ventured across to the Vietnam War Memorial, which I had visited before and which had always struck me powerfully, probably because the 58,000 names of the dead on the Wall were men and women of my generation. But I noticed that here, too, there was no reference to the people these memorialized men and women were there to protect. It was as if, in these two conflagrations, only the Americans could be cited, only their deaths mattered: not even the place or the call-to-arms merited more than a glancing note.

One of the most remarkable aspects of American wars is how little we discuss the victims who are not Americans. The costs of war to the populations and common soldiers of the "enemy" are rarely found in the narratives and dissections of conflict, and this habit is a durable feature of how we remember war. As a nation that has long thought of itself as built on Christian ethics, even as an exceptionally compassionate people, this coldness is a puzzle. It is in fact more than a puzzle, for ignorance or indifference has consequences for the victims of American wars and for America itself.

Wars can kill a great many people, and innocent people, which everyone knows but few consider more closely; it seems to be a regrettable but unavoidable fact of armed conflict. Throughout the twentieth century, it was apparent that war was killing by direct violence more and more civilians as a share of total deaths, flipping the one-to-nine ratio of civilian-to-soldier mortality in the First World War to nine-to-one in many of the ethnic conflicts that occurred after the Cold War ended. Whether this startling reversal of fortune is exactly correct is less important than the underlying reality of breathtaking civilian tolls. In that same, gruesome century, only gradual fluctuations in attitudes about war and its human cost were discernible. The horror of the carnage of the Great War in Europe probably had the most lasting impact, deflating the glorification of war that held sway for so many centuries.

Since then, however, a bleak sensibility of war's necessity has persisted, chiefly in the United States, which mostly has been spared devastation since our Civil War and has regarded itself as safeguarding the free world against fascism, communism, and terrorism. We have altered the dynamics of death in wartime—more efficient killing, more civilians than soldiers dying—but we have not altered how we think about the human consequences of war. Even the Cold War could sustain nuclear weapons of such power that the casualties in a full-out U.S.-Soviet war were estimated in the hundreds of millions, and this risk was thought acceptable by large numbers of Americans (so much so that the risk continues even though the conflict has vanished).

In the wars since the two-time use of nuclear weapons ended the Second World War in 1945, the U.S. military has been in three major wars: Korea, 1950–53; Vietnam, 1964–75; and Iraq, 1991–present.*

---

* The war in Afghanistan, now America's longest, is much smaller than the other three in the numbers of casualties among the local population. Several aspects of Operation Enduring Freedom are considered, however, as it fits patterns explored in this book.

Between one and three million people have died in each of those wars. Most of the dead were civilians. The Vietnam War and the invasion of Iraq in 2003 were of doubtful legality, making those high casualties all the more vexing. The U.S. military did not kill those six to seven million people alone. The adversaries—North Korea and China, North Vietnam and the Viet Cong, the Saddam Hussein regime in Iraq and dozens of insurgent groups—did plenty of killing, as did the armies we supported. There was a rationale attached to each American intervention, not always a compelling rationale, but one that was shaped by both a sense of national destiny and specific, perceived threats. These three wars were enormous conflicts, and with a couple of exceptions—the Chinese Civil War, which took eight million lives, and the war in the Congo, which by some estimates has five million dead—the American wars are the largest since the Second World War. So we have had, as a people, ample opportunity to experience war, if remotely, and to debate the consequences of those wars that were, paradoxically, distinct expressions of the Pax Americana.

Each of these interventions was initially popular among the American people, but they ended in political failure and public disappointment. (While I explore the Iraq War as one venture from Operation Desert Storm to the present, declining public favor applies to the main phase beginning with the 2003 invasion.) The disintegration of support for war follows notably similar patterns in each instance. "Rally-round-the-flag" zeal soon crumbles as reports of setbacks on the battlefield and American casualties mount. Whether antiwar voices are prominent or muted seems not to affect the downward cycle of public distaste for the conflict. Nor does this growing aversion in each instance stem from concern about the bloodshed spilled by the populations in the war zone. Apart from yellow ribbons and occasional hero status accorded the American troops (a recent trend) the home front was indifferent to the human costs of war. The Vietnam War (itself a misnomer, as the United States carried the war into Cambodia and Laos) generated more aversion to these human costs by peace activists and the news media than did Korea or Iraq, but even then the war opposition mainly built its case on the growing numbers of U.S. casualties and the futility of their sacrifice.

Pondering what was happening to the civilians in the distinctive kinds of mayhem that characterized each war was typically reserved to some scattered depictions of hardship in communities the United States supported (and stories of GIs rescuing them), or, far more troubling, reports of atrocities. The nature of war, and the new wars in which combatants mix with civilians routinely, yields atrocities on all sides. It perhaps bespeaks American innocence that My Lai or Haditha could provoke bursts of surprised and tearful outrage. But they did, at least initially, and for a brief time focused a dimming spotlight on the conduct of a few misbehaving soldiers or marines. Such episodes of war coverage were perhaps typical of the news media, fixating, however glancingly, on a spectacular case and missing the quotidian reality of what war does to a society that is torn by opposing forces, suffers saturation bombing and house-to-house incursions, has millions forced from their towns and villages, copes with poisoned soil and water and ruined crops, and feels and sees death everywhere. For years in each place, this suffocating trauma of war—the senseless brutalizing of civilians—escaped Americans' notice or sympathy, appeared very rarely in literature or film, stirred virtually no debate or calls for new policies, and never seemed to be at the roots of disgust with the war.

The question, then, is why: why were civilians so badly mistreated? Why does this mistreatment persist under U.S. political and military leadership? And why are Americans so indifferent to these massive human tragedies?

Several suppositions litter that series of why's, and in the following chapters I address each one empirically. Did civilians suffer excessively? Certainly, the scale of mortality and displacement, to say nothing of postwar traumas, is very high. Was the United States responsible for this suffering? In league with others, yes, though I suggest that in Indochina and Iraq, the United States has primary culpability. The harder question is how much of this "collateral damage" is intentional, or merely callous. That American elites and the broader public do not seem to care much about innocent bystanders in the wars we begin is not really in dispute. But, again, the question is why: is it a product of political culture, as many suggest, or a more universal response to war by major powers that are not suffering from war's disturbances? And does this indifference matter?

This topic has been missing from public discourse and academic studies alike. Most academic treatments of war look at causes, behavior of states, military strategies, effects on other states, and the like. Some interest in analyzing genocide is surfacing, but it has little to do with America. The human element, apart from a nascent interest in human rights, is almost entirely missing. A new emphasis on "human security" (in contrast to the security of states) has not gained much footing inside the university, much less U.S. politics. Sociology and anthropology view wars more closely and with more attention to impacts on humans, but the work of these traditions in the war zones of Korea, Indochina, and Iraq is very limited. So, too, are the voices of the victims, at least in English, and this constrains the scholar's ability to address the social consequences of war (particularly as in two of the venues I examine a repressive state that remains in place, and in Iraq the grappling with war's effects is only beginning). As a result, the study of war stays focused on causes, military strategy, and relationships between states.

One cannot escape the sensation, however, that the lack of attention to this topic derives from more than just indifference or oversight. During the Israeli-Hezbollah war in the summer of 2006 and the Israeli siege of Gaza in 2008–2009, for example, the major American newspapers had dozens of editorials and many news stories about the targeting of civilians, as well as the consequences of that action. Why so little attention to the Iraq War, which during the summer war in Lebanon was frenzied with violence, with as many people dying in any two days as were killed in Lebanon during the entire skirmish? Large natural disasters—the tsunami in Asia in 2004 and the earthquake in Haiti in 2010—earn extensive news media coverage and an outpouring of generosity from Americans, both of which are laudable, but neither of those disasters actually caused as much human damage as has the long war in Iraq. One wonders if the American-made disasters are simply too painful to discuss, even by those policy makers, journalists, and academics who are meant to do so.

The squeamishness Americans feel about addressing the very raw questions posed in this book is perhaps normal. It is not likely that Britain or France, with their many colonial wars, have been more forthright about their occasionally brutal behavior, to say nothing of the Soviet Union. But this is a book about the United States, and it is notable how little we discuss American wars in any but very rote ways about winning, toughness, American heroism, and letting "slip the dogs of war." The consequences for American society—the financial costs, the flotsam of American casualties—also earn some uneasy attention for a time. Academic discourse follows the same path. And this is a country that has a lot of wars and a lot of popular literature and films and television programs about war, and yet the interest in what happened to the Koreans, Vietnamese, and Iraqis is almost nonexistent.

When civilian casualties are discussed, it is typically undertaken in ways that explain how carefully the U.S. military avoids collateral damage. This, too, is to be expected, since U.S. policy makers and other elites have often demonstrated sensitivity to the potential for a negative public reaction if the United States appears to be too unsympathetic to civilian suffering. (The political and military leaders tend to be more worried about foreign opinion than American, and that is a correct perception, since it is mainly foreigners who express disgust at war's destruction.) So, for example, Lyndon Johnson disavowed intent to harm civilians in the bombing of North Vietnam, and Donald Rumsfeld stated that Americans don't kill civilians, terrorists do. The apologists for American behavior range across the political spectrum and typically settle on a few devices to ward off closer inspection: the U.S. military has rules in place to protect civilians; the bad behavior of a few do not reflect the broader conduct of soldiers in the war; the enemy and its sympathizers exaggerate civilian casualties; the other side is worse, and so on. The topic of culpability for very large-scale civilian suffering is deflected by reference to the essential rightness of the war, its ultimate benefits to those very populations under siege, and the good intentions of Americans abroad. Actual practices and consequences are thus shuffled to the side, and the conventional wisdom is secured.

Concern with civilian death is channeled toward the academy and jurisprudence, namely, a philosophical interest evolving over the twentieth century that addresses "noncombatant immunity," now drawing on a legal basis in the Geneva Conventions. The Conventions, which became international law in 1949 (with Additional Protocols in 1977) sanction warring states and occupying forces from "violence to life and person, in particular murder of all kinds, mutilation, cruel treatment and torture . . . [and] outrages upon personal dignity, in particular humiliating and degrading treatment," among other strictures, specifically with reference to civilians. The rules imbedded in the Conventions are subscribed to by the U.S. government, and while there has been ample discord on their scope and application in Washington, the United States generally accepts the moral and legal obligations the Conventions embody. Treatment of detainees came under special scrutiny during the "war on terrorism," precisely because the Conventions were being violated. The protection of civilians more broadly gains less attention—there was far more coverage of a few detainees at Guantanamo than of the entire civilian population of Iraq—but the Geneva accords remain the legal norm to which military and civilian leaders pay homage.

This legal and philosophical tradition is useful: it is taught in war colleges and finds its way into some military training, as it does engage directly the matter of whether attacks on civilians can ever be justified, and tries to set out some rules for this quandary. In many respects, this is a narrowly legal discourse and largely divorced from the realities of war. What policy makers and legal advisers claim the U.S. military is doing and what is actually happening on the ground may be—and often are—two entirely different things. Concerns with noncombatant immunity also draw on a "just war" discourse that is significantly unsuited to the vagaries of contemporary conflict. If one were to take the thrust of "just war" arguments and apply them to the Iraq War, one could claim that all insurgent attacks on Americans are justified because the invasion was not legal, was conducted under false pretenses, and therefore, every single American in Iraq is fair game. By the same reasoning, all deaths caused by the U.S. military are wrong and possibly could be classed as war crimes. Conversely, since nearly all Arab Iraqis in the 2004–2007 period wanted the U.S. military to leave, and many thought attacks on Americans were justifiable, then an argument could be made that (if one considered the invasion to be legal, perhaps post hoc) U.S. attacks on civilians were justifiable on the basis of their support for insurgency. In other words, the just war tradition, however well meaning, and accompanying arguments about noncombatant immunity, are not merely detached but malleable and thereby not compelling. A strict constructionist reading of the Geneva Protocol is far more useful.

Legal strictures notwithstanding, more constraints on the use of military firepower against civilians will come about only if we understand fully the human consequences of war. Whether or not this book fills in some of the gaps in our understanding of civilian suffering in war remains to be seen. It was spurred by my involvement with one attempt to account for the dead of Iraq. I was struck by how little attention there was to civilian deaths and displacement in Iraq from the outset of the 2003 war. The first attempt I knew of —the article published in a British medical journal, *The Lancet*, in October 2004 estimating that 98,000 Iraqis (not just civilians) had died in the first eighteen months of the war—got virtually no attention at all. I spoke with the principal author, an epidemiologist at the Johns Hopkins School of Public Health, a leading institution, and found myself drawn to this topic. Apart from the emotional impact of learning about the scale of killing, this magnitude explained, as no other account did, why the insurgency rose so quickly and ferociously in Iraq. Other explanations, notably, that Sunni Arabs were deprived of their status, seemed inadequate or at least incomplete. The killing or roughing up of Iraqis by U.S. troops, putting many thousands in a Dickensian detention system, disrespecting social norms, and so on, had alienated many tens of thousands; and in the dense kinship networks of Iraq, this sparked obligations of revenge and of defending one's community. And this would be significant only if the killing itself had been sizable. Heuristically, then, this appeared to be a significant finding: the U.S. military was battling an insurgency that was to some important degree one of its own making, and the methods of battling it only intensified that very response of resistance. To explore this further, I commissioned another household survey with a different lead researcher, also at Hopkins, from a program I headed at the MIT Center for International Studies. This survey, taken in the late spring of 2006, found an astonishing 655,000 "excess deaths" attributable to the war, 90 percent by violence, and about a third attributed to U.S. firepower. If this was indeed the case, if even half true, then the violence of the war was far more understandable than its being an ethnic rivalry or loss-of-status issue. The Iraqis were being attacked, and they were fighting back. But another aspect of the mortality study we commissioned was disturbing—the public remained utterly unmoved by this scale of carnage, and indeed the pro-war advocates dismissed the findings altogether (including

President George W. Bush in a press conference the day after the survey's release). The news media, after a one- or two-day flurry of articles, largely misinterpreted the survey techniques, making the results seem less credible. The downward trend in public support for the war at that time did not appear to be affected by the survey's results, although pollsters in the United States rarely ask about concern for the populations in war zones. So, again, the public indifference was glaring, and in my view needed to be investigated in tandem with the indifference of policy elites and indeed the policies and practices toward civilians. At the suggestion of my editor, this inquiry was expanded to the Korean and Vietnam Wars, which showed the same tendencies and patterns, the same ideological gloss, the same grisly outcomes.

As this work evolved, then, a set of patterns in American attitudes and consequent actions emerged. The argument of the book is as follows. The U.S. military, despite policies that claim to protect civilians in war zones, do not in practice do so adequately or consistently. Field commanders are given considerable leeway to deal with local conditions, particularly when U.S. troops are possibly vulnerable to attack. In Korea, initially deployed troops were poorly trained, operated in an intense "fog of war," and believed they had an acute problem of discriminating civilians from North Korean infiltrators. The saturation bombing of North Korea was conducted with nearly complete disregard for the civilian consequences. In Vietnam, discrimination was a daily challenge and led to the wholesale destruction of villages suspected (often without evidence) of communist sympathies. Officers were pressured by commanders for high body counts. Aerial bombing and artillery shelling were frequently excessive and indiscriminate. In Iraq, discrimination again appeared as a major problem, but high civilian casualties also resulted from U.S. force protection, the methods of house-to-house searches and checkpoints, detention of tens of thousands of Iraqis, and, by 2005, the inability to provide order. All of these actions in three wars led to the killing of an astonishing number of innocent people. There has been, in effect, a two-tiered system of a policy that avows to uphold the Geneva Conventions but an unacknowledged practice with priorities that frequently victimize civilians, people who are discardable because they are gooks or hajis or, simply, "savages." The U.S. government's dissembling about civilian casualties radiates into elite discourse, which appears less as an intentional strategy than as an absence of discourse, or merely draws upon the old tropes of the frontier, the civilizing mission of American force, and the consequences for those who get caught in the crossfire. Reinforced by or causative of public indifference, this lack of concern may also be a state of passive denial; no public demand for different behavior is forthcoming as a result. The denial is not merely cultural or political; it is psychological—avoidance of the trauma of so many dead, wounded, and displaced, and even reactions leading to blaming the victim.

Put another way, we can view this set of phenomena as a type. The United States is drawn into a tense situation where diplomacy may have failed (or was given short shrift) and moves toward war. The impending war is framed in America as a righteous and necessary mission, and it is popular. War commences. For a variety of strategic or tactical reasons, the military campaign takes enormous numbers of civilian lives. One consequence is to drive many indigenous young men to join the enemy. At home, civilian casualties in the war zone are not discussed. The war is unpopular because of the failure to win combined with high American casualties, which is the nearly exclusive focus of the news media on the human element. Indifference, or diffidence, at the top reinforces or reflects indifference in the public, which is not culturally prone or cannot psychologically cope with the killing abroad.*

The public's blasé attitude toward non-American casualties is the central mystery in this scheme. That civilians often "get in the way" of soldiers is not new, though as noted it is more prominent in wars of the last fifty years. That states and their leaders say one thing about civilians and do another is also not news, although the breach between ideals of noncombatant immunity and the reality of high civilian tolls is worth exploring. What is less easily grasped is the absence of concern, the want of sympathy, which is so evident in Americans' response to the human costs of war. This collective autism has several dimensions and consequences. One is the evident disrespect for global legal norms,

---

* It is worth noting in this that "casualty aversion," a supposed result of the Vietnam War, has been much discussed in academic and policy circles as a political factor in choosing intervention (so much so that "force protection" became paramount in Iraq), but the casualties are only those of U.S. military personnel. The ratio of those Americans killed to the dead of Korea, Vietnam, and Iraqi is on the order of 1–100 (Korea), 1–40 (Vietnam), and 1–200 (Iraq).

which can have severe reverberations in America's international relations and global politics; other people notice the lack of concern or even the denial of responsibility, and this erodes U.S. standing. Political divisiveness in the United States of a vicious kind is also fostered by this denial of responsibility, as skeptics of war policies and criticism of the U.S. military's behavior toward civilians are depicted as disloyal. The very topic of culpability for civilian suffering is essentially out of bounds in the echo chamber of Washington political discourse, and thus the idea that civilian casualties are unsettling to the American public and that the resultant outrage serves as a check on military behavior is nonsense. The human costs simply are not discussed in any sustained or probing way; even the scattered attempts to account for the dead is a highly charged endeavor. More disturbing still is the appearance of a "blame the victim" mentality: that to the extent the American public reacts at all, it sees the civilian deaths, injuries, disease, and displacement as (if not "normal" in wartime) something the war-zone population has brought upon itself.

How and why do these attitudes emerge, and emerge so reliably, in the wars of the last sixty years? One ready explanation comes by way of notions of American "exceptionalism," about which much has been written. I find the work of Richard Slotkin to be most compelling in this regard because through a close study of American culture and politics he links the notions of exceptionalism and destiny to the use of violence: Americans essentialize those we invade as savages in a wilderness to be tamed, and the taming itself is rewarded with a material bounty. That this pattern—what he called the myth of the frontier—appears sturdy and vibrant in U.S. history is relevant to my inquiry precisely because the moral claims of the frontier myth excuse all manner of violence in what the Puritans called "the errand to the wilderness." That we do still refer constantly to frontier imagery and types in our political and especially our security discourse speaks volumes of its abiding power, even if those who analyze these issues are unaware of this cultural and political resonance. There remains, however, a question of whether exceptionalism or the frontier myth can fully account for the vast carelessness of the American people when extraordinary human suffering is afoot in American wars. Why is America different from Britain or France, with their bloody histories of colonial dominance? Did the ordinary Briton or Frenchman care any more about the

Indian or Algerian who was unjustly killed by their occupying armies? It is very likely that they did not care much more, if at all, although there is a literature about this callousness that is more introspective than anything produced in America. Slotkin makes the point that self-glorified colonialism did not contain the key concept of "regeneration through violence" that is so central to the American experience. That may be true, but the justifications, the ideology of violence, do not fully explain Americans' emotional apathy toward suffering. The apathy is particularly puzzling in view of a prominent, normative counterclaimant (Christian ethics), the dominant cultural influence on Americans' thinking; given Jesus' teachings about compassion, one would expect deep sympathy in America for those who suffer in these wars. For that reason, I suggest we need to look beyond the particular cultural environment, however potent, to psychological explanations of coping with others' suffering. Some attempts have been made in this regard, particularly Just World Theory, which provides a proven explanation for public indifference—that is, that observers of those who suffer protect themselves psychologically by denying responsibility for the source of suffering; indeed, that such suffering cannot be authentic in our just world. Such social psychology does not absolve the frontier myth or neocolonialism or other more specific political impulses in America, for even those responses of "blaming the victim" are culturally conditioned—understood through certain cultural frames of reference. The combination of the cultural and psychological accounts explains why the American public in effect gives permission to its powerful military to conduct operations in ways that result in such colossal misery.

Here we explore the wars, how they were conducted, how the local populations were treated and what they say about that treatment, and what the reaction of the American public has been in each conflict. My intention here is to start an argument—to prompt a new epistemology of war—which others will take up seriously to pursue empirical inquiries that provide more insights. The first place to start would be with extensive surveys of Americans and of the populations in the war zones. Another would be an effort to give voice to the people of those wars, the "subaltern" narratives that are far too few. Histories of the wars concentrate almost exclusively on the machinations of political and military leaders, descriptions of the great battles—Inchon, Hamburger Hill, Falluja—and the decisions leading up to the war, or its end. The "people's history," to borrow a phrase from my late friend Howard Zinn, is not represented, not the people that the war affected most. Perhaps such a people's history would affect the American people's perception of war.

What such deeper inquiries would reveal, I submit, is an essential verification of notions nurtured by intellectuals like Pierre Bordieu, Michel Foucault, Noam Chomsky and others—namely, that a "system" for knowledge production dominates our political and cultural discourse, and this production is an expression of (and a reinforcement of) power and the powerful. The massive, unjustifiable deaths of civilians challenge the relationships of power as few topics of war can. Not even failure in war is as problematic, because failure can be attributed to bad timing, circumstances, tactical judgment, or luck. Failure of that kind can actually enhance the power of the military-industrial complex because such an outcome can be attributed—and often is—to inadequate supply or manpower, or to the rules of war that prevent victory. The morality of killing innocents, however, is unambiguous. As a result, it cannot be discussed if it becomes an impediment to U.S. power projection and those that benefit from that power. While I claim no competence to develop these themes further, it strikes me that the cases explored in this book demonstrate their validity (though what often appears as systematic is frequently less so, at least as intention). But one salient effect of indifference or callousness toward large-scale human suffering in U.S. wars is to permit *more* such wars, and so the insights of critical theory deserves a hearing.

The argument I am prompting should not include the notion that this is about "blaming America." That is not my intention. This same analysis could likely be written about other countries, "great powers" that tend to exert force in other places. The individual soldier, marine, sailor, or airman is not the focus of any moral disapproval, either, although clearly some are culpable. Those who have unnecessarily killed civilians have been caught up in a system of acculturation, training, vulnerability, and commands. Soldiers are trained to do violent things. A famous study of the Second World War found that only one in seven soldiers fired their weapons, a problem taken up by militaries subsequently and solved by bringing the firing rate up dramatically—to 95 percent. This and the anecdotes of atrocities, which are social behaviors, suggest how much killing is a group activity, so to speak, learned and reinforced, driven by peers or superiors.

When reading personal accounts of the Vietnam War I found myself, against all expectations, deeply moved not only by the experiences of Vietnamese, but by those of American soldiers. They were young men who wanted their dads and girlfriends to be proud of their courage and manliness; many were frightened of combat, of the sheer danger in their surroundings, and those who were wounded often cried out for their mothers. It was moving, I expect, because I was like them and not like the Vietnamese. And in that emotional response was the microcosm of the quandary I was confronting intellectually.

The book follows a self-explanatory path. I take up the cultural predispositions to violence first, including the "precursor" war in the Philippines, then move toward the three main conflicts. In each, I provide some context drawing on political culture for the advent of war; a rendering of the war itself; the war from the perspective of the native population; and the war in the eyes of the American public. This scheme is adjusted for Iraq, where I include Operation Desert Storm and Operation Iraqi Freedom as the bookends of a twenty-year conflict. Interspersed are short chapters on strategic bombing in the Second World War, and the Reagan Doctrine (war by proxy), all of which reflect gainfully on the three main wars considered. I briefly take up the U.S. war in Afghanistan ("Operation Enduring Freedom"), the "good" war compared with the errant mission in Iraq, which nonetheless is regarded indifferently at home. Then we look at three atrocities—No Gun Ri in Korea, My Lai in Vietnam, and Haditha in Iraq—to regard the pattern of public reactions and equivocations over "rules of engagement." The controversies spurred by how Americans in particular account for the dead in wars is then taken up, showing how neglected and politically fraught this mechanical exercise has become. Finally, the matter of public indifference is explored using psychological theory and cultural explanations.

Three thoughts guided this inquiry. First is the obvious moral question, which itself raises the most hackles of protest. Second is to understand war and its consequences more clearly by considering how the conduct and course of military interventions are confounded by high civilian casualties. Third is this poison of indifference and fractiousness over the topic of civilian deaths in American wars. If anything, after years of considering these questions, I am more amazed than ever at how little attention has been brought to them—a saddening symptom of the maladies I describe.

CHAPTER 2

American Wars and the Culture of Violence

America has witnessed numerous wars since the first European settlers arrived 400 years ago. America first used war as an instrument of gradual continental expansion to the Pacific Ocean against indigenous tribes and competitors for that land (Britain, France, and Mexico). Then, America became a growing world power that fought on every inhabited continent. From small skirmishes to world wars, America has defined itself by never shirking a necessary battle. Like every hegemonic power in history—Persian, Greek, Roman, Chinese, Spanish, Ottoman, British, French, and Soviet, among others—America's global power was forged by the sword and the cannon. The durability of its power is due to more than firepower; America posseses remarkable political and social organization, economic vitality, and cultural diversity. But war has nonetheless occupied a central place in the American experience.

To this day, America's political and popular culture ennobles above all the sacrifices of Americans in those wars. The major wars* have nearly all been nested in a comfortable norm of necessity or right. The lesser conflicts, including those of the continental expansion, occupations of neighboring countries, and briefer interventions in dozens of

---

* The Revolutionary War, the War of 1812, the Mexican War, the Civil War, the Spanish-American War, the First World War, the Second World War, the Korean War, the Vietnam War, Operation Enduring Freedom (Afghanistan, 2001–present), and, in Iraq, Operation Desert Storm (1991) and Operation Iraqi Freedom (2003–present).

countries afar, sometimes became depicted as wayward, overly exuberant, or unfortunate mistakes. American losses are no less honored in those cases. But actual tragedy—in which one's own qualities dictate a monumental loss—is widely attributed to only one of our scores of conflicts: the Civil War. Even there, the necessity of war was always a prominent rationale during and after the conflict. Whether or not destined by slavery to suffer this great sorrow, the United States in the popular mind sustained this as uniquely tragic because everyone who died was American.

By the time of the occupation and counterinsurgency campaign in the Philippines at the end of the nineteenth century and the beginning of the twentieth, a pattern of public discourse and opinion about war had begun to form. The American "expeditionary" force sent to the Philippines to pacify the islands—a result of Spain's concession of the colony to the United States in 1898—met with a ferocious, indigenous resistance that produced a lengthy and bloody war. Somewhere between 200,000 and 400,000 Filipinos, and possibly more, were killed, many of them civilians, in a gruesome and grinding U.S. military campaign. In the United States, the war was depicted as a struggle to bring civilization to the savage islands, as securing a bridge to Asia for American interests, and as a rightful conquest. Concern for the American forces' discomfort and casualties was nowhere matched by concern for the sizable death toll of the Filipinos.

The war was, in fact, a rallying cry for a new American imperialism, the first salvo of expansion and muscle flexing outside North America. The pattern of the American public's response to the war was repeated in every subsequent conflict abroad—the righteous cause, the brave American soldiers, the brutish enemy, and, in the consequent horror of the war, the deep mourning for fallen Americans and the cold indifference to the suffering of the natives. The U.S. political and military decision makers naturally cultivated such feelings, as all leaders do, not least because the heavy civilian toll was intentional, another harbinger.

Other imperial powers have displayed similar blends of moralistic violence and callousness, camouflaged by sentimentality in their national memorials. But Americans would be repelled by the notion that they share such attitudes with Soviets or Ottomans or British overlords. This evident pattern, however universal in certain ways, is in the United States shaped by a history of conquest that has special characteristics—cultural and political attributes that are distinctly American.

Though explaining much of the American public's attitudes about war, the entire pattern of brutality toward civilians, hero-worship of U.S. soldiers, and neglect of "enemy" populations does not wholly derive from culture. Some of the indifference—in particular, toward others' suffering—is a more universal psychological defensiveness, which will be taken up later in this book. However, the cultural dimensions of this phenomenon, the American attitude toward war, alone have exceptional explanatory power. And it all began at the very beginning.

THE WILDERNESS: TAMING THE CONTINENT

America has long been depicted as a violent country, as a society that tolerates violence and the instruments of violence more than any other advanced industrial country. These attitudes are mainly discussed with respect to violence *in* American society—the instances, like the Columbine and Virginia Tech shootings, which shock the nation with some regularity—but rarely is this violence-prone ethos related to the experience of foreign wars. The place of violence in the nation's self-image, the uses of violence as a fulfillment of goals and even norms, and the reflexive interpretation of the meaning of particular instances of violence have not been part of common discourse. However fundamental these topics are—from the fervent insistence on the right to keep weapons to the ubiquity of violence in popular entertainment—they rarely earn much scrutiny as socially constructed attitudes of long standing that brace, for example, aggression by the state.

The roots of this set of attitudes about violence and its utility, necessity, and morality are found in the earliest period of the European "settlement" of America. The original Puritans and their immediate successors faced a daunting and threatening environment: both the vast and wild wilderness that even in the seventeenth century was unknown in Western Europe, and the indigenous peoples who populated that wilderness, the many tribes that came to be known as Indians. The tiny English settlements along the shore of Massachusetts and neighboring areas were almost immediately in a perilous relationship with both the wilderness and the tribes. They faced a life-and-death challenge daily, and the emergent ideas about who the Puritans thought themselves to be, how they situated themselves in the new land, and what their relationship was to the native tribes were quickly taking shape. And those ideas became foundational for the entire American experience.

The outlooks of these first English settlers as they arrived to the new land were not a tabula rasa. They were part of an emerging Atlanticist race myth, the white supremacy that has been evident throughout the recorded history of North America. "Herein lie the deepest ideological (as opposed to economic) roots of what we now call whiteness, whose purported superiority rests on its racially inherited, mastering capacity for freedom," wrote literary scholar Laura Doyle in the aptly named *Freedom's Empire*. "To be white is to be fit for freedom, and the white man's burden is to lead others by forging the institutions . . . required to practice proper freedom, even if along the way this requires enslaving, invading, or exterminating those others who may not (yet) be fit for freedom."[1] This cardinal notion of "freedom" (from the shackles of monarchy, Europe, geography, even history) is the strong tailwind of the Atlantic crossing and continental (and global) expansion, both its energy and its idol.

The particular expression of freedom and all it implied for a settler nation was embodied in the Puritans' set of ideas that evolved into a myth, the myth of the frontier. The frontier myth became an underlying architecture of American politics and culture. As the historian and cultural theorist Richard Slotkin described it, "the conquest of the wilderness and the subjugation or displacement of the Native Americans . . . have been the means to our achievement of a national identity, a democratic polity, an ever-expanding economy, and a phenomenally dynamic and 'progressive' civilization."[2] This conquest, he explained, was not only pursued for its own tangible rewards—security, land, and riches—but for and by a morally cleansing series of "savage wars" that conveyed upon the pioneers a "regeneration through violence." It was at the frontier, where civilization confronted wilderness, that American values were forged. It provided abundance for those courageous enough to realize and seize it, contrasting sharply with the European metropolis and its scarcity, squalor, and discontent. The frontier myth came to be the über-narrative that encompassed values often linked to Americans—individualism and self-reliance, producing goods from the wilderness, and other "democratic" values, as well as later ideological bents like Social Darwinism and Manifest Destiny. The myth has been endlessly replayed and elaborated through the cultural power of novels, journalism, films, and television.

In Slotkin's formulation, the frontier myth involved separation from the metropolis as one set out for the frontier, a "regression" to a more primitive state of living, and finally a "regeneration" of national purpose and citizenship achieved through the necessity of violent conflict, the "savage war": "The premise of 'savage war' is that ineluctable political and social differences—rooted in some combination of 'blood' and culture—make coexistence between primitive natives and civilized Europeans impossible on any basis other than that of subjugation. Native resistance therefore takes the form of a fight for survival . . . 'wars of extermination' in which one side or the other attempts to destroy its enemy root and branch."[3] The "other"—for the first two centuries, almost always the Indian—is ever responsible for the savagery. As the frontier myth and the nation of European Americans grew together, the justification for outward expansion was elaborated as a mission of civilizing the savages and taming the wilderness, a Jeffersonian expression of yeoman democracy, and a dynamic resolution of the class conflict that beset Europe increasingly from the nineteenth century.

Virtually all the heroic figures of American lore—Leatherstocking, Daniel Boone, Andrew Jackson, Davey Crockett, George Custer, and so on—were the embodiment of the myth. The myth and its heroes are bound as symbiotic organisms. A powerful, national narrative must have heroes; the American heroes bring forth the qualities of adventure, ambivalence toward pristine wilderness and its inhabitants, the ultimate choice of civilization, and virtuosity in the necessary violence that redeems the settler communities on the frontier, and their essential goodness as agents of progress. The encounter with natives was ambivalent for the famous Indian fighters because they recognized the extraordinary qualities, however primitive, of the adversary, just as they dwelt in the majesty of the wilderness. Both had to be conquered, however, and through this Herculean effort, a "new, purified social contract was enacted." This was possible, even inevitable, because "the Indian wars are, for these heroes, a spiritual or psychological struggle . . . to defeat savagery on its native grounds—the natural wilderness, and the wilderness of the human soul."[4]

That the European settlement of America was a violent affair, arguably genocide, is well established. The significance here is how that experience, lasting nearly three centuries, shaped Americans' attitudes toward war, particularly the depiction of the enemy, the civilizing impulse of expansion, and the rewards—materially, physically, and spiritually—of violent conquest.

The frequent explanation of these attitudes is condensed into the term "American exceptionalism." The concept has a mixed parentage. Many if not most of the Puritans and other early English Americans saw their move to New England as a divine mission. The oft-quoted sermon by Massachusetts Bay Colony governor John Winthrop, "that we shall be as a city on a hill," is the linchpin of this exceptionalist idea.* It was elaborated by another minister, Peter Bulkeley, at the same occasion (the launching of the Winthrop fleet from Southampton in 1630), where he implored the people of New England

> to shine forth in holiness above all other people. . . . We are as a city set upon a hill . . . the eyes of the world are upon us, because we profess ourselves to be a people in covenant with God, and therefore not only the Lord our God, with whom we shall have made covenant, but heaven and earth, angels and men, that are witnesses of our profession, will cry shame upon us, if we walk contrary to the covenant which we have professed and promised to walk in.[5]

The "errand into the wilderness," the divine covenant to spread the word of God to the heathen, was not merely missionary, but military. The exceptionalism of the new colonists thus embraced a warrior ethos very soon upon its encounter with the indigenous tribes. Compared with their experience in Europe, the early settlers could scarcely imagine a clearer dichotomy of a community of believers and a community of nonbelievers. This contrast fed their sense of mission and exceptionalism. When

---

* Winthrop was borrowing from Matthew 5, Jesus' Sermon on the Mount: "Ye are the light of the world. A city that is set on an hill cannot be hid. Neither do men light a candle, and put it under a bushel, but on a candlestick; and it giveth light unto all that are in the house. Let your light so shine before men, that they may see your good works, and glorify your Father which is in heaven."

it came time for war—"defensive war," no less—there was no doubt of its rightness. By the end of the seventeenth century, when Puritanism itself was in decline, Cotton Mather took up some of the themes of his father and other early ministers to describe the bloodshed between the English and the Indian in apocalyptic language, as God's scourge against his chosen people who had fallen off the path of righteousness. The agent of God's fury was the Indian. "The spirit of God against whom we had *Rebelled*, permitted the *Devils*, from the *Depths of Hell*, to assault us, with as Prodigious Vexations, as ever befell any People under the whole *Cope of Heaven*."[6] This identification of Satan with the Indians was not unique to the Mathers but part of a much broader lament among the righteous. The context—that the original mission of the Puritans was losing its integrity and the Indians were God's retribution—underscores the contest between the "exceptional destiny" of the Puritans and their spiritual, historical, and physical opposite—the Indians. As one historian of the period explained, the heated sermons "attest to an unswerving faith in the errand; and if anything they grow more fervent, more absolute in their commitment from one generation to the next."[7] In that commitment, moreover, and particularly after the major armed conflict of that century, King Philip's War, the Indians were widely regarded as satanic.

The war itself is instructive, a prototype of later encounters with the Indians and the "other." King Philip, a name given by the Puritans to Metacom, the sachem or chief of the Wampanoags, initiated hostilities in 1675 after a series of encroachments by the English, some of them violent and provocative. The fourteen-month "civil war" engulfed most of New England, killing perhaps half of the 18,000 indigenous peoples and about 10 percent or more of the 60,000 English settlers. Accounts of casualties vary wildly, another pattern that would be repeated; but this war indisputably was "devastating . . . brutal, vicious, and violent,"[8] most certainly a "savage war." Roger Williams described the Narragansetts, an ally in the Pequot War (1637), as "barbarous men of blood who are as justly to be repelled and subdued as wolves that assault the sheep." A day later, the English raided the tribe and burned down a village and slaughtered everyone, including children. It was another example of the Puritans' strategy of "total war," first on display in the Pequot extermination and again in King Philip's War, where the very survival of the English was at stake. Those not killed were sold into slavery or taken as slaves, essentially, in English settlements or among allied tribes, such as the Narragansetts. This brutality in war was turned on its head—that is, attributed to the Indians and deployed by the Puritans only *because of* Indian savagery and the "sufficient light from the Word of God for our proceedings."[9] If one's errand is divinely sanctioned and threatened by heathens in league with Satan, then any form of violence is both necessary and redemptive.

From this fatal encounter came both a principal literary form of the seventeenth and eighteenth centuries, the captivity narrative (in which, typically, a white woman is captured by Indians, but survives through faith), and the mythic form of the heroism derived from the Indian fighter, Benjamin Church, whose troop killed Metacom. Both became essential to a broader understanding of establishing the template of the wilderness as tempting, plentiful, and godless, and the necessary use of violence. The Puritan narratives of the war (the Mathers were preeminent in establishing this form) located the English settlers as victims fighting a defensive war, wars signaling their own failures to sustain the moral rightness of the errand and the new Jerusalem they set out to create. This was a complex theological matter. But the use of righteous violence, the evil associated with the Indians and the wilderness, and the divine sanction of the errand— the expansion outward from the initial coastal settlements—was rarely if ever questioned. The frontier and its powerful myth were under way.

The Secular Republic

By the middle of the eighteenth century, the Puritan mission was all but dissipated, but the sense of an exceptional American mission was no less vibrant. It was reshaped by Enlightenment values—the revelation now enabled by reason, the exceptional quality of the American experiment being the realization of natural rights, the first in the world, and again in sharp contrast to the moral decay of Europe and its aristocracy. This conversion from the highly specific Calvinist vision to a uniqueness based on rights and rationality was quite remarkable. It is the foundation for the assertions of American exceptionalism ever since, though the claims have sustained an elemental Christian dimension as well.

The Constitution and the Declaration of Independence became the sacred documents, subtly detached from the religious underpinnings of the colonial origins while sustaining the inherent authority of natural rights and their divine origins. Benjamin Franklin, a central actor in this transition, explained Deborah Madsen, "powerfully redefined the Puritan mission; recasting the terms of success, . . . where the collective salvation of the community was transformed into a form of government that would protect the rights of all citizens." It sustained the "city on a hill" status in the eyes of the founders, but would "also be the world's guardian, regulating the conduct of other nations, and representing the world's last and best chance at salvation."[10]

The American experiment was by the 1770s an exercise in nation building, with expansion as an explicit yearning. As a result, the frontier myth became, along with the rights and reason revolution, a foundation of nationhood and the American "project." The notion of a project, or experiment, is integral—it conveys verve, dynamism, pioneering, and growth. These many related qualities defined the emerging nation. But notions like "expansion" and "project" and "dynamic" are empty and rhetorical if untethered to an engagement with land and people, and this is where the myth of the frontier was indispensable.

Among its manifold effects, the new republic loosened British restraints on westward expansion into Indian territory. Within two or three generations, this push toward the Pacific encompassed most of what are now the lower forty-eight states. The Louisiana Purchase (1803), the war with Mexico (1847), the Oregon Treaty (1846), and the hundreds of conflicts with the indigenous tribes secured this territory for the United States. Each of these thrusts had cultural winds at their backs, first shaped by the Puritans but renewed and strengthened by the more secular ideas of the late eighteenth and nineteenth centuries. The largest single expansion, the Louisiana Purchase, was popularized in the day as an outlet necessary, in the Jeffersonian idiom, to sustain the yeoman democracy—an image of the small farm as the font of American values that remains vivid today. As the thirteen colonies pushed outward, as they did almost instantly, the rationale pivoted on the fertile and cheap land available to develop, either that taken from Indians or land purchased from Spain and France. It is worth noting that the early

Republic was governed mainly by the Virginia plantation class (Washington, Jefferson, Madison, and Monroe), and their decisions about land and expansion favored the planters over the farmers.[11] Plantations in the South ruined the soil and economically crowded out small farmers, creating new pressures for expansion.

The West's powerful leaders, Jackson and Clay, dominated politics after the Virginians, with the interests of their own frontier constituency at heart, which included their security. Andrew Jackson was known, before becoming president in 1829, as an Indian fighter, the general who defeated Seminoles and Creek and other obstreperous tribes resisting the American migration and harboring fugitive slaves. Jackson traded on the frontier myth early on, identifying himself with the ultimate frontiersman, Daniel Boone; and in this was the first U.S. president molded explicitly by this myth. In keeping with that, his principal legacy was the Indian Removal Act, which made into official policy what had been occurring for decades in the Southeast. In his message to Congress promoting the legislation, Jackson asserted:

> It will place a dense and civilized population in large tracts of country now occupied by a few savage hunters. By opening the whole territory between Tennessee on the north and Louisiana on the south to the settlement of the whites it will incalculably strengthen the southwestern frontier. . . . It will relieve the whole State of Mississippi and the western part of Alabama of Indian occupancy, and enable those States to advance rapidly in population, wealth, and power. . . . What good man would prefer a country covered with forests and ranged by a few thousand savages to our extensive Republic, studded with cities, towns, and prosperous farms, embellished with all the improvements which art can devise or industry execute, occupied by more than 12,000,000 happy people, and filled with all the blessings of liberty, civilization, and religion?

Jackson expressed concern in this and other messages that honored the "aborigine" and noted his best intentions for his well-being, a quality present among all the frontiersmen from Church and Boone onward. In frontier myth, the pioneer "knew" the Indian and appreciated his skills and nature, thereby legitimating the expansionist claims for land, war, and "removal." Jackson is an essential figure in this, elevating the warrior frontiersman in politics as well as culture, a set of qualities that has frequently appeared in national leadership ever since. Not least among these characteristics was elaborate equivocation on the fate of the five nations of indigenous peoples who, during and shortly after Jackson's presidency, were sent on the "trail of tears" that wasted away thousands. Jackson's grip on national politics attests to the popularity of such policies, and the men who followed him to the White House were either protégés or cut from similar cloth—Van Buren, Harrison, Tyler, Polk, and Taylor.*

Through the first half century or so of nation building, then, the expansionist tendencies of the European settlers, now Americans, were nearly uncontrollable and largely supported by a political culture that celebrated the frontier ideology of rough-hewn pioneering. It was, as Jackson's statement earlier makes clear, an expansion that was no longer the divine errand into the wilderness. It was more about the development of the land and the "improvements" that free men could bring to it. The bounty of the frontier, in plentitude and freedom, was the secular vision.

"Trails of tears."

Texas and Mexico

After conquering the land east of the Mississippi River, expelling the indigenous peoples, and acquiring the vast tracts of the Louisiana Purchase, the next hunt came in the form of the first significant war with another nation-state apart from Britain. That was the war of Texas independence (1835–36) and the consequent larger war between the United States and Mexico (1845–48). Both were expansionist at their root. Both excoriated the Mexicans as racially inferior, the first such depictions of an adversary (apart from the Indians, of course). Both had larger designs than the territory immediately at stake. And both, significantly, accelerated and intensified the idea that the entire continent was meant to be

---

* Martin Van Buren was Jackson's vice president. William Henry Harrison, a general and Indian fighter, was from Indiana and Ohio, still then the western frontier. James K. Polk was governor of Tennessee and a Jackson acolyte. Zachary Taylor, also from Tennessee, was the leading general in the Mexican-American War and a longtime Indian fighter. John Tyler, who became president upon Harrison's death, was a throwback to the Virginia planters' class but was initially a Jackson supporter. From the founding of the Republic until 1850, but for the two single terms of Adams father and son, the presidency was essentially in the hands of the planters or the frontiersmen.

absorbed, quickly and beneficently, into the United States of America. The latent imperialism of the earlier expansion became quite explicit in an act of war against another sovereign state.

Texas was a Spanish and then Mexican possession to which American settlers gradually migrated in the 1820s and 1830s. The disputes centered on governance, immigration, and eventually the role of the Texas militia, which the Mexican government sought to disarm. Thus began armed conflict. The seven-month war ended with Sam Houston's victory over the Mexican president and general, Santa Anna, and Texas became an independent republic as a result. The conflict, and especially the Battle of the Alamo, was the stuff of legends—in addition to Houston, there were James Bowie and Davey Crockett, both of whom died at the Alamo—which have been sustained to the present day. Houston and Crockett, both Tennesseans, and Bowie, from Kentucky, all fulfilled the by-then contoured role of frontiersman, bringing into sharp relief the heroic quality of this war as a familiar and nourishing chapter in the master narrative of American expansion.*

In the next several years, a national debate ensued about Texas becoming a part of the United States, a debate that mainly broke along the bitter fissures of the slavery question. Some 6,000 slaves were owned by 30,000 whites in Texas at the time of independence, and abolitionists opposed the annexation of Texas because it would likely be a slave state. Jackson and Van Buren would not bring annexation forward; John Tyler did as a campaign ploy in 1844 and managed (even though he failed in the election) to enact a bill of annexation in early 1845—in part because Polk, an avid expansionist, had won a large victory in the election of 1844 and supported annexation, as did Jackson.

The Mexicans never recognized Texan independence and were no more pleased with the annexation. Polk, in an act of preemption or provocation, sent Taylor and troops to the Rio Grande—south of the

---

* The historian Vernon Parrington described Crockett as a "frontier wastrel" typical of "the slovenly world of the frontier," with its excesses of drinking and corrupt politics and destruction. "He was a hunter rather than a farmer, and the lust of killing was in his blood. . . . Davey was but one of thousands who were wasting the resources of the Inland Empire, destroying forests, skinning the land, slaughtering the deer and bear, the swarms of pigeons, the vast buffalo herds." *Main Currents in American Thought*, Harcourt Brace and the World, 1930, v. 2, 178.

actual border—following a deployment occurring within days of the final acceptance of annexation. An "incident" of the kind that sparks many wars, a murky occurrence of a disappearance, led to skirmishes that led to battles that led to the Mexican-American War in 1846, "It looks as if the government sent a small force on purpose to bring on a war, so as to have a pretext for taking California and as much of this country as it chooses," wrote a colonel and aide to Taylor at the time. Indeed, Polk had his sights set on California, already alluring migrants from afar, and the enthusiasm for rapid expansion to the Pacific could quickly be achieved by defeating Mexico and its claim to sovereignty from Texas to the ocean.[12]

The mission was couched in the usual terms of bringing civilization to a morally barren place. The arguments in favor of war, apart from outright pro-expansionism—the term "Manifest Destiny" was coined for this war—hinged on a series of assertions about the superior vigor of American industriousness compared with the exhausted remnants of Spanish colonialism, and even an appeal that war would liberate the underclass of Mexico. War tends to overwhelm subtlety, however, and soon the pro-war discourse was sotted with racist depictions of Mexicans. The highly racialized context of the war then provided to the American political debate a well-known type—the "savage war." The progress of the war, in which U.S. troops swiftly defeated the Mexican army and occupied the capital and other major cities, stirred an interesting controversy about whether to annex all of Mexico. This urge, by no means as popular as the war itself, was seemingly at odds with the ideology of expansion, which held that the wilderness was its locus and sparse, primitive tribes the only people to be conquered. Mexico, with substantial cities, a complex social system, and the history of previous European conquest, was unlike the grounds of the frontier myth. A sizable number of opponents of the war and annexation were so persuaded by the distasteful possibility of an intermingling of races that might ensue. The annexation urge was resisted, apart from the sizable taking of California and much of what is now the U.S. Southwest, which were "sparsely populated" and therefore more in keeping with the previous continental expansion.

The war was popular. Celebrations of victories were common, the new "penny press" was captivated by the war's successes on the battlefield, the anticipation of bounty excited all sectors, and one of the war heroes, Zachary Taylor, was elected president at war's end. Howard Zinn makes the plausible case for widespread dissent against the war, including large desertions and difficulties in military recruiting, and the famous tracts of New England ministers, Thoreau, and abolitionists. There were fierce class antagonisms in America that often surfaced in the penumbra of the war. But the general outcry for expansion, whether or not engineered by elites and the press, was a powerful force. The death toll of about 13,000 American soldiers—mostly from disease—far outnumbered the deaths in other conflicts, but appears secondary as a source of discontent; the numbers of Mexicans killed is not known, but was surely double or more the U.S. total.

When casualties stirred controversy, it was occasioned by charges of U.S. soldiers' brutality toward Mexicans, typically found in the foreign press. These charges were fiercely rebuked in the American press. In fact, the Americans committed so many atrocities that one of the commanders, General Winfield Scott, among other eyewitnesses, testified to his distress at the rampages of the Americans: "Our militia & volunteers, if a tenth of what is said be true, have committed atrocities—horrors—in Mexico, sufficient to make Heaven weep. . . . Murder, robbery & rape on mothers & daughters . . . have been committed all along the Rio Grande."[13] Zachary Taylor voiced similar laments. Historian Paul Foos correlates the atrocities with volunteers, a large segment of the fighting force, who were significantly an economic underclass seeking material rewards of conquest: "the propaganda surrounding the war effort was nakedly opportunistic and expressly promised plunder," he wrote. "Their proclivity for racist, religious, or nationalist rationales for their crimes took up the language of manifest destiny, suffusing their criminal activity with the heroism and comradeship implicit in that cause."[14]

For all its messiness, the venture to Mexico was hailed in elite political culture as a demonstration that a democracy could prosecute war as efficiently as a despotism could. That gold was discovered in the newly conquered California just after the war was won seemed to provide ample proof of a just reward. Polk's judgment in December 1848 was that "our beloved country presents a sublime moral spectacle to the world."[15] A new epoch had arrived, in the view of many

Americans, an exertion of national power that expanded the terrain for the frontier myth to unfold in the latter half of the nineteenth century.

THE GRAPES OF WRATH

The Civil War is the great divide of American history, not only the bloody cleavage over slavery and sovereignty, but the interruption of continental expansion and the suspension of the frontier myth. It did not literally stop expansion, of course—the transcontinental railroad was begun in 1863 and finished in just six years—and the war's aftermath fed the frontier with all manner of men and stories that provided their own embellishments to frontier ideology.

The war was gruesomely violent. Massive armies were mobilized, and the technology of killing was much advanced from earlier conflicts. "Men slaughtered each other with a zeal we still grope to understand," wrote one historian.[16] Most historians depict it as a "total war," and while not entirely new, it was unprecedented on this scale. Six hundred thousand perished, and Sherman's "march to the sea" imposed destruction on civilian property. This level of violence is contested. Historian Mark Neely has calculated figures scarcely one-third of that "iconic" total, or 135,000 for the North and 66,000 for the South—a very controversial assertion—and it may be that the numbers of dead were manipulated to inflate the scale of sacrifice. In this sense, Sherman's own reckoning, that the numbers of dead provide the "epistemology of the war," is striking. Were 200,000 killed on the battlefield less ennobling than 600,000? The bundling of the numbers of war dead, moreover, is revealing. It is part of the gloss of postwar reconciliation and memorialization, Neely said, that uniquely combined the casualties for this war in a way not represented in other conflicts.

Contemporary accounts reveal both abhorrence and delight in the killing, which, even in the lower calculations, was profound. Military leaders would declaim the violence as un-Christian or even inhuman—sentiments widely cited in conventional histories of the war—but pursue war strategies that maximized its ferocity. That Americans were killing other Americans did not seem to matter much in the event; the regret on that score would come later as a reflection on the horror of this particular conflict, a depiction of war as tragedy that is unique in the American narrative. During the war, the familiar rationales were prevalent. "While southerners most often appealed to self defense against invasion as the source of the war's justness," noted Drew Gilpin Faust, "they invoked as well the notion of divine sanction for a holy war in which they served as Confederate crusaders."[17] The Union readily pointed to the "just cause" of keeping the nation intact.

For the most part, the nineteenth-century rules of war were observed, sustaining a distinction between civilians and soldiers in the torrent of violence. It was, therefore, not a total war in the more recent definition. Like the Mexican-American War and many that followed, however, there existed a gap between the commanders' conception of the war—namely, what they considered to be their fidelity to principled conduct—and what occurred in the field. Sherman, in his fullest expression of war doctrine, professed an interest in protecting civilians, but that "it is almost impossible to lay down rules, and I invariably leave the whole subject to the local commanders." As Neely comments, "Leaving 'the whole subject' to local commanders nevertheless permitted considerable latitude for pillage or destruction and was in itself an important principle. . . . [Sherman] thought a volunteer army, the product of America's ultra-individualistic society, would inevitably loot and burn private property. His conservative social views thus led to a career-long fatalism about pillage."[18] However restrained Sherman might have been, a legend about his brutality, and the war's brutality more broadly, has insinuated itself into the standard military narrative of this seminal conflict—essentially, that every war must become a "war of annihilation."[19] The scale of killing, in the popular image, "brother against brother," enabled and possibly even encouraged a similar scale of killing in future wars.

Just as revealing is the place of black soldiers in the war. If a certain gentlemanly attitude of the two warring armies existed at times between them, no such rules applied to nonwhites. The Confederacy had as a policy the killing of black soldiers no matter what the circumstances. Blacks were killed as prisoners on countless occasions, at times in large-scale massacres. General Robert E. Lee was complicit in one such mass murder.[20] The executions were of a piece with the harsh experience of slavery itself. Slavery's violence and the abrupt abrogation of this practice and ideology for southern whites made black Union soldiers particularly vulnerable to their vengeance. Indeed, white Union officers with black soldiers under their command were routinely executed if captured. The plantation system that was so central to the early Republic and its leaders required slave labor. But it was a system of violence, one carried into the frontier, particularly Texas. That so much of the ideology of the frontier as the spring of democratic values came from Jefferson and the planter class, and from the early western heroes like Jackson—all of whom were proponents of slavery—presents a painful self-contradiction in American history that entangles the frontier myth as well.

religious ←

The religious establishment was central to the violence of expansion and was similarly attendant to the Civil War. The unfathomable carnage and grief was explained by Christian ministers as necessary to defend the values and virtues of North or South. The concept of the "good death" came to dominate the cultural responses to the dying that seemed to touch every family. Such passing was in full acceptance of the Christian god's design, each of the fallen having served his cause nobly and selflessly—conceivably an unintentional enabler of the ferocious violence in a war largely fought by volunteers. "Americans came to fight the civil war in the midst of a wider cultural world that sent them messages about death that made it easier to kill and be killed," wrote a historian of the culture of death, and that these notions, largely based on the promise of heaven, created a "wider cultural climate that facilitated the carnage of war."[21] Just as often the messages were explicit. Lincoln, like many pastors of North and South, positioned the blood sacrifices as biblical in nature: "if God wills that . . . every drop of blood drawn with the lash shall be paid by another drawn by the sword, as was said three thousand years ago, so still it must be said, 'The judgments of the Lord are true and righteous altogether.'"[22]

In many firsthand narratives of battle, however, was a vast incomprehension of the cruelty and suffering of armed conflict. This inability to articulate the depths of war was nonpartisan, even as its utility for the preachers and hagiographers served only one side or the other. Finding meaning in such violence was not an easy matter. Most attempts reflected the religiosity of the time, as divine retribution or providence, and others sought to place it squarely in the ongoing story of American exceptionalism. The violence was regenerative if the cause was emancipation rather than union alone (the latter problematic in view of the promise of the Declaration for dissolving the union), and so the cause of abolishing slavery—arguably a secondary mission for the North at the war's onset—became central and ennobling, joining again the terrible, swift sword with the glories of freedom.[23]

After the war, rituals of remembrance grew that were decades long in evolution. In the immediate aftermath of the war, the national government refused to allocate funds for Confederate cemeteries, reflecting a deep northern animus toward the rebels. The capacity of the country as a whole to honor the dead from both sides, as it is now meant to do on Memorial Day—originally a Union commemoration (Decoration Day, decorating the graves), with competing days for rebels—was perhaps a concession to nation building and unity, made simpler by the common roots of the dead. But this took time to achieve. William McKinley took the Republican Party in 1896 from its emancipationist narrative, by necessity one that excluded any valor for the South, to one of reconciliation. McKinley's purpose, as a tactic of his successful campaign for the presidency, was in part to link his opponents, then proposing economic reform against the growing power of corporations and monopolies, to the secession of 1861, contrasting their class warfare with his message of national unity.[24]

After some years had passed, the tendency in the South to use the war's commemoration as a political rebuke to emancipation remained sturdy, as did the glorification of rebel military leaders, notably Robert E. Lee. But that had less to do with the war itself than the postwar promotion and tolerance of institutionalized racism. Even by the mid-twentieth century, the horror of war was subsumed by a patriotic gloss on the conflict, which was taught in American schools (for example, as the War between the States that tragically resulted from a dispute over states' rights). In tragedy there is honor. After the sting of death and division had passed, both sides could empathize with the suffering and sacrifice of the other: "the dead, the dead, the dead—*our dead*—or South or North, ours all (all, all, all, finally dear to me)," wrote Walt Whitman, "the infinite dead—(the land entire saturated, perfumed with their impalpable ashes' exhalation in

Nature's chemistry distill'd, and shall be so forever, in every future grain of wheat and ear of corn, and every flower that grows, and every breath we draw)."

It was a magnanimity that has never been accorded to other American wars.

THE LAST STAND

The Civil War left many legacies, among them the growing power of the federal government, large debts, and devastated national and local economies, an enormous number of battle-hardened men, many military officers seeking more such adventure, and a desire by countless Americans to leave it all behind. The frontier was one place where all these consequences could find a common stage.

The postwar period was marked significantly by westward expansion across the Mississippi River. While population growth was rapid for the entire United States, due mainly to ample flows of immigrants from Europe, the migration to the West is striking. In 1850, all the territories and states of the "Western division" of the U.S. Census—the Rocky Mountain states to the Pacific—had just 178,000 people, more than half of those in California. By 1890, the total was more than three million. In 1870, the West had less than one million; the white population of the West more than tripled from the end of the Civil War to the last census of the open frontier.[25] Two economic factors were at work throughout the nineteenth century that explain much of this migration: population growth that exceeded what the land and factories of the East could sustain, and lowered transportation costs for migration to the West and shipment of goods back and forth.[26] The migration from the East, and among them many Civil War veterans, meant that the pressure on Indian lands and people was severe. The encroachments are well known. But the embellishments of the frontier myth proceeded apace as a particularly violent period of warfare ensued.

The clashes with indigenous tribes quickly came to a head. A new U.S. policy of forcing tribes onto reservations was instituted in 1868, and those that resisted were subjected to scorched-earth military campaigns. General Philip Sheridan, a major figure of the Civil War, prosecuted the war against the natives using tactics like those he and Sherman used against the Confederates—attacking villages with guns and torches. He promoted the destruction of the buffalo herds of the Great Plains to deprive Indians of their main source of food. All of this was pursued mainly on lands that were legally Indian territories. The fighting was particularly notable in areas of mineral wealth, such as the Black Hills, which came to symbolize the "savage wars" that this period witnessed—the savages, in popular lore, being the Sioux led by Sitting Bull and Crazy Horse, and the heroes being the U.S. cavalry led by George Armstrong Custer. The politics of the time elevated Custer into a national icon in a symbolic contest of the two sharply differing approaches to all challenges to the status quo—those who favored "philanthropy" toward the Indian, the working class, and the Negro, and those who insisted on stout discipline to preserve and strengthen the gains of the settlers and the entrepreneurial classes. The wealthy industrialists, the expansionists, and others of like mind—many newspapers in particular—made Custer the fallen hero of the latter approach.

The most fundamental cultural archetype in American history, the taming of the wilderness and the regeneration of the nation through savage wars, was invoked not only for expansion, but for enforcing the new industrial system on the immigrants toiling in the factories. As a number of observers saw at the time, including Mark Twain, the old ethos of the frontier as a place of small farmers and democratic values had been overwhelmed and essentially disappeared, in favor of an industrial colossus and the imperatives to feed it. It surely ranks as bitter irony that the industrial demiurge consumed the frontier and subverted the supposed values of the pioneering experience. Writers like Melville also saw the obliteration of the natural environment as a self-defeating juggernaut. From the perspective of the conquered peoples, of course, the two phenomena—the industrial and geographical expansion—were of a piece. "It was an incredible era of violence, greed, audacity, sentimentality, undirected exuberance, and an almost reverential attitude toward the ideal of personal freedom for those who already had it," wrote Dee Brown in his seminal *Bury My Heart at Wounded Knee*. "During that time the culture and civilization of the American Indian was destroyed."[27]

Three and a half centuries after the Puritans devised the errand, the wilderness itself was all but vanished and its people vanquished. The massacre at Wounded Knee in 1890 is generally considered to be the last of the indigenous tribes' resistance to the takeover of much of the continent. This remarkable expansion, undoing the designs of the Old World powers and the firmer claims of the Mexicans, in addition to the unassailable sovereignty of the native populations, was a triumph of a certain kind of imperialism. It can also be called genocide; the numbers that died are not easily grasped, but they are in the hundreds of thousands by violence, and with disease included in the range of four million.[28] The European American dominance of the continent blended the instruments of other, mainly European imperialism of the period—growing state power, military acumen, restless economic development, and forms of racism—with the particular attributes of the frontier myth. The expansion was seen not as conquest, but as an expression of democratic values.

THE GLOBAL FRONTIER

The massacre at Wounded Knee concluded the Indian wars and in effect closed the continental frontier. While it was a triumph for the expansionists and an unparalleled disaster for the indigenous tribes—85 percent of which were extinguished—the end of the frontier raised a troubling specter for the Republic. If so much of Americans' self-identity was interwoven with the frontier myth, if the uniqueness of American political institutions and cultural élan was derived from the pioneer experience, what would become of the American experiment now that its dynamic venue had been subdued, consumed, and transformed?

This was not just a question for intellectuals in the late nineteenth century, but a galvanizing concern for political leaders. The end of the frontier was apparent. The concern did not stem from a fear of overcrowding or land scarcity—the West was still sparsely populated. Rather, the alarms were set off for economic recovery and growth, and for the democratic virtues that sprang from the frontier experience.

It was also an age of imperialism, and the European powers had long since claimed much of Asia and Africa. As a former colony with its own

expansion of territory by war..

anticolonial narrative, the United States and its most prominent leaders largely eschewed empire (at least the form of empire that pivoted on territorial acquisition, outside of the "natural" settlement of the North American continent). The world as an American frontier was, in this sense, a relatively new idea when Theodore Roosevelt, Woodrow Wilson, and a few others assayed the closing of the continental frontier and inverted its significance: it was not the end of the frontier, only the end of its first spatial aspiration.

Roosevelt was a central figure in this realization. His lament about the closing frontier drew on an essentially racist notion of how Americans—or Americans of a certain heroic class—subdued the savage and thereby burnished their virile qualities and their moral capacity to lead. The historian Frederick Jackson Turner promoted the more palatable idea that democratic self-reliance was a consequence of the American frontier experience, and that the closing of the frontier (which the Census Bureau proclaimed in 1891) was a threat to American democratic virtue. The frontier had also provided a safety valve for development in the United States, unlike Europe, where socialism and class antagonisms supposedly marred the political landscape. The economic stagnation America was experiencing in the 1890s was a riveting political issue, and so the end of the bounty and promise of the frontier was a clanging alarm to many.

Turner, a student of Wilson's at Johns Hopkins, delivered his now-legendary paper, "The Significance of the Frontier in American History," at the 1893 Chicago Exposition, where the American Historical Association was meeting. (Just a stone's throw away at the Exposition from where Turner spoke was the popular entertainment, Buffalo Bill's Wild West Show. African Americans, however, were barred from participating in the Exposition at all.) Turner's framing of the frontier was thoughtful but dramatic. "The frontier is the outer edge of the wave—the meeting point between savagery and civilization," he said. "The advance of the frontier has meant a steady movement away from the influence of Europe, a steady growth of independence on American lines. . . . the most important effect of the frontier has been in the promotion of democracy." The engagement with the frontier, then, represents both the uniquely American dimension of our history, its democratic core, and the confrontation between the civilized and the savages. This framing of the frontier experience became crucial to the outward push of the ensuing decades of the twentieth century because the rationale for global expansion could be rooted in the nurturing of democratic values worldwide.

If the end of the frontier was a crisis for democratic and manly virtue, Roosevelt and Turner had an answer: extend the frontier elsewhere. As the historian William Appleman Williams described it, Turner "was the apostle of a revival movement that restored the faith of the conquerors of North America and made them individual crusaders." The historian Brooks Adams, who exerted considerable influence on Roosevelt, echoed Turner in many respects and pressed an explicit imperialist agenda as a natural historical process. According to Williams in his remarkable 1953 essay, "The Frontier Thesis and Foreign Policy," Adams advised Presidents McKinley and Roosevelt to "use economic and military power to expand the frontier of the United States westward to the interior of China." Long before the USS Maine was blown up in Havana harbor, Roosevelt advocated war with Spain, which bestowed the Philippines to the newly minted American empire and provided Roosevelt and his cohort with the "savage war" and foothold toward Asia that were, in their view, the very antidote to the frontier's demise in North America.

Once that was under way, the responsibility to sustain our global role was apparent. "If we are to be a really great people, we must strive in good faith to play a great part in the world," Roosevelt told the posh Hamilton Club in Chicago in 1899, when newly governor of New York and fresh from his four-month colonelcy in Cuba. "While a nation's first duty is within its own borders, it is not thereby absolved from facing its duties in the world as a whole; and if it refuses to do so, it merely forfeits its right to struggle for a place among the peoples that shape the destiny of mankind." The doctrines of those "foolish sentimentalists" who would have resisted the winning of the West itself, T.R. said contemptuously, "condemn your forefathers and mine for ever having settled these United States." The comparison is redolent: if the likes of anti-imperialists like William Jennings Bryan have their way, we would be sacrificing our mission to extend the primacy of our race and values across the world.

Woodrow Wilson was less bombastic but no less committed to the extension of the American idea. "The spaces of their own continent were occupied and reduced to the uses of civilization; they had no frontiers wherewith 'to satisfy the feet of the young men,'" he wrote in *A History of the American People*. "These new frontiers in the Indies and on the Far Pacific came to them as if out of the very necessity of the new career before them." In the White House—where Roosevelt persisted with suppressing the Philippines rebellion and building the Panama Canal, both with high human tolls—Wilson invaded Mexico, Nicaragua, the Dominican Republic, and Haiti before entering the First World War. All of these actions, supposedly on behalf of democratic ideals, prefaced his attempts to make the world safe for democracy. While he was, in contrast to Roosevelt, increasingly anti-imperialist, he was no less expansionist—in Williams's words, the "very model of Turner's crusading democrat."

By the end of the nineteenth century, then, it was widely assumed that the United States would take its place among imperial powers. This was a contested view, to be sure, but dominant among political and opinion elites. American empire qua American frontier meant that the rules and rationales of expansion, forged over nearly three centuries of conquest on the continent, would then be deployed to a global venture. How those rules and rationales were realized in practice was very quickly apparent in Cuba and the Philippines.

The Spanish-American War

The short war with Spain occasioned by a Cuban insurrection against Spanish rule and the sinking of the Maine was justified on grounds since familiar: national honor, abhorrence of Spanish atrocities against Cubans, protection of Americans and their property in Cuba, and regional peace. "Under most circumstances war is to be deplored," states a contemporary chronicle of the conflict. "But history shows that even with so peace loving a nation as our own, there comes times when aggravations under which we have patiently suffered can no longer be tolerated with honor and self-respect." Spain, with its "abhorrent barbarities continuing with such cruel persistence" had to be dealt with harshly, and so it was dealt by "the sturdy manhood of America," with one result being the "exaltation of the United States among the nations of the earth."[29] But the war was hardly a last resort, as many contended at the time, including McKinley's message to Congress asking for authorization to intervene. The expansionists were fairly itching for war, and Roosevelt, then an assistant secretary of the navy, bluntly represented this view: "All the great masterful races have been fighting races, and the minute that a race loses the hard fighting virtues, then, no matter what else it may retain," he told the Naval War College in 1897, "it has lost its proud right to stand as the equal of the best. Cowardice in a race, as in an individual, is the unpardonable sin." That same year, he wrote to Admiral Alfred T. Mahan, the architect of the global navy, "Until we definitely turn Spain out of those islands (and if I had my way that would be done tomorrow), we will always be menaced by trouble there."

For McKinley, the decision to go to war and the lure of overseas expansion were fortuitously wedded. The public seemed to abhor the maltreatment of the Cubans, but not enough to start a war, despite the rhetoric of Roosevelt and a few others in the Senate and the sensationalizing press.[30] But pressure mounted, particularly after the Maine disaster, and McKinley sought authority to intervene in Cuba, which prompted Spain to declare war in April 1898. A matter of days later, Admiral Dewey destroyed the Spanish fleet in Manila, and an army was mobilized to invade Cuba. The war lasted only until August. Spain agreed to Cuba's independence (though with tight U.S. controls) and ceded the Philippines, Guam, and Puerto Rico to the United States.

The "splendid little war" was significant in two ways. It gave the United States and the expansionists a relatively painless taste of victory and molded a narrative—Spanish atrocities and American humanistic rescue—that drew upon the frontier images and informed later military ventures abroad. Second, it married this narrative of an ethics-driven adventurism with the imperatives of trade and bonanza economics. W. A. Williams points out this powerful set of incentives, the hope of selling "surplus" abroad and the need to establish stepping stones to Asia in particular, was a view shared broadly in society. While pecuniary motives were one constant engine of continental expansion, they suddenly became paramount in the economic doldrums of the late nineteenth century. The war also provided a platform to unify the country still torn by the Civil War; McKinley's appeal to reconciliation (at a time of growing attacks on blacks) altered the long festering politics of recrimination, created a new frame for understanding the Civil War, and helped recruit Southerners for the patriotic war against Spain. The act of violence (the invasion of Cuba) redeemed the paternalistic racism toward Cubans and Filipinos while regenerating the frontier ethos in the new wilderness of Asia.

The Philippines: The Howling Wilderness

The prize of the war with Spain was the Philippines. The archipelago had been a Spanish colony since the sixteenth century (its name is from King Philip), and it was ceded reluctantly in the Treaty of Paris in 1898. The islands provided America with the perfect stepping stone to Asia, the largest jewel in the Pacific crown that in a matter of months added Guam (from Spain), Samoa (through seizure), and Hawaii (via a U.S.-engineered coup). But the Philippines were not an easy acquisition. The Spanish were swiftly overcome by U.S. naval power at the outset of the war, but that conflict soon gave way to resistance by Filipinos, indeed, a declaration of their independence and establishment of a republic. The ensuing war lasted for about a decade. In many respects, Washington's war to suppress Filipino independence was a model and a prelude to the major interventions following the Second World War, both in military strategy and outlook, and the attitudes of the American public.

In the most intense period of the war (1899–1902), the familiar ideas that justified the "winning of the West" were applied to the Philippines. The conflict was a savage war, fought against primitive cutthroats who resisted the beneficence of the U.S. occupation—rejecting civilization itself. The conflict was depicted from its outset as a racial contest, and the intensity and popularity of this racial frame increased as the war progressed. The racial aspect was twofold: the likening of the Filipinos to American natives was pervasive, with all the implications for how war was to be conducted; and references to the Filipinos as "niggers" at a time when racial attacks (lynching of blacks, mainly) in the United States were rampant. The implication to Theodore Roosevelt (who became president in September 1901) and others in the imperialist camp were obvious: the war challenged the white, enlightened way of life, and thereby was imperative to win. That large segments of Filipino society were relatively sophisticated, with educated and productive classes and cultural diversity, mattered little to the depiction in America of an ungrateful and septic place that required

Roosevelt thought war was a challenge & enlightenment.

the hard hand of discipline. "We will not renounce our part in the mission of our race, trustee, under God, of the civilization of the world," Albert Beveridge of Indiana proclaimed on the Senate floor, in exalting the markets of China and the natural wealth of the Philippines. "It has been charged that our conduct in the war has been cruel," he continued. "Senators must remember that we are not dealing with Americans or Europeans. We are dealing with Orientals."[31]

A number of key U.S. military leaders in the "expeditionary force" of 20,000 were veteran Indian fighters, no less, accustomed to a certain strategic objective—annihilation of the enemy. This strategy was enlivened and rationalized by the guerrillas' occasional acts of terror. Emilio Aguinaldo, the Filipino leader, was prototypical of twentieth-century insurgent strategists, using hit-and-run tactics and popular propaganda against the occupiers. The leadership of the Philippine republic and society more broadly was fragmented by the years of difficult resistance to Spanish colonial rule and the catastrophic war to defend independence against U.S. occupation. The cause of independence was broadly popular.* But not all Filipinos, particularly the monied class, were willing to oppose U.S. military power. As a result, the Americans could describe the resistance as not being broadly representative and therefore not legitimate. This form of disqualification—that those the United States was fighting were a marginal and therefore violent faction—also anticipated later wars.

In fact, it was the considerable popularity of his cause and his élan as a military leader that drove the U.S. leadership to adopt a very aggressive war strategy toward Aguinaldo and his followers. And because of the resistance fighters' embeddedness and their popularity among Filipinos, the Americans felt the need to adopt ever more violent tactics and practices. "Our men have been relentless," wrote a Philadelphia journalist, "have killed to exterminate men, women, children, prisoners, and captives, active insurgents and suspected people, lads of ten and up, an idea

---

* General Arthur MacArthur, a key U.S. military figure during the war (and father of Douglas MacArthur), said during the conflict: "When I first started in on these rebels, I thought Aguinaldo's troops represented only a fraction. . . . I did not like to believe that the whole population of Luzon was opposed to us. . . . But after having come thus far, and having been brought much into contact with *insurrectos* and *amigos*, I have been reluctantly compelled to believe that the Filipino masses are loyal to Aguinaldo and the government which he heads." Quoted in J. H. Bount, *The American Occupation of the Philippines* (Putnam, 1913): 529.

prevailing that the Filipino, as such, was little better than a dog. . . . It is not civilized warfare, but we are not dealing with civilized people. The only thing they know and fear is force, violence, and brutality, and we give it to them."[32] And so they did. One general estimated that one-sixth of the population of Luzon, the major island that includes Manila, was dead from the war, either by killing or disease. A major massacre on the island of Samar led to the prosecution of several U.S. officers; the testimony of one major noted that the commander, General Jacob Smith, "instructed him to kill and burn, and said that the more he killed and burned the better pleased [Smith] would be; that it was no time to take prisoners, and that he was to make Samar a howling wilderness."[33]

After the main period of resistance was over, Aguinaldo surrendered and the Republic essentially ended; scattered resistance continued for several years, with the U.S. military continuing to respond to outbreaks. Most notable in this period was an uprising of the Moros, a Muslim people in the far south, in which a rebellion against U.S. rule was broiling for years, in part as a result of American duplicity in not granting the Moros the autonomy promised in an 1899 treaty. General Leonard Wood, who won a Medal of Honor in the last campaign against Geronimo, was dispatched to put down the Moros. "The U.S. troops had arrived on a mission of liberation, promising to uplift the oppressed," military historian Andrew Bacevich wrote. "But the subjects of American beneficence, holding views of their own, proved recalcitrant. Doing good required first that the liberators pacify resistance and establish order. Before it was over, the Americans' honor had been lost, and uplift had given way to savagery."[34] The savagery was particularly gruesome as the Moros would not yield to U.S. power. The emblematic event of this contest was a 1906 massacre on the island of Jolo in which one thousand men, women, and children were shot dead at close range by U.S. troops, with no Moro survivors. "Now then, how has it been received?" Mark Twain asked sardonically of the news from the Philippines. "The splendid news appeared with splendid display-heads in every newspaper in [New York]." He reported President Roosevelt's cable to General Wood about the "battle": "I congratulate you and the officers and men of your command upon the brilliant feat of arms wherein you and they so well upheld the honor of the American flag."[35] The Moros continued their resistance well into the next decade, and the U.S. actions remain redolent in the lore of Muslim resistance to Western imperialism.

The war in the Philippines took 4,000 U.S. soldiers' lives, most by disease. Filipino mortality ranges from a fairly specific 34,000 military and another 200,000 civilians dead, to a broader calculus of indirect deaths totaling one million due to a cholera epidemic. Several other accounts have the death toll ranging between 300,000 and 500,000 in a population of 7 million.[36] As usual, separating out what is directly caused by war and what is indirect (in this case, the cholera epidemic), and when to stop counting—several "local" insurrections continued in the Philippines at least to 1913—is vexing. Because the Filipino resistance was highly localized, drawing on regional grievances and social structures, some provinces suffered disproportionately. However one regards the violence, it was an enormous, prolonged, ravaging of civilian life, and with few apparent moral qualms on the part of the occupation forces and their political leaders.

Throughout the war, firsthand accounts documenting American violence and atrocities were numerous, not least because the policy appeared, as Twain noted bitterly, to be popular. The "necessity" to respond in kind to a savage enemy was the basis for the broadsheets' relentless editorializing in favor of the war policy. The old habit of setting the white American against the brown insurrectionist was the reflexive stance of the political and opinion elite, and still, like the 1870s, set against a background in the United States of labor unrest, immigration from southern and eastern Europe, and racial turbulence. But there was an ideological quandary for the war's supporters, and for imperialists generally—the absence of the "wilderness" in the war's narrative. It was not the "wilderness" of Samar that could justify American actions, for General Smith was making it *into* a wilderness of destruction. The initial acquisition of the Philippines and the harsh suppression of Filipinos' own aspirations for independence were instead described as a necessity—America's need for a Pacific presence—as well as by the frontier myth's claim for financial good fortune, and the impulse to teach the uncivilized (in this case, the upstart Filipinos) a lesson in which race would rule. But the "errand into the wilderness" was not among the core rationales. It was particularly vexing because the reliable excuse of evangelizing Christianity was frustrated by the fact that urban Filipinos were already Christian, having been forcibly converted to the Church of Rome by the Spaniards.

The American war in the Philippines has long been relegated to a scarcely noticeable episode in U.S. history, frequently overlooked in textbooks and generally grasped as a brief adjunct to the Cuban triumph. "Amnesia over the horrors of the war of conquest in the Philippines set in . . . the summer of 1902," wrote historian Stuart Creighton Miller, who makes the bold case that the anti-imperialists essentially exonerated the public, and preserved "American innocence," by placing blame for the war on opaque, elite decision making. McKinley and Roosevelt's imperialism was, in this account, popular for the bonanza it seemed to promise. "When the dream soured," he concludes, "the American people seemed to take their cue from their leader in the White House by first putting out of mind all the sordid episodes in the conquest, and then forgetting the entire war itself."[37] The U.S. role in the war was repeatedly depicted by Roosevelt and his associates as one of restraint, honoring the principles of the flag, and a civilizing mission against savages. But it passed from a prominent place in American iconography quickly, never to return.

—

Imperial Anticolonialism

Like the period of the Mexican war, the war with Spain and the Philippines had many detractors, even as the actions likely were favored broadly in American society. The metrics of public opinion were scarcely developed then, and any sense of popularity is based on an imprecise calculation of the relevant direction of elections and congressional action, the temper of the press, personal accounts, and positioning by leading figures of the day and institutions like labor unions and churches. The detractors were, most prominently, the Anti-Imperialist League, a movement that was an amalgam of many different sorts—intellectuals like William James, Ambrose Bierce, John Dewey, and Twain; social reformer Jane Addams, steel magnate Andrew Carnegie, some (but not all) labor unions, African American activists, and clergy. The political debate was shaped by Democrats suspicious of Republican motives and those like William Jennings Bryan who were forthrightly opposed to this form of imperialism. As several historians point out, however, many in the anti-imperialist camp were disinclined to overseas adventures because annexation of countries like Cuba or the Philippines could bring brown-skinned people in great numbers into the United States.[38]

The argument between the likes of Roosevelt and the likes of Bryan pivoted on the exact form of American expansion overseas—whether, for example, the United States would have actual colonies—rather than a stark contest between imperialist and anti-imperialist positions. "It is more illuminating," explained W. A. Williams, "to view it as a three-cornered discussion won by businessmen and intellectuals who opposed traditional colonialism and advocated instead the policy of open door for America's overseas economic expansion . . . a brilliant strategic stroke which led to the gradual extension of American economic and political power throughout the world."[39] That these "imperial anticolonialists" won the argument could be seen not only in Roosevelt's administration (which included the important commercial project of the Panama Canal) but in that of Wilson, the paragon of liberal internationalism, who (with Bryan's help as secretary of state) invaded Mexico, Haiti, Cuba, and Panama. U.S. troops also occupied Nicaragua, and in most of these ventures, the political decision making was held firmly in Washington's hands.

Wilson's global activism, however, brought the frontier myth fully into the twentieth century, not least because his interventions near and far introduced a more normative element, as his interest in spreading democracy and good governance was evident well before his turn at the Versailles Peace Conference in 1919. This activism in effect brought the "errand" back into the mixture of motives driving America to become a major world power, for it was that sense of mission—moralizing, self-referential, "Christian," and Enlightenment-based—which was a necessary, or at least useful, accompaniment to the exercise of raw power in opening markets to American corporations and farmers. The entry into the Great War further established the U.S. global mission. Paired with Wilson's assertive stance at Versailles, by which he became the world's model anticolonialist, the participation on the winning side of the war deepened American involvement in world politics, an essentially irreversible course despite the Senate defeat of U.S. membership in the League of Nations.

Wilson set in motion or accelerated three cardinal trends in U.S. foreign policy and domestic political culture. The first was fostering the deep involvement of the United States in global affairs, creating an image of America as the champion of the colonized against the European imperialists, while simultaneously enabling the steady accretion of economic power. The second was linking the frontier myth's moralism with U.S. expansion globally, by bringing democracy and self-governance to the oppressed. The third was a growing anticommunism at home and abroad.

All of this was undertaken by a man who was more than a little imperialist at heart—Wilson was guided by racist ideas as much as Roosevelt was, if less obviously. And as with all military interventions, "errands," or economic domination, racism helps justify what might otherwise be considered morally questionable actions. Wilson's piety also drove his assertiveness, so the Christian element was galvanizing. In addition to racist ideas and his embrace of self-determination as America's calling card in the world (an embrace of inconsistent pressure), Wilson's legacies were an affirmation of the "corporatist" model of global economic policy and the related determination to block the relatively new, contesting model of socialism. Corporatism, which is often associated with Herbert Hoover, was a continuation of the "open door" policies generated under McKinley, advanced by Theodore Roosevelt, and nurtured again by Wilson. This nonterritorial form of empire continued to be refined and practiced by the United States, which occasionally would find the application of military force to be useful.

Wilson grabbed for that military force quite readily when suddenly confronted with the first successful revolutions inspired by Marx, most significantly in Russia. Wilson not only supported the allies' intervention on behalf of the White Russians fighting the Bolsheviks, but initiated covert action specifically aimed at regime change.[40] He regarded the emerging Soviet state as the antithesis of the Christian, democratic, capitalist ideal he was promoting elsewhere. Within the United States, moreover, Wilson acted repeatedly to suppress socialist trade unions in particular and stirred the first Red Scare in 1918. Federal law enforcement created a list of 450,000 "subversives," including hundreds of newspapers, and the scare rippled across America to solidify a fear and loathing of leftists. Between November 1919 and January 1920, some 4,000 people were arrested, many of them immigrants who were quickly deported. (J. Edgar Hoover was in charge of the Alien Radical division of Mitchell Palmer's Justice Department and did much of the dirty work in what came to be known as the Palmer Raids.) The effects of this outburst, which was both nativist and anticommunist, were powerful in politics and popular culture. Labor union membership fell dramatically, with the more militant unions destroyed altogether. The press, generally supportive of the government crackdown, was intimidated, with leftists purged and leftist sympathies silenced. It was a brief but powerful antecedent to the McCarthy period that followed the next world war, and it set the antagonism between Americanism and "communism" as an official, punitive frame of reference that would last for more than seventy years.[41]

By the 1920s, the contours for U.S. foreign involvement were shaped. The cultural and political impetus of frontier mythology powerfully affected American actions and their justifications in the world, a world that by 1945 was very much an American playing field. Williams traced the power of the frontier thesis in U.S. foreign policy to 1953, noting Franklin D. Roosevelt's occasional reference to the closing of the frontier and his interest in expanding the reach of the U.S. economy as a way of coping with economic stagnation; in Williams's estimate, FDR "was sure . . . that America's frontier was the world." Harry Truman's use of the frontier metaphor was evident in the rapid widening of America's global scope after the Second World War. Slotkin uncovers the pervasiveness of the myth in American popular culture—particularly novels and films—as well as politics, and finds certain manifestations of the frontier ideology recurring: the need and obligation to tame the wilderness; the morally purifying violence of savage wars; the civilizing mission of expansion; and the endless promise of economic rewards from expansion.

As the twentieth century rolled toward the Second World War and beyond, the tropes of the frontier myth remained vibrant. Increasingly, and especially after 1945, the "Indians" were Soviet communists and their allies. The "wilderness" was any country under the sway of Marxism-Leninism and the global south generally, released from European colonialism and reverting to a kind of political and moral wilderness that matched its physical and demographic attributes. The "bonanza" of the frontier was domination of the world economic system itself, the resource riches of Africa and Asia, and the cheap labor everywhere south of the equator. The stage was set for the global expansion of the American frontier.

CHAPTER 3
Strategic Bombing in the Second World War

The two world wars that came between the end of the continental frontier, and the beginning of the series of "savage wars" America has waged in Asia in the last sixty years, conditioned our views of death and destruction. In the aftermath of the colossal carnage of Great War of 1914–18, Americans and Europeans acted time and again to abolish war, armaments, and causes of conflict. That such efforts failed—the Kellogg-Briand Pact in 1928 outlawing war appears quaint today—does not discount the widely popular sentiments driving their creation. By the late 1940s, the good intentions undergirding the United Nations were similar to those ambient sentiments of the interwar period. But the destruction wrought during the Second World War, destruction of unimaginable magnitude, may also have numbed Americans to the human cost of righteous violence.

The antiwar movement in the United States in the interwar years was a significant political force, particularly when combined with the "America First" isolationists pressing against foreign involvement. Whatever its composition, this broad opposition to war was powerful enough to make Franklin Roosevelt, even following his landslide victory of 1936, hesitate to act against the Nazi menace in Europe and Imperial Japan's aggressiveness in Asia. The appeasement that much later became synonymous with cowardice was in the late 1930s a viable and relatively popular policy in Britain and the United States, occasioned by the horror of the war that had ended only twenty years earlier.

This apparent abandonment of the tenets of frontier ideology was more hiatus than retreat, not only born of revulsion of phenomena like the trench warfare of 1914–18, but also of the Great Depression, which gripped America and the world in 1929 and had not loosened much by the late 1930s. Europe was not a "frontier," one of the bonanza-laden virgin terrains that were promised by the myth. Defending the French and British (much less Russians) from German depredations was a very different errand from the familiar taming of the wilderness. It was this altogether different and less compelling mission that FDR had to sell. That the United States remained outside the conflict, officially neutral more than two years after Hitler invaded Poland, is a testament to the aversion Americans felt toward war.

The aversion was mobilized by very sizable peace organizations, often led by women, which provided a broad political legitimacy to antiwar sentiment stirring among the legions of poor, unemployed, or barely viable Americans. This echoed similar if more resolute pacifist opinion in Europe, which had borne the brunt of the Great War's grinding destruction. This aversion, or deep anxiety at the very least, was evident in much of the popular interwar writing—Hemingway, Dos Passos, Trumbo, among others—which had depicted the 1914–18 war as an immensely bloody and pointless endeavor. "By the late 1920s," says one analysis of the literature, "the anti-war view of Dos Passos and Hemingway, previously confined to a small group of 'disenchanted' writers and intellectuals, began to gain a wider acceptance."[1] The war's purpose was also questioned by new historians, playwrights, and novelists. There were others who glorified the experience from afar—Willa Cather and Edith Wharton among them—but the ambivalence present in the literature departed from the earlier dominance of can-do Americanism the world over, whether of TR's blustery kind or Wilson's more high-toned interventionism. Americans approached the 1940s rather firmly in the no-war camp, even as it loomed in Europe; indeed, FDR at first congratulated Neville Chamberlain on his deal with Hitler at Munich, reflecting the contemporary view of appeasement that avidly sought to avoid war. The Wilsonian president failed to intervene against fascism in Spain's civil war, too, partly in response to the Catholic Church's pressure and partly from a more general distaste for such involvements. Even after Hitler invaded Poland, France, and the Low

Countries, the political difficulty Roosevelt faced in trying to aid Britain was rooted in the ground of antiwar, not merely isolationist, principle and feeling.

The war fought was total war, the likes of which the world had never seen. The cost in every way was immense. By its end, some sixty million people were dead and another fifty million homeless, many of them refugees. The United States helped repair much of the damage, to its credit, and concern for the human cost of the war was evident in hundreds of efforts to rescue orphans, rebuild cities, aid refugees, and so on—efforts more apparent after the war's conclusion. During the war, the suspension of active concern was driven by the apparent need to use every means possible to stop the Germans, Italians, and Japanese. Even before widespread knowledge of Nazi death camps, the depiction of Hitler and his rancid ideology as utterly inimical to American values was a given. Japan's ravages in China in the 1930s had been widely reported—the 1937 "rape" of Nanking perhaps most gruesomely conveyed to a large audience—and while seeming to be distant at the time, Japanese aggression was a cause of wariness. The attack on Pearl Harbor was in keeping with the popular suspicions of Japan, one that required a ferocious rebuttal.

Trench warfare and chemical weapons were the great scourges of the First World War, but for the most part they affected only soldiers. The cardinal difference in how war was fought merely a generation later was air power. The development of bombardment from airplanes changed all calculations. (In the earlier conflict, bombing from the air was used, but was scarcely comparable to the next world war in scale or lethality.)[2] From an early stage, the British and Americans used *strategic* bombing, which was meant to have a broader effect than simply the destruction of a military target, such as the war industries. After a meeting of Churchill and Roosevelt at Casablanca in 1943, a directive was issued to increase strategic bombing, not only to impair Germany's war industries—armaments, steel, energy, transportation—but also to destroy the morale of the German people. That meant bombing and killing civilians. The British conducted many of these raids in the early going, particularly the devastating attacks on Hamburg in the summer of 1943, intentional firestorms that resulted in 40,000 casualties. W. G. Sebald, the German novelist and literary critic, described the firebombing in a lecture:

1) strategic bombing
2) kill civilians too.
3) A LOT of BOMBS

First all the doors and windows were torn from their frames and smashed by high-explosive bombs weighing four thousand pounds, then the attic floors of the building were ignited by lightweight incendiary mixtures, and at the same time firebombs weighing up to fifteen kilograms fell into the lower stories. Within a few minutes, huge fires were burning all over the target area, which covered some twenty square kilometers, and they merged so rapidly that only a quarter of an hour after the first bombs had dropped the whole air space was a sea of flames as far as the eye could see. . . . [A] firestorm of an intensity that no one would ever before have thought possible arose. The fire, now rising two thousand meters into the sky, snatched oxygen to itself so violently that the currents reached hurricane force.[3]

Many more bombings followed. While in the popular mind, strategic bombing in Europe is mainly associated with the horrific firebombing of Dresden in 1944, killing about 30,000 to 40,000 people and demolishing the city center, the tactic was utilized hundreds of times in fifty German cities, destroying two-fifths of all residential dwellings and making 7.5 million civilians homeless. In the words of the Strategic Bombing Survey, the official U.S. account following the war, civil defense was nearly useless in these attacks, apart from the most resilient concrete bunkers: "Fire storms occurred, the widespread fires generating a violent hurricane-like draft, which fed other fires and made all attempts at control hopeless."

There was an outcry against the bombing of Dresden in Britain particularly; the war seemed to be won and the incineration of one of Europe's most graceful cities struck many as excessive if not immoral. Some protests followed in the United States. "The *New York Times* gave page one coverage to a protest by twenty-eight prominent Americans, mostly clergy, against 'obliteration raids' on German cities," according to a journalist's account. "The protestors called upon Christians 'to examine themselves concerning their participation in this carnival of death' and to acquaint themselves with 'the realities of what is being done in our name in Europe.'"[4] Secretary of War Henry Stimson ordered an investigation, but the policy was already in effect and would continue until the surrender of Germany in May 1945.

Targeting Japan came later, with the main aerial bombings starting in December 1944, as its islands were out of range of sustained attack in the early years of the war. Apart from the atomic bombings, the most important of the strategic attacks was the raid on Tokyo in March 1945. Incendiary bombs easily set aflame a city built of wood, and more than 185,000 casualties resulted. The firestorm, by all accounts, was hellish. The fire destroyed half of a city the size of New York, and many more incendiary attacks, using napalm, followed on other large Japanese cities under the command of General Curtis LeMay, who innovated the raids by flying lower to the ground at nighttime; "bomb and burn them until they quit," he said, and he halted the firebombing only because he ran out of incendiaries. "LeMay said, 'if we'd lost the war we would have been prosecuted as war criminals,' and I think he's right," said one of his top aides, Robert McNamara. "He, and I'd say, I, were behaving as war criminals." At the time, the bombings were greeted with relief in the United States. "The American reaction at the time was that they deserved it," said historian John Dower. "There was almost a genocidal attitude on the part of the American military, and it extended to the American public."[5] *it was like a genocide . .*

The firebombing of Tokyo was neither a unique event nor one that suddenly entered the plans of decision makers late in the war. The famous Doolittle raids of 1942 also dropped incendiaries on Tokyo, and the tactic was always in play. "The shift from precision attacks on factories to area attacks on major Japanese cities had been part of U.S. plans for years," wrote one military historian. "Japanese civilian casualties were not accidental or incidental, but an explicit goal of the incendiary raids on Japanese cities."[6] Not only did the number of casualties and physical damage from the firebombing of Tokyo rival that of Hiroshima and Nagasaki, but the air raids on cities drove nearly nine million Japanese into the countryside. Malnutrition—a result of war itself rather than the aerial bombardment—became acute in the last months of the war, contributing to the despair that overcame many Japanese (likely a majority) even before the shock of the atomic attacks.

The decision to use the "gadget"—Oppenheimer's piquant code name for the atomic device—as a weapon was predicated on its shock value. After all, it could have been detonated somewhere without civilians to demonstrate its awesome, destructive power. It could have been dropped once. But it was instead used twice, on sizable cities, just when Japan was nearly exhausted and by some accounts close to surrender. This decision, subjected to heated debate that continues to this day— particularly the common assertion after the war that atomic bombings

killed Japanese (2 bombs) .. even though they were about to surrend.

were necessary to defeat Japan without a bloody invasion—was in any case taken to deal a final and fatal blow to Japanese morale. The terrible swift sword of the fission bomb leveled the center square mile of each city and killed immediately 80,000 in Hiroshima and 50,000 in Nagasaki, with many more dying in the coming months from radiation poisoning.

Strategic bombing, according to the conservative estimate of the U.S. survey, killed 305,000 civilians and wounded 780,000 in Germany; in Japan, 330,000 civilians died, another 476,000 were wounded. In fact, the Japanese total was higher, due to the lingering effects of the atomic weapons. This scale of mayhem, meted out by the particularly frightening weapon of the incendiary bomb—hence the tactic's contemporary name, "terror bombing"—had its intended effect of demoralizing the enemy population. The survey found that "the morale of the German people deteriorated under aerial attack. The night raids were feared far more than daylight raids. The people lost faith in the prospect of victory, in their leaders, and in the promises and propaganda to which they were subjected. Most of all, they wanted the war to end." The conclusions of the survey were somewhat controversial; one of its leaders, John Kenneth Galbraith, later declared that strategic bombing was ineffectual, and the tactic has been roundly debated ever since. But there was no controversy about the purpose of terror bombing: to kill civilians massively and terrorize those who survived. This was official U.S. policy.

One striking question is less about the damage and the population's morale than whether morale actually mattered. Do ordinary people in totalitarian or authoritarian states have any voice in such circumstances? Organized dissent or opposition to continuing the war was not evident. Productivity in German industry declined only slightly until the last year of the war. The situation in Japan was more chaotic by the spring and summer of 1945, but possibly more due to near-famine conditions. So the very foundation of the strategy of demoralization was questionable from the beginning. Only killing on a truly colossal scale would have impaired the German or Japanese leadership from carrying on, if its military had had that capacity; strategic bombing of industry had more obvious benefits for the Allies. Another question is whether damaging war-making industries could have been accomplished without the scale of human loss that occurred.

The scorched earth policy did not produce much of a protest in American society. The scale of the war, the manifest evil of Hitler and Tojo, and official insistence on the necessity of the bombings to end the war, all convinced the public that this was the right course. The relief that the world war was over trumped all other thoughts. Hitler and Tojo were by any measure monstrous in their war aims and conduct. The Holocaust and devastation in Europe and the genocidal practices of Japan in China were reasons that the American public found the war's end—by any means—morally justified.

Debates about the morality of the bombing aside, the significance of strategic bombing with regard to civilian casualties may be found in a numbing effect, or at least a renewed sense of trade-offs in war that justified civilian losses when the cause was righteous. The Germans in particular, while under the sway of an extraordinary political madness, were too like Americans ethnically and culturally to regard them as "savages;" but the Japanese were another matter. The images of the Japanese and the atrocities they committed were more dominant than anything attributed to the Germans in American popular culture, with the growing presence of Hollywood leading the way. This provided the emotional fodder for total war.

But in both cases, civilians were fair game because of a calculation that killing the enemy was preferable to the potential of more loss of our own troops. This perhaps was always true, and broadly true in this war. What is different is the scale of killing: its quickness, lethality, and ferocity. There was nothing incidental about the deaths of hundreds of thousands of essentially innocent human beings; and once this threshold was crossed, the next time might be easier.

This scale and type of killing was also associated with a heroic feat, the creation of the atomic weapon, American ingenuity as a savior of the nation. It fulfilled a decades-long fantasy sparked by the rise of the airplane and its transformative qualities for warfare. This power, and the unique nature of atomic warfare, were a talisman of sorts, able simultaneously to project destructive power and thereby, in the moral musings of its proponents, make a case against war itself. So the use of the atomic bomb, for example, was justified by the secretary of war, Henry Stimson, as a "horrible" event that "could awaken the world to the necessity of abolishing war altogether." As historian Michael S. Sherry noted in *The Rise of American Airpower*, "If the bomb promised either deliverance or doomsday, if it loomed as either scourge or savior of mankind, then its psychological awesomeness became all-important, and questions regarding its immediate consequences for Japan's cities seemed almost trivial in comparison." The atomic weapon, and indeed the firebombing that preceded it for two years, were framed as a redemption through violence—not precisely in the Puritan sense, to be sure, but no less striking—in which the very act of destroying the ultimate evil of fascism was redeeming for the Allies, not only in the commonly understood ends-and-means moral equation, but also because the very scale of destruction was redemptive for all humanity as it could lead to the abolition of war. Thus the U.S. decision makers, wrote Sherry, were acting in a "tradition of prophecy" about air power that "allowed destruction to proceed almost unquestioned, while the moral energies of responsible men remained focused on man's historical fate."[7]

The attempts to make a few of the inventors of the bomb into heroes did not succeed. Oppenheimer and the others working in the New Mexico hills to develop the weapon were brilliant scientists, but not swashbucklers. Oppenheimer himself was hounded from government service as a result of several unfounded rumors that rendered him a "security risk." In addition, many of the most prominent atomic scientists were Jewish immigrants, a sizable portion of whom, along with many of the native-born scientists, were stoutly opposed to further development of the atomic arsenal—not the stuff American heroism is made of. (It is ironic that these actual frontiersmen, men who explored and altered our understanding of physics and war, and organized science's relationship to each, could never quite catch on as heroes in the mode of the frontier myth.) As a wife of an atomic scientist, Alice Kimball Smith, described the mood after the first blush of euphoria that the gadget had worked, "the revulsion grew, bringing with it—even for those who believed that the end of the war justified the bombing—an intensely personal experience of the reality of evil."[8]

The Second World War's dramatic conclusion also ended two sentiments about America's place in the world. Far more than Theodore Roosevelt or Woodrow Wilson might have imagined, America was a global power of unprecedented scale. The indelible image of Eisenhower's ticker-tape parade down Fifth Avenue seemed to encapsulate America's new sense of power. We had won the war. The homeland was nearly unscathed. We had half the world's economic output. The "wise men" were crafting the postwar world.

The other sentiment laid to rest was the innocence of war. The loss of innocence, or ignorance, about the sheer brutality of war had started long before—especially for those who experienced it—but the Second World War affected so many so directly, and had been waged with a ferocity previously unknown, that any remaining notions of war as a noble and personal endeavor were fundamentally challenged. Total war as an application of deadly force by technological means was suddenly the norm. All calculations of American war-makers would begin with that as the premise.

America had global power & half the world's economic output.

− 3,000,000 deaths.

CHAPTER 4

The Korean War

The Hegemony of Forgetting

The three-year war in Korea took three million lives and ended in a stalemate, with the lines demarcating north from south nearly the same at the moment of cease-fire as they were at the moment of outbreak. The war was variously depicted as a civil war, a superpower competition, the opening shots of the Cold War, and an effort to establish U.S. containment of the Soviet Union and China. To the extent that it stirred passions in the United States, those hinged on outsized personalities—MacArthur, Truman, Acheson, McCarthy, and Eisenhower. For most of its three years, the attitude toward the war was less one of obsession and more of negligence: once the war looked like a loser, the American public turned away from its carnage and mainly quibbled over its domestic politics.

Three aspects of the Korean War are worth exploring here. First is its politics, the reassertion of anticommunism as a central fixation in America, unique in its features and cultural resonance, which preceded the war but was fueled by the conflict and also shaped public perceptions of the war and its stakes. Second is the strategic implications of the war: what, after all, could justify such a bloody war, aggressive tactics, and contemplation of the use of nuclear weapons in this out-of-the-way peninsula? Third is the colossal loss of life and the sharp juxtaposition between American indifference and Korean suffering. The entire deathly, inconclusive enterprise could be summarized in the solders' complaint that they were there "to die for a tie."

The longer view of Korea's importance remains obscure. The South Koreans have taken up long-repressed memories and grievances in a Truth and Reconciliation Commission (TRC) that is reshaping their understanding of the war, the American role, and their own leadership. South Korea long suffered under authoritarian right-wing regimes until the 1990s, regimes that were both a cause and a consequence of the war. The North remains in the grip of its peculiar leaders, repressive of its people, isolated, and episodically dangerous.

The interpretations of the war by journalists and historians were frequently intended to teach lessons about Vietnam but may be more relevant to Iraq. Ill-defined objectives and expectations, the use of war as a signal of resolve to other adversaries, and a bitter fractiousness in domestic politics characterized all three wars. But with Korea, as with Iraq, public indifference swiftly took hold, absolving American leaders of responsibility for the human costs of the war, while its proponents practiced the politics of reductionism—that is, presenting the war as a stark choice between good and evil. The intellectual discourse about the Korean War's meaning, apart from predictable lamentations about the limits of U.S. power, never grappled with the magnitude of loss. This, too, is the apparent fate of the failed venture in Iraq.

For the American public, the Korean conflict has frequently been regarded as the "forgotten" war, forgotten not by others but by Americans themselves. The losses on the battlefield, the alternately desultory and vitriolic politics, and the cruel price for an inconclusive outcome all shaped perceptions. "For many Americans," David Halberstam concluded in his massive history, "Korea became something of a black hole in terms of history. In the year following the ceasefire, it was a war they wanted to know less rather than more about."[1] Its "forgottenness"—this collective silence—says much about Americans' attitudes toward war. That so much could have been sacrificed without serious regard, introspection, or even remembrance is telling. The catastrophe of war could not be confronted, its moral lessons buried by indifference, avoidance, and even relief.

THE NEW ENEMY

Communism was believed in America to be an insidious threat long before the North Koreans crossed the 38th parallel to begin what we know as the Korean War in June 1950. From the time of the Bolshevik Revolution at the latest, communism was considered by most Americans as the antithesis of the U.S. credo of freedom, capitalism, and religiosity. While there was a resilient interest in democratic socialism, mainly evidenced in labor unions and in a small but visible Socialist Party, affinity in the United States for Marxism-Leninism as practiced in the Soviet Union was scant. Yet the national obsession with communists internally and the growing communist world abroad was a fulcrum of American politics in the twentieth century. It began most spectacularly with the Palmer raids in 1920, which demonstrated the government's seriousness under the liberal President Wilson to eradicate leftist organizations. Socialists and other leftists, even liberals, were confused for communists and were ensnared by the broad net of J. Edgar Hoover and countless legislative investigators.

The mounting attention to communists occurred almost simultaneously with the closing of the American continental frontier, mainly a fortuitous coincidence but not without connections. The business elite and the press often compared the labor strife and newly arrived immigrant workers in the late nineteenth century with the wars against Native Americans. One New York newspaper in 1886, in decrying a labor "riot," called for a ban on further European immigration: "Such foreign savages, with their dynamite bombs and anarchic purposes, are as much apart from the rest of the people of this country as the Apaches of the plains are."[2] The taming of the wilderness was paralleled by the taming of the urban masses throughout the latter nineteenth and early twentieth centuries, and the language and norms of "savage war" were applied with equal vigor to both. That many in this new labor force belonged to left-wing unions solidified the depictions of the "savages" as communists, and communists as savages. The attacks on the leftist workers were frequent and often violent, as with Haymarket affair in Chicago in 1886 and the Ludlow massacre of mineworkers in Colorado in 1914. The left-wing unions, particularly the Industrial Workers of the World, or Wobblies, were militant and confrontational, not surprising given the deplorable working conditions, low pay, and gross disparities in the nation's distribution of wealth. So the owning classes, including the newspaper barons, sought to depict them as mortal threats over many decades. As communism appeared viable in Russia in 1917 and Europe experienced postwar convulsions that were in part driven by Marxists, the new threat in America seemed all the more apparent to the powerful. The communists schemed to eliminate "all science, art, and every advance of civilization," declared Senator Miles Poindexter, a

Republican from Washington state, on the Senate floor in 1918. "Their ideas are foolish in the extreme and if carried out would bring about a reversion to savagery and mean the end of all civilization."[3]

The militancy of labor increased in the 1930s after a period of relative quiescence that followed the Palmer raids and other anti-union actions of the federal authorities. The Federal Bureau of Investigation, newly created and used by Palmer specifically to hunt Reds, quickly became an effective instrument of state power in the 1920s, and the task of rooting out communists became Hoover's very public obsession. But the Depression turned the tide again and gave rise to a new labor activism buoyed by a public sympathy for the unions' views that was both durable and widely shared. No longer socially marginal and often aligned openly with the American Communist Party, this activism helped propel some New Deal reforms but also produced a response from conservatives—themselves shunted to the margins by FDR's popularity—which gradually laid the groundwork for a new Red Scare. The House Un-American Activities Committee (HUAC) was created in 1938, chaired by a conservative Texas Democrat, Martin Dees, and immediately went after the New Deal itself by associating some members of the Roosevelt administration with communism. At the same time, a burgeoning anti-communist coalition was taking root, nourished by the Catholic Church. "The American working class was largely Catholic and, in order to maintain the church's influence over its flock and especially over its dwindling male membership, some Catholic activists undertook to drive the Communist party out of the labor movement," observed historian Ellen Schrecker. "In the late 1930s, a handful of enterprising priests and laypeople began to organize anti-Communist nuclei within a few left-led unions. Though ineffectual at first, these efforts were to provide the organizational structure for later, more successful campaigns to eliminate the party's influence in the labor movement."[4] Men of the cloth like Charles Coughlin, Francis Spellman, and Fulton Sheen were voluble anticommunists who helped leverage Catholicism's social conservatism. So a decade that began with broad appeals for relief and fairness, organized in a socially diverse movement, ended with an increasingly and bitterly polarized society still beset by an anemic economy.

Dees' committee was short-circuited by the Second World War, and it could never quite gain a foothold in the political milieu of the late 1930s, but its tactics and ideology informed the more consequential congressional investigations following the war. Events abroad fed the momentum of right-wing anticommunism. Josef Stalin's harsh internal repression in the 1930s drove many from the party in the United States to become celebrated anticommunists. The Soviet Union was encouraged by its role in defeating the Axis powers and asserted itself as a postwar global power in Central and Southeastern Europe and East Asia. This startling expansion of the Soviet sphere was seen quickly in America as a formidable challenge, spurring renewed attention to the internal presence of communists. Stalin's moves into Central Europe mobilized Americans whose ancestors had emigrated from those countries. The USSR developed nuclear weapons—its first atomic test was in 1949—and kept an enormous army mobilized. Across the Asian continent, Marxism-Leninism was also on the march, most prominently in China, where Mao's forces took power in 1949. Communist or leftist parties were prominent in India, Iran, Southeast Asia, and indeed much of the global south emerging from colonialism.

In Washington, such events occasioned a sense of panic that very soon became the political equivalent of a house-to-house search for traitors in government and society. The high-profile cases, such as Congressman Richard Nixon's pursuit of the diplomat Alger Hiss, or HUAC's war against the Hollywood 10, were aimed squarely at institutions the right wing abhorred—in these cases, the United Nations (with which Hiss was associated) and the leftist segment of the entertainment industry (which was also significantly Jewish). Through the Depression, the influence of communists or other leftists in these institutions was discernible, but judging by the film industry's overall output, Red influence was insignificant and any ideational sympathy was a far cry from fealty to Stalin. What is remarkable about the anticommunist enterprise was not the attempt to ferret out "disloyal" employees from government and other institutions (a practice that President Truman also supported), but the widely proffered conception of a certain type of enemy—the communist subversive at home and the communist foe abroad. They were not merely believers in a strong central state, communal ownership, a godless and classless society, and so on, but comprised a heinous race necessitating the cleansing of America and a fresh commitment to U.S. militancy to battle them overseas.

The two depictions were vitally linked and therein laid its unique lethality. "The web of subversion is not primarily a domestic growth," wrote organizational theorist James Burnham, a former Trotskyite who became a fierce anticommunist. "It is the domestic extension of an international organism . . . the spinning of the web."[5] This perception of an insidious peril, which stirred a new genre of science fiction movies in the 1950s, depicted communists as aliens, like insects or monsters, or in apocalyptic Christian imagery, with Stalin as the Antichrist. Or the communist was a brute, a new version of the horde. Or a cancer, a disease. "Communism is to the social body what leprosy is to the physical body; in fact it is more serious, for Communism affects personality directly, while disease affects the mind and soul only indirectly," Bishop Sheen told his television flock. "Communism is intrinsically evil . . . because it submerges and destroys personality to the status of an ant in an anthill."[6]

Whatever the imagery used, the central anxiety about communism was its intention to take over America and force it into the Soviet mold. The communist-hunting publication *Red Channels*, which was a prime source for lists of suspected communists and fellow travelers in television, put it starkly: "the Communist Party will assume control of this nation as the result of a final upheaval and civil war."[7] This fear, repeated with metronomic frequency in much of the popular press in the late 1940s and early 1950s, insistently connected internal "subversion" in American society, the Soviet influence and agents in the U.S. Government, and the actions of the Soviets abroad. In this way, much of U.S. foreign policy was regarded as not merely a fatally weak response to Soviet designs, but weak precisely because American communists were weakening it. Potentially worse were the harrowing doubts about the American character, its moral decline and self-indulgence, which made the work of the enemy all the easier. This self-recrimination was a replay of the Puritans in the second and third generation, and its potency as a springboard for violence—the violence of repression at home, and war abroad—would replicate itself years later as well.

The Phenomenology of McCarthyism

By 1950, the postwar machinations of anticommunism were at full throttle. HUAC and several other committees on Capitol Hill and in state legislatures had been conducting highly publicized hearings for years that sought to expose the extent of communist influence in government, academia, lower schools, the entertainment industry, the legal profession, the news media, and others. Rhetorical, public floggings of leftists and dismissals of thousands of academics, journalists, and others from their jobs for sympathy with liberal and leftist ideas accelerated through the late 1940s. The Soviets' test of an atomic weapon in 1949, their grip on Eastern Europe, and the "loss" of China in October of that same year underscored the apparent need for a wholesale commitment to resist communist expansion. The Truman Doctrine, articulated by the president in 1947 when the Soviets were meddling in the Greek civil war and in Turkey, put the United States at the forefront of the "free world," and against totalitarianism. "The free peoples of the world look to us for support in maintaining their freedoms," Truman told Congress. "If we falter in our leadership, we may endanger the peace of the world—and we shall surely endanger the welfare of our own nation." But this policy did not satisfy many who wanted to roll back communism, or saw the U.S. policy of containing Soviet influence as too weak, uncertain, or ambiguous. It seemed clear that communism was on the march, despite the Marshall Plan and containment, and those in the United States intent upon raising the alarms focused not just on Stalin and his designs, but on his helpers in America.

These alarms reached a new volume in the winter of 1950 in the person of Senator Joseph McCarthy, Republican of Wisconsin, who made repeated, sweeping, and largely undocumented charges of a vast Soviet spy network in the U.S. government. In the launch of his jeremiad, he proclaimed:

The reason why we find ourselves in a position of impotency is not because our only powerful potential enemy has sent men to invade our shores . . . but rather because of the traitorous actions of those who have been treated so well by this Nation. It has not been the less fortunate, or members of minority groups who have been traitorous to this Nation, but rather those who have had all the benefits that the wealthiest Nation on earth has had to offer . . . the finest homes, the finest college education and the finest jobs in government we can give.

I have here in my hand a list of 205 . . . a list of names that were made known to the Secretary of State as being members of the Communist Party and who nevertheless are still working and shaping policy in the State Department.[8]

For four years McCarthy held sway in his Senate investigation and in the news media as the great scourge of communists in government, industry, and universities. The heightened public sensitivity to risks posed by Soviet agents or others with sympathies for communism—driven by the Hiss case and amplified by McCarthy—added to a sense of insecurity that had several other roots. This made "McCarthyism" and anticommunist fervency a salient political force in the decision to initiate an ambitious war in Korea (and, later, in Indochina), a perilous nuclear arms race, and confrontations all over the world for the coming four decades.

Among those factors was anxiety about the global U.S. role. In the late 1940s there remained a debate about Roosevelt's drawing the United States into the Second World War: that he somehow used trickery (Pearl Harbor) or was seduced by the British into a bloody and costly involvement.* The argument about FDR was just as much about postwar engagement in the ambitious act of creating the United Nations, occupying Germany and Japan, confronting the Soviet Union, devising the Truman Doctrine and Marshall Plan—all signaling an enormous role for the United States. The anxiety this role provoked reinforced the isolationism always present in American political culture and both fed anticommunist sentiment and clashed with it. Confronting the Soviets and Chinese and their growing web of subversion, repression, and expansion would mandate global leadership in Washington. But global engagement meant, in the first half of the twentieth century, two world wars and colossal costs: $340 billion for the Second World War, with 400,000 Americans killed. A shooting war with the Soviet Union—which sacrificed twenty million of its people to help defeat the Nazis—appeared in the late 1940s as a genuine possibility.

The dread of that prospect was intensified by the onset of the nuclear age. Once again, the Soviet menace was alarming not merely because it possessed an atomic bomb, but because a spy ring in the United States

---

* A cultivated suspicion of the English and their American "imitators"—Hiss, Acheson, and others—was fostered as part of this sense of conspiracy, a sentiment held mainly in the German and Scots-Irish "hinterlands" of the Midwest and South. This perception of class difference based on nationality was remarkably strong. It recalls Isaiah Berlin's explanation for fascism as the anti-Enlightenment reaction of the Germans in the nineteenth century, who resented French attitudes of superiority.

had apparently provided atomic secrets to the communist state, adding betrayal to the danger. The arrest of the Manhattan Project physicist Klaus Fuchs in January 1950 for passing secrets to Moscow, followed by arrests of Americans Julius and Ethel Rosenberg, among others, for being couriers of the bomb secrets, were sensational charges that remain contested. But in the hyperbolic climate of 1950, the haunting thought that American spies—communists—were undermining U.S. security in the most devilish ways gripped the nation. The atomic espionage fed the perception that only the theft of the bomb's secrets could enable the backward Russians to engineer their own weapon (another doubtful assertion, but soon the conventional wisdom). So the specter of another war, within a few short years of the last world war and compounded by the terror of atomic weapons, both escalated the public's fear and anger about the communist "web" and drove the calculations—logistical, political, and emotional—about a military confrontation with Stalin and Mao.

Anticommunism had other dimensions. It was another way to play out the ongoing drama of race scarcely eighty years after Emancipation, just when flows of black migrants headed north to look for industrial jobs. African Americans were becoming politically engaged as never before; in Louisiana, for example, black voter registration leaped from 7,000 in 1946 to 161,000 in 1956.[9] During the war, Martin Dies warned that "subversive elements" were urging blacks to assert rights to social equality, and the nascent civil rights movement was in many quarters framed as communist agitation. Major African American figures like W. E. B. Du Bois and Paul Robeson were vilified when questioning the Red hunt and the burgeoning conflict with the USSR.[10] Combining racial politics with peace activism was a particularly incendiary mixture, as Martin Luther King, Jr., would discover in the mid-1960s, and it fueled anticommunism's perfervid search for internal enemies.

American culture at the dawn of the Cold War was reawakened to self-doubts about the toughness necessary to battle communism. This was a manufactured anxiety of conservatives and some anticommunist liberals who worried about passive, emasculated men and the consequences for the protection of the free world. Such sentiments were not new—Theodore Roosevelt made a career of modeling himself as the avatar of masculinity—and would reappear in other times of war and international stress. The masculinity crisis, oddly appearing just after millions of American men had courageously fought across the globe

made masculinity. "Roosevelt."

against fascism, became a rhetorical tool rather than an ideology, but one that prodded male leaders nonetheless. It was, in the words of one historian, "a political culture that put a new premium on hard masculine toughness and rendered anything less than that soft and feminine and, as such, a real or potential threat to the security of this nation."[11] The invocation of masculine, warrior virtue, and the disparagement of the "softness" of diplomats and their appeasement, or the conformity exacted by communism, ran rife through politics and culture and has not ceased. *Anticommunism = economics.*

At its roots, however, anticommunism was about economics and politics. Labor unions in particular had grown stronger during the Second World War and strikes were widespread immediately after the war ended. The union powerhouses ratcheted up both their demands and the way they wanted to bargain, a new assertiveness that alarmed industry leaders and spurred a concerted effort by the Republican Party, which won a majority in Congress in 1946, to rein in labor. The Congress of Industrial Organizations (CIO) and United Auto Workers (UAW) were openly leftist, with a number of members in the Communist Party. This provided the Republicans with the needed ammunition to pass anti-union legislation—particularly the Taft-Hartley Act—which linked the unions ever more directly to communism by requiring that union leaders declare they were not communists. The economic future of the United States appeared to be played out in this struggle, a high-stakes contest that continued into the 1950s and 1960s, but was at its fiercest and most polarized in the late 1940s.[12] The very origins of HUAC in the 1930s were rooted in anti-New Deal sentiments among conservative southerners, and union leaders were regular targets of the investigatory committees in the 1940s.

That intervention was also driven by politics, namely the Republican frustrations with being the out-of-power party. On the eve of the 1946 congressional elections, for example, which the Republicans did win, the party's House leader Joseph Martin proclaimed that "the people will vote tomorrow between chaos, confusion, bankruptcy, state socialism or Communism, and the preservation of our American life."[13] So the political impetus was apparent in the immediate postwar election and only accelerated as it appeared to be a winning strategy—communism or Republicanism, as Democrats were repeatedly associated with Russian aims. The political grievance was intensified by Truman's upset of

New York Governor Thomas Dewey in the 1948 presidential election. Many of the most sensational episodes of the search for internal enemies—the Hiss case, the Rosenbergs' atomic spy trial, the peak of the Hollywood blacklist, McCarthy's rise itself—took place in the wake of the 1948 election. After McCarthy's fall in 1954, the analysis of anticommunism and McCarthy's role engaged several prominent intellectuals, Richard Hofstadter, Daniel Bell, David Riesman, Talcott Parsons, and Seymour Martin Lipset among them, much of it about status and "out groups." But the most likely answer for the rise of HUAC and McCarthyism was politics: Nelson Polsby demonstrated by a relatively simple examination of polling and election data that supporters of McCarthy were hard-core Republicans, a conclusion expanded upon in the 1960s by Earl Latham and Michael Paul Rogin. McCarthy and his kind did not have much popular depth; the public concern for subversives in government or other institutions was shallow.[14] His support was thoroughly Republican, particularly the midwestern right wing. Democratic leaders often ran scared or were silent, as were leaders of many other institutions, but Democratic voters were not McCarthy backers.

Anticommunism served three important purposes in the late 1940s and early 1950s by shackling the unions, resisting the blacks' social movement, and returning the Republicans to power. These were not consequences, but causes, of the period's anticommunism. That feckless Democrats, occasionally including Truman, could not mount a decisive counterattack was likely due to the steamroller effect of the anticommunist surge (supported by much of the nation's press) and events abroad—the Soviet challenge in Europe, the U.S.-USSR atomic rivalry, unrest in former colonial states (including Korea), and, above all, Mao's stunning victory in China. These required a response, and the militancy of the response frequently followed domestic politics, the growing salience of anticommunism most poignantly, and the growing scope and authority of the national security imperative that was one of its outgrowths.

The "Loss" of China

By the time the Second World War ended in 1945, China had been in turmoil for a century. Beset by a declining monarchy and rebellions and wars that took tens of millions of lives, China entered its modern period in the 1920s as a failed state divided and ruled by warlords. The modernizing military officer Sun Yat-sen, with the aid of the Soviet Union, built an alliance with the Chinese Communist Party (CCP) to tame the warlords and bring the nation under control of his nationalist party, the Guomindang, a nearly realized achievement brought off by his protégé Jiang Jieshi (Chiang Kai-shek) after Sun's death in 1925. After defeating the warlords, Jiang turned on the CCP, sparking the Chinese Civil War that would continue to 1949. A hiatus ensued between the two warring parties to form a common resistance to Japan, which invaded Manchuria in 1931, waged a sporadic war until launching a full-scale invasion in 1937, and ruthlessly occupied much of China until its surrender in 1945. Until 1937, the Guomindang was largely winning the civil war and appeared to many observers to be in an advantageous position at the end of the war with Japan; Roosevelt and Churchill had elevated China to a great power status precisely to bolster the nationalists' chances of unifying China and becoming a Western-friendly democracy.

The Chinese Civil War resumed in late 1945. At the end of the war with Japan, the United States was substantially involved with Jiang and the armistice in China. In fact, the U.S. left Japanese troops locally in place for a time to avoid a power vacuum that the CCP could exploit, and landed 50,000 Marines to secure the coastal cities. Considerable financial aid was flowing to Jiang as well. In the autumn of 1945, U.S.-brokered talks between the Guomindang and CCP resulted in a political agreement on the future of Chinese governance; but it quickly came apart as a result of bad faith on all sides. Truman saw the situation rather clearly: the United States wanted a united China (fears of warlordism persisting) and no civil war, and, if possible, an outcome that would diminish Soviet influence. The Soviets occupied Manchuria at the end of the war with Japan (partially as a result of the Yalta agreement), and the concern this produced in the U.S. government was palpable. Truman sent George Marshall, just then retired as army chief of staff, to serve as an adviser and mediator. For more than a year, Marshall engaged the parties assiduously, set up workable cease-fire committees, helped craft political agreements, and gauged and reported the situation more broadly to Truman, including the viability of Jiang, the military situation, the Soviet role, and so on. In January 1947, just before he was appointed secretary of state, he concluded that no agreement between Jiang and Mao could stick and ended his China mission.

At the same time—and against America's popular image of communist solidarity—Stalin was playing a diplomatic game by negotiating with Jiang to gain control of Outer Mongolia and access to Pacific ports, a game that worked against Mao's designs. A Soviet representative at some of the talks recalled that "Moscow's decision on non-interference [in the Chinese Civil War] amounted to a refusal to support Mao's adventurist policies, which could have created a situation leading to global conflict."[15] Stalin apparently expected a war with the United States but did not want the Chinese communists to bring it on. He withdrew from Manchuria and did not insist on a sizable role for the USSR in the ongoing attempts to negotiate a settlement, an expression of moderation or even indifference that reassured Washington that deeper U.S. involvement was not required.[16]

Truman saw the episode in terms of exasperation—"the Chinese began these endless, oriental negotiations between themselves, and only an expert chess player can follow them. . . . It was an old Chinese way to be sure nothing would happen." The Americans, including Marshall (and Stilwell, the commander of the region during the 1941–45 war), saw ineptness in Jiang as a leader and had little confidence in his capacity to prevail. Jiang, said Truman, "would not heed the advice of one of the greatest military strategists in history and lost to the Communists."[17]

The Guomindang forces scored some early victories but could not sustain their success, and the tide quickly turned. The communists were better organized, more attuned to people's needs, and driven by a coherent worldview. "The impoverishment of rural societies in parts of China as a result of wartime dislocation and destruction provided the Communists with a social laboratory for land reform," wrote historian Odd Arne Westad. "The high level of collaboration with Japanese authorities, especially in the coastal cities, effectively split the prewar Chinese elites. And the onslaught of the Japanese army . . . reduced the [Guomindang] regime's reserves of military power, economic resources, and morale."[18] There was virtually no hope for Jiang inside the U.S. government, and in August 1949, Truman stopped the flow of money, much of which was being carried off to private bank accounts abroad. Mao proclaimed the People's Republic on October 1, 1949.

The volume of recriminations escalated in Washington quickly. For a country already beset by fear of communist advances, espionage, and the Soviet atomic weapon, the "loss" of the world's largest country to the Chinese Communist Party was an apocalyptic setback. Truman, his secretary of state Dean Acheson, and even Marshall, among others, were accused of cowardice and worse. As with the atomic arms spy cases, betrayal was central to the political charges. Several State Department advisers were fingered as communist agents who shaped policy in favor of Mao, including Hiss, whose role in Yalta figured prominently. Also targeted were a few "China hands" who had predicted Jiang's weakness and the likely CCP victory, and were excoriated for such analysis (and in some cases prosecuted). Senator Robert Taft, a respected Republican leader, stated from the Senate floor that "the State Department has been guided by a left-wing group who obviously have wanted to get rid of [Jiang] and were willing at least to turn China over to the Communists for that purpose."[19] The search for scapegoats in the China debacle paralleled, and for some months was the leading edge, of anticommunism—indeed, until the Korean War erupted nearly ten months after the CCP took control of China. McCarthy, for example, called out the "'egg-sucking phony liberals' whose 'pitiful squealing . . . would hold sacrosanct those Communists and queers' who had sold China into 'atheistic slavery.'"[20]

Jiang himself did not blame the lack of U.S. material support for the nationalists' defeat; he was quite clear-eyed about his army and his party's deficiencies. "To tell the truth, never, in China or abroad, has there been a revolutionary party as decrepit and degenerate as we [the Guomindang] are today," Jiang complained to his own officers in 1948, "nor one as lacking spirit, lacking discipline, and even more, lacking standards of right and wrong as we are today. This kind of party should long ago have been destroyed and swept away!"[21] These were sentiments he voiced often, and they mirror the assessments of the China hands who were vilified in Washington, as well as those of Marshall and U.S. military leaders. The vilification proceeded as a political act, too, because the Republicans had never offered an alternative policy for China—certainly not U.S. troops—during Jiang's descent.

However strong its political roots, the lamentation for China did not exclusively spring from the anticommunist dirge. China had for generations persisted in the American mind as a vast imaginary, a land of peasants happily encountering Christian missionaries, gradually casting off the yoke of cruel emperors and warlords and Japanese. A prayer book of Maryknoll Fathers, for example, described the Chinese as "sitting in darkness and the shadow of death" and a "field ripe for the harvest."[22] This imagined country—so central to Theodore Roosevelt's notions of American expansion, redolent in the 1930s' novels of Pearl Buck, and powerfully represented a decade later by the *Time* magazine of Henry Luce, himself (like Buck) raised in China by missionary parents—thus embodied a kind of purity violated by the communist revolutionaries, a massive betrayal all the more shocking for its contrast to this abiding image. The revolution itself was foreshadowed in literature and journalism by the so-called Boxer Rebellion (1898–1901), the violent rejection of all things foreign, which revealed the anti-Christian savagery to which the Chinese masses could fall prey, as they did indeed, in this account, later in the twentieth century in the menacing form of the Communist Party. Given the scale and the aspirations of both the Christian missionaries and the China trade, the country represented, perhaps more than any other place after the Battle of Wounded Knee, Americans' "errand into the wilderness." As a result, the "loss" of China was doubly traumatic: a major encroachment on the free world by the ever growing forces of communism, and the end of the American dream of China, the closing of that most promising frontier, with both blows delivered by the worst possible adversaries—the heathen savage, and the traitor.*

Given the magnitude of this loss, then, it is not surprising that the bitter politics engineered after Jiang's fall shaped American elites' attitudes about the Korean situation. While the Truman administration was castigated for seeming to downgrade Korea's importance in the new global contest with the Soviets and Chinese, appearing instead to favor Europe, the all-out attack in June 1950 earned an immediate pledge by Truman to reverse the North's advances. To many, this sudden commitment to defend South Korea was unexpected, but Truman articulated a rationale based not so much on the importance of Korea itself, but in standing up to Stalin. The loss of China, the onset of

* This sense of betrayal is visible in the founding of the right-wing John Birch Society, named for another member of a missionary family in China who was allegedly murdered by communists in 1945 while on a reconnaissance sweep in northern China. Among his exploits was the rescue of Jimmy Doolittle when his plane was shot down. The John Birch Society was the rock bed of anticommunism for twenty to thirty years.

McCarthyism, the anticommunist anxiety generally—all weighed on this decision. The tactics of war, the base requirement to demonstrate resolve and toughness, thus flowed from the decision to wage war, the need to not lose, and the increasing cacophony of domestic politics.

Rollback

The policy disarray occasioned by the turmoil in China in the late 1940s and the Soviet assertiveness in Central Europe and the Middle East stirred U.S. policy makers to reconsider FDR's "internationalism" in favor of a more muscular posture toward communist expansion. The Truman Doctrine was one such response, and support for anticommunist forces in Greece, the Berlin airlift to break the USSR's blockade, and the creation of the North Atlantic Treaty Organization (NATO) signaled the Americans' determination. These policies elevated national security and the national means to provide that security, worldwide, on a permanent basis, into what some came to call the "national security state."[23] It was less reliant on Roosevelt's notions of collective security, clearly, but something short of a garrison state. For a country that had prided itself on its relatively small military, the idea of global responsibility braced by atomic weapons, formal alliances, intelligence agencies, and a large, permanent army occupying distant lands was novel. Truman and his coterie of talented policy intellectuals were aware of the unease this might provoke among the public and sought to assuage it with appeals to the nation's founding principles. George Kennan, no less, the consummate realist, articulated this in his seminal "X" article in the July 1947 edition of *Foreign Affairs*, his anonymous version of the long telegram he posted from Moscow: "The issue of Soviet-American relations is in essence a test of the overall worth of the United States as a nation among nations," he wrote. Providence itself was stirring the American people to accept "the responsibilities of moral and political leadership that history plainly intended them to bear."

Much of the new national security attention was focused on Europe, conforming to an evolving doctrine of containment of communism. For Asia, the shape of containment and other responses to communist advances was vague, because the war, Japanese occupation, anticolonial movements, and the continent's sheer vastness exerted powerful, changeable, and unpredictable effects in the five years after Japan surrendered. Containment, in fact, was a recognition of limits—the exhaustible resources of the United States in the face of the capacities of the Soviet and Chinese communists to expand. Containment was, in Kennan's words,

> to cease at that point making fatuous unilateral concessions to the Kremlin, to do what we could to inspire and support resistance elsewhere to its efforts to expand the area of its dominant political influence, and to wait for the internal weakness of Soviet power, combined with frustration in the external field, to moderate Soviet ambitions and behavior. . . . Stand up to them, I urged, manfully but not aggressively, and give the hand of time a chance to work.[24]

By this he expected the United States and the Soviet Union to avoid the war that many thought was brewing in the late 1940s and to preserve the gains of the Second World War. This simple formulation made sense, particularly where lines could be drawn and a manly stance made; Europe was Kennan's main concern, too, though he recognized the fundamental need to keep Japan in the American orbit. Containment was adopted by the Truman administration as a strategy, though it was applied more broadly and more militantly than Kennan was advocating even in its earliest years.

To the anticommunist right, however, containment was excoriated as appeasement. It was defensive and passive. No single event in the 1940s appeared to expose this passivity more than the U.S. response to the communist takeover of China. Despite the nearly universal assessment of the U.S. military that intervention would be foolish and that the years of support for Jiang were wasted, the inability of the United States to prevent this enormous prize from falling into the hands of Mao and Stalin became a call for an entirely different strategy, the strategy of "victory" over communism.

The avatar of this view was James Burnham, who published three books in the late 1940s and early 1950s extolling the necessity of "rollback" of communist advances. The first of these, published the same week as Truman's momentous speech to Congress in 1947, was entitled *The Struggle for the World*, which argued that the United States and the Soviet Union were in a life-and-death struggle, and to survive, the free world would need to go to war with the Soviets to pursue victory. His views, in that book and plentiful essays, were popularized by the Luce publications and essentially adopted as the foreign policy of the conservative wing of the Republican Party. The rejection of containment was explicit and unrelenting, all the more so when the Soviets seemed to consolidate their gains in Europe and Mao triumphed in China. Burnham was articulating a view that was in fact widely shared in the postwar anxieties of rising Soviet power, the expectation of war with the USSR among the more prominent. Truman and the containment liberals of his presidency embraced some of these ideas in moderation by organizing covert operations in Eastern Europe that sought reversals in some of the "captive nations" newly in the Soviet sphere, such as Albania. Years later, Eisenhower and his secretary of state, John Foster Dulles, were openly enthusiastic about rollback until it came up against the hard realities of Soviet atomic weapons. They failed to support the Hungarian resistance in 1956, possibly as a result of that concern.[25] But rollback nonetheless became entrenched as the alternative to containment, or, more accurately, as an adjunct of containment, the more assertive tactic often implemented discretely, and offered up for public consumption by Republican politicians in particular who could score easy points in the tense and complex world of the late 1940s and 1950s. Burnham, who became co-editor of the *National Review*, the most important intellectual vehicle of the right in the postwar years, was described by founder William F. Buckley as "the number-one intellectual influence" on the magazine, and rollback was his core contribution to foreign policy thinking, one that has been a permanent fixture of conservative ideology ever since.

It was not wholly limited to the right, however. That rollback had its prominent niche in the Truman administration (and later, with Kennedy and Johnson) was not surprising given the fierce domestic political pressures at work and the legitimate concerns about ultimate Soviet intentions. For a time, however, the small but vocal popular agitation for rollback focused on Asia, whereas Eastern Europe remained central to government calculations. Europe and the hardening line that separated the Soviet sphere from the Western sphere appeared as the more likely arena of conflict and the one with higher stakes. Given the Soviet deployments in its newly captive nations, rollback was scarcely feasible as a military aspiration. Many of the right-wing advocates of victory, however, saw Asia as the Promised Land, and increasingly focused their energies there.

The notion of victory gained momentum inside the U.S. bureaucracy in part as a reaction to the China debacle. By 1949, several strands of policy formation recommended not only containment, but more brawny "action." Some rather wildly ambitious ideas were floated about roll-back in China, though none were considered seriously, despite some support from MacArthur and the China Lobby before the Korean conflict. But the possibilities of rollback were nonetheless in play in high government circles. NSC 48, a National Security Council policy guidance document issued in the summer of 1949 and presaging the doctrinal NSC 68 issued nine months later, spoke of the necessity "to check and roll back" communism in Asia.[26] NSC 68, written by Paul Nitze and approved by Truman before the Korean War began, argued that "our policy and actions must be such as to foster a fundamental change in the nature of the Soviet system. . . . It is not an adequate objective merely to seek to check the Kremlin design." Throughout all the talk of rolling back communism, the advocates of rollback took pains to express the goals of U.S. action as liberationist, as freedom's march. "If we can make the Russian people our allies in the enterprise we will obviously have made our task easier and victory more certain," NSC 68 continues.

What made the dream of rollback plausible was a new confidence in air power, so dazzling in the Second World War, and the means of projecting American power in the great expanse of Asia without actually getting involved with the local populations. As a strategy, it conformed to the superficial acquaintance that people like Luce and MacArthur had had with Asian peoples throughout their lives. Air power also included the atomic bomb, accentuating the fantastic possibilities of using the chain of islands won over the previous half century—the Philippines, Hawaii, Guam, Japan, and so on—to leapfrog the ocean on the way to China, Indochina, and Korea to defeat the communists from 10,000 feet high. "Rollback, drawing on the 1930s isolationist currents in the changed circumstances of the 1950s, represents a reaction against both [internationalism and isolationism]," wrote historian Bruce Cumings. But, he continues, rollback shares "with isolationists of the 1930s a general lack of real interest in or connectedness with the rest of the world."[27] This was verified time and again as U.S. decision makers failed to perceive strong popular sentiments in the target nations, from China to Korea to Vietnam and Iraq, among other venues, clinging to their own narrow perceptions of how those primitive populations—if their sentiments were considered at all— had been manipulated by America's enemies. A lack of empathy, or basic knowledge, about the peoples to be liberated by the application of massive air power or invasion, is a reliable tool in understanding America's wars.

It also connects the global ventures with the continental imperialism of the seventeenth to nineteenth centuries, and the push out into the world at the turn to the twentieth century. Cumings noted that the ideological content of the rollback philosophy is indebted to "frontier expansionism and Indian wars as models . . . and a restless search for new ventures, markets, and raw materials."[28] The men who were most influential in America's long military involvements in Asia were those who "knew" the Asians, who sought to Christianize, globalize, and even Americanize the peasant masses, and who acted to protect for American development the limitless bounty of Asia. The concept of imperialism does not quite capture this phenomenon, with its implications of colonization and crude exploitation, but the fusion of the state's military power and capitalism's need for markets and expansion is unmistakable,* and very much in keeping with the neocolonial expansion later described by William Appleman Williams, Gabriel Kolko, and Richard Barnet, among others.[29] While rarely an explicit rationale of the emerging American globalism, the positing of a Manichean contest between freedom and slavery (utterly regardless of the wishes of the local population) encompassed these more prosaic goals of business.

* Hannah Arendt's exploration of the origins of imperialism (and totalitarianism) is informative in this respect, linking the historical trends of the expansion of capitalism and the projection of power abroad, precisely at the end of the nineteenth century. She asserts that "only through the expansion of the national instruments of violence could the foreign-investment movement be rationalized. . . . The first consequence of power export was that the state's instruments of violence, the police and the army, . . . [were] promoted to the position of national representatives in uncivilized or weak countries. . . . [Foreign investments] became a permanent feature of all economic systems as soon as it was protected by the export of power." *The Origins of Totalitarianism* (Harcourt, 1951, 1968): 136–37.

"Rollback," then, was the policy manifestation of the liberationist impulse, the regeneration through violence, so central to the first three centuries of the American experience. And it became a much-heralded strategy in the improbable venue of Korea.

THE WAR

The conventional narrative of the Korean War begins after Japan surrendered in 1945 with the division of Korea into two occupied zones: the south in the hands of the United States and the north occupied by the Soviet Union, with the 38th parallel as the dividing line. The drama of the ensuing five years was played out on the international stage as relations between those two powers worsened, though they both withdrew their forces as agreed. In the north, the communists under the wartime resistance leader Kim Il Sung held sway; in the south, Syngman Rhee, an opponent of Japanese occupation and a friend of the United States, was essentially installed as president of the Republic of Korea (ROK). The ROK itself was created in August 1948, and the Democratic People's Republic of North Korea (DPRK) was established a month later. Social unrest notwithstanding, the Americans demobilized from the south in 1949; the Soviets departed the north at the end of 1948. This left a country not merely divided with the two halves increasingly hostile toward each other, but one where each leader publicly vowed to unite all of Korea, if necessary by force. It was a volatile situation and known as such in all capitals, but Korea was not considered a priority by Stalin or Truman, and the emerging pressures of the Cold War appeared to be elsewhere.

Force was indeed applied on June 25, 1950, when the North Korean People's Army (NKPA) invaded the south, a sudden and largely unexpected attack, significant in scale, and initially very successful. They quickly seized Seoul, the capital city, and continued to drive south as they overwhelmed the poorly trained and equipped South Korean army. Truman reacted immediately. Informed of the attack while spending a weekend in Independence, Missouri, he flew back and convened his top advisers, who agreed to his assessment that the United States could not allow what they saw as Soviet-inspired aggression. Truman ordered MacArthur, U.S. commander in the Pacific and the head of the occupation in Japan, to deploy air and sea support as quickly as possible. Acheson was dispatched to Lake Success, New York, then the headquarters of the United Nations, to gain its support and its sponsorship of the military mission to resist the DPRK aggression. The American role in the war, while paramount, was henceforth in the form of a United Nations force.*

It was apparent to MacArthur that the South Korean army would be unable to hold their half of the peninsula, and the hopes of U.S. policy makers that they could limit involvement to bombardment from air and sea were dashed. Troops would be required, and soon. By late July, the Eighth Army was deployed in the south at a strength of 45,000 troops. With another 47,000 South Korean soldiers, they defended the southern port of Pusan and environs as a last stronghold against the invading North Korean force of 120,000 men. It was the first of six phases of the war. As military historian Adrian Lewis described, each phase had its own objective, improvised according to the circumstances on the ground: "delay and defend (the Pusan Perimeter); the offensive turning movement (the Inchon Landing); pursuit and exploitation (the advance to the Yalu); retreat, delay and defend (war with China); attack to regain the 38th parallel (Ridgeway's offensive); and negotiating while fighting (the static war of attrition)."[30] While the military action sought to secure a strategic objective, the course of war from the beginning held many surprises, including the entry of Communist China to fight with the North Korean army, a rapid series of changes of fortune on the battlefield in the first year, and a raging political controversy in Washington over Truman's handling of the war, most particularly, his dismissal of MacArthur in April 1951.

The Eighth Army did secure the Pusan perimeter in the summer of 1950, and by September MacArthur planned a risky amphibious landing at Seoul's port city of Inchon. The military and civilian brass in Washington was skeptical of its chances for success, due to the exceptionally difficult geography and tides, but MacArthur's standing made it virtually impossible to oppose. Its success cut off the North Korean

* While the American forces were in this sense UN forces, along with several other countries that contributed to the allied cause, principally South Korea, I refer in this chapter to U.S. or American troops where appropriate, and South Korean forces where appropriate; the command structure and decision making was very much in the hands of the United States.

army in the south from its supply lines, and the complexion of the war changed instantly. The Eighth Army was able to drive up from Pusan and MacArthur's landing force took Seoul, routing the North Koreans and essentially reestablishing control of the entire south for Rhee and the ROK. Truman's vow to expel the invaders had been fulfilled in three months.

At that point, the second key U.S. decision of the war was taken—to cross the 38th parallel and carry the war to North Korea, with the goal of annihilating its army. MacArthur was a keen advocate of this action to win the war outright, insisting that the one condition Truman feared, the entry of China into the war, was very unlikely. With the enemy on the run, most of the administration was in favor of liberating the north and dealing a blow to Stalin that could affect his calculations for Europe. MacArthur, supremely confident as always and now untouchable after the Inchon triumph, prevailed over any residual cautions in Washington and moved the UN forces rapidly north to the Yalu River, Korea's border with China. The rollback of communism in Korea seemed complete. But MacArthur and U.S. intelligence were grossly mistaken about Beijing's intentions.

China had been alarmed at the outset of the war by Truman's ordering the Seventh Fleet into the Taiwan straits, an action prompted by anxieties about the Korean attack being part of a broader communist strategy in East Asia. Mao began to mobilize to support the North Koreans, not least because he feared a U.S. presence on China's border. The crossing of the 38th parallel was the trigger for Chinese forces to enter the war—remarkably, forces undetected by the United States until the UN army tangled with the Chinese forces in late November near the Yalu. The scale of the Chinese forces, and the surprise, forced MacArthur to retreat, draw back below the 38th parallel, give up Seoul again, and reorganize efforts to repel the new enemy. The winter of 1950–51 was a low point for the Americans: its fortunes suddenly reversed, in the strange position of retreat and near defeat at the hands of a new and darkly imagined enemy on the frozen fields of Korea and riven by bitterness in Washington. The entry of the Chinese changed many calculations, not least the possibility of an attack on China that could include nuclear weapons. The decision to sack MacArthur, due to his public disagreement with the president about limiting the war to Korea, became a political fulcrum of the war. The new commander, Matthew Ridgeway, was able to mount a counteroffensive that again brought the opposing forces face to face at about the 38th parallel—one of several thrusts from each side—and there a stalemate ensued that never broke, even as fighting continued to be intense and U.S. bombing of the north escalated. An armistice negotiation began that lasted nearly two years, stuck in the distrust between the antagonists and volatile issues such as the status of prisoners of war. When Dwight Eisenhower was inaugurated president in January 1953, he threatened the use of atomic weapons, which he believed hastened the final cease-fire in July 1953. More likely, it was the sudden death of Josef Stalin in March 1953, creating great uncertainty in the communist states, which enabled an end to fighting.

War through a Different Prism

The conventional narrative serves a primary purpose of placing responsibility for war exclusively on the communists in the Soviet Union, China, and North Korea, and locating the conflict as the first significant confrontation of the Cold War, one that the United States could not fail to engage with massive armed force. As a result, the sacrifices of the war—some two to three million killed, and possibly more—are justified as a larger, global struggle between oppression and freedom. While this account is not false, it is incomplete, and its inadequacy as an explanation for why the war began and the goals of U.S. policy and action obscure the very meaning of "sacrifice"—who sacrificed, who brought on that sacrifice, and why. This additional prism reveals what was significantly a civil war that was "internationalized" to become a superpower conflict and a readily seized opportunity for rollback that could extend to China.

From 1945 to the outbreak of the June 1950 hostilities, Korea was roiled not only by occupation, but by a low-intensity civil war. The dimensions of that unrest are complex, but, in the south, they involved the old elite and military classes that had been mainly aligned with Japan during its occupation and were favored by the American occupation chieftains as well, arrayed against both democratic forces opposed to the terms and practice of U.S. occupation, and more militant leftists (some communist) who were linked, formally or emotionally, to the forces led by Kim Il Sung in the north. Korea was emerging not only from the

Second World War, but also from decades of harsh Japanese occupation and a feudal land ownership system. The emerging leaders of the postwar nation were resistance fighters in one form or another and other anti-occupation advocates, but these groups gradually lost out to the collaborators and those, like Rhee, who used the old system of privilege and power with great aplomb and a helping hand from Washington.

Due to Japanese repression during occupation, political movements inside Korea were not well formed, but the demands to alter the old oppressive systems were enormous and sprang up very quickly in 1945 and 1946. Sentiments were strong to unite the country and resist further occupation. "The basic issues over which the war in 1950 was fought were apparent immediately after liberation," wrote Bruce Cumings. A civil war broke out that claimed 100,000 lives—by any standard, a sizable conflict—wrought by "peasant rebellion, labor strife, guerrilla warfare, and open fighting along the thirty-eighth parallel."[31] The United States, as one of the principal occupiers, contributed to the instability by refusing to acknowledge legitimate social aspirations—land and labor reform, for example, long overdue—and left-liberal organizing that could have resulted in a unified country. At the moment of the Second World War's end, Koreans had formed local political committees that met to create a nationwide Korean People's Republic, which was stunted and then overturned by the U.S. occupation. Seeing communist infiltration and designs under every rock, the occupation authorities acted to quash popular sentiments, including repressing labor and land-reform activism, empowering the same police that had been part of Japan's harsh occupation, and eventually installing a republic and Rhee in contravention of multilateral agreements. A longtime resident of the United States and a tactician in the China Lobby mode, Rhee moved swiftly to eliminate liberal and leftist opposition in the south, frequently by force—including a crackdown of an uprising on Jeju Island in spring 1948 that resulted in 30,000 deaths. That in turn led to other outbreaks of rebellion and violence over the coming months. So opportunities to stabilize and even unify Korea on acceptable terms—acceptable to the United States—were plentiful but squandered.

As it happened, a number of U.S. leaders were not convinced in those early postwar years that Korea merited even the modest attention it was receiving. American troops after V-J Day were stretched thin; Americans wanted and expected a demobilization, and the key places for occupation—Japan in Asia, Germany in Europe—were demanding enough. Korea, in the calculations of both Pentagon and several civilian policy makers, was not strategically important enough to bother with. They did not want to leave it to the Soviets, to be sure, but the effort to make Korea a pivotal venue of U.S. commitment was not a fetching idea in Washington. The rote anticommunism and support for repressive measures in the south by General John Hodge, the U.S. commander, was in part a reflection of this lack of interest—leave it to the familiar elements (Japanese police units, then Rhee's own police state) rather than creatively engage with the complexities of nascent democratic activism. Hodge had even recommended a quick, joint U.S.-Soviet withdrawal in 1945 to "leave Korea to its own devices and an inevitable internal upheaval for self-purification."[32] This laissez-faire attitude gave way as U.S.-USSR relations worsened, the Truman Doctrine was promulgated, and the anticommunist juggernaut inside the United States gained momentum. It was always viewed in Washington as easier, in effect, to allow and even lead the steady drift toward right-wing authoritarianism in South Korea as the most plausible anti-Soviet response. It was not an especially partisan issue then, either, because the Republican Congress actually cut appropriations for the occupation and saw Korea as an afterthought in their far more obsessive attention to the decline of Jiang in China. After Rhee was installed (in an election in 1948 that leftists and liberals boycotted), it was widely agreed in Washington that the U.S. military could begin withdrawal. So Korea was not high on the list of American strategic concerns well into early 1950, and U.S. carelessness in dealing with a politically unique opportunity showed this lack of interest. The easy option of empowering Syngman Rhee, who was detested in the high circles of American decision makers from start to finish, signals more than anything else this essential irresponsibility. It was a pattern that would become a rigid habit of the Cold War, repeated elsewhere.

When the formal war began, one of Truman's first actions was to move the Seventh Fleet into the Taiwan Straits between mainland China and Formosa. "The invasion of Southern Korea cannot be regarded as an isolated incident," stated the minutes of Truman's meeting with his advisers on the day of the North Korean invasion. "It alters the strategic realities of the area and is a clear indication of the pattern of aggression under a general international plan. Quick affirmative action by the United States in other Far Eastern trouble spots will contribute to the disposal of the Korean situation."[33] (Acheson, at the same meeting, recommended support for the French position in Vietnam.) This situation in Korea clearly meant, in army chief Omar Bradley's words, "that we must draw the line somewhere" against the communists, and this would be it; the president agreed.[34] So the immediate support for the ROK from MacArthur's forces in Japan and bolstering Jiang's position in Taiwan sprang from the U.S. leadership's perception that a concerted communist "takeover" was under way.

In fact, the sailing of the Seventh Fleet, more than any other action, brought the Chinese communists to the fore because the U.S. naval maneuver was in effect an intervention into the Chinese Civil War, still active in the sense that Jiang and his supporters in America envisioned his triumphal return to the mainland some day, and because Beijing considered Formosa to be theirs. Acheson, just the previous January, had in a widely noted public speech excluded Korea from the "U.S. defense perimeter" in Asia. This was a controversial stance, but by subsequently committing large forces to Korea and injecting itself into the Straits, America seemed to Mao to be setting the stage for an action against China. Why else take these actions if America thought Korea was so unimportant? The rollback drums had, after all, been beating in Washington for months. China had accepted the early July initiative by Nehru to restore the status quo ante in Korea, which the United States snubbed, further stirring suspicions. Over the following weeks, Mao had to consider that American rollback ideology would be applied to China, and, by all accounts, his entry into Korea was an excruciating decision given how unprepared the Chinese were to confront the United States. Stalin had left the decision up to him. The decisive factor appears to have been Mao's geostrategic judgment that it was better to fight the Americans then and there rather than after the United States had defeated the North Koreans and occupied the entire peninsula. The decision appeared all the more necessary when MacArthur moved rapidly north of the 38th parallel and was driving toward the Yalu River, the nearly 500-mile border with China. "The crossing of the 38th parallel and the need to defend North Korea," wrote China scholar Thomas Christensen, "not a desire to 'liberate' South Korea per se, [were] the key triggers for expansion of the war by Beijing."[35]

Stalin's role is still a historical controversy, but it seems that he was not a decisive voice for the North Korean attack or for Chinese intervention. He played a wily game, now and again encouraging Kim Il-Sung, and then leaving the decision for North Korea's attack to Mao. He provided some logistics and air support during the war, important but hardly anything decisive. He most certainly did not want to get drawn into a world war. As the Cold War was taking shape, he was no doubt gratified to see the United States bogged down in Korea. He could afford to be far less concerned than Mao was that the Korean operation was an opportunity to reverse communist gains in Asia. Yet Stalin and his designs loomed large in the American imagination, a latter day King Philip threatening civilization, and as such, a necessary foil for the U.S. intervention in Korea.

In some key respects, Mao was correct. Rollback *was* an objective of U.S. policy makers from the start of the war (though, for most policy makers, only for Korea, and even then not unanimously). But pressure to operate above the 38th parallel came within days of the war's onset, first from the air force and its many adherents (believing, as they did, that the North Korean advance and perhaps North Korea itself could be defeated solely with air and sea power) and then by civilian policy makers. George Kennan recalled in his diary a U.S. position to be tabled at the Security Council in early July in which we would demand "that the North Korean forces . . . should surrender their arms to the United Nations commander and relinquish authority to him in order that he might create order throughout all of Korea."[36] The notion that we could not leave Korea "half slave and half free" was in the air, embraced by Republicans, and suddenly an intoxicating idea. Rhee, of course, was one of the instigators of this view, and indeed he had proclaimed his intention from 1948 on to unite Korea under his leadership by armed force, and was never effectively rebuked.

The rollback quest gained unstoppable momentum after Inchon, especially with MacArthur's assurances that China would not enter the war ("there is no indication at present of entry in North Korea by major Soviet or Chinese Communist Forces," he cabled the joint chiefs) and with the green light from Marshall to move north. In Marshall's words, "we want you to feel unhampered tactically and strategically to proceed north of the 38th parallel." Here is where MacArthur's own vision of rollback took over—his "strategic plan for North Korea," he cabled back to Marshall as the troops moved north, was to persist "unless and until the enemy capitulated."[37] It was a vision enabled by his exaggeration of U.S. prowess and the public disparagement of Chinese capabilities. He was willing to risk so much—intervention of the Soviets, which is what Kennan most feared; and a U.S.-China war that would soon include direct attacks on Chinese cities—to defeat not only the communists in Korea, but communism in China.

The rollback in China was very much on MacArthur's agenda, an active part of his promethean ambitions, and was apparent throughout his short tenure as commander in Korea. Shanghai was viewed by MacArthur as a landing area for rollback in China, using 100,000 of Jiang's troops; this would not only force Mao to redeploy from Korea, he thought, but would provide the leading edge of a rollback in China that would overthrow the communist regime.[38] Naturally, the broader vision's first step was the annihilation of the enemy in Korea: even when the tide began to turn on the battlefield, he implored Truman "with all the earnestness that I possess that there be no weakening at this crucial moment and that we press on to complete victory," which he thought was assured by U.S. air power and America's "indomitable will."[39] In that desultory winter of 1950–51, MacArthur flew to Korea and upon landing declared, "This is exactly where I came in seven months ago to start the crusade. The stakes we fight for now, however, is more than Korea—it is a free Asia."[40] Indeed, it was MacArthur's threat that he could provoke a military collapse of China that, among other loose talk and insubordination, brought on his dismissal.

Truman's firing of MacArthur, which Marshall and the joint chiefs supported, created a political firestorm in the United States: denigrating the relatively new concept of a "limited war," so easy to do in the victory culture of America, was a self-glorifying exploit by MacArthur to impugn Truman, even as it was apparent that a broader war would risk a major conflagration. Coming as it did in the midst of the anti-communist witch hunt (McCarthy's hearings barely a year old), the change of leadership in Korea electrified the volatile climate as few actual events would. "The country's most famous general was all but accusing the . . . administration of appeasing the enemy," wrote David Halberstam. The Republican right wing wanted "to win China back without the loss of a single American boy on Chinese soil."[41] MacArthur kept the pressure on Truman after leaving the army, speaking widely and offering himself as a presidential candidate, a willing factional leader to spur a major war against communism in Asia. This was a role that Republicans and the China Lobby eagerly embraced, all but accusing Truman of treason. While Truman was adept at fending off such attacks, the political pressure was influential; America could not be seen as losing the war or giving in to communist demands at the negotiating table. The result of this largely one-sided public cacophony was a reversion to brutal war-making in the conflict's final year.

MacArthur's ideas for expanding the war were not his alone in government and military circles. The possibility of using Nationalist Chinese troops in Korea was a topic of keen interest among military decision makers. Manchuria was always in play as a bombing and invasion target, as were other sites in China and even Russia, as Truman's own diaries attest.[42] But it was in MacArthur's startling ambitions and willingness to articulate them that the true crusading spirit of the war and the aspirations for rollback were presented with such great clarity (and could be later disparaged as a vain old general's fantasies). MacArthur and a significant number of others not only envisioned the widening of the war to China, but winning that war by the liberal use of atomic weapons.

The Nuclear Option

It was widely believed at that time that the bombings of Hiroshima and Nagasaki brought Japan to its knees in August 1945, and that this singular weapon could do the same to China and the North Koreans. The threat alone, in this view, might be enough. The possibility of such an attack was never disavowed, and indeed it was at virtually every juncture an active option from the beginning of the war.

That the atomic arsenal could come into play then is remarkable given what was known of the atomic blasts' effects in Japan. By 1950, the radioactive poisoning and long-lasting impacts of the bomb were well known. John Hersey's postwar account, *Hiroshima*, among others, had brought this home. Disarmament advocates, including most of the atomic scientists, were energetic in their insistence that the world needed to abolish nuclear weapons, and they prompted a significant public campaign in Europe and the United States. The debate quickly fell into the Cold War mold, particularly when the Soviet Union tested its atomic device in 1949, and the American discourse on the acquisition and use of the "ultimate weapon" thereafter became a symbol of political divisions over the conduct of the superpower rivalry. In considering its use in Korea, then, the innocence of 1945 was no longer possible: everyone realized it was an astonishingly destructive weapon, indiscriminate in its gruesome methods of killing, and with effects that endured long after the initial blast. It could not be contained to military targets and was in essence a terror weapon, aimed at civilians or at least putting them very much in harm's way. That Truman and Eisenhower, and the joint chiefs, were amenable to its employment against an adversary that did not have the weapon and posed no threat directly to the United States speaks volumes about the attitudes toward noncombatants.

The potential use of the nation's growing arsenal of atomic bombs—nearly 500 by then*—was on the decision agenda from the outset of the war. After the conflict moved to its stalemate phase, the United States more actively considered the use of atomic weapons. Truman had already said publicly that he had not ruled out the possibility of an atomic attack as the war turned sour in late 1950, and that MacArthur had the authority to use the bombs (a statement later "corrected"). He was in fact reflecting a pervasive panic among American elites, several of whom were recommending atomic attacks. A squadron of planes carrying atomic bombs was deployed to the Western Pacific in April 1950, verifying Truman's seriousness about the threat. One account of that decision holds that deploying the weapon near the theater of operations was the price for the support of the joint chiefs to fire MacArthur.[43] While the recommended use of atomic weapons is most often associated with MacArthur, and then Eisenhower after he became president, the field commanders repeatedly requested, and Pentagon chiefs repeatedly approved, their availability. But MacArthur's musings

* They were at that point atomic, or "fission," bombs of the type used on Japan in 1945. At the same time, however, the far more powerful "fusion" or hydrogen bomb was being designed and tested, itself a source of controversy because some scientists opposed its development. By 1951, U.S. authorities knew the new device would work. The first such bomb was tested in the Pacific atoll of Enewetak in November 1952; it was 450 times more powerful than the atomic explosion that destroyed Nagasaki.

about nuclear use are no less striking. He later claimed that "I would have dropped between 30 and 50 atomic bombs . . . strung out across the neck of Manchuria" forming a "belt of radioactive cobalt."[44] The broader interest in atomic weapons is clear from the deployment of the weapons after MacArthur's sacking and their active consideration thereafter. While these weapons were often discussed as a tactical measure against enemy troops and airfields, the U.S. weaponeers had not satisfactorily designed a tactical nuclear weapon by 1951, even as the public was being regaled with reassuring stories in the news media about how tactical use of the atomic weapon would minimize or even eliminate civilian casualties.[45] Instead, the air force was carrying out "dummy runs" with B-29s over North Korea in 1951, simulating, in effect, the atomic bombing of Japan. Later, in Truman's final year in the White House, he escalated the application of armed force, part of which involved further planning for both the use of nuclear weapons and attacks on China at the behest of Ridgeway's successor as field commander, General Mark Clark.[46]

Eisenhower rose to the presidency in part by promising to end the Korean War, with nuclear weapons, if necessary, and this possibility was raised in his war council within days of his assuming office. John Foster Dulles, his secretary of state, pushed the idea of using small nuclear detonations on enemy troops, in part to break the nuclear taboo—as Dulles put it to the president, "the moral problem and the inhibitions on the use of the A-bomb." Through the winter and spring of 1953, as negotiations to end the war were tangled on issues of prisoner of war (POW) repatriation, Eisenhower kept hinting at atomic use. By May, Dulles was signaling to Mao through several channels that if the war was not resolved soon, the United States was prepared to use atomic weapons on the battlefield and against China.[47] But Mao apparently was willing to take an atomic blow, something he calculated early in the war. But it was Stalin's death, by most accounts, that was the decisive alteration of the war's dynamics, not the nuclear posturing.

The frequent atomic threats from the United States worried allies and earned the opprobrium of important neutrals like India. On first hearing Truman's threat in 1950, British prime minister Clement Attlee tried to pry assurances from the president that no such weapons would be used in Korea, fearing that the world would see that we "have a low regard for Asiatic lives."[48] But Attlee's worried reaction,

reflecting aroused European opinion and his attempt to gain some concessions from Truman on China to settle the Korean War, caused barely
a ripple in U.S. decision making. The regard for Korean or Chinese lives
never seemed to enter the calculations about atomic use; restraint was
based far more clearly on the concern that an atomic attack could lead
to a world war with the Soviets, who had largely stayed out of the
Korean conflict, or other factors leading to restraint.[49] As with so many
of Washington's decisions about Korea, its people seemed rarely to surface as a concern at all.

THE PEOPLE

In 1953 the Korean peninsula was a smoldering ruin. From Pusan in
the south to Sinŭiju in the north, Koreans buried their dead, mourned
their losses, and sought to draw together the shattered remains of their
lives. . . . At American military encampments on the outskirts of the
capital, masses of beggars waited to pick through the garbage that foreign soldiers tossed out. In the north, modern edifices scarcely stood
anymore; Pyongyang and other cities were heaps of bricks and ashes,
factories stood empty, massive dams no longer held their water. People
emerged from a mole-like existence in caves and tunnels to find a
nightmare in the bright of day.[50]

The "smoldering ruin" of Korea was the consequence of a war that was
the responsibility of several players. It was not solely an American-
caused tragedy, to be sure; China employed a military strategy that
resulted in massive casualties. But U.S. actions were more prominent.
The popular effort to create a unified and sovereign Korea was suffo-
cated by the U.S. occupation in 1945 and a revanchist state and
strongman installed in the south in 1948, one dedicated to unification
by force. The war itself could have been stopped before the Chinese
entered, after Inchon, if the Americans had not implemented a rollback
strategy, a vision that animated U.S. attitudes toward Korea and China
time and again in the early 1950s and may itself have been the spark
for China's intervention. When American compromise at the negotiations was excoriated by the right wing, U.S. war-makers escalated mer-
cilessly. Strategic bombing of cities in the north, including the use of
napalm, and the destruction of dams that flooded thousands of acres

of farmland and villages, was the U.S. response to the tangled armistice talks, which were snagged on the minor issue of repatriating 16,000 Chinese POWs. Rarely if ever was there a public discourse in America about the human costs of the war to Koreans, and the absence of such concern allowed the military to exert maximum force.

Those human costs were colossal. The war dead may have totaled more than three million. While accounts differ, as they always do, military historian Adrian Lewis wrote that the South Koreans suffered 415,000 killed or missing in action and between a half million and one million civilians dead. North Korean mortality was 1.5 million, military and civilian combined. Most other accounts are somewhat lower, although the proportions of military and civilian vary significantly. Roughly, civilian deaths were three times the military deaths on both sides. The wounded, or the severity of wounds, is largely unaccounted for, but serious injuries likely range into the millions. The foreigners involved in the war, particularly Americans and Chinese, took significant casualties—34,000 Americans died in combat in Korea, and perhaps 500,000 Chinese.[51] Many more thousands died from noncombat causes.

These totals for Korea are higher than for the American Civil War, the Vietnam War, and the Iraq War, and they occurred in only three years. Apart from the world wars in the twentieth century, very few conflicts took so many lives, and those that did (notably, the Chinese Civil War, the Congo wars of 1886–1908 and again in the last twenty years) extended over much longer periods. The Korean War was an exceptionally bloody affair, and more than half of the dead, perhaps much more than half, were civilians.

Americans' violent encounters with Korean civilians were threefold. First, and beginning before the war, the United States acceded to or actively aided repression by South Korean authorities, including approval or ignoring of massacres of "leftists." Second was the indiscriminate bombing and artillery shelling of North Korea during the war, with the intention of dealing a massive blow to civilians. And the third type—the most intimate—was killing civilians who were refugees or who were "in the way" of military missions. Each proceeded with a logic of its own, with opportunities for U.S. military and civilian leaders to disavow violence, assure the public that any harm to civilians was incidental and rare, and present the ferocious warfare as a necessary evil to prevent a greater calamity for the people of Korea.

Rhee's Repression

The U.S. decision to boost Syngman Rhee to power through the creation of the Republic of Korea in 1948 was momentous on several
counts. As the occupying power with the legal authority through a UN
Trusteeship to prevent such a codification of the peninsula's division
(or at the very least to insist on a fair election), the United States' folding
to Rhee's designs immediately resulted in rebellions large and small
that the regime put down harshly. Using police trained by the Japanese
occupiers, and in many cases, led by Korean officers who had been
in Japanese security forces, Rhee was uncompromising in his determination to silence all leftist opposition in the south. The repression
stemmed from two perceived needs of the burgeoning state. It was
aimed to eliminate legitimate political rivals, such as those born of the
people's committees at the end of the Pacific war. As important was the
desire to eradicate those who sought to unify Korea through cooperation with their northern counterparts, whether communist or not.
Rhee was determined to unify Korea by force with himself as head of
state.[52] He doubtlessly felt emboldened in his anticommunist fervor by
the permissiveness of the American occupation and the growing Red
scare in the United States, and he enjoyed the aid of a political network
in America spearheaded by the Catholic Church.[53]

The rivals to Rhee in the south were liberal nationalists who were
keen for a unified Korea, and it was these opponents whom Rhee
methodically eliminated. Korea was, after the Pacific war, much like it
had been for centuries: dominated by a very small elite that was politically powerful and economically dominant over a poor and largely
peasant population. This elite, the CIA understood in assessments at
the time, was aligned with a hard right wing that had collaborated with
Imperial Japan and needed someone like Rhee, without the taint of
Japan, to govern a new semifeudal state. The CIA had no illusions that
he was anything other than a demagogue "bent on autocratic rule."[54]
The "ordinary" repression of trade unions, liberal newspapers, leftist
political parties, and the like proceeded apace; some of that work had
been done by Rhee and U.S. authorities before the ROK was created.
In 1946, for example, General Hodge had approved and funded the
creation of Rhee's Korean National Youth, a paramilitary used extensively in repression, as were several other organized youth gangs,

most of which had links to the occupation authorities. These gangs supplemented what Hodge considered as the other bulwarks against a challenge to Rhee, the police forces that were also bolstered by the occupation authorities, and an army created by the U.S. military. As the Americans fully realized, South Korea was fast becoming a police state. "The harsh truth is that the United States as a matter of high policy vastly preferred the south police state," concludes Bruce Cumings. "The repression of the Rhee regime, in other words, had a joint Korean-American authorship."[55]

Thousands of dissidents were jailed by military authorities in the period of U.S. occupation. When Rhee assumed formal authority with the creation of the Republic of Korea, he enacted laws that virtually eradicated any published dissent or educators not aligned with the state. All of this was aided and abetted by American advisers, aid, and muscle. Rhee and the authoritarian apparatus he quickly constructed would plainly not have been possible without the fulsome support of the United States. It is noteworthy that the U.S. government, having just led the worldwide battle against fascism, would instantly create and sustain what was an authoritarian state in Korea, one that lasted forty years. Its rationale was completely grounded in anticommunism, even though most of the opponents of the Trusteeship, the occupation, and Rhee were noncommunist nationalists—a fact that the Americans were told repeatedly by their own intelligence services.

The repression led directly to a series of militant protests and rebellions. Most serious were actual armed rebellions such as the peasant uprising on the island of Jeju, which began after the police killed six people without apparent cause in April 1948, four months prior to the founding of the ROK. The rebellion grew into a defiance of the plan to divide Korea, and for several months the South Korean army, until August under U.S. supervision, responded with overwhelming force. Although the rebels offered to negotiate, the army and its militias—with the consent of Major General William Dean and an American military adviser, James Hausman—killed thousands of islanders. The first commander of the South Korean troops refused to carry out the attack orders—one among other mutinies—and was replaced; he later described the action as a war crime, but his successor on Jeju was more compliant. "From the [U.S.] point of view," said South Korean writer Do Khiem, "the massacre was vital to establishing a U.S.-supported puppet government in South Korea."[56] The devastation wrought in putting down the Jeju Uprising, as it came to be called, was extensive. "The ROK army under the direction of U.S. Korean Military Advisory Group (KMAG) burned villages and killed those suspected of collaborating with the enemy," noted another scholar's account. "The estimated number killed reached 30,000, about ten percent of the island's population. Some 70 percent of the island's 230 villages were burned to the ground."[57] As with nearly all these cases, innocent villagers were victimized by the state-sponsored violence. This rebellion led to others at Yosu and Sunchon, altogether known as the Autumn Harvest Uprisings, but were quickly put down. "James Hausman, an army counterinsurgency expert who helped organize the suppression, reported that so many loyal civilians were killed that 'people are beginning to think we're as bad as the enemy.'"[58] Yosu was burned to the ground.

Those battles led to a guerrilla movement in the mountains. South Korean soldiers used starkly violent methods to deal with suspected communists, what fascist youth gangs called a "purification" of South Korea. Rhee imprisoned 60,000 as a result of these episodes, including some police and legislators. The guerrillas taking to the southern mountains, and particularly the Chollas islands right after Jeju and Yosu, fought ROK troops for months, and an intensive campaign to eradicate the guerrillas enveloped many civilians, with likely 10,000 or more killed in those operations of 1949–51.[59] While the insurgencies of this southern tip of the country were characterized as beholden to North Korean influence, there is little evidence of that; most historical accounts now see them as genuine, popular outbursts against the forced division of Korea and Rhee's authoritarianism. It is believed that 70 percent of the population at that time in the south would have preferred a leftist, even communist, government. It is not wholly surprising then that this popular rebellion was met by Rhee with a scorched earth policy, which one American journalist described as a "cloud of terror that is probably unparalleled in the world."[60] Overall, in the prewar turmoil of South Korea, 100,000 died in political violence,[61] mostly from the South Koreans under the U.S. occupation and the ROK.

Even after the U.S. troops of the occupation had departed in 1949, Americans were prominent in organizing and directing anticommunist activities for Rhee. "The monitoring and exterminating of Rhee's political enemies before June 25," wrote a member of the Truth and

Reconciliation Commission, "may have been carried out under the leadership of U.S. Special Intelligence agents in Korea. The most important figure was Donald Nichols, who commanded a . . . unit assigned not only to guard U.S. air bases in Korea but also to go after 'Korean communists' for President Rhee." He had trained a large number of the South Koreans who engineered executions. Notably, "in two cases of execution, in April 1950 near Seoul and the June 28 Suwon massacres, he was at the very site of the executions and took many pictures."[62]

The outbreak of the war and the North Koreans' initial military advances drove the South Koreans quickly south, toward Pusan (Busan), and the frantic retreat had enormous consequences for civilians. Among them were massacres of political prisoners in jails that would soon be overrun by the North Korean army and could have been recruited or pressed into the North Korean military. The decision was taken by South Korean authorities to execute the prisoners. In the words of journalists Charles J. Hanley and Jae-Soon Chang, "With U.S. military officers sometimes present, and as North Korean invaders pushed down the peninsula, the southern army and police emptied South Korean prisons, lined up detainees and shot them in the head, dumping the bodies in hastily dug trenches. Others were thrown into abandoned mines or into the sea. Women and children were among those killed."[63] The Truth and Reconciliation Commission in Korea, which investigated these stories and located mass graves, estimates the total murdered is about 30,000, which equaled the number of political prisoners at the time. At one prison, Daejeong, some 7,000 prisoners were executed. A British journalist claimed that a sizable number of U.S. officers "supervised the butchery," and Americans even photographed the gruesome scene. "About three hours after the executions were completed," wrote a U.S. army sergeant at the scene in the village of Dokchon, "some of the condemned persons were still alive and moaning. The cries could be heard somewhere from the mass of bodies piled in the canyon."[64]

A parallel set of killings was under way, probably larger in scale, and at times intermingled with the others. Korean jurists who had been Japanese collaborators and were close to Rhee had created a "reeducation" program, the National Rehabilitation and Guidance League, known as the Bodo League, which communists and other leftists were mandated to join. It was modeled, as so many things were in Rhee's

Korea, on the repressive mechanisms of the Japanese—their Bodo League was designed to corral anti-Japanese agitators. In April 1949, the new Bodo League started its roundup, eventually including 350,000 South Koreans. It was part-and-parcel of a sweeping set of security laws, assassinations, disappearances, and jailings of anyone opposing Rhee. "The Bodo League was established in this atmosphere of state-sponsored political terrorism," recalled a Korean filmmaker who produced a series on the Bodo League. "The fact of the matter is that, by 1949, most of the real leftists had been either purged or had escaped to North Korea and the 'leftists' left behind in South Korea were mostly poor farmers and left-leaning artists in Seoul."[65] Many and possibly most of the "members" were not communists or even liberals or leftists; they had been put in the Bodo League to fulfill local police quotas; as many as 70 percent were nonpolitical. All were monitored in the coming year.

When the war started in June 1950, Rhee issued an order to take all the Bodo League's members into custody, which was done mainly by the local police—part of a harshly effective anticommunist security apparatus. Within days and weeks, after digging their own graves, nearly two-thirds of them—as many as 200,000—were executed.[66] There were several eyewitnesses among Westerners, including a United Press reporter who was with a UN observer team. "He wrote that he witnessed a scene 'behind American lines' in which forty Korean prisoners had their backs broken with rifles wielded by members of Syngman Rhee's military force. He wrote that the prisoners were later dragged away and shot."[67] A large number who were in seaside villages were "forced into a boat and executed in the middle of the sea without gunfire. The police tied the people together, took them far from land, and kicked them into the sea."[68] The Japanese apparently lodged a complaint that their shores in Okinawa were awash with dead bodies. Killings took place in batches of hundreds or thousands all over South Korea in the first weeks of the war. Notably, many of the same police units that had willingly registered people they knew were not leftists, were those people's executioners.

At least one U.S. lieutenant colonel is on record as having approved the executions, telling the South Korean's Colonel "Tiger" Kim, who was in charge of the executioners, that he could kill a sizable number of prisoners in Busan if the North Korean army approached.[69] Such a mass execution of 3,400 South Koreans did in fact take place near Busan that summer.[70] Several other eyewitnesses demonstrate widespread knowledge among American officers of the mass executions. MacArthur, when told of the practice, described it to aides as an "internal matter" and, according to a U.S. official with MacArthur, "refrained from taking any action."[71] Some American officers objected to the executions without due process, but others observed without stated reservations or, more important, orders to desist. (The British, by contrast, not only objected but seized "Execution Hill" near a similar scene in occupied North Korea later that autumn to prevent more mass killings.) The executions persisted beyond those first, panicky days. When Seoul was recaptured in late September, an estimated 30,000 South Koreans were summarily deemed collaborators with the North Koreans and shot by ROK forces.[72] In some villages, whole families, including young children, were executed.

The killings were not confined to the Bodo League. The South Korean security forces were quickly recognized as particularly cruel and cavalier, and this "savagery" was even reported in the early weeks of the war. "The South Korean police and the South Korean marines whom I observed in front line areas are brutal," wrote the legendary correspondent John Osborne. "They murder to save themselves the trouble of escorting prisoners to the rear; they murder civilians simply to get them out of the way or to avoid the trouble of searching and cross-examining them. And they extort information . . . by means so brutal that they cannot be described."[73]

MacArthur had complete control over the ROK security forces from July 14, and the U.S. ambassador and military advisers like Hausman and Nichols were essentially first among equals in any deliberations before and during the war. Without a doubt, the U.S. authorities knew of the massive, countrywide executions, may have given consent, and possibly even prompted them. "All U.S. military reports about the executions by Korean troops described the scene without mentioning how they knew the executions were to take place and how they came to be on hand for them," noted an analysis by the Truth and Reconciliation Commission. "U.S. headquarters and a villa of the UN Commission stood yards away from the field of atrocities in the case of Pusan."[74] Reports from American officers on the killings were suppressed for years, and whenever rumors of the mass executions surfaced, the U.S.

government attributed the shootings to the "barbarism" of the North Koreans. In South Korea, one could be imprisoned for repeating stories of the atrocities many years later. This dishonesty—and complete suppression of information—persisted for nearly a half century.

Casualties of the Air War

During the war, millions of soldiers were fighting in a relatively small space with heavy weapons and air and naval bombardment utilized liberally. Apart from small island nations, the Korean peninsula, and especially the south, was and is one of the world's most densely populated areas. This was the fundamental physical reality of the Korean War that partially explains the high casualties. The conduct of the war, however, was brutal from all sides. As a matter of policy and attitude, the United States pursued a variety of strategies ranging from limited operations to nearly total war on the peninsula; but in all cases, the protection of civilian lives did not appear to be a priority. This is evident not only in the consideration of nuclear use or stated intentions to annihilate the enemy forces, but in the considerations of war tactics and strategy by uniformed and civilian leaders, the actual military operations, the accounts of Koreans and others, and the absence of concern in American political culture. In the first months of the war, the U.S. commanders were reluctant to bomb civilian areas of cities. "There is little evidence that American leaders were motivated primarily by humanitarian concern for sparing civilians," noted historian Sahr Conway-Lanz. "The limitation of attacks on cities was part of a strategy to avoid provoking a war with the Soviet Union."[75] MacArthur and the air force generals were willing to devastate cities apart from that caution—LeMay urged the destruction through firebombing of the five major cities of the north from the outset—and when the war began to go badly, or the armistice negotiations were not progressing, the policy of restraint was quickly abandoned.

The decision to bomb dams in the north when the armistice talks stalled in the spring of 1952 is an example of this set of attitudes. Ridgeway was opposed to bombing these large facilities because he thought it might spur the Chinese to escalate their own violence. Sites on the Yalu and near the Soviet border were off limits for the same reason. When Clark replaced Ridgeway, he adopted the more aggressive tactic and requested permission from Washington to bomb. Upon receiving it in June 1952, he commenced a major air campaign on the hydroelectric complex and, later, on irrigation dams; over three days, 1,200 bombing sorties were flown against the power plants. As to the reaction in the United States, "the question of why the power complex had not been bombed earlier was raised in Congressional and other quarters," said one army history.

> Clark could do little to help the [Joint Chiefs of Staff] answer this query since he saw no reason why they should have been spared so long. On 19 July, [Secretary of Defense Robert] Lovett told a congressman that seven factors had forestalled prior efforts to strike the power targets: 1. the postwar reconstruction problem; 2. the knowledge that some of the plants had been dismantled and only recently reconstructed; 3. the status of excess capacity in the plants; 4. possible losses of [UN Command] air forces; 5. use of North Korean power in Manchuria and in the USSR and possibility that destruction of the plants might invite a Communist offensive; 6. estimated effect upon the armistice talks; and other priority targets.[76]

The hydro dams were then producing electricity mainly for civilians since manufacturing had been nearly obliterated by prior bombing, and weeks-long blackouts resulted. Long-standing restrictions on bombing the dams on the Yalu were lifted. Some of these facilities were bombed repeatedly over weeks or months. Bombing of the irrigation dams in 1953 resulted in flooding 75 percent of the land used for food production in the north just at the time of planting, which was aimed to cause, in the words of an air force report, "starvation and slow death."[77] Pyongyang was also flooded by the "devastating torrent" of water unleashed by the destruction of the dams.

It was not the first bombing campaign of the war, to be sure. The air force command from the beginning embraced terror bombing as a way to break the North Koreans' will: the commander spoke of "putting a very severe blow on the North Koreans" that would include "burning five major cities in North Korea to the ground." Another air force policy document asserts that "the psychological impact of bringing the war to the people is a catalyst that destroys the morale and will to resist."[78] This "punishment" strategy, once under way in the winter of 1950–51, never really abated after the brief occupation of the north, when a ferocious amount of bombing accompanied the retreat from the Yalu in late 1950 and early 1951. In November 1950 alone, 3,300 tons of napalm were used on northern cities and villages.[79] One city and town after another were reported to be 90 percent destroyed. "One B-29 bombardier said that with the switch to incendiaries in November, the bombers had 'completely wiped out innumerable cities in North Korea'" before the Chinese advance. A year later, the air force reported they had destroyed 145,000 buildings in the north.[80] So the bombing of North Korea in the advance north and the subsequent retreat was constant and all-encompassing, using napalm, and making minimal if any attempts to spare civilian areas.

The 1952 "air pressure" strategy, implemented long after the eventual armistice lines were reached and the war was supposedly stalemated, clearly demonstrates the attitudes toward civilians in the north. The air campaign was three-pronged: destroy the dams and hydroelectric plants; use napalm bombs again on Pyongyang; and destroy villages and towns across the north that purportedly harbored or were sympathetic to the enemy. Operation Pressure Pump, against Pyongyang, began in July and "practically every operating unit in the Far East was to have a part in the savage assault," which included 1,254 sorties on the first day, unloading 23,000 gallons of napalm on the city.[81] The village eradication program was equally impressive, also using ample amounts of napalm. Seventy-eight villages and towns were targeted for the napalm attack and delayed-fuse bombs, but these attacks were halted by the State Department short of their objective because of concerns about the propaganda value to the communists, particularly when some reports of the horrific consequences—children burned, relatives killed by the delay-fuse bombs when they were tending to their wounded, and so on—sporadically appeared in the press. These reports prompted Acheson to try to censor any such news coming out of the northern war zone (although censorship was in effect from early in the war). "By 1952 just about everything in northern and central Korea was completely leveled," Cumings wrote. "What was left of the population survived in caves."[82]

The control of the news media reports included an insistence throughout the war that the massive bombing was all intended for military targets and industry alone. Even privately, the joint chiefs denied that civilians were targeted, as in a heated exchange between the air force chief of Britain and his counterpart in Washington in August 1952; the U.S. commander said that the joint chiefs "were not radically opposed to indiscriminate bombing," only that such tactics would not work.[83] That the military leaders were dissembling to their principal ally is remarkable. "Despite public claims that only military targets would be attacked, in fact, target selection focused on undermining civilian morale," observed Robert Pape in his seminal study, *Bombing to Win*. "To hide the true nature of the attacks from public scrutiny," the air force planned, in the words of an operations chief, that "attacks will be scheduled against targets of military significance so situated that their destruction will have a deleterious effect upon the morale of the civilian population."[84] There is some disagreement among historians about the effectiveness of the bombing—737,000 bombing sorties flown during the war—on civilians and morale, or even the immediate military objectives, just as the impact of strategic bombing during the Second World War is contested. But the implementation of the strategy is indicative of the U.S. policies toward noncombatants: they were viewed as fair game to win the war.

The notion of "winning the war" was a controversial matter, too, and instructive. In the charged atmosphere of domestic politics—1952 was a presidential election year—the sentiment was growing that the military should be "allowed" to win or withdraw, and the Republicans relentlessly charged that Truman was either appeasing the communists or had no strategy to win.[85] That the massive bombing of 1952–53 was a result of the Republican fusillade would be overstating the case, since the right wing had not relented in its criticisms of Truman's foreign policy since 1946; however, the combination of politics and the widely advertised need to break communist intransigence in the negotiations led to the new bombing campaign.* Since the war of attrition on the ground was unlikely to exert much influence one way or the other, and the U.S. air force had nearly complete control over the skies of the peninsula, the air war took on this special prominence. The military would frequently claim that its air assault was working: "Our

---

* Truman was apparently contemplating far more drastic measures. In his diary he wrote of several possibilities, including a blockade of China, destruction of bases in Manchuria, and "all out war" on the Soviet Union and China. As noted, he frequently contemplated using atomic weapons as well. (Foot, 176)

around-the-clock air operations brought to all North Korea the full impact of war," boasted one field commander in an internal memo. "The material destruction wrought, the panic and civil disorder created, and the mounting casualties in civilian and military populations alike became the most compelling factors in enemy accession to an armistice."[86] Apart from the net assessment of scholars that the strategic bombing of that period did not have the intended effects, however, the question of who was being intransigent remains a lively and important one. The ultimate cease-fire line and the POW issue were the sticking points, and on neither was there a principle at stake that could warrant the terror bombing and nuclear threats. For their part, the British apparently saw the Americans as the more rigid. "The British tended to blame American recalcitrance and inflexibility rather than the obstructiveness of the communist side for the deadlocks,"[87] concludes one account. The final terms of the armistice could likely have been reached many months sooner and without the bombing campaigns of 1952 and 1953.

The air war against the north exacted an enormous casualty rate, though it is impossible to gauge precisely how many Koreans in the north died as a result. If one million North Korean civilians died, and a great many of them were killed in the air raids—the most likely cause of civilian mortality in the north—then the responsibility for those deaths lies mainly with the U.S. air force, which had nearly complete command over the skies of the north during the war.

Just as morally notable is the air war in the south during the opening weeks of the war. The U.S. command had clearly provided permission, if not direct orders, to shoot civilian refugees in particular due to a belief that North Korean infiltrators could be among them. In one memorandum entitled "Policy on Strafing Civilian Refugees," a U.S. air force colonel stated that "the army has requested that we strafe all civilian refugee parties that are noted approaching our positions."[88] Given the very large number of refugees in the war and frequent changes of occupation of many areas, the war zone in the south and near the 38th parallel would have had a constant presence of civilians on the roads, almost invariably approaching U.S. positions.

Survivors who filed complaints with the Truth and Reconciliation Commission, testimony that logically represents only a small fraction of total incidents given the six decades that passed, speak of many strafings of villages and refugee columns by U.S. warplanes. "Through the use of napalm bombs and machine guns, the U.S. military killed civilians and burnt villages," concludes one investigation by the Commission. "The witnesses testified that the victims were killed while engaged in their daily activities, such as working or resting at home. One witness stated that 'the U.S. Forces bombed mostly ordinary houses.'" Dozens died in this one incident at Uiryeong in August 1950, and "the victims included the elderly, women, and children." As with most of these incidents, the victims' families regarded the military action as completely unwarranted. "The petitioners testified that 'at the time of bombings, there were no North Korean troops at all'" in the vicinity.[89] Using testimonies and U.S. National Archive documents, the Commission uncovered several other strafing and bombing incidents of that kind. For example, in January 1951 the U.S. air force bombed a northern province of South Korea "where refugees were hiding, and strafed civilians running out of the cave. . . . [M]ost of the victims were minors and women, and it is presumed that over 200 civilians were murdered in the incident."[90]

Another incident uncovered by the TRC occurred in 1951 near the village of Gokgyegul, 120 miles south of Seoul. Ordered by local authorities to leave the village, a large contingent of villagers was blocked a few miles from their homes by a U.S. armored division; they eventually took shelter in a large cave, the Cave of the Crying Stream. Days later, U.S. F-51 Mustangs hit them. "They dropped oil drums," said one survivor, referring to napalm, "and the fire incinerated everything and spread into the cave." That survivor, then a nine-year-old boy, watched a friend strafed, torn apart; "his mother fell down and cried over his body in the shower of bullets." More than 300 people were killed by the American raid.[91]

More such attacks have come to light. Near the site of the Inchon landing, a few days before MacArthur's great triumph, U.S. warplanes napalmed and strafed Wolmi Island, killing dozens of civilians. "When napalm hit our village, many people were still sleeping in their homes," reported a survivor. "Those who survived the flames ran to the tidal flats. We were trying to show the American pilots that we were civilians, but they strafed us, women and children." Another attack, in 1951, was carried out near Tanyang, where 167 refugees in a cave were napalmed to death; the pilots reported "excellent results."[92] Associated

Press reporter Charles Hanley interviewed some of the U.S. airmen involved, and they acknowledged that "we're not lily white" and "I know at times we were ordered to strafe refugees. . . . I pulled fighters off refugees at times." They got orders to destroy "all buildings showing signs of occupancy" and to "hit anything that moved."[93]

On the Ground

During the war, a Korean Catholic priest provided a striking insight into Korean views of American soldiers: "Do you know that if you held a plebiscite in South Korea, the Communist vote would be more than seventy-five percent? We are sick of war and ruin. . . . Your armies have not behaved well to the people, and we dislike you all. . . . [The people] are afraid of the bombs and the burning and the raping behind the battle line. . . . You all appear to despise us."[94]

The American culpability for the ruin of so many lives and families in Korea is not total, of course, given the predations of the communist forces, both Korean and Chinese, and a ruthless South Korean regime. Writers who have delved into the social and familial consequences of the civil conflict and the wider war are struck by how tragically divisive it was, far more so than the harsh years of Japanese occupation and the Second World War. Families were broken up, villages were torn by ideological loyalties and subterfuges, political repression, and the ravages of war. Few places escaped such impacts. Seoul, among other cities, changed hands several times, and experienced air raids and house-to-house battles each time. Cities were burned to the ground and sent refugees fleeing into free fire zones. The traditional, supportive environment and values that served the Korean people well for generations were obliterated. But the most abiding sensibility may be the feeling of being used wantonly for purposes having little to do with their homeland. "The typical Korean reaction to the war was bewilderment and self-abandon," said one account. "Koreans had a sense that the war was neither caused by them nor fought for them."[95]

That perception was rooted in the bombings and strafing incidents most profoundly, but other U.S. actions and policies left large numbers of civilians in mortal danger. When Seoul was under attack from the North Korean army early in the summer of 1950, there was an instant surge of people seeking to flee south. "Millions of people were heading toward the Han River like sheep toward a cliff," recalled Korean-American writer Mira Stout. She described a scene of panic when the flows of people from Seoul tried to cross the Han River to find that retreating South Korean forces had destroyed the bridges. The same scene was replayed when Seoul was taken again in the winter of 1951, when, trying to cross the Han they were blocked by Rhee's troops, who opened fire on those making their way across on the cracking ice of the river. The U.S. commanders, including Ridgeway, issued explicit orders to prohibit any refugees from using the main routes out of Seoul. Three million refugees were in flight at the time, but the American orders were to shoot anyone who was on the road or bridges. The Eighth Army commanders issued a "sweeping directive to 'stop all civilian traffic in any direction.' It instructed subordinate commands that 'responsibility to place fire on them to include bombing rests with you.'"[96]

Very few journalists at the time reported on the civilian massacres, and reports have filtered back, many uncorroborated or very general, of sizable killings at the hands of American troops. The typical phrasing is that the U.S. soldiers would shoot at "anything that moved," or that atrocities were committed in a state of panic about infiltrators. "Fear of infiltrators led to the slaughter of hundreds of South Korean civilians," wrote one American correspondent in September 1950.[97] The Truth and Reconciliation Commission in its first three years investigated cases denoting 7,533 civilian massacres, and classified 1,222 as genocides, of which 215 are attributed to U.S. soldiers. (Some 552 are attributed to South Korean soldiers and police.)[98] The most notorious of them, and indeed the massacre that led to the establishment of the Commission, was the incident at No Gun Ri.

Charles Hanley and his Associated Press colleagues revealed this in a 1999 news feature. Five weeks into the war, U.S. troops were digging in around the hamlet of No Gun Ri, about 100 miles south of Seoul in central South Korea. They sent villagers from their homes ahead of advancing enemy forces, and several hundreds from No Gun Ri were on the road going south. They came to a U.S. roadblock and were directed to a railroad track instead of the main road; U.S. soldiers inspected their belongings as the tired Koreans rested briefly and had something to eat. The soldiers left, and soon U.S. warplanes appeared and began to shoot their machine guns at the refugees on the railroad tracks. About

100 were killed by the strafing. Taking refuge below a railroad bridge, the villagers there sustained three days of gunfire from soldiers of the U.S. 7th Cavalry. Surviving Koreans from the onslaught described in detail the chaotic panic they experienced; having believed the Americans were protecting them, they then saw the U.S. troops fire indiscriminately at men, women, and children at the scene. No infiltrators were among them, and none of them were armed. Those that Hadley interviewed for the article, men who were U.S. soldiers at No Gun Ri, "corroborated the core of the Koreans' account: that American troops kept the large group of refugees pinned under the No Gun Ri railroad bridge and killed almost all of them." They said they had orders that no civilians should cross the front lines, and one artillery commander told his troops, "The hell with all those people. Let's get rid of all of them."[99] Overall, some 400 Koreans were killed by American troops in those three days. There were survivors, and they told their tale. Many also clearly were traumatized for years to come.

It now seems clear that the U.S. command had in fact issued guidance, somewhat ambiguous but sufficiently robust, that refugees were not allowed to cross the front lines and that they should be stopped, by force if necessary, after a warning. Some leafleting of Korean villages explaining this policy was done later. The policy supports the claim, however, that civilian shootings were authorized from the top, an assertion verified by the report of a meeting by U.S. Ambassador to Korea John Muccio—a high-level meeting of key decision makers in Korea—which oddly enough took place during the same week of the No Gun Ri episode. Their conclusion: "If refugees do appear north of U.S. lines they will receive warning shots, and if they then persist in advancing, they will be shot."[100] This report was written to Assistant Secretary of State Dean Rusk, indicating that the upper echelons in Washington very well knew the policy, even as Rusk would later aver that American troops were taking every precaution not to harm civilians. There were several other orders from the Eighth Army commanders and other military brass in the theater of operations—for example, a directive that "all civilians seen in this area are to be considered as enemy and action taken accordingly."[101] The difficulty of preventing infiltration by North Koreans presumably could have been solved (and in many cases was) through inspection of refugees, which was operationally a bit cumbersome and a bit dangerous, but would conform the U.S. military actions to international law.

Time magazine's Osborne, in a vivid passage, described the dilemma faced every day by U.S. officers. He was writing in August 1950.

It is midnight and all around the hills are astir. Here a sharp burst of small-arms fire, there the flashing life & death of an American shell, searching out the enemy who we know are gathering within 5,000 yards of this command post. One of the field telephones rings, an officer of the staff picks it up, listens a moment and says, "Oh, Christ, there's a column of refugees, three or four hundred of them, coming right down on B company." A major in the command tent says to the regimental commander, "Don't let them through."

And of course the major is right. Time & again, at position after position, this silent approach of whitened figures has covered enemy attack. Finally the colonel says, in a voice racked with wretchedness, "All right, don't let them through. But try to talk to them, try to tell them to go back."

"Yeah," says one of the little staff group, "but what if they don't go back?"

"Well, then," the colonel says, as though dragging himself toward some pit, "then fire over their heads."

"O.K.," an officer says, "we fire over their heads. Then what?"

The colonel seems to brace himself in the semidarkness of the blacked-out tent.

"Well, then, fire into them if you have to. If you have to, I said."

An officer speaks into the telephone, and the order goes across the wire into the dark hills.[102]

The massacre at No Gun Ri was the largest of its kind reported from the war; and then nearly fifty years after the fact, it was disputed by the military and became a topic of heated controversy (a topic explored in a later chapter of this book). What seems clear is that the "rules of engagement" that Osborne described were not followed carefully—or at all—in the No Gun Ri massacre. Some American officers were careful, some were not. Unknown is how many other incidents there were of Americans shooting refugees without warning or other forms of brutalizing noncombatants. Given the broad orders and the colossal number of refugees, the house-to-house combat in Seoul and other cities, and the air campaigns, the human toll of civilians was surely very significant. British journalist Reginald Thompson noted in his memoir of reporting from Korea that a new approach to fighting was employed in Korea that, above all, sought to minimize U.S. casualties and failed to protect civilians. "This is the new technique of warfare," he wrote in *Cry Korea*. "It is certain that it kills civilian men, women and children, indiscriminately and in great numbers, and destroys all that they have."[103] That included use of overwhelming force when fired upon, rampaging through villages, reflexive use of air power to suppress enemy fire, and so on—for the most part justified by the rules of engagement, but devastating to Koreans all the same. "Every enemy shot released a deluge of destruction," Thompson said of the drive north of the 38th parallel. "Every village and township in the path of war was blotted out. Civilians died in the rubble and ashes of their homes. Soldiers usually escaped."[104]

One common observation by historians is how ill-trained the Eighth Army was for this battle; they had been an occupying army in Japan before being shipped suddenly to Korea, and their readiness for combat was low. Not only did this lead to "wild fire" on the ground, but it led to heavier use of artillery and air strikes to compensate for the ineffectiveness of ground troops. "General Van Fleet has stated many times that one of our major advantages over the Reds is our ability to mass supporting fires rapidly on any target," noted a U.S. marines training bulletin during the war. "In X Corps in late 1950 and early 1951 we found that ability primarily in the artillery; the infantry was not making maximum use of the weapons available."[105] The result of the poor training, then, was not only civilian deaths caused by fearful soldiers at close range, but more reliance on the indiscriminate heavy artillery of marines, army, and navy (such as the navy's 861-day siege of the northern city of Wonsan, which reduced it to "a cluttered mass of ruins"),[106] as well as "close air support"—strafing and bombing from the air.

In American conflicts, the Korean War stands as the most deadly to civilians as a proportion of all killed, a dimension of war largely left out of reporting back home. It was a forgotten war in several respects, and the human toll was one of its most important characteristics that was overlooked, repressed, or ignored. Osborne described his August 1950 report as "the ugly story of an ugly war" that displayed not just the usual savagery of war, but "savagery in detail—the blotting out of villages where the enemy may be hiding; the shooting and shelling of refugees who may include North Koreans . . . [and] savagery by proxy."[107] Thompson's recounting the first recapturing of Seoul speaks of the same horror:

> Slowly, day by day, the tragedy unfolded as death and destruction inexorably consumed Korea and its people, and the fears of one day became the knowledge of the next. Handfuls of peasants defied the immense weight of modern arms with a few rifles and carbines and a hopeless courage which would not—or could not—know defeat. The shots of the doomed came from the rice paddies and the shattered ruins of the few concrete buildings, and brought down upon themselves and all the inhabitants the appalling horror of jellied patrol bombs and the devastation of rockets and heavy artillery.
>
> Slowly the American troops advanced through the smoking rubble, pausing until the opposition was crushed under the air strikes and the bombardment. Civilians died in the hundreds, and presently in thousands.[108]

The carnage was not entirely hidden from the view of American society, and the question then is how or why it was not more fully regarded, acknowledged, or discussed—which brings us back to the political and psychological climate of America in the early 1950s.

THE AMERICAN PUBLIC

What we came to know as the culture of the Cold War was in its infancy when the Korean War began, and the war helped shape that culture but not with the abrupt and decisive impact that wars often do. The 1941–45 "good war" had only just ended, and it dominated novels, films, comic books, and the new medium of television in the opening years of the 1950s. Its heroic ideal and the totality of the fight against worldwide fascism fairly leaped over the Korean conflict to lend its template to the total, global fight against communism. That Korea was the actual template, with all its tough ambiguities, was not a notion easy to digest. The political culture that was in thrall to the anticommunist dramas was certainly germane to Korea, as if the necessity of Truman's police action was proof of the insidious threat about which Nixon, Chambers, and McCarthy had warned, and at the same time was a weak, inadequate riposte, as MacArthur, Luce, and Dulles were warning. The fatigue wrought by the Second World War and the lack of clarity about the purpose and scale of the U.S. commitment in Korea chilled any enthusiasm for the new war once its fortunes fell quickly in the "coldest winter" of 1950–51. While the war's goal remained beholden to anticommunism, it was an imperfect mission, to be sure, derived from the missed bounty of China; and, after rollback, it was routed by the very Chinese who spoiled the American dream of Asia, leading to retreat and self-doubt.

The anxieties of the period issued from the rapid social changes afoot. The hopes of the New Deal and the triumph over fascism had quickly been overwhelmed by the cacophony of anticommunism and the mounting bitterness over the war itself. Playwright Arthur Miller's drama "The Crucible"—drawing parallels between Puritan self-righteousness and the present—was staged in 1953; he noted later that the hysteria generated by the right wing "was capable of creating not only a terror, but a new subjective reality. . . . It was as though the whole country had been born anew."[109] The insular nature of this new reality, the terror, the search for demons inside American institutions, and the stunted expansiveness of 1945—not only the battlefield triumph of 1945, but the vision for a different kind of world where American liberal values would reign—was not a culture where empathy for the war's local victims would be nourished.

The Public and the News Media

The ways that the public's perceptions of foreign policy are affected by the news media, and vice versa, is always an intriguing question, particularly in times of war. Opinion about Korea was trifurcated: those who supported U.S. prosecution of the war, those who felt Truman was not being aggressive enough toward China and the Soviets, and those who opposed the military action in whole or part. The third group rose in salience from the time of the Chinese intervention and the U.S. retreat in the winter of 1950–51. Support for Truman's stewardship of the war diminished, and those who backed a more expansive war—essentially, MacArthur's "no substitute for victory"—remained a prominent minority. The news media—most important, the leading news services and dailies—were largely pro-war, at least in support of the "limited" war Truman was pursuing to contain the Soviets or Chinese. It was rare, however, in the mix of opinions—changeable as they sometimes were, frequently pinned to political personalities, and always shaped by the contours of anticommunism—to see much concern for the Korean civilians who were victimized by the conflict.

Opinion surveys demonstrate declining support for the war after the early surge of patriotic enthusiasm. Scholars argue about the effect of casualties on public opinion—American combat casualties, of course, not those of civilians—and in Korea, the U.S. military sustained most of its casualties in the first nine months or so of the war. As a result, the opinion surveys show variable but generally declining public support for the U.S. war policy. In the first months, there is the "rally effect" and then decline; in Korea, the battlefield fortunes of the U.S. effort changed radically in the first seven months—retreating to the Busan tip of the peninsula, retaking South Korea, and marching to the Yalu, all within four months; then the Chinese intervention and a quick retreat back south, losing Seoul to the communists in the first week of January 1951. So, in July and August of 1950, a very difficult first few weeks of the engagement, American support reached levels of 75 percent, and then declined slightly, until peaking at 81 percent after Inchon and the routing of the NKPA from the south in September. Then, the decline, gradual but inexorable, until the war was opposed by a plurality (those who said it was "a mistake") or even an outright majority in 1952.[110]

Survey methods were just being honed in the early 1950s, and the measured variations in opinion were likely greater than in later wars. Among the findings of several of the survey pioneers was that Americans had an abysmally low grasp of international issues. One account of this series of analyses in the immediate postwar period noted that "despite the dramatic events of the previous decade—including World War II, the start of the nuclear era, the nation's emergence as a world leader, and the onset of the Cold War—many Americans remained remarkably uninformed about even the most elementary aspects of international affairs."[111] In fact, those studying this troubling ignorance, or indifference, concluded that opinion on foreign matters generally was volatile and lacking in coherence, but that the views of the public had very little impact on government decisions. What tends to matter, then as now, is the trend of opinion—elite opinion in particular, typically conveyed through the news media and some institutions like universities, think tanks, and unions—and expressions of strong popular sentiments at particular times of crisis, usually signaled through social movements and other political organizing.

During the Korean War, the major institutions likely to exert influence were largely supportive of the war. The Republican Party, oddly, was all over the map—the isolationists worried about deep involvement, the right wing charging appeasement and incompetence (stemming from the loss of China), fiscal hawks worried about the costs of war. Democrats warily supported Truman throughout, with some on the left increasingly skeptical. A peace movement of sorts appeared, based mainly in the progressive Protestant churches; but it was not prominent, certainly not when compared with later antiwar movements. The news media and other major players on the national scene, such as the trade unions, tended to the anticommunist orthodoxy and the relatively safe haven of Truman's leadership. So institutional power formed along predictable lines, and the change in public opinion then likely followed the bad news from the front: the retreats, the Chinese intervention, the sacking of MacArthur, the accumulating U.S. casualties. Much of the growing distaste for the war occurred during the long stalemate, indicating war weariness was at work; although to some extent the public did not think withdrawing from Korea early was a good option, even when they saw U.S. involvement as an error.

One interesting survey of college students in 1952 produced two unexpected and noteworthy findings. As a group, they were evenly split on the wisdom of going to war, or, more generally, of fighting a major war against communism. Among the questions was: "Would you like to see our government show more concern for conditions in other countries, or would you prefer us to show less concern?" Many more of those who answered "more" or "much more" concern—a sizable plurality when combined (46%)—favored the war in much larger numbers than those who answered "less" concern. By about the same margins, those who thought the work of the United Nations was effective backed the war. War supporters also scored high when asked if we are fighting for an ideal—that is, freedom versus dictatorship. So there seemed to be a correlation, a fairly strong one, between "idealism" and support for the war. And those favoring the war scored higher on questions demonstrating political knowledge. This survey used a large sample, more than 4,000, of male students at eleven universities.[112] Very few, however, were keen to enlist and fight themselves, suggesting a certain idealism by remote control.

The survey of students may have pinpointed a phenomenon of American attitudes—namely, a genuine if detached concern for South Korea as a venue of Cold War conflict, a place where we had to remain fighting so that the Soviets and Chinese would be deterred from further expansion; but little empathetic concern for the human costs of achieving that result. Pollsters don't ask questions that reveal much in this regard. But there is also a problem of knowledge in assessing the public's attitudes toward the carnage in Korea: how much did the news media convey about these human costs of war? How much did Americans know?

While television news began to play a more prominent role in the first three years of the 1950s—ownership of TV sets went from about three million at the beginning of 1950 to about 20 million in 1953—newspapers, radio, and weekly magazines were the main sources of information. News from the front was reported by a relatively small number of correspondents, as most newspapers would publish the stories from the wire services, the Associated Press and United Press, and a few others mainly from major newspapers. Censorship was an issue from the beginning, although formal censorship did not occur until what MacArthur called the "Disaster School of Journalism" became prominent, when China entered the war and the U.S. retreat from the north commenced in December 1950. Censorship was invoked to deny the enemy useful information about troop whereabouts and movements, but the reporters were always careful about that; more likely, the military and civilian brass were alarmed by the negativity of some reporting and its effect on home front morale.

That negativity emerged from the sheer brutality of the war, which many correspondents, who were veterans of reporting the Second World War, were ready to portray. The genre of interviewing or profiling the U.S. infantryman was well used, and those men, particularly during the retreats in either the steamy hot summer of 1950 or the bitterly cold winter of 1950–51, were terribly burdened. Many were openly puzzled about the reasons they were there and the tactics used by American leaders. It was a war, too, in which it was not entirely clear who the enemy was.

The scale of the killing, and the price paid by civilians, occasionally came through in the dispatches. The deadly work of the B-29s and other bombers was not fully explored, to be sure, but reports filtered out. In August 1950, an A.P. story headlined "B-29 Armadas Rain Death on 60,000 Reds" noted that "when it was all over the pilots and bombardiers didn't know whether they had done any good. They had hit the target on the nose, and knew that. Results were uniformly reported as 'excellent.' 'But that means we dropped all our bombs and hit the assigned area,' one Air Force officer said. 'But it doesn't mean that we killed gooks because we just don't know whether they were there.'"[113] For the most part, however, the reporting on the extended bombing campaigns in the north emphasized—indeed, insisted—that the American flyers were hitting only industrial or military targets and taking pains to avoid civilians.

There were exceptions. After questioning the plausibility of air force communiqués about bombing northern villages and not harming civilians, journalist I. F. Stone, one of the few independent voices in print media, remarked that a "complete indifference to noncombatants was reflected in the way villages were given 'saturation treatment' with napalm to dislodge a few soldiers," he reported. The raids on villages, he continued, reflected none of "the pity which human feeling called for, but a kind of gay moral imbecility, utterly devoid of imagination—as if the fliers were playing in a bowling alley, with villages for pins." He quoted a pilot from an air force operational summary saying, "It's hard to find good targets, for we have burned out almost everything."[114]

While the breadth and frequency of bombing at least suggested considerable costs to civilians, the on-the-ground operations were more difficult to capture in the news media. Adding to that was the growing censorship by U.S. officials, including, as an early guidance document from MacArthur's office put it, "the vilification of armed forces personnel."[115] Echoing the John Osborne story cited earlier, Charles Grutzner of the New York Times reported in late September 1950 about the difficulties of identifying enemy soldiers among the civilian populations, especially refugees. "Fear of infiltrators led to the slaughter of hundreds of South Korean civilians, women as well as men, by some United States troops and police of the Republic," he wrote from the front. "One high-ranking United States officer condemned as 'panicky' the shooting of many civilians last July by one United States regiment."[116] Another

New York Times story later in the war spoke of a massacre of South Korean villagers—as many as one thousand in a village of 1,400—by ROK troops in a region of guerrilla activity. The government was concerned about bad publicity in light of the mass executions in Seoul in December 1950.[117]

Another aspect of the war that received scant attention was misconduct by troops. One story midway through the conflict described a trial of Canadian soldiers for murder and attempted rape; the report noted that "Koreans are keeping an intense watch on this case as possible proof finally that United Nations authorities mean to crack down on misconduct and outbreaks of contempt that already have created a deep animosity among large sections of the Korean populace." The reporter, George Barrett of the New York Times, was notably more outspoken than most. His story continued to note something exceptionally rare among journalists' accounts: the Chinese "have impressed many Koreans with the discipline of their troops. Many residents of Seoul seem to go out of their way to tell about good Chinese behavior, and especially about executions of two rapists the Chinese are said to have held."[118] (A story in the London Times made much the same point about retreating North Korean troops, who did not—as the UN troops would—torch the villages left behind.)[119] Such a comparison was rare because in virtually all stories of U.S. or allied misbehavior, the actions were set in the context of worse communist practices that infected nearly all reporting. The trial Barrett spoke of was, to Koreans, a "symbol of the widespread contempt held by many United Nations soldiers for the people of this country, a contempt emphasized every day in the way the Koreans are pushed around."

Barrett reported later that autumn about the hardships civilians were facing ("civilians in the northern Communist areas are suffering even more," he added), and concluded: "Every Korean this correspondent has talked to during the last few weeks about present and future seems to feel only despair, disillusionment or angry resentment—or all three."[120] Such observations were unusual; most reporting was about the to and fro of the military operations, and if hardship was mentioned, it focused on those faced by the GIs. War-front bylines by correspondents like Homer Bigart and Marguerite Higgins focused on the stories of individual American soldiers, many of whom criticized their leadership and lamented the conditions; several veterans of the Second

World War told these reporters that the violence in Korea was worse than anything they had experienced in the earlier war. These stories had enormous popular appeal back home and were widely syndicated, and the reporters were asked for more by the *Saturday Evening Post* and other publications.[121] So hardship as reported from Korea for American audiences was overwhelmingly associated with the difficulties faced by American infantrymen, not Korean civilians.

Television was if anything more restrained, more self-censoring, than the newspapers. There were few reports from the front. Television cooperated with the government in ways the print media never would, airing documentaries that were essentially propaganda and generally reflecting Washington thinking, particularly the Cold War context. When seasoned reporters sought to be more penetrating in their observations and analysis, they were typically beaten back by network executives. One example of this practice was Edward R. Murrow's August 1950 report, which never aired, in which he said, "When we start moving through dead valleys, through villages to which we have put the torch by retreating, what then of the people who live there?"[122] Later, television's most prominent contribution was Murrow's "See It Now" broadcast in which he followed individual soldiers through their daily routine and had them speak to the television audience. He also noted solemnly that half of those had become casualties of the fighting.[123]

Television's peculiar role aside, the reporting from the war zones was ample enough to signal to the American public that a vicious war was under way, one in which readers or listeners could readily infer that civilians were victimized in very large numbers. Casualty figures were rolled out at somewhat frequent intervals. MacArthur himself, in a one-upmanship show at a widely watched Senate hearing after his dismissal, claimed that one million casualties had been suffered by civilians in Korea, and were "horrible beyond conception."[124] After nearly a year of the war, the United Press mentioned in a short item the 4.7 million total casualties and that such a figure "was fast shaping up as one of the deadliest in history."[125] At times, the press inadvertently tipped their readership to the scale of ruin by endorsing, for example, the extensive bombing of North Korea. "Inevitably a campaign against military targets in and near cities will result in civilian casualties and the destruction of homes—and it will make very little difference to the victims what the moral purpose of the raid was," argued the *Washington Post* in a 1952 editorial insisting the bombing campaign was not "terroristic."[126]

The political opposition also spoke out on occasion in ways that underscored the high civilian toll. In a remarkable speech on the Senate floor just as the Chinese were overrunning Seoul in January 1951, Senator Robert Taft, the leading Republican in the Senate and a leading candidate for president, said, "We have saved Korea at the expense of the destruction of every city in Korea and the killing of an infinite number of Korean civilians. I do not believe we are so welcome in Korea today."[127] A few conservative columnists likewise questioned the prudence of the bombing, as did a writer in the periodical *Human Events*, for example, in referring to the "barbarities of aerial warfare."[128]

Americans could avoid the implications of these "barbarities" by swallowing whole the assurances about the relentless B-29 bombing campaign only hitting strategic targets, or the insistence that the communists' tactics forced the allies to make difficult choices on the battlefield. There were acknowledgments of the high costs of the war for civilians in relief efforts undertaken by the U.S. government and, after a time, by a consortium of private relief agencies (many of them church based) to send clothes and food to South Korean civilians, mainly refugees and children. While these efforts were well publicized, it is difficult to gauge the extent to which there was significant public participation, or what that participation meant politically. The efforts were genuinely humanitarian, but many in the government doubtlessly saw them as necessary for public relations, given the sharp criticism of U.S. bombing tactics, for example, among the nonaligned countries. The relief and reconstruction both were meant to signal the free world's superiority over communism as well and to reward South Korea for making such sacrifices to fight communism. As the war was winding down, an opinion survey showed just over half of Americans agreeing that some money should be allocated in South Korea to repair the physical damage wrought by the war, a relatively weak response given how important reconstruction was to the overall mission.[129] The principal agency within the military tasked with civilian assistance had as part of its mission the reconstruction of primary education, which, in the north during the brief occupation there, included curriculum overhauls to exclude any tendencies toward communism.[130] Some of the private relief efforts also were undertaken in the spirit of anticommunism. So even the simple acts of generosity that some Americans undertook were fraught with Cold War politics.

The government's attempts to control information and remind Americans of the fundamental importance of the mission did not succeed as intended, to be sure. But to the extent that the "Disaster School of Journalism" triumphed, it was all about the plight of the GI and the humiliating retreats. So the public debate revolved around issues of American casualties, the war's worth, the Truman-MacArthur controversy, and the new and wrenching responsibilities of the Cold War. In such a dense jungle of concerns, civilians were hard to find.

The Hegemony of Forgetting

The constant references to "the forgotten war" beg for explanation. In the most obvious sense, the war was forgotten after the fact in that it failed to elicit the glorification typically accorded American combat (although the Philippines venture was similarly set aside). The defeats in Korea do not square well with the roseate picture that American pop culture now paints of the 1950s. But the "forgotteness" also signals the attitudes at the time. The question is: Why was it forgotten so soon, virtually while the war was being waged? And what precisely was the nature of this forgetting?

In a thoughtful essay, David McCann asserts that the rhetorical tradition of glorifying war, stretching back to Pericles' funeral oration, died in the unspeakable carnage of the world wars, and that there was a "predisposition not to seek literary heroism in connection with the war in Korea."[131] The McCarthy deluge was a suppressing agent—the possibility of honoring the dead of Korea of any nationality was complicated by the "terror" and consequent risk of taking a stand. That suppression, or self-censorship, worked across the political spectrum. For the forgetting was not incidental or cavalier, but intentional. "Forgetting, Nietzsche said, is not mere result of inertia: 'It is rather an active and in the strictest sense positive faculty of repression,'" Bruce Cumings observed. "'Forgetfulness is like 'a doorkeeper, a preserver of psychic order, repose and etiquette.'" For both liberals and conservatives, who took away different lessons (if any) from the war, "it merely symbolizes an absence, mostly a forgetting, but also a never knowing,"

Cumings wrote. "The result is a kind of hegemony of forgetting, in which almost everything to do with the war is buried history."[132] If indeed forgetting, or apathy, is a mechanism of repression, what was being repressed? What memories needed to be expunged?

The answer at hand is "defeat," or at least a frustrating ambiguity about the results of the war and its human costs in American lives and treasure. It was often said at the time that America had never lost a war, and while Korea was not a clear-cut loss, it was—particularly with respect to the seminal loss of China—a dispiriting endeavor, particularly after the rapid march north following the landing at Inchon appeared to be on the way to redeem the loss of China. Rollback was tantalizingly within America's grasp, within the grasp of the hero-warrior, when he was pulled back by the bureaucrats and feckless politics of Washington.

It's worth noting in this regard how popular culture was treating— or not treating—this very sizable conflict and the political currents shaped by it. The Korean War stirred little in the way of literature or films, certainly not during the conflict, and those that came later, like the sardonic movie and television series *M*A*S*H*, could have been about any war. Movies about the Second World War were prominent in the early 1950s, and the few movies that were exclusively about Korea were box office failures. Many of the most popular films made during the war were apolitical entertainments like *An American in Paris*, *The Quiet Man*, and *The Greatest Show on Earth*. But one genre did speak to the frustrations spurred by China and Korea, and that was the Western. Consider, for example, the immensely popular (and Oscar-winning) *High Noon*. Often interpreted as a Cold War tale, it depicts the honorable and brave sheriff, played by Gary Cooper, saving a town of spineless citizens from violent invaders. But he casts off his sheriff's badge, throwing it to the ground at the end, signifying the hero who acts outside the "system."

Unmistakably, the use of the Western as the dominant allegorical form about the use of force says as much as anything about the mood of the country at the time. *Rio Bravo, Shane, The Gunfighter*, and numerous others were popular and followed a cultural form, the frontier myth, which spoke directly to the frustrations of Americans who saw Korea as a letdown from what they knew to be the heroics of the American past, a heritage in which the invaders, the savages, the untamed territory, and the bounty were invariably ours. Notably, the conflict in the Western movie was always resolved by a "singular act of violence," explained Richard Slotkin. "Since the Western offers itself as a myth of American origins, it implies that its violence is an essential and necessary part of the process through which American society was established and through which its democratic values are defended and enforced."[133] No wonder, then, that Americans supported the use of the atomic bomb to end the Korean War and possibly destroy communism in China—it was that "singular act of violence" that would redeem American suffering.

That this errand took Americans to the Asian wilderness explains in part the capacity to forget the carnage. Racism feeds all explanations of how and why civilian misery was largely ignored. The references to Koreans as "gooks" or "coolies" were commonplace; prevalent political attitudes were less vulgar but, at a minimum, patronizing. The belief in the racial and moral inferiority of Koreans was rooted in a broader attitude about the "Orient" that was European first and absorbed by Americans, and it reared its head before the war and since.[134] In the early part of the occupation in 1945–46, for example, the widespread notion among Washington elites was that Koreans and their people's committees were too immature for self-governance (as well as too "leftist"). That attitude directly fed the tragedy unfolding in the ensuing eight years. And that perception—more accurately an applied, preexisting cultural bias— conforms very closely to Edward Said's definition of "orientalism," specifically the political implications of orientalism: that Asians were morally vacuous, supine if not effeminate, prone to accept despotism, and utterly devoid of democratic virtues. At the same time, somewhat paradoxically, they were "barbarians." The notion that Koreans do not value life as much as Americans do, a sentiment that General William Westmoreland (who also served in Korea) voiced during the Vietnam conflict, was at work as well. No less than the lead lawyer in the 1945–46 Nuremberg trials, Telford Taylor, could say without fear of rebuttal that "individual lives are not valued so highly in Eastern mores," nor will the Korean soldier "follow our most elevated precepts of warfare."[135] Many commanders in Korea were on record with similar views, and they were usually much more demeaning. That it was not merely the emotions of war that drove such stereotyping, but institutional racism, is evidenced by the anti-Korean laws and practices in effect in America in the twentieth century, including laws proscribing marriage to whites, ownership of land, or, in New York City, eligibility for more than two dozen types of jobs.[136] Truman was often congratulated, rightly, for integrating the armed forces in the Korean War, but the underlying racism of the war itself, the shameless attitudes of the political and military elite, and the consequences of those attitudes are rarely mentioned— and are almost always completely absent—from the histories of the war and the period. It scarcely needs to be said that if one regards a people as "half men," "barbarians," "a shade of above the beast" (words of top journalists and generals), then killing them indiscriminately is not a problem for policy or practice. And perceptions of the war in Asia smoothly repeated the tropes of the "Indian wars"—the same attitudes, the same depictions of the savage, the same civilizing mission, the same regeneration through violence—to the point that those wars and images were frequently invoked in Korea by the fighting men of America, and, as noted, were a prominent metaphor for examining the war's failures in popular culture.

It could be argued that the act of forgetting, of foresaking the human toll of Korea, was part of the larger narrative of the frontier myth, the epic of the Second World War, the emergent epic of the Cold War, and reflexive and persistent orientalism—all of which are "hegemonic." They involved powerful forces, culturally, politically, and psychologically, and were almost wholly braced by popular entertainment, the educational system, the news media, and politics. As will be explored later, the psychological processes at work both deterred and submerged any sense of responsibility to victims of war as well. But the setting for this collective denial of the reality of death in Korea, particularly the gripping climate of anticommunism, may have provided its own fog of war to ignore civilian casualties. Naming the enemy as subhuman, as a mortal and insidious threat, as a denier of American destiny, resulted in a slaughter of the innocents in numbers—hundreds of thousands?— which even then was too easy to ignore and thereby forget.

CHAPTER 5

The Vietnam War

The High Cost of Credibility

America's interest in Vietnam was slow to rise in the 1950s, vacillated in the Kennedy years, suddenly escalated in the mid-1960s, then subsided gradually until the last helicopter infamously departed from the embassy roof on the last day of April in 1975. For several of those years, it shaped American politics and society as few wars ever have. While the objectives of U.S. leaders were like those of the Korean War—stopping the takeover of a divided Asian country by Marxist forces and dealing a blow to world communism—the fighting itself was quite different and the arousal of American society starkly contrasted with the war of 1950–53. While still beset by a kind of rote anticommunism, American society had changed, too, and this made for a lively and skeptical scrutiny of the war that was far more broadly based than in the Korean or any other war.

Yet for all the attention focused on the Vietnam experience, the concern for Vietnamese civilians in the war zones was merely episodic. The body bags that drew sympathy and provoked anger were those carrying American soldiers home for burial, a ritual that was soon a symbol of a misbegotten war. Those war dead, some 58,000, stirred a public anxiety that has ever since informed U.S. military interventions and launched a discourse among military analysts about "casualty aversion," a copious literature in which "casualty" is implicitly understood to mean that of an American soldier and no one else. That one to two million Vietnamese civilians (or more) died in the war, which is not the source of the politician's aversion, remains an obscure and scarcely relevant number. Despite the anti-war antics and heroics of the late 1960s and early 1970s, and the news media's intensive reporting and occasional cynicism about the U.S. role in Vietnam, the topic of the war dead was and is mostly an all-American affair.

That this was so, and remains so, is all the more remarkable for those two social and political phenomena—a massive and often radical opposition to the war, and a newly questioning press corps that undertook remarkably brave and insightful reporting from the battlefields of Indochina. Both of these lit and focused a searchlight on the warriors' misbehavior in ways not previously done. The war's opponents, who grew in numbers and militancy quickly after the war escalated in 1965, repeatedly inveighed against the bombing of North Vietnam and Cambodia, the use of napalm, and the seemingly indiscriminate killings in villages of the South. The press corps—for all its apparent willingness to expose the misdeeds of both the U.S. military and the client state of South Vietnam, including the signature massacre of the war at My Lai—as a whole came only gradually to disapprove of the war and even then was seen as carping and even disloyal. Still, with all this attention to the carnage in Vietnam, the protests and the press turned the American public only on more mundane grounds—the costs of the war to Americans—and even then, only after the U.S. military had been involved in Southeast Asia for nearly a decade.

Like Korea, certain personalities dominated the political landscape and became lightning rods for discontent—Lyndon Johnson, Robert McNamara, William Westmoreland, McGeorge Bundy, and Richard Nixon, among them. Unlike Korea, the Indochina war created opposition figures and groups that also acquired larger-than-life persona who were folk heroes to the dissidents while vilified by the war's supporters—the Chicago 8, the Black Panthers, Students for a Democratic Society (SDS), Jane Fonda, the Berrigan brothers, and the counterculture, among many others. We tend to remember the war through those characters and the domestic political tumult they engendered. But the war itself was conducted much like other wars, with strategies and allies and deployments and air power and rules of engagement and designs for victory—the stuff of war as fought and experienced—and it was there on the ground that the war's human costs were exacted. The war at home, as it was often called, came to affect the war in Vietnam mainly through interpretation; namely, how it was viewed by the public and political leaders. Protest and the mounting antagonism of the intellectual elite might also have restrained the war policy's worst tendencies and brought the war to a sooner end. The "real war" was the savage war fought by all combatants for hamlets and hearts and minds, America's punitive bombing in the North and the tactical bombing in the South, the promiscuous application of napalm and Agent Orange, and "free fire zones." These were the constituents of the mayhem that left so many dead.

THE WAR

The memory of the war tends to gravitate to the late 1960s when the violence in Vietnam was at its height and the dissonance at home was growing and diversifying into street protest, countercultural outbursts, and reactions of the "silent majority" to both. However, the war was under way earlier in ways that set its course through the volatile times. Truman and Acheson saw Indochina as a key theater in which to contest expanding Russian and Chinese communism, and they supported the French in their attempt to recolonize Vietnam after the Japanese were defeated in 1945. Unable to reassert its imperial position in the face of resistance from the Viet Minh, the Marxist and nationalist forces led by Ho Chi Minh, France agreed to a peace accord signed in Geneva that divided North from South Vietnam in 1954 and promised elections to reunify the country in 1956. The United States instantly braced the South Vietnamese government and denied the validity of the peace treaty. Eisenhower and Dulles thereby brought to Saigon an American presence that steadily accreted the American stewardship of war-making and state building. From the earliest days of Eisenhower's advisory mission, to Kennedy's fascination with counterinsurgency, to Johnson's rapid escalation, to Nixon's violent denouement, the U.S. purposes in Vietnam were shaped by the same fears and aspirations that informed the Korean War—the defeat of communism and establishment of predominant American influence in Asia. America wanted to influence Asia.

Eisenhower, soon after becoming president and while the French were being routed by Ho's forces, spoke darkly of the falling dominoes in Indochina, those teetering pro-Western regimes that could collapse from the destabilizing aggression of communism from India to the Philippines. Not only would this be politically intolerable, he said, but it would deprive the West of valuable resources, a rationale for involvement that persisted into the 1960s. The "domino" principle was apparent in decision-making circles from the time of the Chinese Revolution and was usually applied to Southeast Asia; primary among its feared consequences was the loss of resources. As noted by a 1952 National Security Council (NSC) memorandum: "Southeast Asia, especially Malaya and Indonesia, is the principal world source of natural rubber and tin, and a producer of petroleum and other strategically important commodities. The rice exports of Burma and Thailand are critically important to Malaya, Ceylon and Hong Kong and are of considerable significance to Japan and India, all important areas of free Asia."[1] John Foster Dulles, Ike's secretary of state, went further. "There is the risk that, as in Korea, Red China might send its own army into Indochina," he said in a 1954 speech. "The Chinese Communist regime should realize that such a second aggression could not occur without grave consequences which might not be confined to Indochina."[2] Even as they felt handcuffed by the French debacle (the United States was supplying 80 percent of the French war budget by 1954) and worried that direct intervention would smack of imperialism, Eisenhower and Dulles considered Vietnam a top priority and sought ways to threaten China while scuttling the Geneva accord and militarizing the new South Vietnamese state.

Eisenhower's activism sprang directly from the well of both right-wing discontent with the Korean War and anticommunism more broadly. Both were commanding the political heights even as McCarthy began to self-implode; the more cautious Eisenhower was offended by McCarthy's crudeness but was willing to ride the wave of anticommunism. The old guard of the GOP was frustrated with Truman's containment policy and in the 1952 campaign "argued that the time had come to move beyond containment to retaliation and even liberation of those areas that had fallen under communism." The 1952 Republican platform, which Dulles helped draft, specifically called for the liberation of "captive peoples."[3] So the evergreen ideology of rollback was imbedded in Dulles's guidance of U.S. foreign policy even though he and Eisenhower were fully aware of how that proclivity failed after General MacArthur's march to the Yalu. Anticommunism in America survived the death of Stalin and the demise of McCarthy and entrenched itself as a social value and political lodestar over the coming decades. The Soviets played their role in this, of course, expanding their nuclear arsenal; repressing democratic movements in Eastern Europe; making inroads into the Middle East, Latin America, and Africa; and escalating their verbal assaults on the West, even as they dealt quietly with their own demons of Stalinism and could not avert a split with Mao. The new face of communism in the late 1950s was the Ukrainian peasant Nikita Khrushchev, a neat caricature of a Soviet strongman and the suitable foil for Americans' embrace of a stout-hearted confrontation with Moscow. He openly welcomed third world rebellions, challenged Washington in Europe through strong communist parties in France and Italy and brutal repression in Hungary and Poland, and shocked Americans with the launch of the Sputnik satellite. Communism was on the march, it seemed, and marching with it was anticommunism in the United States. In the decade following the cease-fire in Korea, the center of political gravity shifted in America, moving anticommunism from its right-wing origins to something more mainstream, bipartisan, and relatively unchallenged, if less panicky than during the Truman years.

The 1950s were relatively prosperous, engendering the growth of a sizable middle class and suburban living. Anticommunism spoke mainly to this rising middle class by warning that the Soviets, Chinese, and their agents could take away the newly acquired comforts. A poster for war bonds during the Korean conflict shows Uncle Sam pointing to a land of plenty and suggesting that we fight to protect "all we have," a commonplace image of that era. Communism had always been depicted as an insidious and alien force. A telling portion of Cold War culture in the 1950s and early 1960s was dedicated to the machinations of spies and double agents or aliens from outer space—all of whom were invasive, sneaky, and utterly lethal. Not all the Hollywood, television, and print treatments of this type were successful commercially. But they did reify, or reinforce, an institutional emphasis, even an obsession, with unorthodox ideas and personalities.[4] The conformity to an American way of life was strong—a life of faith, the nuclear family, and free enterprise—and nothing threatened that credo more than com-munism. The excesses of McCarthyism faded, but the fundamentals of anticommunism remained as sturdy as ever for years after his demise.

The East-West confrontation in Europe was the focal point for U.S. policy makers in the late 1950s, a stable, if dangerous, configuration of armed force. Security was conditioned by a singular anxiety, the "new look" of massive retaliation fostered by the Eisenhower administra-tion, in which the tripwire in Germany would trigger a nuclear holo-caust against the Soviet Union. In addition to the tensions inherent in the endless "what ifs" of the new nuclear doctrine, U.S. policy makers were alarmed by the advances of Marxists elsewhere as the colonial empires of Britain and France disintegrated and the old Spanish pre-cincts of Latin America all became fertile grounds for revolution.

It was difficult to separate the democratic aspirations of people in these very poor countries from communist intrigue, in part because anti-colonial struggles were by nature about redistribution of power and wealth. It is no small irony that the ideas of Woodrow Wilson gave shape to so many of these movements for self-determination in the wake of the First World War and stimulated the organizing to achieve sovereign rights in dozens of third world countries. (Among those early organizers was Ho Chi Minh.) Franklin Roosevelt gave voice to these aspirations, too, but the onset of the Cold War flipped America's stance as history's great-est anticolonial advocate into a force for stasis, looking to keep the status quo of pro-American regimes no matter what their record on human rights. Eisenhower instigated Central Intelligence Agency (CIA) coups against democratically elected governments in Iran and Guatemala, driven by dubious suspicions of communist leanings.* Other rebellions surged in the 1950s—in Malaysia, against the British; in Algeria, against the French; in the Congo, against the Belgians; and in Egypt, Syria, and Iraq, against monarchies, some installed by the Allies after the First

---

* These coups had enduring consequences. The one in Guatemala ushered in a long period of repressive, mainly military regimes; in the 1970s and 1980s, large-scale massacres of mainly indigenous populations resulted in an estimated 200,000 deaths and one million displaced, according to an independent commission created by the UN in 1999. In Iran, the repressive reign of the Pahlavi monarchy and the destruction of the secular nationalists and leftists meant that only the religious leaders remained as the opposition. This brought the Khomeini clique to power in 1979, reverberating throughout the region, and empowered political Islam in other Muslim countries as well.

World War. Latin America, which had thrown off its Spanish overlords in the early nineteenth century, was convulsed by leftist revolutionaries battling oligarchies and the military, which typically had strong ties to America. The United States had intervened at will in many of the nearby countries for more than a century—in Mexico, Cuba, Nicaragua, and elsewhere, almost always siding with the *caudillos*. So the Latin American upheavals, often aided by the Soviets covertly, were linked very directly to U.S. power and interests, and the revolutionaries consciously saw their insurgencies as a fight against American imperialism.

To say that Washington saw this as a worrisome trend is putting it mildly: the third world appeared in the late 1950s to be moving rapidly into anti-American, as well as anticolonial, rebellion. An enormous bloc of countries became part of the nonaligned movement, supposedly rejecting fealty to either superpower, but generally sympathetic to liberation movements. Eisenhower had no viable answers for these popular uprisings, and the combination of the communist countries and the nonaligned cornered the United States and Europe in a small minority bolstering the old ways. The "new look" military doctrine, relying on nuclear weapons and air power (even the army was being adapted to the "nuclear battlefield"), was ill-suited to this challenge as a task of the armed forces. Meanwhile, the nonmilitary activities of covert operations, propaganda, and foreign aid were also inadequate and often at cross purposes—the trumpeting of freedom was discordant when the CIA was assassinating leftists or undermining governments, or when political backing went to right-wing despots. Aid and development were frequently insensitive to local needs, appeared to be self-interested, or became a well for corruption.

The aftermath of the French retreat from Vietnam was for U.S. leaders shaped by this swirl of forces. Among those was a determination to prevent communist territorial gains; the loss of China and the Soviet domination of Eastern Europe provided ample proof of this need for containment. That goal of stopping communist expansion was backed by an American society fearful of such gains worldwide and supportive of some mix of containment and rollback. Yet the arsenal of democracy appeared to house too few effective tools, military or civilian, which were matched to those objectives. Eisenhower's approach in Vietnam was to circumvent the Geneva Accords and support a separate state of South Vietnam, supplying it with military hardware and advisers. The attitude toward the Geneva conference in the spring and summer of 1954 was grudging. Dulles, more than Eisenhower, sought to find ways to intervene militarily on behalf of the deteriorating French position, but Eisenhower insisted that a united action among allies had be a prerequisite for intervention, and participation from allies like Britain was not forthcoming. The administration uniformly saw the conference—which included China, the Soviet Union, France, Britain, and representatives of what would become the two halves of Vietnam—as a losing proposition. Conceding territory to the communists appeared inevitable. As a result, the United States wanted to keep some diplomatic distance from the likely outcome. When the accords were signed in July, U.S. leaders' public expressions about the agreement were a studied ambivalence. As recalled in the *Pentagon Papers*,

> Even as the Administration could not do more than agree to "respect" and "take note" of the Geneva accords, it had to concede that they represented a reasonable outcome given the chaotic state of Allied relations before the conference, the rejection by France of a possible military alternative, and the undeniable military superiority of the Viet Minh beyond as well as within Vietnam. On the other hand, the settlement . . . also contained the elements of defeat. Part of the Free World's "assets" in the Far East had been "lost" to the Sino-Soviet bloc (much as China had been "lost" to Mao Tse-tung's forces).[5]

This displeasing outcome, coupled with public expressions of how important Vietnam was to U.S. interests and the general anticommunist tenor of American politics, meant in effect that the United States would feel compelled to sustain the zone of the South, in effect the Government of South Vietnam, as a noncommunist country. When the leader in the South, Ngo Dinh Diem, declared a sovereign state after Geneva and rejected the promised nationwide elections, the United States acceded. Diem, a nationalist, had rejected the Geneva Accords outright. Among many Vietnamese, including those in the North, the partition was an outrage, inviting more conflict and disrupting the years of struggle for an independent and unified country. This magnetic vision for Vietnam thus pitted two strong personalities against each other, Diem and Ho, both intending to unite Vietnam under their own leadership. In this, the situation resembled Korea in the late 1940s. But Diem also could not abide by the expectation of negotiating the elections with the Viet

Minh. Everyone knew that Ho would win an election, so there was, in Diem's and America's view, little point in holding one.*

A provision of the Geneva Accord that was upheld was voluntary migration between zones, and the highly publicized movement of nearly one million northerners to the South was claimed as proof positive that the Vietnamese really preferred the alternative to Ho's communism. Many of the refugees were Catholics, as was Diem, which in itself prompted further sectarian fissures in the South. But the refugee movement provoked a politically potent stimulus to further U.S. support for Diem. Just after Geneva, Dulles engineered the new South East Asia Treaty Organization, or SEATO, which provided additional justifications for U.S. involvement in Vietnam. After an initial blush of successful state building in the South, however, Diem's regime grew more authoritarian, with "reeducation" camps for 50,000 or more suspected Viet Minh, failed land reform, clampdowns on the press, corruption, and all that typically goes with an increasingly fearful and unscrupulous leader. Some of his actions replayed Rhee's governance of South Korea from 1948–50, particularly a ruthless drive to root out Viet Minh in the countryside with scant concern for civilians. The United States nonetheless stuck with Diem as the only game in town. Even though U.S. intelligence had poor information sources in the countryside, the CIA accurately predicted as early as 1954 that Diem and his government had little prospect of success and that the grievances of the peasants—nine-tenths of the population—would eventually grow into armed opposition; the Viet Minh were already a powerful presence throughout the South. The gloomy assessments of the agency throughout the late 1950s, however, did not appear to affect policy making. "Assist Free Vietnam to develop a strong, stable, and constitutional government to enable Free Vietnam to assert an increasingly attractive contrast to conditions in the present

---

* In the *Pentagon Papers*, the secret government memos leaked by Daniel Ellsberg in 1971, is one fascinating speculation reflecting some wider views among Vietnam watchers. It holds that the United States could have embraced Ho Chi Minh, who was, above all, a nationalist, and thereby could have helped him become the "Asian Tito," that is, a communist independent of the USSR and China. Ho had asked for U.S. support just after the Second World War to stop France's attempt to reimpose Vietnam's colonial status, a request that was denied. Even as Eisenhower and others recognized Ho as the "father of his country" and a formidable leader, the politics of anticommunism in the United States would prevent such an acceptance of Ho as the rightful leader of Vietnam.

Communist zone," said a 1956 NSC policy directive, "[and] work toward the weakening of the Communists in North and South Vietnam in order to bring about the eventual peaceful reunification of a free and independent Vietnam under anti-Communist leadership."[6] Given the pessimism of the agency's intelligence estimate, this rollback aspiration was remarkably misplaced: the survival of Diem's regime and state was what was actually at stake. That in itself was a variant of rollback, however; from the earliest days of U.S. involvement, the Viet Minh controlled or were more popular in much of South Vietnam, and the American struggle there was always about rolling back that influence.

The American enthusiasm for Diem and the anticommunist mission was backed by ample economic and military aid. Throughout the 1950s, Vietnam ranked as one of the top worldwide recipients of U.S. assistance, and at least four-fifths of that aid went to the military or other security apparatuses. Security spending crowded out aid for economic development and sometimes was diverted from human needs to projects like road building that had military utility. By the end of the Eisenhower administration, a recognition that the Diem regime's heavy hand was feeding the peasant rebellion—the National Liberation Front, initially a broad-based coalition that included noncommunist opponents of Diem, was founded in 1960—dawned on U.S. policy makers, and a shift to anti-guerrilla training and tactics became the order of the day. Eisenhower never committed many military personnel, and the presence of the CIA covert operation there was significant but not sizable. But by the end of the Eisenhower era, the United States was prominently committed to the defense of South Vietnam as an anticommunist priority. It had initiated a new emphasis on fighting the guerrillas in the countryside, remained publicly supportive of Diem in spite of his growing dictatorial style, and saw the entire enterprise not only in terms of military action but political persuasion inside South Vietnam. All the elements of the oncoming war were in place.

The Kennedy Mistake

John F. Kennedy was elected in 1960 as the paragon of a new generation, seeking new ways to extend American power and keenly interested in Southeast Asia. Kennedy was willing to try innovations in military doctrine and he came to relish the new emphasis on counterinsurgency ideas. Perhaps more than anything else, it was this infatuation that led the United States into trouble in Vietnam. Kennedy had decried the French presence in Vietnam in the early 1950s, saying the French were unable to rally the Vietnamese people to fight the Viet Minh: "the war can never be successful unless large numbers of the people of Vietnam are won over from their sullen neutrality and open hostility to it and fully support its successful conclusion."[7] Throughout his eight years in the Senate, he described Vietnam and Indochina more generally as crucially important to U.S. interests, and criticized Eisenhower for doing too little to protect the pro-Western regimes from communism. So he was as committed a cold warrior as any on the national scene; his own inaugural address called on the American people to "pay any price and bear any burden" to see that freedom triumphs.

Kennedy's appeal to Cold War values was perfectly consonant with where the American public seemed to be in 1961. We tend to see the height of the Cold War as a thing of the 1950s, but the same messages warning of the constant dangers of communism were strong in the early 1960s as well. In fact, communism's apparent success in many "wars of national liberation," as Khrushchev helpfully called them just a fortnight before Kennedy's inaugural, created a new set of concerns to accompany the nuclear confrontation.

What was different in Kennedy was not ideology as much as a new approach to fighting the Cold War. The Kennedy style is much remarked upon, but it was not the First Lady's elegance or Kennedy's youth or breeding or wit that was germane to his policies in Vietnam. What mattered was a sense of his own heroic status, a self-consciously generated image. Norman Mailer captured this in a renowned essay in *Esquire*. "America was the land that still believed in heroes," he reported from the convention that nominated JFK in 1960. "It was almost as if there were no peace unless one could fight well, kill well (if always with honor), love well and love many, be cool, be daring, be dashing, be wild, be wily, be resourceful, be a brave gun" and "grow on the waves of the violent." This, Mailer said, *was* Kennedy, this new kind of hero, in contrast to "the fatherly calm of the General" and the dull predictability of Nixon.[8] It was in that convention's acceptance speech that Kennedy spoke of the New Frontier, no less, a call to action based on America's most redolent myth. He honored the past: the pioneers who settled the

American West "were not the captives of their own doubts, nor the prisoners of their own price tags," he told the convention. "They were determined to make the new world strong and free—an example to the world, to overcome its hazards and its hardships, to conquer the enemies that threatened from within and without." But then he went on with a more interesting twist:

> Some would say that those struggles are all over, that all the horizons have been explored, that all the battles have been won, that there is no longer an American frontier. . . . Beyond that frontier are uncharted areas of science and space, unsolved problems of peace and war, unconquered problems of ignorance and prejudice, unanswered questions of poverty and surplus. It would be easier to shrink from that new frontier, to look to the safe mediocrity of the past, to be lulled by good intentions and high rhetoric. . . . I believe that the times require imagination and courage and perseverance. I'm asking each of you to be pioneers towards that New Frontier.

Kennedy used the older mythic call as a "race for mastery of the sky . . . the ocean . . . the far side of space, and the inside of men's minds," and while his inflection of the frontier myth was more than territorial expansion, it posed the challenge of national purpose as a global project, wrought from a uniquely American character, and one of battles—righteous battles—to be won.

Invoking the frontier and posing as the hero was politically shrewd, reminding the public of his own heroism in the Pacific War and situating himself and his candidacy squarely in the frontier myth. This was a cultivated image, but it also sprang from an attitude that was in keeping with the frontier mode of engaging the third world, the new wilderness. Kennedy urged compassionate intervention in the wilderness through the Peace Corps, the Alliance for Progress, and other programs, and at home in the War on Poverty. But he also was a warrior, seeking that mantle and all it implied.

The idea of the frontier was more than a metaphor or a single speech. The Kennedy circle referred to themselves as the New Frontiersman, and the label was self-consciously applied like FDR's men used the notion of the New Deal. The excitement sparked by the president's élan infected popular culture and a newly mobilized and purposeful youth culture, too, but one in which communists were clearly understood to be the savages that we were destined to meet in the "long twilight struggle." The frontier spirit was a propellant for Kennedy to engage the savage in many places and in the most dramatic scripts. It also drove a search for new ways to confront communism, ways that could be matched to the unique qualities of the wilderness as it was just then being perceived, which was the "third world." The wars of "national liberation" could not be fought as if they were the Battle of the Bulge or even Inchon. New ways had to be found that were matched to the frontier and its own logic and language.

The answer came in the form of counterinsurgency doctrine and a strong emphasis on covert operations. Of the latter, Kennedy got an early opportunity to roll back communism in Cuba by adapting a CIA plan from Eisenhower to land Cuban exiles on the island and foment a popular uprising against Castro, which would then be followed with overt U.S. support. The chosen locale for the landing, the Bay of Pigs, is now synonymous with catastrophe—an ill-planned, half-baked, and poorly executed catastrophe, nearly comic in its stumbles. But the Bay of Pigs had several consequences, not least Castro's fresh dedication to Marxian revolution. One reverberation from the Cuba debacle was Kennedy's reluctance to intervene in the Laotian conflict, which bore some similarities to the one in Vietnam. Instead, he opted that same spring for a negotiated settlement that provided for a coalition government. Robert Kennedy later said that "if it hadn't been for the Bay of Pigs, we would have sent troops into Laos"—that is, chastened by the military snafu in the Caribbean, another venture just then could have been hard to pull off.[9] But it also meant that the "neutralist" solution for Laos, which earned the president the usual brickbats from the right wing, led several in the administration to see Vietnam as a place to draw a line. For the president, the humiliating experience of the Bay of Pigs was relatively painless in terms of domestic politics. "The political damage was more evident abroad than at home," wrote Lawrence Freedman, "where there was seen to be nothing intrinsically wrong in having a go at Castro."[10] But Kennedy used the experience to systematize his approach not only to covert operations but also to counterinsurgency.

In fact, Kennedy had approved a counterinsurgency plan for Vietnam within a week of becoming president, and the day after the Bay of Pigs fiasco, he summoned his advisers to examine anew the Vietnam policy. What seemed clear from the outset were three facts. First, the Viet Cong were controlling large areas of the South, essentially winning the contest with Diem's forces. Second, the U.S. military was providing little in the way of suitable options for intervention, relying, as was its wont, on large-scale warfare that was insensitive to local conditions. Third, the loss of South Vietnam, along with what was viewed as a retreat from Laos and the Cuba disaster, would surrender the initiative to Khrushchev and Mao, possibly inviting further challenges to important allies like Japan and Western Europe. Kennedy and most of his advisers saw Vietnam, then, as a place to take a stand, although the "how" was now more vexing than the "why."

What ultimately drove the "how" was the "why." The line-in-the-sand attitude was occasioned not just by setbacks in Laos and Cuba, but by a nuclear posture that was unrealistic and extremely dangerous. At the time of Kennedy's inauguration, the United States held a roughly four-to-one or better advantage in nuclear warheads, and had the long-range bombers and missiles to deliver them. In the Berlin crisis of 1961, Khrushchev threatened to push the North Atlantic Treaty Organization (NATO) out of West Berlin. East Germany was losing thousands of citizens per month in emigration across the then-unwalled and unguarded border between East and West Berlin, an accelerating movement that could provoke a collapse of the East German state and the rickety structure of Soviet vassal states in Eastern Europe. Khrushchev had to do something, and the Vienna summit of June 1961 gave him a chance to confront Kennedy on the Berlin issue. This deeply angered and frustrated Kennedy, who now saw Khrushchev as a risk-taker and potentially willing to go to war over the status of Berlin. Around the same time, the national security adviser, McGeorge Bundy, at the urging of a young defense analyst, Daniel Ellsberg, asked the Joint Chiefs to provide the president with the military's top-secret warfighting plan; this, Bundy and Kennedy were astonished to learn, ordered a rigid, automatic escalation of a conventional conflict with the USSR—just the sort of scrum that could be provoked in Berlin—to a full-scale nuclear attack on Russia, an attack that would essentially destroy the USSR and kill tens of millions of people and a million or two in America should the Soviets manage to launch some of their weapons. Eisenhower unaccountably had forfeited decision making on a nuclear launch to military commanders as well. (Biographer Kai Bird tells the story of how difficult it was for Bundy to get the Joint Chiefs to reveal to JFK what the plan actually was, a sign among others of the military's obstreperous attitudes.)[11] Kennedy steadily moved this posture toward one of "flexible response," which allowed for more options in the event of war before the use of nuclear weapons.

Even with this flexibility, however, the Berlin crisis, in which contingency plans were drawn up for a nuclear first strike, convinced the Kennedy team that the United States needed to demonstrate resolve below the nuclear threshold; it needed to signal unambiguously to Moscow that intimidation and "wars of liberation" and other communist assertiveness could be challenged and turned back without resort to nuclear threats or nuclear attacks. Vietnam then became an attractive venue for just such a show of resolve. Unlike Korea, where the June 1950 invasion from the north was a precipitating event in the Cold War to which Truman could not fail to respond, the Vietnamese communists in the South were largely an indigenous movement in 1961, had had control over much of the countryside for several years, and were more popular with the peasants than the corrupt officials attached to Diem. As a result, everyone realized that the tasks in Vietnam required a different kind of war. But the guiding—indeed dominating—rationale for entering Vietnam more forcefully was embedded in Cold War thinking. A limited war with small contingents of U.S. combat forces, which would bolster Diem and demonstrate resolve to Ho, Mao, and Khrushchev, would send just the right signal. "A victory here would produce great effects all over the world," Bundy argued in a memo to the president. Given Diem's parlous position, a defeat would not be seen as an enormous setback. And the choice of Vietnam was one posed in contrast to Laos: "Laos was never really ours after 1954. South Vietnam is and wants to be."[12] Others argued in favor, too, pointing out that Vietnam had a long coastline that enabled the navy to play a prominent role and made it infinitely easier to supply, compared with the landlocked and mountainous Laos.

So the "why" was about the Cold War and demonstrating resolve, just as the Korean War was, but the "how" was still vexing. Vietnam remained a relatively second-level concern within the White House in 1961; Laos, Berlin, and Cuba were paramount. But momentum for its cause was building. The actual terms of engagement remained complex, partly because Diem's corrupt state made it difficult to intervene with confidence on his behalf. This was not just a moral question about Diem's legitimacy or popularity. It was also strategic—the way a limited engagement would be fought relied crucially on the capacity of the government of South Vietnam (GVN) to reform itself, to end the police brutality in the countryside, to curb the excessive corruption, to be, in effect, worthy of the fight not only to Washington, but to the Vietnamese people. And it is here that the counterinsurgency ideas became both indispensable and frustrating.

Counterinsurgency doctrine held that the keys to defeating guerrillas was to destroy the infrastructure of their networks, their supply routes in particular, and to build close relationships with the civilian populations—essentially to earn their trust and cooperation, since good intelligence was the sine qua non of success. The doctrine was derived significantly from the experience of the British in Malaysia and the successful 1950 campaign in the Philippines engineered by the legendary Edward Lansdale. General Lansdale was one of the models for the exceptionally influential treatise-cum-novel of counterinsurgency, *The Ugly American*, a best seller in 1958 (and endorsed by Senator Kennedy). He was involved in advising Diem in the early days of the GVN and was recruited by Kennedy to be, in effect, the major domo of the new effort in Vietnam. He understood that the "hearts and minds" of the people were the real battleground, and they could be won only by achievable aspirations for a better life conveyed by good government and professional military conduct.

The flurry of activity in the spring of 1961 was occasioned by intelligence assessments that from 1959 through 1961 were uniformly dire. The Viet Cong were gaining; Diem seemed incapable of producing economic well-being or reform. After Lansdale went there in January 1961, he reported that "the Viet Cong hope to win back Vietnam south of the 17th parallel this year, if at all possible, and are much further along towards accomplishing this goal than I had realized from reading the reports received in Washington."[13] Lansdale was a proponent of getting U.S. combat troops into Vietnam, but Kennedy would commit only 400 more advisers in May 1961 and kept delaying a crossing-the-Rubicon decision about combat forces. The actual actions of the South Vietnamese army, using a cobbled together counterinsurgency strategy, was following U.S. army predilections of attacking guerrillas directly before carrying out the tasks of winning hearts and minds. The tactics failed to protect civilians, who were often direct victims of the operations, but the joint chiefs continued to cling to this approach. In the coming two years, many more U.S. military "advisers" and hardware flooded in to support Diem, including military and economic assistance, and a growing repertoire of covert operations. But the bleak assessments by the CIA, journalists like David Halberstam and Neil Sheehan, and the president's steady stream of emissaries never ceased. Seemingly every memo to the U.S. decision makers stressed that "it is now or never" to save South Vietnam because the Viet Cong were at the doorstep of Saigon. With a few exceptions—notably, Walt Rostow, a top lieutenant to Bundy and then head of the planning staff at State—the observers saw the Viet Cong as a genuinely indigenous and popular force, not, or at least not clearly, a vassal of the North Vietnamese, Moscow, or Beijing.

The Kennedy effort from late 1961 increased the support to the GVN while insisting on a counterinsurgency that included the Strategic Hamlets Program. The idea was to clear areas of the countryside of Viet Cong with the South Vietnamese army and police, secure certain areas—the strategic hamlets, as many as five thousand—and cultivate social and economic programs to win the allegiance of the peasants. The program, combining anti-guerrilla fighting and "pacification," or rural development, was doomed by its repeated emphasis on the security operations over the pacification activities. The Strategic Hamlets initiative was "similar if not identical to earlier population resettlement and control efforts practiced by the French and by Diem," noted the *Pentagon Papers*. "The long history of these efforts was marked by consistency in results as well as in techniques: all failed dismally because they ran into resentment if not active resistance on the part of the peasants at whose control and safety, then loyalty, they were aimed. U.S. desires to begin an effective process of pacification had fastened onto security as a necessary precondition and slighted the historic record of rural resistance to resettlement."[14] Peasants did not want to be resettled, did not identify with the Diem regime, and resented the harsh treatment from GVN forces. One of Kennedy's inner circle, Michael Forrestal, revealed in 1964 that "both our army and the Vietnamese army tended to want to fight the Viet Cong by whatever mechanical means they had at their disposal (artillery, air power, napalm—anything that you could get) and without much attention being paid to the populace." The U.S. air power being unofficially applied to the war (as it was in Laos) was particularly devastating, Forrestal admitted, since the air force was "bombing the hell" out of villages from which the Viet Cong had already evacuated. "We and the Vietnamese ended up bombing peasants." Similar tactics were used on the ground, burning down villages.[15] When the destruction of villages was not pursued outright, the destruction of the peasants' way of life was. In most cases, the Strategic Hamlets program forced villagers into a choice: either build new houses with their own money and labor after their homes had been destroyed intentionally as part of the program, or relocate to a new place where they also had to build at their own expense, far away from their home village (which was the basis of their entire existence, including, importantly, the graves of their ancestors, their source of worship).

Reports from the field to Washington glossed the essential failure of the program and projected a picture of success, reports that fooled Kennedy during 1962 and led him to think that the war was being won. As a result, the counterinsurgency effort intensified, despite the fact that senior military and civilian leaders in the United States knew it was, at best, haphazardly and ruthlessly applied by Diem. Not only were the fundamental flaws of relocation and brutality overlooked, but the choice of hamlets was chaotic and corruption was rife—for example, food and building materials provided by the United States were sold for profit by local officials. The numbers of "advisers" in Vietnam rose steadily during Kennedy's tenure, an ersatz combat force that numbered 16,000 by late 1963, but Diem's regime was nonetheless coming apart. The CIA supported a coup against Diem, who was murdered. But the next junta supported a negotiated settlement with the Viet Cong, an intolerable betrayal; they, too, were deposed. The fundament of the moral argument for defending the GVN was shaky and would remain so for the next twelve years.

Kennedy's assassination is often viewed as a turning point in Vietnam: his innate caution was no longer a restraining influence. His war council—Bundy, Rostow, McNamara, Secretary of State Dean Rusk, the joint chiefs, and many others—were largely in favor of an expanded role for the U.S. military in Vietnam. The question of whether Kennedy would have expanded the war as Lyndon Johnson did is hotly debated to this day, but whatever Kennedy *might* have done, what he *did* do was to deeply involve the United States in Vietnam: the counterinsurgency effort, the growing numbers of special forces, the covert operations, the raids in Laos, and, most decisively, the insistence that Vietnam was a momentous arena of the Cold War. All of this made possible the programs that were resulting in sizable human costs and creating a trajectory toward the colossal carnage that was soon to come.

Lyndon Johnson's first year in office was an election year, and he was reluctant to escalate the war even as the stream of assessments about the capacity of the coup-prone government of South Vietnam, and the lack of progress in the war itself, strongly suggested that a change of course was needed. For much of the year, a debate raged within the administration about "taking the war North"—openly attacking North Vietnam. This rose from a miscalculation long persistent among Kennedy-Johnson advisers, namely, that the Viet Cong were wholly tools of the North, not an indigenous rebellion, and that putting severe pressure on the North would therefore yield a stronger bargaining position should the GVN appear able enough to stand on its own. The generals in the South were keen for U.S. bombing of the North; some even saw a chance of defeating Ho outright and unifying Vietnam under a noncommunist leadership. U.S. policy makers thought the best that could be achieved was a "neutralist" solution for the North—a North Vietnam untethered to Moscow or Beijing—and a noncommunist South. There was a recognition that bombing entailed a much larger war, one that could even result in the use of nuclear weapons.

During that election year—the Republicans nominated the militant conservative, Barry Goldwater—Johnson dithered over whether to bomb the North or commit many more troops to the South. He was haunted by the "loss of China" syndrome and always saw Vietnam in the line of dominoes. The thinking on China worked two ways: amplifying LBJ's fear that another loss in Asia would be politically disastrous, but also acting as a constant restraint on U.S. bombing in the North (no one wanted China to enter the war as it did so decisively in Korea). Nor was there any taste for a negotiated settlement that would allow the United States to withdraw but would surely result in an eventual communist takeover of the South. A small number of advisers urged such a course—Undersecretary of State George Ball most famously among them—but nearly all others were urging Johnson to stay and adopt a northern strategy.

A precipitating event made up LBJ's mind for him. North Vietnamese patrol boats attacked a U.S. destroyer in the Gulf of Tonkin in August 1964, an incident that may have been provoked by U.S. covert operations against the North launched from ships in the area. An alleged second attack, widely publicized, never took place. Johnson used the incident to gain authorization from Congress to "take all necessary measures to repel any armed attack against the forces of the United States and to prevent further aggression." Only one dissenter, Senator Wayne Morse of Oregon, voted against the resolution. Like Korea, the Vietnam War proceeded without a formal declaration of war.

By early 1965, Maxwell Taylor, then ambassador to Vietnam, was urging a stepped up U.S. military campaign, as were Bundy and McNamara. All saw the GVN sinking, wracked by infighting and corruption, unable to hold its own against the Viet Cong—an assessment like virtually all others over the previous four years. Their response to the near-collapse of their client regime was to recommend a bombing campaign against the North. Bundy, in Vietnam on a fact-finding visit in February, awoke one morning to learn that the Viet Cong had attacked a U.S. base at Pleiku, inflicting serious casualties. He conveyed to the president his firm conviction that the time had come for a very sharp and sustained response, to which Johnson and his other advisers, gathered in the White House, agreed. The next day, 132 naval warplanes attacked North Vietnam. The major combat phase of the war was on.

By late March, a regular and sizable air campaign against military targets and infiltration routes was under way. Operation Rolling Thunder reflected McNamara's "graduated response" strategy of steadily increasing pressure on the North via the bombing, a variant on what Bundy and Taylor were urging. The bombing campaign, Taylor said in a memo to the president, should be aimed at demoralizing North Vietnam: "what is bad for Hanoi is generally good for Saigon. Effect of the physical destruction of material objects and infliction of casualties will not, in our judgment, have a decisive bearing upon the ability of [North Vietnam] to support [the Viet Cong]. However, degree of damage and number of casualties inflicted gauge the impact of our operations on Hanoi leadership and hence are important as a measure of their discomfort."[16] Bundy was keen on the bombing to bolster the GVN. U.S. military commanders were more aligned with Taylor, regarding the bombing to be most prominently a signal of America's determination. All were in agreement that the basic objective of bombing was to protect U.S. credibility in the world. In one formulation, Assistant Secretary of Defense James McNaughton described U.S. objectives as

70%—To avoid a humiliating US defeat (to our reputation as a guarantor).
20%—To keep SVN [South Vietnam] (and then adjacent) territory from Chinese hands.
10%—To permit the people of SVN to enjoy a better, freer way of life.
ALSO—To emerge from crisis without unacceptable taint from methods used.
NOT—To "help a friend," although it would be hard to stay in if asked out.[17]

All of LBJ's advisers publicly fostered the view that the bombing was intended to prevent North Vietnamese assistance to the Viet Cong, a point repeatedly asserted but at that time, early 1965, promoted with scant evidence. That and the other rationales for Rolling Thunder— mainly, raising GVN morale and reducing Viet Cong military activity— were not working, McNamara acknowledged in a July review; but he urged continuing. The misunderstanding at the root of the bombing campaign about Viet Cong autonomy was the pivotal and ignored explanation for the lackluster results of the bombing; while North Vietnam was just then increasing its support for its allies in the South, such aid was not strictly necessary for the Viet Cong to sustain its insurgency. Much of its firepower, for example, was from captured U.S. weapons. By the beginning of 1963, "the United States had potentially furnished the Vietnamese communists with enough weapons to create an army in the South capable of challenging" the South Vietnamese army, reported Neil Sheehan. "The Americans had distributed more than 130,000 firearms," a cornucopia of weaponry and ammunition and radios, "to Saigon's Civil Guard and Self-Defense Corps militia and to a menagerie of irregular units financed and equipped by the CIA." As this figure was multiplying quickly and the munitions were being captured, they could easily supply the 23,000 guerrillas and their local supporters.[18]

When Operation Rolling Thunder began in the spring of 1965, General Westmoreland requested combat troops and helicopter units to rectify the deteriorating situation in the South. Johnson approved. The initial deployment of marines was intended for counterinsurgency; one army brigade went in to secure air bases, a common rationale during the buildup in 1965. By April, some 80,000 troops were authorized for service in Vietnam. Three other countries were sending combat troops, about 7,000 total, including South Korea (a contingent that grew to 50,000). The American public was kept in the dark about the extent or purposes of the additional deployments, which widened what was becoming tagged a "credibility gap" in official Washington explanations of the whys and hows of the Vietnam War. Sharp criticism of the war among students and intellectuals was mounting as the bombing continued, and the introduction of combat troops raised the temperature of dissent even more. Cracks in the administration's consensus on the war policy began to appear, particularly as Westmoreland requested ever larger supplies of soldiers, which by mid-summer appeared to be headed to 200,000 or more as a total commitment. During the whole of 1965, about 160,000 troops were shipped in, adding to the 23,000 there at the beginning of the year.

U.S. troops executed their first search-and-destroy operation in late June 1965, and from then on this was a primary mode of operation. Westmoreland reasoned that even with the difficult, high-casualty U.S. operations, the enemy was suffering killed-in-action ten times greater. The Viet Cong and the North Vietnamese army, which began to appear in the South in 1965, could not sustain such losses indefinitely, so the American commanders believed the war of attrition on the ground and the air war in the North would defeat the communists. The ground operations relied on a three-part sequence. First was "Search and Destroy, to find, fix and fight the enemy's 'big units,' battalion size and above. This was followed by 'Clearing Operations' to seek out and find guerrilla forces in an area in which big units no longer operated because of the success of the Search and Destroy operations. The final phase consisted of 'Security Operations' to eliminate local [Viet Cong] VC, and create and maintain a stable environment in which the pacification program could advance."[19] Increasingly, even with troop levels that exceeded a half million, the search-and-destroy operations relied heavily on air power and artillery. B-52 bombers, which were the large, strategic bombers that were central to the nuclear force, were used in these operations, as were helicopter gunships and other aircraft.

The American strategy also relied on two crucial, nonmilitary elements that in the event were elusive. First was the chronic weakness and venality of the South Vietnamese government. It was believed by virtually everyone in the Johnson administration that the war would end in defeat if the government could not right itself to deliver goods and services to its people and professional soldiers to the war effort.

This was never achieved. Second was the strategy of pacification, the "other war" in which U.S. civilian and military experts would, with the GVN, help to economically develop the areas that were free of the Viet Cong. This also failed. The "hearts and minds" idea, which we will examine more closely later, was perhaps doomed by cultural difference as well as a lack of adequate dedication by the military command.

So the war simply escalated, steadily and seemingly inexorably. A war of attrition requires a lot of men, and a lot of men were supplied—in 1966, more than five divisions, in 1967 another two and then some. Even with these additional troops, the mood among U.S. leaders was pessimistic. Early in 1966, for example, McNamara told the president "the odds are about even that, even with the recommended deployments, we will be faced in early 1967 with a military stand-off at a much higher level, with pacification [still stalled, and with any prospect of military success marred by the chances of an active Chinese intervention] *hardly underway and with the requirement for the deployment of still more US forces.*"[20] And the principal rationale for this escalation was also pessimistic, in McNaughton's words: "*The present US objective in Vietnam is to avoid humiliation. The reasons why we went into Vietnam to the present depth are varied; but they are now largely academic. Why we have not withdrawn from Vietnam is, by all odds, one reason: (1) To preserve our reputation as a guarantor, and thus to preserve our effectiveness in the rest of the world.*"[21]

The air war escalated apace. At first confined in its targeting to military barracks, railroad yards, the infiltration routes, and the like, it gradually expanded. In 1965, 55,000 sorties were flown, one-third over the North. Hanoi and Haiphong were said to be off limits, due to the fear that China or the USSR would enter the war should the bombing be too severe (and hit some of their assets, like Soviet supply ships in Haiphong harbor). McNamara stressed that the bombing was targeted to set back North Vietnamese support of the Viet Cong, even though privately decision makers also regarded bombing as hurting the North enough to drive them to negotiate. At the same time, there were many who urged escalation of the air campaign. "The hawks were very much alive," said an analysis in the *Pentagon Papers*, "and there was mounting pressure to put more lightning and thunder into the air war."[22] Officials often chafed at the restrictions—"75 percent of the nation's population and the most lucrative military supply and [communications] targets have been effectively insulated from air attack,"[23] the CIA noted in an early 1966 memo—and the military pressed hard for more extensive bombing and permission to hit more targets. As the initial bombing did not seem to be having any of the desired effect, the hardliners gradually won more targets to hit. The air strikes included in December 1966 heavy strikes on Hanoi—power plants, petroleum storage facilities, waterways, steel plants, and other such facilities were increasingly targeted. Yet the North Vietnamese, while protesting the civilian loss of such raids, were unbowed. Ho said he would bargain only if there were a permanent cessation to the bombing of his country.

The air war in the South also picked up steam as the ground operations intensified. An air force study described heavy "enemy attrition in South Vietnam at an extremely low cost in U.S. loss of life" with tens of thousands of sorties, including 3,300 heavy bomber (B-52) strikes over the two years after escalation. The air force flew more than 200,000 bombing missions during that period in the South alone. The navy and marines were also flying thousands of missions, mainly to bomb North Vietnam, totaling nine million tons of munitions in 1964–73.[24] The navy's figure of 7.6 million tons (other reports have it much higher) is itself more than all the bomb tonnage dropped in the Second World War.

The action on the ground was ferocious. Westmoreland knew he could not occupy every village even with 500,000 troops. As a result, the army and marines continued with search-and-destroy missions. The relocation of peasants sent many going to the cities, nearly tripling the urban population of Vietnam. The countryside became a maelstrom: the U.S. military used defoliants to denude the forests, continued to drop napalm, and created "free fire zones" that permitted the use of unlimited force. The military strategy of attrition meant that accumulating enemy body counts became an obsession. Yet visit after visit by top officials and increasingly skeptical reports in the news media revealed little progress, either in the effect of bombing in the North or the winning of a decisive edge in the South. In fact, media coverage was becoming a major thorn in LBJ's side: Harrison Salisbury's firsthand reports for the *New York Times* detailing the effects of bombing in the North, CBS News and the other networks' capacity to bring the war into American homes, and many other damning reports were driving the administration into a political dead end.

The key moment of the war was the Tet offensive of February 1968, in which the North Vietnamese army and the Viet Cong attacked several major cities in their largest operation of the war. The U.S. military turned back the offensive. However, the fact that the communists could even mount such a challenge after three years of pounding by the Americans displayed a resilience that shocked both policy makers and the public. Westmoreland, wanting 200,000 more troops, was instead recalled to the Pentagon and replaced by Creighton Abrams. Johnson, stung by growing and vociferous political opposition, withdrew from the 1968 presidential race and opened peace talks in Paris. His five-year leadership of the war ended with Richard Nixon's inauguration in January 1969.

Nixon's Peace

The conduct of the war was under relentless criticism by early 1969. Books and articles excoriating the military strategy as either too harsh or too weak were commonplace. Editorials in once-reliably supportive newspapers were openly dubious of government claims and intentions. The antiwar movement had grown quickly. Nixon ran on a promise that he had a "secret plan" to end the war, and his victory over LBJ's vice president, Hubert Humphrey, was another sign of the public's uneasiness with the war.

Nixon famously exhibited erratic behavior during his presidency, some of it intentional. His "madman" pose to scare opponents, notably a cultivated ambiguity about the use of nuclear weapons, was a tactic he claimed that he borrowed from Eisenhower's threats toward North Korea. This on occasion included Vietnam, though the possibility of nuclear strikes was never significant. But he did alternately seek "peace with honor"—essentially meaning an American withdrawal while a noncommunist government was still in power in South Vietnam—and at the same time racheting up the bombing in the North, in Laos, and in Cambodia, the last being a new tactic begun early in his administration. In fact, he escalated bombing overall, another signal of U.S. resolve, while withdrawing U.S. ground troops gradually in an effort at what he called in November 1969 a policy of "Vietnamization" of the war.* He did indeed carry out this policy, though the war remained broadly violent.

The bombing in Cambodia and Laos was justified as a Vietnam action. The two countries, also with legacies of French colonialism, were used as sanctuaries by the Viet Cong and routes for the North Vietnamese to supply their allies in the South. Laos, which the United States had secretly bombed on and off for years, had its own civil war between a U.S.-backed government and the communist Pathet Lao. The bombing in 1969 in the Plain of Jars was intended to interdict the supply routes from North to South Vietnam but was indiscriminate, hitting many villages of Laotian civilians. Nearly 750,000 tons of bombs rained down on Laos during Nixon's years. A similar pattern obtained in Cambodia, to the south. Some say the pro-Western Prince Sihanouk was not even informed of the bombing campaign before it commenced; in any case, he was deposed in a coup that the Nixon White House welcomed. The initial air campaign in Cambodia—Operation Menu, which would have phases of Breakfast, Lunch, Snack, Dinner, and Dessert—involved nearly 4,000 sorties by B-52s with 104,000 tons of bombs dropped, a total that doubled by March 1973.[25] The bombing helped destabilize the country and set the stage for the horrors that were to come in the next decade. Nixon even invaded Cambodia, briefly and without gaining anything militarily; he encouraged the coup leader Lon Nol to start a military campaign against a weak communist force in Cambodia, which was suddenly mobilized by Sihanouk, in Beijing, and his new partner, Pol Pot. In both countries, Nixon could use heavy bombardment with few U.S. casualties to send messages of his toughness to Hanoi, a pattern that he would pursue in Vietnam itself. Air power was used to increase leverage at the bargaining table, not in the belief that it would succeed militarily. "'No one cares about B-52 strikes in Laos,' Nixon told Kissinger after an NSC meeting on February 27, [1970], 'but people worry about our boys there.'"[26]

---

* Nixon had hinted at this policy earlier, most notably during the splashdown of the July 1969 astronauts from the first moon landing. There, in Guam, he articulated what became known as the Nixon Doctrine—that the United States would not fight wars like Vietnam again but would instead supply allies facing communist challenges with ample armaments and other support. This doctrine became, after 1971, particularly consequential in the Persian Gulf with the lavish arming of the Pahlavi regime in Iran.

What occurred in the rest of Indochina was a sideshow compared with the bombing campaign in Vietnam. Nixon's policy was a combination of diplomatic maneuvering to gain a plausibly "honorable" exit. But he braced diplomacy with a brutality of bombing and other aggressive tactics that Johnson would not use. In addition to the bombing of Laos and Cambodia, Nixon ordered the mining of Haiphong harbor and some airstrikes that inadvertently hit Soviet supply ships. He told an aide, "The bastards have never been bombed like they're going to get bombed this time."[27] Nixon doubled the number of B-52 sorties and overall stepped up bombing in the region by 25 percent over what Johnson had authorized. So while Nixon was steadily withdrawing troops from the ground operations in the South, he was expanding the air war dramatically in an attempt to appear to gain a victory.

Even with the withdrawals, the war in the South continued at its ferocious pace for many months. More Americans died in Vietnam in 1969 than in any other year. The North Vietnamese were, more than ever, supporting their comrades in the South with intervention, and the first offensive came soon after Nixon took office in the dry season around February–March. It was, by all, accounts, among the bloodiest periods of the war, including the infamous battle over a single place in the Central Highlands, "Hamburger Hill," a gruesomely violent confrontation that took several weeks. The battle took 242 American lives and occasioned a decision at the top to scale down ground operations.[28] The carnage only slowly declined, however. The air campaign intensified, as did pacification, particularly its lethal Phoenix program, an effort to "neutralize" Viet Cong.

Negotiations at the Paris Peace Conference were fitful, punctuated by more bombing and threats. Nixon ordered a bombing campaign in the North in April 1972 called Linebacker, which caused enormous damage in Hanoi and Haiphong, after the North's Easter offensive commenced. But the final paroxysm of violence erupted after an apparent deal had been reached—Kissinger said that "peace is at hand"—but became snagged in details. This action, Linebacker II, utilized hundreds of aircraft targeting Hanoi in particular, a relentless attack of 3,400 sorties, with three-fourths of the tonnage dropped by the B-52 "Stratofortress." The damage to Hanoi was profound. Civilian casualties were low only because of the evacuation of the city when the bombing campaign commenced. Still, many residential areas were devastated. "As the Nixon administration hoped," wrote

Kimball, "there was terror on the ground from the sheer intensity of the bombing . . . and with many believing Nixon was mad to be killing civilians."[29]

The war ended for the United States in January 1973. The terms of the agreement varied only in details from what was on the table for months; in any case, it was merely a face-saving gesture for the United States. No one expected the Republic of South Vietnam to survive, and it was overrun twenty-seven months later. The entire war effort from about 1966 on was steeped in American pessimism and dissembling, a war carried out to protect American credibility abroad and to prove anticommunist mettle at home at a cost of millions dead and homeless and a region upended in bloodshed for years after.

THE PEOPLE

The war was unlike any war the United States has fought. The nature of much of the fighting—in jungles, among areas possibly controlled by the enemy, with no clear lines of a front—meant that distinguishing between combatants and civilians was a frustrating and thankless task. With a conscripted army, the U.S. military pursued the search-and-destroy mission in the South with often frightened, disaffected, and traumatized young soldiers. The fitful effort to win over the South Vietnamese peasants alienated many of them and subjected them to violence from both sides. As the American war became bogged down, technological solutions proliferated—more bombing as "close air support," more firepower, more chemical agents. Even the metrics of the ground war were conveyed in technical terms—the all-important body counts, the "neutralization" of suspected enemies, the "other war" of "pacification."

The bombing campaigns in the North, as well as Laos and Cambodia, were reminiscent of those of earlier wars and took up uncritically the adoration of air power as a solution for all problems. That the B-52s and advanced fighter-bombers were called upon as the ground war stalled (and as each reform of South Vietnamese governments stumbled) indicates how air power was actually regarded—namely, as a way to compensate for the failures of what were, by all reckonings, the main requisites of success. That so many bombs exploded in Vietnam, North and South, over such a long period of time, with widespread knowledge of their impact, says everything about Americans' attitudes toward the Vietnamese people.

In the South

The Americans' routine of search-and-destroy missions would begin with entry into a village, often with as many as 5,000 residents, via an air drop of soldiers or armored convoy. The soldiers would search the village, house by house, to look for Viet Cong fighters, and interrogate villagers about their possible support for the VC. Men might be taken to a district headquarters to be questioned. Those resisting or fleeing were in danger of being killed if not captured. If U.S. troops were fired on, anything from a sniper to a larger outbreak, the American officer in charge would call in artillery or air strikes, often obliterating the village before interrogations, since the gunfire would be evidence of communist partisanship. When no such fighting occurred, the Americans would tell the villagers to take some belongings and prepare to evacuate. Trucks or large Chinook helicopters* would move them from their village to a refugee camp, a "strategic hamlet," or another, now-overcrowded village. The target village then, in all likelihood, would be destroyed by a methodical bombing, often using napalm, which would destroy most of the buildings—mainly peasant huts—as an attempt to deny sanctuary to the VC. In the event the village was not evacuated that time, chances are it would be later, or be bombed or burned as a result of some real or perceived resistance. In the lowland jungles or the highlands, livelihoods might be devastated by the use of defoliants or the bulldozing of enormous tracts of land that denuded the countryside in order to deprive the enemy of its cover.

Bombing was sometimes preceded by leafleting or megaphoned announcements from helicopters warning the villagers (in cases where there was no evacuation), but that would also alert the enemy; so often the U.S. commanders would forgo the leaflets and bomb without warning.

---

* Oddly, the modern-day cavalry, which is airborne in helicopters, names its aircraft after the Native American tribes it once subdued: Black Hawk, Kiowa Warrior, Chinook, Iroquois, Sioux Scout, Cheyenne, and Comanche among them. The marines add the Apache. In Vietnam, the helicopters were often decorated with Indian warrior "face paint" in intimidating expressions.

Frequently, air strikes were called for in less-organized fashion, to chase a small group of VC who might have staged an ambush, for example, or even a single person found in an area that had been evacuated. Neil Sheehan described one such incident, after a small battle nearby that went badly for the U.S. side, where some women and children in a sugarcane field were spotted by the U.S. air force. The communists who might have been in the vicinity were "long gone," and the women, knowing the tendencies of the pilots, stayed in the field as a sign of their innocence even as the fighter-bombers buzzed low over the fields. Finally, the planes dropped napalm. A "young woman was the only survivor of the eight in the field," Neil Sheehan reported. After having walked to another village for treatment, where she was questioned, it was found that "both of her arms were burned so badly that they were going to have to be amputated. She would never be able to close her eyes to sleep again because her eyelids had been scorched away."[30] The rules of engagement were such that any suspicious behavior—fleeing at the sight of a helicopter gunship would qualify—enabled crews to fire. "We flew over a large rice paddy, and there were some people working in the rice paddy, maybe a dozen or fifteen individuals, and we passed over their heads and didn't take any action, they were obviously nervous, they didn't try to hide or anything," recalled a warrant officer. "So we then hovered a few feet off the ground among them with the two helicopters, turned on the police sirens and when they heard the police sirens, they started to disperse and we opened up on them and just shot them all down."[31]

The air war within South Vietnam accounts for a large number of the civilians killed there. Jonathan Schell, another of the most insightful independent journalists in the war, described a mid-1967 tour of the province of Quang Ngai, along the coast and highlands north of Saigon, with a spotter plane, a small Cessna. In each village, 50 to 90 percent of the houses in the province had been destroyed, unless used as a friendly outpost. Some were bombed, some were burned to the ground by marines or army units, some were bulldozed. "Although most of the villages in the province had been destroyed, the destruction of villages in large areas was not ordinarily an objective of the military operations but was viewed as, in the words of one official, a 'side effect' of hunting the enemy."[32]

Once evacuations were completed in a certain area, it could be designated a "free fire zone" under the assumption that anyone remaining was VC. It could then be hit by long-range artillery or bombing, or if ground troops were involved, with armored vehicles, helicopter gunships, or by patrolling infantry. The bombardment seemed to be random and without any refined military purpose. Harassment and interdiction fire, as it was called, "went unobserved—no U.S. observers were there to see who or what was hit," according to one account; but it was enormous in scale, from half to two-thirds of all such ordnance used. Artillery fires, said one captain, "did nothing but kill a lot of innocents and alienate us from those we were supposedly trying to help."[33] The shooting from helicopters (some with rockets) was carried out in a fury or with a sense of "sport" that unnerved those who witnessed it, but the larger share of casualties resulting from the air and artillery were random or routine—napalm strikes and other bombing; shelling; strafing where the enemy, or its supporters, were purported to be. Often, fighter-jets were used for "prep work"—clearing an area with their weapons in advance of an infantry operation.

The ground operations were possibly more ghastly, given the proximity of the killing. One massacre, typical of many others, was recalled by a girl who survived a 1968 incident in Vinh Cuong Hamlet No. 3, when, following artillery shelling, U.S. troops arrived and ordered everyone out to the center of town. Her mother told her to crawl through the high reeds in back of their hut and hide. She met an uncle near a river and "heard the crack of weapons firing. That evening, another uncle brought her back to the hamlet. As they emerged from the tall grass, they saw a pile of bodies outside the bunker. 'It was raining. Under the rain, they lay dead in cramped positions, some on top of each other. Dead bodies scattered all around.'" Two siblings and her mother had been shot dead; a three-year-old sister had been crushed to death by the falling bodies. A tablet now at the site says that the Americans "barbarously opened fire to massacre 37 of our compatriots, among which were 16 elderly and 21 children."[34] The attitude toward destruction seemed cavalier. "When we went out, I would say about 50 percent of the villages we passed through would be burned to the ground," said a marine. "There would be no difference between the ones we burned and the ones we didn't burn, it was just if we had the time we burned them."[35]

The pressures of battle and fatigue, the indistinct enemy, the clear hostility from many peasants angered by what the war was doing to their village—all preyed on the American soldier and blurred the ethics of combat. If you came under fire, the rote reaction became shoot, call in air support, destroy the hamlets. But there was more than the emotional traumas or pathologies of war that caused the high civilian toll: there was official sanction, even encouragement, for high body counts, which led to killings that lowered the bar for identifying whether the fallen were actually VC. McNamara had instituted quantitative measures of the war's progress, and among them were the body counts. This emphasis, conveyed down the chain of command by officers whose advancement might depend on such gauges, resulted in orders to shoot "anything that moves" and the indiscriminate killings of civilians who were then counted as enemy dead. The body count mania "was taking its toll on the war effort by making everyone a bounty hunter and a liar," said one soldier. "Yet, with the passage of time, the reliance on it among the top brass of the military, the Defense Department bureaucrats, and the politicians would only increase. The more bodies we counted, went the thinking, the better we were doing. . . . Body count was also well on its way to destroying whatever was left of the moral code of soldiers and officers."[36]

The obsessions with body counts combined with the actual problems of identifying the enemy were a road to tragedy. The Pentagon issued pocket cards with the rules of war listed, with pleas to respect civilians, "to help prevent jittery U.S. soldiers from mistakenly, or intentionally, declaring a suspect village a 'free fire zone,' then destroying it and its residents," noted a veteran A.P. reporter. "All too often, postmortem investigations revealed that such zones had been peaceful and should not have been assaulted."[37] The mistakes or sheer ignorance were so pervasive that the "status" of a village—VC core, mere sympathizers, some villagers and not others, or pro-GVN—could not easily be discerned in the time a military operation had, and even a scouring of the village might not reveal anything definitive. "We would go through a village before dawn, rousting everybody out of bed and kicking down doors and dragging them out," recalled a marine. "They all had underground bunkers inside their huts to protect themselves against bombing and shelling. But to us the bunkers were Viet Cong hiding places, and we'd blow them up with dynamite—and blow up the huts, too." The peasant would be "herded like cattle" into a prison-like holding area to sit in the hot sun; some would be interrogated, often harshly, and the others would be released, perhaps, to return to their demolished village. "If they weren't pro-Viet Cong before we got there, they sure as hell were by the time we left."[38]

This was the long undercurrent of violence that was the daily practice of the war in the South, although the atrocities earned far more attention. The My Lai incident is the best known of these and will be explored in greater depth in a later chapter. It was a case like many others in which a hamlet in the village of Song My along the South China Sea in Quang Ngai province was shelled and then assaulted by a helicopter-borne troop; a captain barked orders over a radio "to waste the Vietnamese and get my people out on line"[39] to the next engagement, and a lieutenant, William Calley, made sure that was done. In that hamlet known as My Lai 4, a total of 347 Vietnamese were murdered on the morning of March 16, 1968. Neil Sheehan described the scene:

> Some of the troops refused to participate in the massacre; their refusal did not restrain their fellows. The American soldiers and junior officers shot old men, women, boys, girls, and babies. . . . The soldiers beat women with rifle butts and raped some and sodomized others before shooting them. . . . They tossed satchel charges into the bomb shelters under the houses. A lot of the inhabitants had fled into the shelters. Those who leaped out to escape the explosives were gunned down. All the houses were put to the torch.[40]

Another ninety were murdered in a nearby hamlet the same morning. The incident, which came to light only through an investigative report by journalist Seymour Hersh the following year, became a symbol of the brutality of the war, but was widely and erroneously viewed in America as an isolated incident. Other atrocities of troubling magnitude were uncovered, some many years later, including the massacre of as many as 100 civilians by "Tiger Force," an elite squad of the 101st Airborne, and the Thang Phong raid involving Bob Kerrey, later a prominent Democratic politician. There were other incidents too.[41]

The atrocities—slow to be revealed in any case, and many likely never revealed—can obscure the mundane reality of violence in Vietnam, however. Had Calley and the others guilty at Song My "killed just as many over a larger area in a longer period of time and killed impersonally with bombs, shells, rockets, white phosphorous, and napalm, they would have been following the normal pattern of military conduct," Sheehan observed.[42] A staff sergeant wrote anonymously to Westmoreland: "Number one killer . . . was the rule that said shoot if they run. . . . Shoot any dude that run. And lots of them did. Run from the GIs, run from the gunships, run from the loaches [helicopters]." The writer, who blamed the body count mania from senior officers for this and other murderous practices, asserted that "we were 'told' to kill many times more Vietnamese than at My Lai, and very few per cents of them did we know were enemy"—a "My Lai each month" for over a year in his brigade.[43] Medals and promotions often hinged on producing high body counts.

The treatment of those considered to be Viet Cong—a wide-ranging and imprecise assessment—also crossed the line on countless occasions. Interrogations frequently surged into torture, and the accused were dealt harsh punishments. An example is a major 1969 operation at Balang An involving 8,000 U.S. troops and shelling by sixty guns from Seventh Fleet warships. The villagers were rounded up to be transported to a holding camp, with some 600 killed in the process. The village was totally destroyed. The 1,200 detained were considered Viet Cong. The "suspects were put into jute rice bags, each in one, with many bags containing two children, and dumped into a number of small fishing boats," according to a survivor. The fishing boats were tied together and towed out to sea, where they were upended by a motorboat piloted by U.S. soldiers. "Jute bags that remained on the surface were strafed."[44] Others accused of being communists might land in the infamous "tiger cages" of South Vietnam prisons: tiny, cramped enclosures where they were subjected to routine torture, many of them for years.

Some American allies were feared as even more vicious. The South Vietnamese army was difficult to control from the beginning, as Sheehan underscores through his portrayal of John Paul Vann, one of the American advisers who was most concerned about the GVN's habits of massacre (and informed the U.S. military brass in Vietnam, only to be met with indifference). The South Koreans, however, earned an even nastier reputation. "In one part of the village [Dien Ban] they burned everything and shot everyone. In another part they just shot everyone in sight but didn't burn the villages," is the way a survivor, an infant at the time, told of an incident that disfigured her for life. She and others were herded into a bomb shelter. "The adults tried to cover the children with their bodies when the South Koreans started shooting everyone in the bunker. As they walked away, I started crying. They came back, realizing not everybody was dead, and threw a hand grenade into the shelter."[45] The Koreans were under the operational control of the U.S. commander.

Most officers and soldiers observed the rules of war, took care to discriminate friend from foe, and aided villagers in various ways. Much depended on the commanders in the field. But the war devolved quickly into one where the use of overwhelming force reigned. "By 1967, only a foolhardy or desperate commander would ever engage hostile elements by any means other than with firepower," said one general. B-52 usage, he noted, went from sixty sorties a month in 1966 to more than 800 a year later.[46] The amount of ammunition expended in Vietnam was higher than in any other American war. The attitudes of officers toward civilians in such circumstances may have been ancillary. Without the personal contact that could tell friend from foe, massive casualties were sustained under such bombardment.

The number of killings of civilians simply cannot be documented because when such incidents occurred, the reports almost invariably described the dead as Viet Cong. Often, "after action" reports claim all deceased Vietnamese are VC. Apart from the eyewitness accounts of probable civilian deaths—surely a tiny fraction of what occurred, given shame, possible retribution, or even the legal liability of coming forward—one can infer from the reports the likelihood of mistaken identities. In the many incidents we know of, a common piece of evidence is the reporting of VC killed in action, but without retrieval of a commensurate number of weapons. One 1972 article in *Newsweek* described a major operation in the Mekong Delta, the fertile area south of Saigon, in which nearly 11,000 enemy were claimed killed, but only 748 weapons were recovered. The reporter, Kevin Buckley, investigated the incident and concluded that 5,000 civilians had been killed.[47] A number of less spectacular stories have similar contours—alleged Viet Cong killed, but with too few weapons or other evidence to be convincing. One air force captain tasked with damage assessments relates a case in the Delta where some villagers in a free fire zone had refused to leave because their village was their whole world to them—not only their homes, but their livelihoods and their burial grounds—which was a common sentiment. After an airstrike topped off with napalm "which would just fry everything that was left," he did his count and found sixty-two corpses. "In my report I described them as so many women between fifteen and twenty-five and so many children—and so many old people," he recalled. "A few days later, I happened to see an after-action report from this village. . . . The report said one hundred thirty VC dead."[48]

A remarkable amount of mayhem was exacted in the name of "the other war," the years-long effort to pacify the countryside. A hand-maiden of counterinsurgency, the pacification campaign, as it was called through several iterations, sought to achieve what is typically now called nation building: the United States was to help the GVN rebuild the villages and create favorable economic and social conditions—or, in the words of its major domo, Robert Komer: "generating rural support for the Saigon regime via programs meeting rural needs and cementing the rural area politically and administratively to the center." At the village level the program was an all-Vietnamese affair, but the Americans were providing security ("deprive the insurgency of its rural popular base") and, through the Phoenix program, attacking the communist infrastructure, or local leadership cadre ("neutralize the active insurgent forces and apparatus in the countryside").[49] Pacification was Lyndon Johnson's sincerest hope to turn the war into something admirable and recalled to him the memory of how things like rural electrification improved lives in the impoverished Texas of his youth. Bringing modernization to the peasants, not incidentally, would lure them away from the attractions of communism. With the GVN in charge at the local level, however, inserting themselves into the hamlets after the U.S. forces had "secured" them, ample opportunities for corruption and settling scores prevailed. The primary goal of cementing the peasants to the GVN was unattainable when the relations between the two were so brittle and mutually suspicious. No less important was the growing urbanization of the Vietnamese peasantry, which in most cases was a forced urbanization, emptying the countryside of those for whom the pacification was intended. The long history—beginning with Strategic Hamlets and continuing throughout the 1960s of evacuating villages—generated a refugee crisis that no authority in the South came to grips with successfully. By most estimates, the numbers of internally displaced people were in the millions by the time LBJ left office, (as many as five million in a country of eighteen million).[50] Those remaining in the villages were in some important measure sympathetic to, or controlled by, the Viet Cong. But the pacification effort, while making some local progress in areas controlled by the GVN, was doomed by the security dimension—the "destroying the village in order to save it" mind-set of the U.S. military—and the sheer difficulties of imposing a theory of development in the midst of war.*

Pacification included assassination via the Phoenix program, a special operations juggernaut that neutralized tens of thousands of South Vietnamese, allegedly communist, by converting them, imprisoning them, or killing them. The number reported killed was about 7,000 at the program's height, 1968–69, with increasing emphasis on assassinations over capture or conversion. But the program often went off the rails, with paid assassins harming civilians and further alienating ordinary Vietnamese in the cities and countryside. "The biggest fear is being falsely accused—from which there is no protection," explained a Vietnamese writer for a Catholic newspaper in Saigon in 1971. "That's why Phoenix doesn't bring peace and security. That's why it destroys trust in the GVN, not the VC."[51] Among the CIA-led program's many problems was the role of the South Vietnamese agents. "The GVN high command in Saigon did not much care if chiefs arrested or killed a few people whom they disliked," wrote two conservative analysts of the war. "Nor did top GVN leaders generally oppose the neutralization of members of opposition political parties and racial minorities. These leaders, indeed, often encouraged the chiefs to neutralize the members of non-Communist groups suspected of anti-GVN activity. Even the senior [pacification] leaders were not overly concerned with these problems." They estimated that 180,000 people were arrested as a result of the Phoenix program.[52]

* The pacification campaign had many authors, but Walt W. Rostow, a prominent political scientist at MIT before joining the Kennedy-Johnson administration, was the academic designer of "modernization" theory, which was the whole cloth of pacification. As a consultant to the U.S. government, Samuel Huntington at Harvard was critical of the application of this theory, with its logical progressions to cosmopolitan bourgeois capitalism, noting that development in Vietnam would find its own way and could not be imposed. Pacification would, moreover, frustrate the U.S. soldiers as peasants showed indifference or hostility to yet another attempt to reshape their lives. It was the end of modernization theory, in effect, which Huntington continued to attack in the 1970s. See Christopher T. Fisher, "The Illusion of Progress: CORDS and the Crisis of Modernization in South Vietnam, 1965–1968," *Pacific Historical Review*, vol. 25, no. 1 (2006): 25–51.

By the latter stages of the war, the enormous flows of people into Saigon and the high numbers of war dead created an urban nightmare. "There are street gangs now in every quarter of Saigon," an American journalist reported in the early 1970s. "Led by army deserters and recruited from among the mobs of smaller children, they roam like wolf packs."[53] Many of the youth were orphans, or abandoned. A startling number of teenage girls and older women sold themselves for sex, and others were raped. "Many of the prostitutes were farm girls, for another collateral effect of the physical destruction of the countryside was to help fulfill American needs for labor and entertainment," Neil Sheehan wrote.[54] Shantytowns and brothels sprang up around U.S. bases, and Saigon swelled with them. Rape was also a too-common occurrence in the more severe search-and-destroy operations.

One study—a survey, published by the U.S. Government, of Vietnam veterans interviewed in the late 1970s—found that one in eleven U.S. soldiers committed "an act of abusive violence, such as torturing prisoners, raping civilians, or mutilating a corpse," and one-third of all soldiers said they witnessed such crimes.[55] Nearly four in five were committed by Americans, the remaining one-fifth by U.S. allies or Viet Cong. Since the number of Americans in combat was nearly one million, and a total of 3.4 million served in Southeast Asia, this adds up to a very high number of these incidents, particularly since some witnesses must have seen more than one Vietnamese abused.

The physical destruction of the countryside was accomplished by many means. Burning, bulldozing, and bombing the villages and fields were day-to-day routines, but U.S. tactics included a form of chemical warfare, too. Counterinsurgency and "big unit" warfare in South Vietnam was fought in a terrain that favored guerrillas; not only did they have the advantages of knowing the countryside and mountains as well as the people's routines and paths, but they also benefited from the cover provided by the jungle itself. This stymied the U.S. military constantly, not least in trying to interdict the Ho Chi Minh Trail of supply from North to South. The failures of the interdiction effort and the Viet Cong's ease in slipping away from battles so vexed U.S. operations that the military pervasively used defoliants, including the carcinogenic dioxin, to eliminate forests. The chemical herbicides, which came to be known as Agent Orange because some were stored in orange barrels, were sprayed from airplanes beginning in 1961 and were used with increasing frequency as the war intensified. Operation Ranch Hand, as the defoliation campaign was called, destroyed 850,000 acres in 1966 and 1.5 million acres in 1967, including croplands to deny food to the enemy, and covered one-fifth of South Vietnam's forests.[56]

The Agent Orange controversy erupted later, after the war, and was mainly concerned with U.S. soldiers who were accidentally exposed. But the effects of Agent Orange were known at the time—no later than 1966.[57] President Nixon's science adviser explained the effects of the defoliants to him in 1969, but their use continued at least until 1971. The chemical warfare, including the use of white phosphorous and napalm, was known at the time and widely publicized by the war's opponents. Peter Davis's documentary of the war, *Hearts and Minds*, visits a small factory where coffins are being made, and a man named Min Duc Giang hammering together a small coffin is interviewed. "They are for children," he said, "eight hundred or nine hundred a week. I have lost seven children myself. Many have died here, though it's nothing like the countryside. Many more have died there." He is asked how all the children died. "Poison, poison you know. These planes keep spouting and spraying the stuff, and so many people have died. It seems to destroy their intestines, this spraying and bombing. Each day, right on time," he continues, looking distraught. "We can't talk about it because we are afraid of the government," the GVN.

Among the chemicals' effects was the poisoning of rice fields and orchards of ordinary peasants, affecting their offspring in some hideous ways and chronically depressing rice output to the point that Vietnam, once a major rice exporter, had to import rice by 1966. The residual effects of the chemicals remain powerful in Vietnam: in the provinces most heavily sprayed, according to an eyewitness visit in the late 1980s, the incidence of birth defects is more than twice their occurrence in the rest of Vietnam.[58] The medical effects of dioxin and related chemicals are contested among scientists, but the weight of evidence points to serious effects of various kinds. It was, moreover, very heavily concentrated in certain Viet Cong-controlled areas of Vietnam that have since experienced unusually high abnormalities. In profiling a fifteen-year-old boy who was born in a heavily contaminated area and has severe disabilities, the BBC reported in 2004 that "in Vietnam, there are 150,000 other children like him, whose birth defects—according to Vietnamese Red Cross records—can be readily traced back to their parents' exposure to Agent Orange during the war, or the consumption of dioxin-contaminated food and water since 1975." An American scientist found levels of contamination there 180 million times what is normal.[59]

The war policies and practice of the United States showed such consistent disregard for civilians that it could not be accepted as "collateral damage," the unfortunate side effect of savage war. Even a partisan of the war effort like John Paul Vann saw this. "Vann was convinced that this 'generating' of refugees and its concomitant toll in civilian casualties was not an accidental outgrowth of an attempt to bludgeon the enemy, but a policy deliberately fostered by the high command," Sheehan explains. "I asked [Westmoreland] if he was worried about the large numbers of civilian casualties from the air strikes and the shelling. He looked at me carefully. 'Yes, Neil, it is a problem,' he said, 'but it does deprive the enemy of the population, doesn't it?'"[60]

A South Vietnamese soldier relates a story about the free fire zones, where he once noticed a thatched hut with two old people living inside. He evacuated them and burned the hut so they wouldn't return. Weeks later he saw a new hut built on the same spot, and he found the old couple there again. He told them it was dangerous and asked why they had returned. "'All my ancestors are buried here and this is our land. We are not going to leave.'" He explains, "the land is unimaginably important to Vietnamese peasants. They were extremely poor and the land was all they had, all they loved."[61]

From the North

In December 1966 the *New York Times* correspondent Harrison Salisbury went to Hanoi, one of the first journalists to do so since the beginning of the U.S. offensives of the Johnson presidency. His reports over the next weeks startled many in the United States, coming as they did at the time of some of the heaviest bombardments of the North since the Gulf of Tonkin incident. He reported that "contrary to the impression given by the United States communiqués, on-the-spot inspection indicates that American bombing has been inflicting considerable civilian casualties in Hanoi and its environs for some time past." He described the use of a fragmentation bomb "said to have fallen on

Phuxa village, releasing 300 iron spheres, each about the size of a base-ball and each loaded with 300 steel pellets about the size and shape of bicycle bearings."[62] While the actual number of casualties he reported in that article were low—in the dozens—the assertion that the U.S. military was hitting civilian areas, and with anti-personnel weapons, caused an uproar, as the administration had repeatedly avowed it had scrupulously contained attacks to military assets. Salisbury pointed out that railroad yards and other such military targets were amid thick settlements, however, and the damage—vaguely acknowledged the next day by the Pentagon when stating "it is impossible to avoid all damage to civilian areas"—around such places was apparent. Salisbury then reported from the country's third largest city, Namdinh, while it was under attack; the mayor told him in a bomb shelter that it was the fifty-first attack since the previous June and that the homes of 12,000 people had been destroyed with 500 casualties, including eighty-nine deaths. She claimed that Namdinh had no military targets. "The Amer-icans think they can touch our hearts," another resident told him. A town of 10,000 nearby was attacked in October, with every house destroyed and only railroad sidings to attract the U.S. bombers.[63]

The following day brought more of the same. Aircraft attacked Hanoi, hitting railroad yards where Salisbury viewed the damage—"Some bombs certainly fell along the railroad. But there are large num-bers of apartment houses close by, and one after another was blasted out."[64] Salisbury returned to Namdinh a few days later and reported that the villagers were contending that the U.S. navy bombers had purposefully hit dykes earlier in the year, causing six breaches, and he witnessed other craters in a line atop the levees. As he noted, the pos-sibility of dyke destruction (advocated by Barry Goldwater and many others) raises memories of the breach of dykes in the Second World War by the Japanese that caused a million deaths. The U.S. government always denied intentionally striking dykes.

The matter of the dykes was only a part of the storm of controversy stirred by Salisbury's reporting, however. His two weeks in North Viet-nam had propelled the issue of civilian casualties to the top of the American political agenda as never before, and the administration, the military, and pro-war journalists and politicians condemned his reports as naïvely conveyed propaganda. But Salisbury had seen much with his own eyes and he was scrupulous about parsing what he saw and what he was told. In a wrap-up article from Hong Kong after departing Hanoi, Salisbury addressed the brewing tempest about casualties. He noted that he did indeed see many military sites that had been hit. But he also saw other areas struck by American weapons:

> Residence areas of Hanoi, substantial areas of mixed housing, small shops, and miscellaneous buildings in the suburbs of Gialam, Yenvien and Vandien in the Hanoi metropolitan area, several schools in the Hanoi area, villages and hamlets along highways leading south from Hanoi, large areas of housing and shops in towns like Namdinh and Ninhbinh and in the Phatdiem village complex. . . . It is easy to establish that widespread harm has been done to civilian housing and non-military institutions and that civilian casualties have been extensive.[65]

"For a while in early 1967 it seemed that Salisbury had replaced Ho Chi Minh as the administration's prime adversary," wrote Stanley Karnow. The *Washington Post* called Hanoi's invitation to Salisbury "as 'clearly conceived' as the Viet Cong's 'poison-tipped bamboo spikes.'"[66] The White House was certainly alarmed and aimed to discredit Salisbury, scrambling to staunch the public relations hemorrhaging, as the *Pentagon Papers* noted: "The matter reached a level of concern such that the President felt compelled to make a statement to the press on December 31 to the effect that the bombing was directed against legitimate military targets and that every effort was being made to avoid civilian casualties."[67] But Salisbury's reports, buttressed by visits by peace activists like Tom Hayden, Staughton Lynd, and A. J. Muste, apparently revealed that the "northern strategy" was taking a significant civilian toll despite the endless protestations of innocence by the military and the nation's political leaders.

In an odd sense, both sides were "right" in that the United States was not aiming to kill civilians, but the reports from the North were nonetheless accurate. Partly from moral considerations, but more emphatically for strategic reasons, the Johnson team did not want heavy civilian casualties because they sought "to keep the hostage healthy," the idea that bombing's power as coercion was the threat of *future* punishment, and to "tighten the noose" around the communist leadership in order to persuade them to negotiate an end to the war.[68] As noted earlier, LBJ was also concerned about potential moves by China or Russia. But the damage in the North was incontrovertible.

Whether as accidental damage or a minor objective (akin to the harassment artillery strikes in the South), the air campaign was killing and wounding civilians. Some of the missions involved high-level flights that could not achieve pinpoint accuracy. Some targets were too close to civilian areas. And, as Salisbury speculated, some navy pilots may have jettisoned excess bombs randomly on their return to aircraft carriers. Malicious conduct cannot be discounted either. Whatever the causes, the remarkable outcome in the North is that fewer deaths occurred than might have because the government had ordered evacuations of Hanoi in particular—its population dropped by half between 1965 and 1967—and had built very extensive bomb shelters throughout the city and in smaller towns and villages. The official U.S. mortality estimates of this phase of the bombing, "Rolling Thunder," were 57,000 killed directly by bombs; the actual number is likely closer to 100,000. But the bombing also caused hardships, which was a primary objective of war planners. As Robert Pape observed, "the physical pattern of Rolling Thunder indicated no intention to kill large numbers of civilians," but the strategy of annihilating the industrial base was intent on "inflicting extreme civilian costs."[69]

The costs did not come in the form of surrender, or even a change in North Vietnam's support for the Viet Cong. Washington decision makers were unanimous in their assessment of the bombing: it didn't work. "Evidence regarding the effect of the bombing on the morale of the North Vietnamese people suggests that the results were mixed," a high-level group of scientists explained in a study for McNamara in the summer of 1966. "The bombing clearly strengthened popular support of the regime by engendering patriotic and nationalistic enthusiasm to resist the attacks. On the other hand, those more directly involved in the bombing underwent personal hardships and anxieties caused by the raids."[70] As nearly all assessments of the time agree, the bombing didn't achieve its intended objectives, but Johnson persisted with it all the same, and Nixon repeatedly used the same strategy through his first term.

The coping strategies in the North, as Salisbury reported, focused on dispersal of the population from large cities and the extraordinary system of shelters. In the 5,000-member commune of Thinh Liet in the Red River delta, for example, villagers would be warned by sirens and loudspeakers that an air raid was about to commence; most would retreat to the shelters, which were ingeniously designed to absorb shrapnel and other ordnance, while a few stayed above ground to shoot at low-flying aircraft with AK-47s and similar weapons. In ten direct attacks during the war, fifty-seven villagers, all civilians, were killed (a quarter of nearly 400 men who fought in the army were also killed elsewhere), with more permanently disabled from injuries sustained during the bombing and strafing. The complete loss of some soldiers' corpses, without possibility of proper burial, and the bombing of graveyards were especially wrenching, given traditional observances regarding the dead. The attacks bludgeoned the agrarian fields and depressed crop yields, too, and the residents went long periods with very little to eat. Food was rationed; rice harvests were requisitioned for soldiers and replaced with Russian or Chinese wheat, which villagers did not know how to bake properly. After bombing paused, Vietnamese all over the country would hold festivals to celebrate, drawing on animist and Catholic traditions that the state disliked but did not stop.[71]

A British journalist traveling far from Hanoi in 1970 noted the complete destruction of bridges—the interdiction campaign that failed—and the damage to villages, most of which, like Thinh Liet, had no obvious military value. Consider the village of Hatinh, home to 12,000. "To judge from the few remaining facades, it was once a rather pretty colonial town," he wrote. It had "a church, a pagoda, a new hospital with 200 beds, an agricultural implements workshop, a small power station for the needs of the town and to assist the rural electrification program. All gone."[72] Even where the people from Hanoi had been dispersed in the countryside, there was terror. "I went to school with other children, but we never gathered in large groups during the day," recalled Tran Luong, who was twelve when the war ended. "If you did, bombs would start falling in fifteen minutes, and in the countryside there were no sirens to warn you of air strikes. We just ran as soon as we heard the airplanes. Sometimes the bombs fell just as people were starting the scatter for shelter."[73]

For the Vietnamese, no amount of preparation can shield from the shock of being bombed. "It is true that at times I was scared stiff and particularly during our 1972 [Easter] offensive when the B-52s were carpet-bombing us," recalled an officer who was in Hanoi at the time. "The atmosphere was like living through a typhoon with trees crashing down and lightning transforming night into day."[74] When Nixon ordered an attack to put concluding pressure on the North Vietnamese leadership, the so-called Christmas bombing, it caught some by surprise: its ferocity was unlike any other period of the air assault, essentially carpet bombing, with much of it falling on residential neighborhoods of Hanoi. "Children hated American pilots because we could see the destruction they rained down on our country," recalled Tran Luong. "The Christmas bombing caught us completely by surprise. Kam Thien Street in the busiest part of [Hanoi] was destroyed by American bombs. . . . The morning after the bombing I went to Kam Thien Street with some older children. I saw pieces of hair and scalp hanging from the trees. It was an indelible sight."[75] Another witness to the Christmas bombing campaign was the father of children killed by the American B-52 pilots. "My eight-year-old daughter was killed, and my three-year-old son; a son, three years old," he told Peter Davis in *Hearts and Minds*, amid the complete destruction of his house, his voice laced with anger and distress. "My daughter died right here. She was feeding the pigs. She was so sweet. She is dead. The pigs are alive. My mother and children took shelter here," he said, pointing to a small mound of rubble. "Here they died. The planes came from over there. No targets here. Only rice fields and houses. Tell them she was only a little schoolgirl."

The civilian toll in the North, despite all the bombing and the attention it drew, was far less than the South. As Bernard Fall commented in 1966, and which held true, "what changed the character of the Vietnam war was *not* the decision to bomb North Vietnam, *not* the decision to use American ground troops in South Vietnam; but the decision to wage unlimited aerial warfare inside the country at the price of literally pounding the place to bits."[76] It is ironic that with all the protestations of restraint in the bombing of the North, with all the claims of concerns about civilians, the United States did not cause more civilian death and injuries there mainly because of the actions taken by the Vietnamese—the shelters and the evacuations that saved many times more lives than were lost.

At war's end, the count of civilians slain in the South was said to be 415,000, a number that fails to account for the pervasive habit of labeling Vietnamese casualties as enemy kills when many—an unknown number—were civilians. The South Vietnamese military sustained more than 200,000 dead. North Vietnam said that more than one million combatants died, including Viet Cong, and two million civilians perished. Some estimates are lower and some are higher. McNamara estimated total war dead at 2,358,000, including 1,200,000 million civilians. And studies since the war have ranged widely, from 1,000,000 to 3,800,000 total war deaths. Like the causes and conduct of the war, the casualties remain mired in embittered controversy.[77]

THE HOME FRONT

The mere mention of the Vietnam War brings to mind not only the conflict in Indochina, but also the turmoil the war caused in the United States. While the protests, the burgeoning counterculture, the critical press, and the decline of LBJ dominate the common memory of the period of the war, the American public remained largely supportive of the war in Vietnam, with many insistent that the war was not being waged with enough ferocity. Our memory of the Kennedy presidency and its abrupt break from the Eisenhower years as well as the "sex, drugs, and rock 'n' roll" counterculture of the late 1960s obscures the essential continuity of American life, culture, and politics from the 1950s to the 1960s. That continuity included the anticommunist habits of mind that had been cultivated for decades. In popular culture, the frontier sustained its dominance well into the 1960s, with television's most-watched program a Western (called *Bonanza* no less, with *Gunsmoke* another popular show) and Hollywood churning out movies like *The Magnificent Seven* and *The Alamo*, the latter yet another John Wayne epic as Davey Crockett. Military dramas were also popular in the early 1960s, with as many as eleven prime-time shows, typically set during the Second World War (e.g., *Combat* and *Twelve O'Clock High*), generally adopting heroic narratives of action, and wholly uncritical of the military (although some were comedies like *Hogan's Heroes*). The "silent majority" that Nixon later celebrated was enamored of the frontier myth and its realization in anticommunism, and Kennedy's call to action worldwide and his apparent gambler's instinct in both the Cuban Missile Crisis and Berlin provided assurances that confrontation would be rewarded in keeping the savages at bay.

Yet the public was inundated with images of the war, certainly many times more than what Americans were exposed to during the Korean War, as well as a vast amount of reporting and analysis of the conflict, its human toll and suffering. As early as 1967, Bertrand Russell held hearings that exposed "war crimes" and published an enormous volume filled with disturbing testimony.[78] That display, like denunciations from other European intellectuals like Jean-Paul Sartre, failed to stir more than a ripple of public response in the United States. More significant, and more direct, were the street demonstrations across America that told the majority that something was deeply amiss in Vietnam, and as popular culture did turn toward the probing, critical, and alternative perspectives of the late 1960s, few Americans could say they did not know an unusually violent war was taking place under the U.S. flag in Vietnam.

Naming the System

While the seamlessness of American culture from the 1950s into the 1960s is apparent, an undercurrent of discontent was appearing in American literature and theater, an uneasiness with the prosperity, and suburban and restless mobility, of 1950s America. While this was largely apolitical, it fed a stream of youth culture that was, more than any other cause in the early 1960s, drawn to the burning social and political issue of equal rights for African Americans, that had been front-page news since the early 1950s and had already witnessed several militant confrontations by the time Kennedy entered the White House. The sharp cleavage that race relations had long suffered was an ugly clash that erupted into police violence in Selma, Alabama, and elsewhere to suppress what was, for years, a black movement built on Ghandian nonviolence. By the time Johnson escalated the war in Vietnam, an array of activists had formed organizations like the Students for a Democratic Society (SDS) and the Student Non-Violent Coordinating Committee (SNCC) mainly to address racial inequality, and they were schooled by the violence and racism that "the Establishment" evinced. This civil rights movement was the foundation of the antiwar movement that quickly emerged in 1965. For many of these radicalizing youth, racism and war were two sides of the same coin: brown people were being sent to Vietnam to kill other brown people, while their brethren at home were being clubbed for asking for the rights to which they were born. In what was at that point the largest antiwar rally in American history, the president of SDS, Paul Potter, spoke to

25,000 students in 1965 in front of the Lincoln Memorial, connecting the demonstrators there with the Vietnamese themselves: "In both countries there are people struggling to build a movement that has the power to change their condition. The system that frustrates these movements is the same," he said, in what became an anthem of the New Left. *"We must name that system.* We must name it, describe it, analyze it, understand it and change it. For it is only when that system is changed and brought under control that there can be any hope for stopping the forces that create a war in Vietnam today or a murder in the South tomorrow or all the incalculable, innumerable more subtle atrocities that are worked on people all over, all the time."[79]

The stage was set, then, for a confrontation between the long-standing values of the American Dream, faith, family, and anticommunism, versus an emerging set of values that rejected corporate privilege, stultifying conformity, the violence of foreign intervention abroad, and repression of dissent at home. Beyond rejection, what this emergent counterculture stood for was less obvious, but it surely embraced a quasi-socialist or even anarchist political ideology, sexual freedom, and growing affinity for the third world peoples the United States was attempting to dominate, including the poor and the blacks in America. This confrontation is fascinating for many reasons, but relevant here is the breadth and depth of antiwar activism, a phenomenon that is unique in American history on this scale. SDS, SNCC, the Mobilization to End the War, and other organizations mounted a massive and militant opposition to Johnson's policies. In demonstrations at the Pentagon and the White House, on campuses, at military recruiting offices, at corporate headquarters of defense contractors and elsewhere, protestors shouted out a message of total denunciation of the war's aims and its conduct. An alternative press sprang up, fueled by counterculture products like rock 'n' roll, but politically charged and dedicated to racial equality and immediate withdrawal from Indochina. A cottage industry of antiwar work grew quickly, with small research outfits, academic explorations and curricula, labor organizing, action collectives, mothers for peace, mobilizing clergy, and the newly popular musicians all contributing in a growing and often chaotic protest against Johnson and then Nixon.

What motivated them was significantly spurred by the violence they perceived in Vietnam. Several leading activists traveled to North

Vietnam and reported the horror of the bombing. Coupled with some journalists' accounts of what was transpiring in South Vietnam, a very deadly enterprise—an American enterprise—was apparent. Veterans of the war, many deeply disillusioned and angry, began to speak out. The protest and these accounts fed upon each other and raised the temperature, attracting more of the same—more critical journalism, more visits to Hanoi, more veterans voicing their painful stories, and more protestors. The photo of a little girl running down a street in South Vietnam ablaze with napalm was, like Salisbury's dispatches, a galvanizing image. Analysts like I. F. Stone and Noam Chomsky exposed the government's persistent dishonesty about the war, the ideology of the body counts, the "progress" and (in)humanity of the American mission. When the major figures of the black liberation movement, notably Martin Luther King, Jr., linked the two struggles—antiracism and antiwar—they decried the same American tendencies of using violence to repress the powerless, and the movement took on an ever-more radical character, challenging not just U.S. foreign policy, but many of the pillars of American society and the state.

The legendary reporting of Sheehan, Halberstam, Schell, Karnow, Ward Just, Gloria Emerson, Homer Bigart, and others was also unprecedented. It was skeptical of the government claims and exposed the gruesome consequences of the American war. Vietnam was in some respects the first "television war," but the actual coverage was limited by the still-cumbersome technology. (One study found that for the five years beginning in August 1965, "of some 2,300 reports that aired on evening television news programs, no more than 76 showed anything approaching true violence—heavy fighting, incoming small arms and artillery fire, killed and wounded within view.")[80] Americans got a flavor of the violence, but the focus was on U.S. casualties. "Because there was little interest in showing Vietnamese, the subjects of the combat footage produced were invariably Americans, who were usually engaged in unspecified, but seemingly successful, military activity," noted another scholar. "The networks simply presented a series of images, mainly of Americans fighting an unseen foe."[81] One school of thought drawn from television critic Michael Arlen's *Living Room War* holds that TV's entertainment programs were so violent that the war footage would not shock or activate the viewers, and apathy about Vietnam's carnage took over. Most assessments of the influence of television and the print coverage conclude that consumers of the news from Vietnam would likely filter the information according to their own predispositions, including their regard for the government and the military, their attitudes toward communism, whether they knew someone deployed in the war, and the like. Few novels or films were openly derisive of the war until well into the 1970s. Popular music was the one consistent pole of opposition to the war and its associated values from early in the conflict.

By the time of the epochal confrontation in Chicago during the 1968 Democratic National Convention, the antiwar movement was driven by many different groups and viewpoints—its fragmentation being one of its crippling characteristics—and represented an array of social groups and causes than spun out from "the movement." It was viewed broadly by the public as being anti-American and tinged with communist influence, even if the core message of the war's wastefulness was gradually accepted by growing numbers of mainstream Americans. Woven into the antiwar message was an unmistakable norm of questioning authority and war, a norm that persuaded more Americans to doubt the tenets of the frontier myth and American exceptionalism than ever before.

The Silent Majority

There was a silent majority, and it was offended and disdainful of the tactics and ideology of the New Left and the more licentious elements of the counterculture. Not wholly convinced of the rightness of the war, particularly since the drafted soldier was likely to come from their ranks, they nonetheless rejected the scorching rhetoric of SDS and other confrontational protestors; they were angered by the growing militancy and violence in the black liberation movements and the city riots they attributed to the likes of SNCC and the Black Panthers. All of these new ideas and their vociferous advocates were very much at odds with what was considered to be core American values (even as many in the protest movements called up the same or similar values, such as democratic rights). As a result, the antiwar message was mixed up with other messages—accusations of racism, capitalist greed, and middle-class conformity—which alienated large segments of this majority, to say nothing of their dislike of the messengers. This conflation of messages and their conveyers possibly diverted the public from coming to terms with the scale of violence being imposed upon Vietnam by the U.S. armed forces.

As would be expected, a reaction to the protest quickly popped up. A number of pro-war novels and films began to appear before those of an antiwar tilt, led by Robin Moore's *The Green Berets* in 1965, made into a film starring John Wayne in 1968. Wayne was the colossus of Hollywood patriotism; it is striking how many Vietnam soldiers recalled later that they imagined being deployed to Vietnam was going to be like a John Wayne movie. The film, exceeding even the book's commercial success, sought to counter the growing cultural drift toward antiwar expression and explicitly promoted racial stereotypes of savage Asians possibly as an argument for why the war should be fought and won.[82] It reflected to some degree reigning attitudes toward the "gooks" in the military ("the racism directed towards the Vietnamese people was of epidemic proportions," one study finds, noting it was cultivated in boot camp; "such attitudes and behaviors became generalized toward all Vietnamese"),[83] a fraught topic when the black liberation movement was becoming more confrontational and a white backlash was simmering, most obviously represented in Alabama governor and segregationist George Wallace's strong showing as a third-party candidate for president in 1968. One could easily imagine the transference of violent anger against black activists to brown Vietnamese, and there was a strong correlation between racist attitudes and support for the war. *The Green Berets* and its imitators often framed the story as a group of heroes fighting not just the Viet Cong but the U.S. bureaucracy that "tied our hands" and would not permit a full-scale assault on Vietnamese communists. This was a favorite complaint of the right wing throughout, and subsequent to, the war.

The public as a whole began to turn against the war with the rise in American casualties, as political scientist John Mueller has shown: polls indicate that Americans called the war a "mistake" steadily more often as casualties mounted—"every time American casualties increased by a factor of 10 (i.e., from 100 to 1,000 or from 10,000 to 100,000) support for the war dropped by about 15 percentage points." He noted the same pattern in decline of support during the Korean War. "While [Americans] did weary of the wars, they generally seem to have become hardened to the wars' costs: They are sensitive to relatively small losses in the early stages, but only to large losses in later stages," in part because in the latter stages of war, the hard-core supporters are less likely to be swayed by bad news. Notably, even as a plurality of those answering yes to whether the war was a mistake was attained and never reversed (by 46–42 percent in February 1968), a sizable number of Americans (70 percent) favored bombing North Vietnam, a number that declined sharply once a partial bombing halt was in effect.[84] This may have meant that some in the "it was a mistake" camp thought more vigorous military action was necessary, and without it the war could be considered a mistake because it could not be won. Those favoring escalation of military action in October 1967, for example, stood at 42 percent (with 47 percent opposed to escalation), with high shares of the public against deescalation *or* withdrawal—65 and 56 percent, respectively. Remarkably, 27 percent favored the use of nuclear weapons to win the war as late as March 1968.[85]

The surveys of opinion about the war seemed to describe two different kinds of opposition. There was the antiwar crowd that opposed the Indochina intervention on moral grounds, and there was a growing number of Americans who regarded the cost of the war—particularly the cost in the lives of the U.S. servicemen—as not worthwhile. The moral arguments of the antiwar students apparently failed to convince a majority of Americans of their outrage (the protestors themselves averaged only a 28 percent "favorable" rating in 1968), even among many who opposed the war.[86] "Disenchantment with the war is based on our visible lack of success in winning it," concluded Howard Schuman, who conducted the large Detroit Area Survey in 1971. "More and more Americans now think our intervention was a military mistake, and now want to forget the whole thing."[87] The British journalist Godfrey Hodgson observed that the opposition to the war mainly grew when American citizens "could see that it was affecting their own lives" and made, with a "large dose of sheer gruff impatience and irritation," the judgment pragmatically "and not out of any sense of moral guilt that the war was a mistake."[88]

Hodgson points out one of the most interesting findings of the Detroit survey, which was the absence of concern about the Vietnamese as a matter of morality or as a reason to end the war. That finding is indeed striking. Of those who were in favor of a quick end to the war—that is, the "doves"—less than half (42 percent) cited the war's casualties as a reason. Of the entire sample of doves alone, 30 percent cited death and harm coming to American soldiers as a reason, and another 7 percent cited "people killed and injured" without specifying who, exactly, they were concerned about. Three percent mentioned the death of, and injuries to, both Americans and Vietnamese as a reason to end the war. In this dovish segment of this large survey, zero (statistically) mentioned death or injury to the Vietnamese alone as a reason to end the war. In a separate sampling of sociology students at the University of Michigan, 10 percent mentioned casualties among Vietnamese only as a reason to stop the war.[89] (Another 1968 poll conducted by Lou Harris found 4 percent were opposed because of the killing of Vietnamese.)[90] As for other reasons to end the war, among the more prominent mentioned was that the conflict was a civil war, and of those, as Hodgson puts it, "84 percent of the Detroiters turned out on further analysis to mean, 'We should get out because *they* are causing *us* trouble.'"[91] Schuman frames this neatly by noting that such a pragmatic outlook "explains why the Tet offensive had such a disastrous effect on public opinion while the My Lai massacre caused hardly a ripple in the polls."[92]

Lyndon Johnson and his top advisers were certainly sensitive to public opinion; the *Pentagon Papers* relay a constant undercurrent of anxiety about what the public would accept in the way of escalation, which was at root a calculation about U.S. casualties. While more obviously alert to the rising criticism of the war in the elite media than in the street protests, the inner circle of decision makers felt the impact of both. Until 1968, electoral gains for antiwar candidates were minimal, but the trends were beginning to display skepticism about the war even before LBJ withdrew from the presidential race in March of that year, when he faced formidable challenges on the war from Eugene McCarthy and Robert F. Kennedy, both Democratic senators. The fractious divisions within the Democratic Party, while dramatic, clearly did not reflect the opinion of the whole electorate. Ronald Reagan, for example, elected governor of California in 1966 in part as a reaction to the Berkeley Free Speech Movement, was already mounting a national presence in 1968, and Nixon—ambiguous about Vietnam but with impeccable anticommunist credentials—and Wallace together garnered 57 percent of the vote in the fall. Even in an atmosphere of rising crisis and bitter divisions over the war, the silent majority exerted its electoral power on behalf of the more anticommunist leaders. And this continued into the Nixon years. Nixon, far more than Johnson, made the antiwar movement an object of scorn and was able to depict the debate about the war as one of "honor" versus "defeat," with the silent majority arrayed against dark forces of revolt and chaos. He understood that this majority wanted to punish the Vietnamese communists and deny them victory, but with a minimum cost to Americans, especially American lives. The cost to the Vietnamese was rarely if ever a consideration for Nixon or his popular base of support, apart from the largely cynical pose that the South Vietnamese would benefit from his policies.

The silent majority, then, acted powerfully in the voting booth to brace the general policy of anticommunism in Southeast Asia that American leaders pursued, with some splits over the scale of the war effort, the pace of withdrawal, and the way the war should be concluded. The extent to which most Americans ever registered doubts or shame about the treatment of the Vietnamese (or Laotians or Cambodians) is not fully known, but the evidence points to scant concern about the violence or its effects on the local people. The supposition that the American military was there to defend free peoples and to defeat and roll back the communist challenge was an article of faith for this majority, and the effects of the war on the people of Indochina were, in this calculation, seemingly worth the desired outcome. Even if the news media were largely compliant with government views, and the "living room war" is more legend than fact, the American public could not claim ignorance of what was transpiring in the war.

Bringing the War Home

The comforting assumptions about the rightness of the American cause in Vietnam and the acceptability of the violence were directly confronted by the antiwar movement and a growing chorus of returned veterans whose voices were angry, accusatory, and persistent. This aspect of the Vietnam experience sets it apart from other wars, too—not merely that there were sizable protests, but that some in those movements used violence as a means of shocking the public into recognition of the war's violence.

For the most part, protest was peaceful if occasionally strident. It was increasingly intertwined with more general counterculture outbursts and black activism, and in both, protest demonstrations frequently offended traditional public sensibilities (but these were nonetheless nonviolent). Violence began to appear in demonstrations and other actions as the violence of the war itself rose and as the local and federal police took more aggressive tactics of their own. But the key linkage is between the violence that began to appear in the race struggle of the mid-1960s and the antiwar movement.[93]

The reactions of police and white supremacist groups is particularly important here, because the nonviolent civil rights movement—while sometimes provocative—was met with very harsh reprisals and little federal protection from those reprisals. The surge in violent street protests and what amounted to a black insurrection stirred a national dialogue about race *and* violence (and new federal initiatives) which was sustained in the stormy antiwar atmosphere of the late 1960s and early 1970s.

Most notable in the serious discourse about violence was a point that militants were attempting to make throughout both the civil rights and antiwar movements: that the violence perpetrated by the state at home or abroad was either hidden or wrapped in moral justifications obscuring its reality, but popular uprisings that used violence were damned as pathological or insurrectionary.[94] The black violence seemed to be a breakthrough of sorts in cracking apart this mold. By the time of the King and Kennedy assassinations of 1968, followed soon by the confrontation at the Chicago convention, violence as a tactic of the antiwar movement became more and more plausible. "Violence was endlessly talked about, feared, skirted, and flirted with," wrote Todd Gitlin, an SDS leader in the 1960s. "The social psychologist Kenneth Keniston astutely wrote around this time that 'the issue of violence is to this generation what the issue of sex was to the Victorian world' . . . violence organized the movement's fantasy life."[95] From the "police riot" of Chicago, campuses witnessed more than one hundred bombings, burnings, and other acts of violence against property, with very rare instances of accidental killings. But the militancy was high, particularly after the invasion of Cambodia in 1970 and the killing of protestors by the National Guard at Kent State University. The Weather Underground, an offshoot of SDS, took this to another level of "revolutionary" violence, seeking to bring the war home in a series of confrontations involving gunplay or bombings.

Perhaps the most astonishing displays, however, were those staged by Vietnam War veterans. With their own protest group, Vietnam Veterans against the War, growing to more than 200,000 members, the veterans became a formidable presence in American society from an early point in the war. Their credentials were unassailable; where campus radicals could be dismissed as pampered intellectuals, veterans had a very different image—working and middle class, once conventionally patriotic, and thoroughly authentic. By 1969, they were taking an active part in organizing their own actions, and many of them were startling. In 1970, thousands participated in "Operation RAW" that sought to recreate battle conditions in Vietnam for public display in small town America; even without weapons or actual violence, their presentation was indeed raw and meant to shock. Acting out search-and-destroy tactics, they distributed fliers in many places, like one in western New Jersey that read: "A U.S. INFANTRY COMPANY JUST CAME THROUGH HERE. If you had been Vietnamese, we might have burned your house . . . shot your dog . . . shot you . . . raped your wife and daughter . . . turned you over to your government for torture. . . . If it doesn't bother you that American soldiers do these things every day to the Vietnamese simply because they are 'Gooks,' then picture yourself as one of the silent victims."[96] To this kind of protest, veterans added a "winter soldier" investigation—a public hearing in which war veterans told stories of atrocities they had witnessed or participated in, an effort to disturb the complacency of the American public. The testimony included stories of unwarranted killing and also rape and torture, and the refrain that mistreatment of Vietnamese had been a part of training from the time they were in boot camp. The hearings, held in Detroit and with a smaller event in Washington, D.C., failed to gain much national media attention but did introduce this narrative into the antiwar movement and caught the attention of antiwar politicians.* Later in 1971, a sizable rally in Washington, complete with guerrilla

---

* It is noteworthy that the main hearings were in Detroit and earned considerable coverage from the *Detroit Free Press*, one of the city's major dailies, in December and early January 1970–71. Just a few months later, the Detroit Area Survey was conducted, and registered little concern for Vietnamese lives. This "natural experiment" is possibly the best evidence of indifference or even hostility toward the victims of the war.

theater, a respectful march to Arlington National Cemetery, a "surrender" of 75 vets as self-confessed "war criminals" at the Pentagon, and lobbying Congress, brought all the tactics directly to the seat of power.

At each place, beginning with the earliest veterans' actions, pro-war veterans of the Second World War and ordinary Americans often ridiculed the Vietnam vets like they did other protestors: as traitors, tools of the communists, or even frauds. At the April 1971 actions in Washington, Nixon apparently "leaked a rumor that two-thirds of the [Vietnam Veteran Against the War] were imposters." Nixon also speedily sought an injunction to deny permission to the veterans to camp on the National Mall, which backfired politically.[97] But it is nonetheless striking how badly treated the veteran protestors were, given the sanctified place American society holds for those who served in the armed forces. It has been much remarked upon that veterans were sometimes confronted by antiwar activists, but far more significant, and far more pervasive, was the indifference of the public generally or, even more notably, the hostility to those who spoke out against the war policies they personally witnessed or implemented. "I never had experiences like, for example, being spit on or called a baby killer or anything like that. On the other hand, I was just kind of ignored," recalled a medic in Vietnam. "I really thought, I guess, when I first came home people would want to know about my experience. . . . They didn't."[98] Robert Jay Lifton, the Yale psychiatrist, held numerous sessions with returning veterans and reported one vet's reaction to indifference, a "rage associated with the man's telling his story of what he had experienced in Vietnam—to a considerable extent laying himself bare—and then being rebuffed. This rage was directed not so much toward war supporters or political opponents but toward those who 'don't give a damn.'"[99] The federal authorities carried out a campaign of harassment, infiltration, and arrests of veteran activists that struck many as a kind of double jeopardy—abused by the war, and abused when they returned.*

---

* The most direct consequence of violence in Vietnam for the vets, apart from those who were physically handicapped, was post-traumatic stress disorder (PTSD), which afflicted more than 30 percent of those who served there, six times the normal incidence of PTSD among the male population. Yet the Veterans Administration hospitals handling these men treated them for years as cases of insanity or with high doses of sedatives and other psychotropic drugs, in effect denying the syndrome and its causes. Like the effects of Agent Orange, the PTSD epidemic was largely hidden from public view during the war.

The vets joined the campus radicals in the "fantasy" of violence, the small acts of damaging property of the government, universities, or defense contractors, and the symbolic representation of violence to confront American complacency in hundreds if not thousands of acts that were reported and analyzed in the news media rather endlessly. For many veterans and activists on the militant left, political violence was viewed as redemptive, an act not only of protest but of expiation for American society's sins of violence against the third world and the long-repressed minorities—a public act of defiance and an exemplar. It is not too much to see the use of violence as regenerative in intent, too, that destruction (of the slum, the recruiting station, the weapons lab) would force society to recreate a different kind of world.

That Americans generally detested this civil violence—whatever its purpose—is well known, as is their distaste for the protestors and the renegade veterans. (There were violent rampages by pro-war militants as well, physically attacking antiwar protestors.) It is often said that Americans grew to oppose the war despite the protests; indeed, every time a major demonstration occurred, support for the war increased. This assessment of the link between protest and public opinion ignores the more encompassing change wrought by the cultural upheaval of the time, one that profoundly affected major institutions of society—the news media and universities especially—and introduced entirely new cultural forms and messages in a uniquely popular way.[100] What was for many years called the "Vietnam syndrome," a vaguely articulated inhibition on America's willingness to commit violence abroad to pursue its interests, grew mainly from the political residue of the cultural revolution of the late 1960s and 1970s, much of which was fueled by sharply critical denunciations of the war and the war makers. The protest movements also raised as never before the charge of American imperialism, of violent mistreatment of third world peoples for the pursuit of corporate interests (rather than virtuous anticommunism). This caused a disruption of the Cold War consensus and has been a point of political contention ever since. And while the broader public did not embrace this critique, it likely affected their view of the war and the condition of American society. As Vietnam grew more unpopular and cultural and political outbursts became more confrontational, the public frequently lumped it all together simply as "a mess."

Even with this new awareness of "imperialism" and the wretched consequences of the war for Americans, the endless debates about violence as well as the testimony of vets about the war's costs for Vietnamese, indifference to civilian casualties or the rightness of American intentions in Vietnam was rarely shaken. Graham Greene, who may have penned the most important novel about the American experience in Vietnam long before the commitment of troops and prestige, famously wrote about the harm that American innocence caused. Twenty-five years later, Ronald Reagan recharged his political career on a revanchist sentiment about the war, telling Americans that they were robbed of victory by appeasement at home and abroad and promising a morally righteous revival of America's promise as a "city on a hill." Reagan in many respects epitomized the denial of American culpability in Vietnam. When demonstrators challenged the ruling orthodoxy about the war when he was governor of California, he vowed, "If it takes a bloodbath, let's get it over with. No more appeasement."[101] He was always a hawk on the war, favoring more bombing and whatever the military sought to win. Later he spoke repeatedly of the "noble cause" of Vietnam and the betrayal inherent in the peace accords, and that the only thing immoral about the war was not allowing our "gentle heroes" to win it. At a Veterans' Day speech at the Vietnam War Memorial in 1988, Reagan, then in his final year as president, furthered his appropriation of the hero: "For too long a time, they stood in a chill wind, as if on a winter night's watch. And in that night, their deeds spoke to us, but we knew them not. And their voices called to us, but we heard them not." This became the defining perspective of not only the remembrance of the war—the nobility of the American warrior, and his betrayal—but of military and foreign policy, namely, that wars should only be fought with both a minimum of American sacrifice and the intention to win. Reagan's insistence that the only thing wrong with the war was political leaders' failure of will to win resonated deeply with the American people, absolving any lingering sense of doubt about that tragic errand to the wilderness. With the heroes honored and the vanquished forgotten, America was ready to move on to the next frontier.

CHAPTER 6

The Reagan Doctrine

Savage War by Proxy

For all his bluster about the use of military power and his plaintive, post hoc calls to action in Vietnam, President Ronald Reagan was restrained in deploying American troops and even more cautious in committing them to combat. His military forays (in addition to bombing Libya) amounted to two ventures. The first was in Lebanon, where he deployed peacekeeping troops in 1983, only to see 300 of them killed in two separate terrorist assaults. He response was to "cut and run," to use the phrase familiar to his followers but rarely applied to him, actions doubtlessly emboldening politically violent groups in the region who must have reasoned that if Reagan could so easily be dislodged and neutered, then Americans were unlikely to take up the fight against them. Within hours of the Beirut debacle—the second bombing there took the lives of 270 marines—Reagan launched an invasion of the tiny Caribbean island of Grenada to depose a leftist leader and protect American students. This action, following policies meant to destabilize the government, was the 135th time U.S. forces had intervened in Latin America and the Caribbean. Supposedly a shot over the bow of Cuba, the message was lost on Castro but was far more successful in diverting the American news media and public from the deadly failure in Lebanon.

These two incidents aside, Reagan's preferred method of military intervention was to use other people to do the fighting, and he took aim at Marxist governments with these would-be liberators. With fulsome support, he set out to undo the Soviet puppet state in Afghanistan (and Soviet troops occupying it), the Vietnamese control over Cambodia, the Sandinista regime in Nicaragua, and the postcolonial state of Angola. The leaders of the last two were liberators themselves, overthrowing centuries of colonial or neocolonial dictators and appearing to enjoy considerable popularity and legitimacy. The Cambodian fiasco was a direct consequence of the U.S. war in Indochina, a war in which Cambodia was fully in play. And the Soviet occupation of Afghanistan, while clearly a catastrophe of their own making, was one of the reverberations of the 1979 revolution in Iran, another signal event with American fingerprints all over it.

In each of these venues, the ideology of rollback was paramount. What came to be known as the Reagan Doctrine—the attempt to overthrow regimes of a pinkish hue by supporting, if not creating, violent insurgencies—grew like a malignancy from the frustrated rollback ideologies of anticommunism's heyday. Unable to commit U.S. troops to such missions because of the failure in Vietnam, Reagan backed the *contras* in Nicaragua, *mujaheddin* in Afghanistan, UNITA in Angola, and a bizarre coalition that included the Khmer Rouge and Pol Pot in Cambodia to undertake what he was unwilling to do with U.S. soldiers: to overthrow these states and usher in new regimes that would be friendly to U.S. interests and "freedom." What once could be achieved with covert CIA coups, as in Iran in 1953, Guatemala in 1954, and Congo in 1961, now required a more sizable undertaking, one that would be aided by U.S. covert operations but also demanded very large sums of money, arms, and political legitimacy. These Reagan willingly supplied, sometimes illegally. But like the attempts at rollback in Korea and Vietnam, the consequences of this ersatz intervention were ruinous for the venues of conflict, not least in their human costs.

REAGAN'S ROLLBACK

The inauguration of Ronald Reagan came at a low point for Americans' sense of their global role. The sting of the Vietnam disaster remained fresh in everyone's memory; only a few years had passed since the shocking sight of Americans and Vietnamese evacuating onto a helicopter from a Saigon rooftop. In Tehran, Americans were seized in

November 1979 and held captive by the Iranian revolutionaries until the day of Reagan's swearing in as president. Meanwhile, Senator Frank Church's hearings about CIA turpitude highlighted a brief but intense period of self-criticism and introspection that the public generally found distasteful. Those events, coupled with what the right wing darkly (and erroneously) warned was decisive Soviet nuclear prowess, left much of America feeling humiliated, set upon, perhaps itching for a fight. In popular films and novels, the itch was apparent: the ambiguity of the Vietnam experience in *The Deer Hunter* or the manic *Dispatches* gave way to the "Rambo" series—in which, in its "cinematic wish fulfillment fantasy, America gets to go back and finish the war that the bleeding hearts and bureaucrats wouldn't let us win the first time around"—and seemingly critical treatments like Oliver Stone's *Platoon* that nonetheless conformed closely to the frontier myth.[1] (*Rambo* was, no less, a captivity narrative, the deepest scar on the national psyche.) At the same time, a new prominence was accorded right-wing evangelicals, reliable anticommunists but with much more visibility in the 1970s and 1980s—partly in response to the 1960s counterculture—and this braced the militant foreign policy wielded by Reagan, with special emphasis on support for Israel as the bulwark against Muslims in the Holy Land. The long obsession with China gradually gave way to a new attention to the "clash of civilizations" in the Middle East.

That sentiment in part led Reagan to deploy marines in Beirut and to approve Israel's invasion of Lebanon, a deviation from the long-standing Republican aloofness from Israel's cause and a new alignment with Likud that would prove momentous over the coming years. Far more quietly, Reagan also lent enormous resources to Iraq to turn back Iran's threat to defeat Saddam Hussein, who had invaded Iran in 1980 only to meet surprising resistance and then, by 1982, likely defeat without American help. Reagan's substantial aid to Saddam—$5 billion in financial credits, political legitimacy and cover, crucial military intelligence, and, finally, the reflagging of oil tankers and a small naval war with Iran—saved the Iraqi dictator and enlarged his ambition in the Gulf. Not only had Reagan nourished Saddam's expansionism, but he made an enemy of Iran (or merely reinforced the regime's convictions regarding the Great Satan). Once Iran recovered from the immensely bloody conflict—nearly one million died—and continued to feel rebuffed by the United States, it began to assert itself against American interests throughout the region.

The Reagan Doctrine was applied elsewhere, however. Sensing, perhaps, the sullen public mood, Reagan provided the stirring call to arms, answered not by Americans but by patchwork bands of "freedom fighters," religious extremists, mercenaries, common criminals, *genocidaires*, and proxies of the old guard. Wars were launched to unseat the left-leaning governments, conflicts that in some cases lasted for more than a decade, leaving each country reeling from the havoc—many thousands (or tens or hundreds of thousands) who were killed, even more made homeless or refugees; economies left in ruins; spillover to neighboring countries; and social disintegration that opened floodgates of disease, criminality, terrorism, and unimaginable waste.

The doctrine emerged gradually from a muddle of anticommunist sentiments and exaggerated fears of growing Soviet influence in the third world. Moderates in the State Department tried to cool the fervor of William Casey at the CIA and the likes of Oliver North on the White House staff, though the latter typically won the debate; this policy mishmash led, as they often do, to blunders and dashed expectations. It was only late in his presidency that Reagan laid claim to an operational philosophy of rollback, even as some of its venues were demonstrating the doctrine's unsuitability. But it nonetheless became one of the signature policies of his presidency. "The attractiveness of the Reagan doctrine was, in large measure, its apparent compatibility with these limitations" exacted by the Vietnam experience, wrote one foreign policy veteran in 1989. "This version of globalism would require very little treasure and, *even more significant, no American blood at all*."[2] It was also rhetorically attractive, as rollback generally is to American audiences. Reagan captured this sentiment neatly in a 1983 speech: "The goal of the free world must no longer be stated in the negative, that is, resistance to Soviet expansionism. The goal of the free world must instead be stated in the affirmative. We must go on the offensive with a forward strategy for freedom."[3] So the old and bitter battle between containment and rollback was joined again, this time with rollback gaining the upper hand.

Afghanistan has long been showcased as the trophy of the Reagan Doctrine. Alarmed by growing unrest in its "ally" state, the Soviet Union saw in 1979 what was occurring in Iran—a full-scale revolution—as a danger not only to Kabul but as a mortal threat to the largely Muslim region of the USSR bordering Afghanistan and Iran. The Soviets, with the decrepit, Stalinesque Leonid Brezhnev still in charge, intervened in their typically clumsy and brutal fashion, sending 80,000 troops in at the end of 1979 to occupy the country and to quell a simmering rebellion, which was in part a revolt of countryside traditionalists against urban-based modernizers. The invasion was a fool's errand from the start; some analysts have speculated that the United States even lured the Soviets into Afghanistan by supporting the traditional tribal leaders. This religious, antimodern resistance, the *mujaheddin*, quickly grew, fighting what seemed to be insurmountable odds but trading on a long history of battling invaders, and was soon joined by Muslims from many other countries in what was heralded as an epic *jihad*.

Reagan was actually a bit half-hearted in supporting the *mujaheddin*; he was doing little more than Carter did in the final year of his presidency. By 1986, with considerable congressional prompting, Reagan had finally upped the ante with a sizable, mainly covert operation to funnel billions of dollars worth of weapons to the anti-Soviet forces, create training and operations bases in Pakistan (requiring the United States to back the military dictatorship of Muhammad Zia-ul-Haq),* and provide other logistical support to the rebels. By the end of the decade, the Soviets—who actually sought a way out much sooner, in the early 1980s, but hadn't the wherewithal to leave and declare victory—were beaten. It was a devastating defeat for the USSR, though hardly the sweeping triumph claimed by Reagan's minions: the U.S. role was important, but defeat was visible before the major U.S. arms shipments came. The collapse of the Soviet Union, which some attribute to the Afghan debacle, was due to a multiplicity of causes in which the Afghan war played only a minor part. More important was what transpired after the Soviets left and American backing dried up: years of chaos and warlordism, a lively export engine supplying the West with opium and heroin, and, by 1996, after years of civil war, the horrifying ascension of the Taliban to power. Reagan never had a plan for

* The U.S. promotion of General Zia had consequences that well matched those in Afghanistan, for Zia aggressively promoted Islamic education, law, and practice, demoting in effect the secular, common law bequeathed by British colonists and setting Pakistan on a road toward religious militancy. This resulted in strong alliances with the Afghani Taliban, the Kashmiri militants, and other extremists.

a post-Soviet Afghanistan, and the consequences of this sheer neglect were the years of a failed state topped by years of one of the most repressive regimes in memory, one that by 1998 warmly welcomed and hosted Osama bin Laden and his al Qaeda headquarters. No one knows how many Afghans died in their resistance to the Soviet Union; the number is in the hundreds of thousands, possibly more than one million, if including civilians and fighters alike.

Nicaragua was meant to be another trophy. The United States had dominated Central America for decades and freely intervened in Nicaragua several times; once it had captured the nationalist hero Sandino, the symbolic patron of the revolutionaries who in 1979 overthrew the classic Latin *caudillo* Anastasio Somoza and created a state that was by turns democratic and intimidating. The outcome rang alarms in Washington because of the fear that another Cuba was in the offing. The Sandinistas appeared to be aiding rebels in El Salvador and were eventually recipients of Soviet assistance themselves. The mood attending U.S. policy in Central America was fractious, and the Reagan team was unremitting in its hostility to the leftists, an attitude emblemized by Jeanne Kirkpatrick's implication that the Maryknoll nuns murdered in El Salvador by the regime's death squads deserved their fate, and, later, by Reagan's backing of the genocidal Ríos Montt regime in Guatemala. Thus commenced from the first weeks of Reagan's tenure an attempt to dislodge the Sandinistas. The Reagan administration essentially created the *contras*, a ragtag band of opponents of the Sandinistas, who launched violent raids into Nicaragua, sometimes killing civilians, engaging in drug trafficking, and besetting the communities in Honduras where they set up camps. "Hoping to show a wavering rural population that the Sandinistas could not establish effective sovereignty," noted one historian's account of the U.S. objectives, "the Contras razed cooperatives, schools, health clinics, and power stations and tortured, raped, and murdered civilians, including foreigners who were helping to rebuild Nicaragua."[4] The Sandinistas were largely incompetent and sometimes doctrinaire rulers, but they were not totalitarians, nor did they threaten neighbors, as Reagan alleged. They were eventually voted out of office—totalitarians generally do not hold elections, of course—and then returned to power by the vote some years later. Unlike some of the other venues of the Reagan Doctrine, "in Nicaragua, aid was to be provided to a resistance that lacked broad support in the population, was led by members of a despised military, and was seen as the creation of the United States."[5] Throughout the 1980s, Nicaragua was plagued by the turmoil created by the contras, isolated and impoverished; Honduras in particular also suffered profoundly adverse effects. Drug trafficking and gang violence were among the furies afflicting Central America after its many years of conflict. The *contras'* war took 30,000 lives.

Angola was the other major venue of the Reagan Doctrine. It had long been a Portuguese colony, and indigenous movements challenged and then upended the colonial order following a coup in Lisbon in 1974. The rebels soon were fighting with each other, but the Popular Movement for the Liberation of Angola (MPLA) emerged victorious and was widely recognized internationally as the legitimate government. But because it was aided by Cuba and hosted other liberation movements aimed at apartheid South Africa, it earned the enmity of America's right wing, which preferred the National Union for the Total Independence of Angola (UNITA), headed by Jonas Savimbi, which had been aided by South Africa. When Reagan came to the White House, a deadly civil war was still under way, complicated by South Africa's recalcitrance over neighboring Namibia, which it controlled. The rollback advocates in the administration chafed at congressional restrictions that limited aid to Savimbi, who became the "freedom fighter" par excellence in southern Africa; the ban was finally lifted—partly due to promises of diplomacy—and tens of millions of dollars in aid flowed to UNITA. "Under the guise of 'constructive engagement,' the United States improved diplomatic and economic relations with South Africa," wrote scholar Michael McFaul, "tacitly sanctioning and circuitously subsidizing South African operations in Angola."[6] So the lethal aid to Savimbi was not only about fighting a communist-tinged state (Angola had Soviet aid and advisers as well as Cubans) but about serving as a guarantor of South Africa's security. The diplomatic track, which eventually did get South Africa out of Namibia in exchange for a withdrawal of Cubans from Angola, was opposed by the rollback partisans, who actively disrupted diplomacy to support South Africa's military incursions into Angola. Savimbi himself was revealed as an authoritarian with a deplorable record of human rights violations; as an obituary in 2002 put it, "For the past 10 years, using the proceeds of smuggled diamonds from eastern and central Angola, he fought an increasingly pointless and personal bush war against the elected government in which hundreds of thousands of peasants were killed, wounded, displaced, or starved to death."[7] The Reagan aid to UNITA merely prolonged the civil war, delayed the resolution of the Namibian impasse, and resulted in colossal human losses—as many as 1.2 million dead and 1.5 million displaced. As is always the case with the Reagan Doctrine, some of the worst consequences took place after he left office.[8]

Afghanistan, Nicaragua, and Angola were the three rings of the Reagan Doctrine (Cambodia was "a minor element of a secondary issue"),[9] and none turned out well. Each place suffered continuing civil war, social dissolution, and large-scale suffering as a consequence of the actions of the American-backed insurgencies. The U.S. culpability varied greatly from case to case. It seems fairly clear that the scale of misery in Afghanistan would not have differed much with an absence of U.S. support for the *mujaheddin*; whereas in Nicaragua and Angola, U.S. meddling was directly correlated to the high civilian tolls. The ill effects of U.S. intervention, including the extraordinary numbers of casualties, weigh heavily in the history of American foreign policy.

REAGAN AND THE REAGAN DOCTRINE

What the American public made of these surrogate wars varied according to the political salience of the specific country and recent events. In general, Americans held slightly favorable attitudes toward supporting aid and arms, particularly if compared with sending U.S. troops. But when asked (in 1986) specifically about economic and military aid to the U.S.-backed insurgents in Angola, Afghanistan, and Nicaragua, only 24 percent supported economic *and* military aid, with nearly half opposed to any assistance. The ambivalence is partially about involvement in the world generally, with "internationalists" favoring assistance more than those who might be labeled isolationist.[10] A sizable "solidarity" movement in the United States opposing aid to the *contras* raised the visibility of the war as well as the human costs, and this may account for *contra* aid being more unpopular than the support of the Afghan rebels and of UNITA in Angola. But *contra* aid was soiled by illegality (the Iran-*contra* scandal) and by the nature of the *contras* themselves, hardly paragons of rebel virtue, and this was more evident to the American public than the human failings of other Reagan favorites. The Afghan issue was linked directly to bad behavior by the Soviets and hence easier to support. Angola's troubles were remote and difficult to understand, and Americans were at that time viewing South Africa with growing distaste, thanks in part to a well-organized anti-apartheid movement on campuses. Those "for" and "against" the policies subsumed under the banner of the Reagan Doctrine tended always to follow political lines, however, and rarely evinced any concerns about the enormous human costs of those wars.

Reagan himself marched to an uncertain drummer. While his anti-communist and pro-freedom rhetoric always soared, it was his underlings who agitated for the riskier and violence-prone policies—Casey, North, defense secretary Caspar Weinberger, aide Elliott Abrams, and the like. "In truth, President Reagan's involvement in the doctrine that bears his name was episodic at best," wrote James Scott in the most complete account of the policy. "Most of the time, President Reagan was a spectator to disputes between advisers."[11] He was active only for a short period of time in his second term, long after the conflicts were essentially decided or close to resolution. And soon after, he embraced Mikhail Gorbachev's initiative to end the Cold War, going far beyond what traditional anticommunism (or his right-wing base) would support, or indeed his own tentative steps before. This was done in part to rebuild his presidency after the Iran-*contra* scandal shook it so badly. The irony was that the most dicey gambit of the doctrine—the sale of missiles to Khomeini's Iran and the illegal diversion of money for the *contras*—would be the piece that necessitated a reversal of anticommunist zeal in order to preserve the Reagan presidency and legacy.

But the legacy did survive. One of its most resilient features was Reagan's capacity to cast himself in the role of the frontier hero, of course, even as he had no credentials on that score, no military service or anything resembling it, no actual encounter with the American or global frontier in his past life. It was a completely manufactured image. But the rhetoric and the go-it-alone tough talk (burnished by his Santa Barbara ranch with all the trappings) reestablished the frontier myth after its years of hardship with the loss of Indochina and the hostage-taking in Iran. He did so not only by talking about freedom fighters and Moscow's evil empire but also by a specific discourse of betrayal and civilizational conflict. He fit the heroic trope of working outside his own system, which itself was filled with cowards and inert officials, and nimbly used that as a lifelong and popular stance. Few presidents in modern memory mobilized mythic belief as Reagan did, and it was thoroughly imbued with the images and norms of the frontier (so much so that the "shining city on a hill" phrase is often attributed to him by his ideological progeny). His wars were remarkably limited affairs, at least for Americans, if wholly savage. The "bonanza" sprang not only from Reaganomics at home, but Reaganomics abroad—specifically, and fatefully, the global policy reversal on third world development that undermined years of steady success via the building of indigenous industry and human capital, to a "free market" ideology that enabled American corporations to buy and control resources and industries while public industries were sold off and institutions like education and health care were starved of funds. The results of these "structural adjustment policies" were setbacks for much of the third world, Africa and South America in particular. Conflict, poverty, and epidemics in many of these places were outcomes of this intrusive and mendacious ideology.

Throughout his political career, Reagan reasserted the American beliefs in global resources being ours for the taking, in military power, and in the intrinsic goodness and prerogatives of America. The Reagan Doctrine combined all of these qualities. He was also a transitional figure of sorts from the multilateralism and global leadership shaped by FDR and Truman, with its emphasis on collective security, containment of communism, and state-led development in the global south, to an ever more unilateralist outlook that renewed the gold rush mentalities of frontier expansionism and gradually recognized a new "savage" in Muslim militants.

It is not surprising that the American public was frequently thrilled by Reagan's tough talk and embrace of getting rich. By effortlessly placing these policies in appealing language—"We have every right to dream heroic dreams," he said in his first inaugural address—he renewed the moral righteousness that was squandered in Vietnam. That two of his next three successors would aim to emulate Reagan virtually guaranteed that the errand to the wilderness would avidly be pursued. And, like those that came before, the costs would be high.

CHAPTER 7

Iraq

The Twenty Years' War

A merica's entry into the Persian Gulf in 1990 was the first large-scale military intervention in the region and the first anywhere since the Indochina wars. The war to remove Iraq from its occupation of Kuwait in 1991—Operation Desert Storm—was followed by a dozen years of U.S. calls for the overthrow of the Iraqi state, economic sanctions, forceful isolation and inspections, and military skirmishes. Those twelve years gave way in March 2003 to an invasion of Iraq, allegedly to protect America from Iraq's supposed capability to attack with chemical, biological, or nuclear weapons. Operation Iraqi Freedom did destroy the regime of Saddam Hussein, but in so doing it unleashed an orgy of violence that has caused hundreds of thousands of Iraqi deaths, millions of displaced people, and a society in shambles. The war involved more than one million American soldiers, sailors, marines, and airmen, trillions of dollars in expenditures, thousands of deaths of Americans, and uncertain political consequences, and continues to this day, spanning the last decade of the old millennium and the first decade of the new, a twenty-year foreign venture for the United States and a devastating reality for Iraqis.

Like Korea and Vietnam, the Iraq War was a response to the injustice and disarray left by colonialism; and like the other wars, it was much more. Where Korea and Vietnam were anticommunist crusades, the Iraq War, particularly the main phase since 2003, was a retort to Islamic militancy and the "clash of civilizations" that the terrorist attacks of September 11, 2001, seemed to symbolize. Among the other causes and rationales are the protection of friends and allies in the region, especially the Gulf monarchies of Saudi Arabia and Kuwait, drawing a "line in the sand" against Arab or Muslim aggression against the West, and transforming the Middle East into states more cooperative with the United States and possibly more democratically governed. Above all, the wars were about that most precious resource of the global hinterlands, cheap petroleum.

Iraq has provided another step in America's fateful evolution and attempt to extend the frontier. It has been, as President George W. Bush implied, a historic mission to free Arab society, bringing the light and fruits of Western civilization. Less overtly, the wars continued a century-long contest for the region's vast resources. These missions were pursued through savage war, sustained applications of deadly force. What the consequences are for the civilizational struggle or the control and utility of oil will not be discernible for years. But the human costs are increasingly known (and increasingly contested), leading America into a dead end: the Iraq wars signal the closing of the global frontier, the incapacity of the United States to sustain a wasteful ideology and lifestyle with wasteful habits and wars.

OIL, SADDAM, AND WAR

The twenty years of conflict over Iraq have been nested in a delusional set of rationales about U.S. involvement. The primacy of oil has at every turn been denied as the raison d'être of such attentiveness to Iraq. This diversion to other reasons—balancing Iran, supporting Israel, protecting the sovereignty of friendly governments, promoting human rights and democratic values—has been practiced by a wide range of politicians and intellectuals, left, right, and center, with infrequent reference to the central fact of the Persian Gulf, namely, that it possesses an exceptionally large amount of petroleum and is controlled by states harboring various forms of hostility to the West and the United States in particular. That this region has been resistant to U.S.-led economic globalization braces the mind-set of U.S. policy elites. But it is the singular significance of oil that forms the backdrop, the incentives, the foundation, and the near-hysteria associated with the region (e.g., animus toward Iranians, slavishness to Saudis), and the primary factor explaining the unshakable obsession with Iraq. Whatever one makes of the outcome of this long war, the costs and its rewards, it has been done for oil.

The oil era in the Persian Gulf began in Iran in 1908. The rights to produce oil were granted by the failing Qajar dynasty to a British entrepreneur, William D'Arcy, who struck wells in Masjid-i-Sulaiman in the Zagros Mountains close by the Persian Gulf. Within thirty years, oil was discovered in Saudi Arabia, Kuwait, and Iraq. The United States did not have the footing in the region afforded to the European victors of the First World War, France and Britain particularly, but the major oil companies—most adeptly the Rockefeller combine and its many Standard Oil companies—made their way to the Arabian peninsula to stake a claim and form the Arabian-American Oil Company, Aramco. Aramco drilled and exported Saudi crude beginning in the 1930s, and won concessions from other, smaller sheikdoms in the Gulf. This very profitable arrangement was reinforced near the end of the Second World War when President Franklin Roosevelt met with Saudi King Abdul Aziz Ibn Saud on a U.S. warship in the Suez Canal and cemented a relationship that became a pillar of American action in the region—namely, American protection of the House of Saud in exchange for preeminent access to Saudi oil.

Franklin D. Roosevelt (FDR) could not foresee the fatefulness of this errand to the desert. The Saudi kingdom was scarcely more than a tribal fiefdom. Iraq, Kuwait, Syria, Palestine, Jordan, and Egypt were all under the "protection" of Britain and France; Arab nationalism was faint and unthreatening. Iran was also under the sway of the Western powers to assure its fealty during the war; Islamic militancy was a barely discernible curiosity. FDR was not favorable to the growing case for a Jewish homeland in Palestine, and thus could not foresee the reverberations of his successor's decision to support the founding of Israel in 1948, a decision that united and gave new meaning to the Arab *umma*, or nation. But Roosevelt's compact with the Saudi king was merely the culmination of thirty years of growing involvement and growing needs: oil was one decisive factor in the world wars, and the United States, once the largest producer of crude oil, was losing its capacity to meet growing domestic demand. The juggernaut of the world oil market was in motion.

Iraq was a principal venue of the oil speculation from early on. The country had been formed from three *vilayets* or provinces of the Ottoman Empire after the conclusion of the First World War. Basra, Baghdad, and Mosul, encompassing three cities and many towns and villages over a large, Texas-sized mountain and desert landscape, were forged together and given a monarch from the Hashemite dynasty, whose authority derived from his being the Sharif, the Mohammad-descended protector of Mecca. Hashemites also populated the new thrones in Jordan (where they remain) and Syria. In fact, the whole of the region, from Morocco to Afghanistan, was a string of monarchies and European guardians, a rickety scheme that soon crumbled with the rise of Arab nationalism. The most prominent of these was the coup in Egypt in 1952 that toppled King Farouk, a cartoonish gourmand, and eventually brought Gamal Abdel Nasser to power. Syrians fought the French for years and finally gained independence in 1946. In Iraq, Faisal, known for his alliance with Lawrence of Arabia during the First World War and briefly king of Syria, was essentially installed as the king of Iraq by the British, who had been granted a mandate in Mesopotamia by the League of Nations to guide Iraq to statehood.* The monarchy finally fell to an army coup in 1958.

By then, Iraqis had established their animus toward British control and indeed had rebelled in 1920, a brief outbreak of violent unrest in largely Sunni areas. The rebellion and subsequent political dynamics were shaped by the colonial history: Ottoman Turkey, the seat of the Sunni Caliph, had empowered the Sunni Arabs over the majority Shia Arabs, and the British continued this favoritism. The Kurds were left to themselves in the northern mountains. But the rebellion was also an occasion for unity of a sort. "Rising anti-British sentiment had been fanned by the nationalists in Baghdad, the *shi'i* religious leaders of the holy cities, and the disaffected mid-Eurphrates tribal leaders," wrote historian Phebe Marr. "All were united by a desire to be free from British rule. A chief feature of the movement was the unprecedented cooperation between the *sunni* and the *shi'i* communities; in Baghdad both used the mosque for anti-British gatherings and speeches, clearly mixing religion and politics."[1]

The British put down the rebellion by bribing sheiks and demonstrating British potency through the use of the military's new air power.

* Faisal was not only a legendary sidekick of T. E. Lawrence but also a serious Arab nationalist, modernizer, and, remarkably, an important Arab bridge to Zionism. Faisal accepted the Balfour Declaration (calling for a Jewish home in Palestine), conditioned on British acceptance of Arab aspirations for nation building, which was not forthcoming. His commitment to Jewish-Arab harmony seemed authentic and visionary. He died in 1933 at age fifty and was succeeded by a much less skilled son and grandson.

The sheiks were also empowered by the British as the link between state and society, rural society most particularly, in a kind of reflection of English political development. Privileging the tribal chiefs in this way had, of course, quite far-reaching consequences long after the British were gone. Exhibiting, moreover, classic orientalism that would later influence or be replicated by U.S. authorities, the British disowned and blocked the political aspirations of the urban elites, who were modernizers, in favor of the sheiks and a romanticized (and infantilized) conception of the Iraqi peasant who required the firm hand of colonial administration. Thus a political architecture was created that relied not only on sheiks and anti-urbanism, but on the Sunni-Shia divisions that would fatefully boomerang in the post-British era.[2]

Shortly after the 1920 rebellion, the British discovered oil near Mosul and Kirkuk, and the importance of Iraq was assured. Through the 1920s, a complex series of negotiations resulted in an agreement dividing up the oil-rich regions, with American interests well represented in Iraq, along with the British, French, and Dutch. The American companies by 1934 were two, the same Rockefeller behemoths—Standard Oil of New Jersey and Standard Oil of New York—that would become Exxon Mobil. This cartel owned 23.75 percent of the Iraq Petroleum Company (IPC). It would later team up with Texaco and Standard Oil of California to form Aramco.

While Britain formally ceded Iraq's independence in 1932, it remained (as in several other countries of the region) its international interlocutor on security and commerce, mainly through the king. "Iraq was a territory inhabited by a diverse and divided population run by a small clique of mainly Sunni politicians who could not control the country without the help of British airplanes," a situation that would, with varying forms of coercion, prevail well into the future.[3] Even after the British Empire receded and the last king of Iraq was deposed and murdered in July 1958, the British (and Americans) kept a stubborn grip on their oil holdings—production levels, control of the fields, pricing, transport, refining—as if the old political order had not just collapsed.

With the 1967 Six Day War that all but ended the Nasser era in Egypt and led to the Israeli occupation of Palestinian territory, the region's politics—rather than the prerogatives of Western oil giants—more than ever began to determine the control of oil. More militant regimes came to power in Iraq, including the long reign of the Ba'ath Party commencing in 1968. These militants were keen to discard the agreements with IPC, which they regarded as vestiges of colonial avarice. The government opted for developing fields with the Soviet Union, a slap at the pro-Israel West and a political move toward the USSR that was broader than oil cooperation alone. Moscow provided technical assistance for the Ba'athists' drive to modernize Iraq, as well as military assistance. Oil revenues rose quickly with the actions of the Organization of Petroleum Exporting Countries (OPEC), the oil-producers' cartel, in the early 1970s, not least the embargo resulting from the October 1973 war between Israel and its Arab neighbors. This enabled Iraq to pour money into education, health, housing, transport, and other sectors, earning the regime popular support. The decade of the Ba'ath ascent, led by Hasan al-Bakr, was also one of consolidation of the state's power, using kinship networks, police repression, propaganda, and material rewards to solidify their authority. Closely allied with al-Bakr was his chief lieutenant Saddam Hussein, who gradually drained al-Bakr of his authority and accumulated political power for himself. By 1979, he was in control. The following year, he went to war with Iran.

The Iran-Iraq war, which began in September 1980—scarcely eighteen months after the end of the fifty-five-year Pahlavi regime and the triumph of Ayatollah Khomeini—lasted until 1988 and was occasioned by long-standing border disputes between the neighbors and Saddam's calculation that Iran was vulnerable following its revolution. It was an opportunity to demonstrate his leadership, not merely of Iraq, but of the Arab world. The attack was encouraged by the United States, but Saddam scarcely needed such a stamp of approval. At first, the war was an apparent triumph for him, but Iran was able to repulse the Iraqis, counterattacked in 1982, and quickly gained a foothold in Iraq. At that point, the United States came to Iraq's aid, calculating that an outright Iranian victory would be catastrophic for U.S. interests, not least the flow of oil. The Gulf Arab states concurred and backed Saddam with money; the U.S. support was mainly in the form of financial credits—$5 billion worth—political legitimacy, and real-time intelligence. Later, in 1987, the U.S. navy protected Gulf shipping and even engaged the Iranians in small naval skirmishes. Washington also turned a blind eye to Iraq's devastating use of chemical weapons against the Iranians and Kurds in northern Iraq. It is not an exaggeration to say that President Reagan saved Saddam Hussein's regime. The war was costly for Iraq; not only were an estimated one million people killed in Iran and Iraq in the eight-year conflict, but the economic costs were crippling. Iraq faced enormous debts, mainly to its Arab supporters, and reconstruction costs. Oil prices, so high at the beginning of the war, were at lows not seen since before the 1973 price hikes; the recession in the early 1980s, caused in part by high oil prices and the full production of North Sea oil by the mid-1980s, depressed prices. Saddam, failing to revive Iraq's economy by normal means, turned to a military option with his aim set on Kuwait.

The United States saw its new relationship with Saddam as a plus in a region long enamored of socialism and an on-and-off embrace with Moscow; the revolution in Tehran signaled perilous flirtations with Islamic militancy, and so cultivating other allies in the Gulf was considered imperative. President Carter had sought better ties with Baghdad during the Iranian revolution, Reagan solidified those entreaties, and President George H. W. Bush in 1989 persisted with policies favorable to Iraq in trade and political gestures. A presidential decision memorandum, NSD 26, a prime directive for all U.S. policy, was issued in October, and it stated quite clearly that the United States sought to find an accommodation with Iraq to enhance the U.S. position in the region. Trade and oil were paramount. Agricultural exports to Iraq, continuing the flow undammed by Reagan, were enormous. Dual-use technologies (those, like computers, usable for civilian or military purposes) were approved for export with few exceptions. In return, Iraq discounted oil to American companies.[4] Republican senators from farm states made their own haj to Baghdad to pay homage to Saddam Hussein.

By 1990, the Iraqi strongman must have felt secure in his newfound friendship and the manifold benefits such friendship brought. President Reagan not only saved Hussein's regime, ignored his use of weapons of mass destruction (WMDs), and provided him with global political standing, but now President Bush was seeking a postwar modus vivendi that would normalize the relations forged during the wartime crisis. When the oil price problem arose—OPEC would not raise the price of oil or lower production, leaving Iraq in a bind—Saddam must have calculated that he could act against the nearest and weakest OPEC member, Kuwait (an old tribal area that many Iraqis, including Faisal, thought should be incorporated into Iraq), and not bear the wrath of his American boosters. On that he was mistaken, and thus began a new and longer conflict in the Gulf, one firmly rooted in the control of oil.

Saddam's decision to occupy Kuwait was a calculation that no major power would be willing to go to war to protect Kuwait's ruling al Sabah family, that the Saudi royal family in particular would come to terms with Iraq to buy their own security, and that he could, perhaps should, reassert his leadership in the Arab world and Iraq by this grand gesture of seizing the "nineteenth province" of greater Iraq. The U.S. ambassador infamously told him that Washington had no view on his burgeoning dispute with Kuwait, a message buttressed by other statements from the administration.* This U.S. passivity, guided by NSD 26 and Saddam's experience with American leaders over the previous eight years, strongly intimated to him that they would bend very far to accommodate his wishes.

Against Saddam's expectations, the move into Kuwait was met by condemnation not merely from his erstwhile supporters in Europe and America, but by the Arab League in an unusual show of unity with the old imperial powers. His isolation was all the greater because the Cold War had essentially ended. Soviet leader Mikhail Gorbachev's reforms and the new attitude of détente had reshaped global politics in the previous three years, including the end of Soviet tutelage over its former satellite countries in Eastern Europe. This meant that the Iraqis could not call on Moscow for the kind of support that likely would have dissuaded a concerted effort to eject Iraq from Kuwait. The United States responded quickly to the August 2, 1990, invasion, amassing 500,000 troops as part of a broad coalition in what President George H. W. Bush called the "new world order," engineered UN approval, and demanded Iraq's unconditional withdrawal from Kuwait.

The colossal effort for the United States of assembling the coalition and putting it on a war footing involved tireless diplomacy, conveyance of favors, money, and weapons to Arab states, to say nothing of the logistical challenges of readying a major military campaign in the

---

* While much blame was later placed on April Glaspie, the ambassador, the State Department spokesperson, Margaret Tutwiler, had made a point of stating publicly that the U.S. had no security commitments to Kuwait, and a direct message from Bush to Saddam on the day before Iraq's invasion of Kuwait reaffirmed the U.S. desire for a better relationship. The threats to Kuwait came after months of intelligence on Iraq's WMD programs and Saddam's vow, six months earlier, that Iraq had chemical weapons and "will make the fire eat up half of Israel."

desert in about twenty weeks. No such exertion would have been feasible, even thinkable, to protect a small monarchy without the salient feature of oil. Not only did Kuwait have the fifth greatest reserves of oil globally, but it borders Saudi Arabia's largest oil fields. So the prize of oil—Iraq already ranking fourth in reserves—was what was at stake. While there were ample rhetorical flourishes on both sides to disavow the central importance of oil, it was apparent that this was what the conflict hinged on. The secretary of state, James Baker, said as much in an unguarded moment before the war began,* but it scarcely needed a slip of the tongue for verification.

The opening of the military campaign began in January 1991 with heavy bombardment of military and other strategic assets, and continued from the air for six weeks. The plan was to begin with the command structure and communications—necessitating an air assault on Baghdad—and on chemical, biological, and nuclear weapons facilities. The hope was that Saddam Hussein might be killed as well—260 missions targeted places where Saddam was thought to be—and that "by destroying the infrastructure of Iraq, by punishing the people, Iraqis could be convinced to rise up and overthrow" Saddam.[5] This reflected a broader strategy, which was not merely to force Iraq's evacuation of Kuwait—the official objective and the language of the UN mandate—but to so cripple Iraq's military and dictatorship that it could not threaten its neighbors again.

With Saddam's command, control, and communications system disabled, the war plan sought to destroy the Iraqi air force and antiaircraft weapons. The rapid neutralizing of the Iraqi air force (which never challenged the coalition forces) and destruction of air defenses demonstrated complete U.S. superiority; Saddam's elite Republican Guard was next on the targeting list, followed by all Iraqi ground forces in Kuwait. The goal in the U.S. command was to do as much with air power as possible, and some thought the war could be won from the air. In retrospect, Desert Storm looks easy as a military campaign, in part due to the extraordinary display of air force prowess. This was not a

* Baker told Terry Gross on NPR's *Fresh Air* in 2006 that every administration he worked in (Ford, Reagan, and the first Bush) "had a written policy that we would go to war to defend secure access to the energy reserves of the Persian Gulf. That's very important to the economic and . . . political interests of the United States."

certainty at the outset, given Iraq's battle-hardened, sizable army and air force, the latter equipped with French as well as Soviet fighter aircraft. But U.S. air power proved itself very quickly; the coalition took control of the air space over Kuwait and indeed of Iraq in a matter of days and began the attrition from the air of the 560,000-strong Iraqi army in Kuwait. In all, tens of thousands of air sorties were flown—116,000 in a forty-three-day war—mainly by U.S. aircraft, including 1,624 B-52 missions, which were responsible for 30 percent of the bomb tonnage dropped.[6]

The ground war began on February 24 and was finished in four days. The Iraqi army crumbled; 200,000 deserted or surrendered, the remainder essentially fled north into Iraq. A few battles ensued as the U.S. armored divisions, backed by airborne forces (mainly Apache gunships) moved north into Iraq, but in the end the Iraqi army was nearly destroyed and what remained quickly retreated or simply fled. In the midst of this retreat was the infamous "turkey shoot," where Iraqi soldiers (and apparently some civilians, including Kuwaitis) were trapped in a pincer maneuver and bombed and strafed through the night. "The slaughtering of the Iraqis as they tried to retreat along the six-lane Highway 80 continued for the next 40 hours, until the truce," wrote journalist Dilip Hiro. Quoting a colleague, he noted it "'was one of the most terrible harassments of a retreating army from the air in the history of warfare.'"[7] Thousands of vehicles were destroyed there and on an adjacent escape route. The images from this gruesome finale convinced U.S. policy makers to end the war the next day.

Desert Storm was certainly a success in the prime objective—removing Saddam's forces from Kuwait. It was also proclaimed to be an astonishing success for precision-guided munitions and the resulting low number of casualties. Television images of this precision abounded. The low number of coalition fatalities—293 U.S. military deaths (half in action), plus seventy-seven others from the coalition—and the ease of dislodging the enormous Iraqi military from Kuwait with seemingly little collateral damage burnished this impression. Finally, its success was a boost to those who sought to bury the "Vietnam syndrome"—the reluctance of policy makers to use massive military interventions to pursue U.S. interests. Those interests would remain fixed on the Gulf for years to come, where U.S. forces would contain Saddam—politically safe but wounded in Baghdad—at a cost of $50 billion each year.

The Storm for Iraqis

The revolution in military technology that was the object of much attention in the 1980s—namely, applying new electronic techniques to war fighting and configuring forces to maximize that edge—did result in vastly more accurate munitions. In significant part this was achieved to minimize the jeopardy for U.S. forces. In the ground offensive in Kuwait, for example, Apache helicopters could demolish Iraqi tanks (old Soviet models) from three miles away, well out of sight of the tanks, using laser-guided Hellfire missiles. The F-16s flying over Baghdad could also hit targets more accurately than was possible in Vietnam. But accuracy was dependent not only on the refined technologies just then coming into use. They were also reliant on good intelligence—knowing where to place munitions with precision—and in this, the U.S. war effort was far less impressive. The consequences of this for ordinary Iraqis were often intense. "I had never seen anything in my entire military service that was a parallel to the incompetence of CENTAF intelligence," said one senior officer, referring to Central Command's Air Force. "Never." Bombers were also releasing their payloads at altitudes that were too high for accuracy, despite the U.S. command of the air. B-52s were employed extensively, too, and they are not precision weapons.[8]

Errant bombs and missiles were one source of collateral damage. The other was the intentional destruction of Iraqi infrastructure to cripple its ability to make war and spur Iraqis to take down the man responsible for their misery. Strategic bombing of this type was an article of faith in American war planning circles, going back to the Second World War, and it was no less regnant despite the mixed results in all wars in which it was employed.

The direct mortality of this bombing has variously been estimated to be between 2,000 and 30,000 civilian deaths. But within months it was clear that the war's devastation was taking a much larger toll, due to the nearly complete destruction of infrastructure—electricity, sewage treatment, water systems, and the like. The war was also devastating for an entirely unexpected reason: the decision to encourage Iraqis to do what the United States was at that point unwilling to do directly (and was outside its UN authorization), which was to destroy the regime.* President Bush openly encouraged armed uprisings by Iraqis following Saddam's defeat. The U.S. military was halted well short of overthrowing Saddam and permitted him not only to remain in power (fearing, in part, Iranian mischief) but to retain weapons like helicopters that he very effectively used to crush the rebellion Bush championed. The Kurds in the north had fought the Baghdad regime off and on for years, but Saddam's wrath still drove tens of thousands across wintry mountains into Turkey in a massive refugee crisis necessitating, after some dithering, an enormous rescue effort and the creation of a no-fly and no-go zone that essentially provided Kurds with their own quasi-state. In the south, however, in the predominantly Shia provinces around Basra, the rebellion fared far worse. Some Shia sheiks supported Saddam as a result of his patronage; and the rebellion in the south was largely urban and failed in part because of the passivity of the rural population, which waited to see who was going to win. Chaotic conditions were amplified by returning soldiers—who in some cases joined the uprising—and fed by exiled clerics in Iran, making for a disjointed rebellion that was ruthlessly put down from Baghdad with no countering action from U.S. or other coalition forces.† Republican Guard divisions that were dedicated to protecting the regime rampaged through the south, "inflicting massive loss of life and destruction in the Shi'i cities." As with the Kurds in the north, the Arab Shia in the south tried to flee: "more than 50,000 refugees poured over the border

---

* As one policy maker put it at the time: "If you're going to go in and topple Saddam Hussein, you have to go to Baghdad. Once you've got to Baghdad, it's not clear what you do with it. It's not clear what kind of government you would put in. . . . How much credibility is that government going to have if it's set up by the United States military?" The policy maker was Secretary of Defense Dick Cheney. Quoted by Adrian R. Lewis, *The American Culture of War: The History of U.S. Military Force from World War II to Operation Iraqi Freedom* (Routledge, 2007): 369.

† At the end of the war, the United States had Saddam at its mercy; it could have set conditions and denied him weaponry, which would have obviated his well-known ruthlessness in advance. For Bush to spur rebellion was a foolish and costly blunder—costly for Iraqis. The United States also had complete mastery of the skies and could have retaliated from the air without being drawn into the quagmire that policy makers feared.

into Saudi Arabia and thousands of others sought sanctuary in Iran, whilst many fled to the marshes of the south in an attempt to escape the vengeful pursuit of the armed forces," wrote historian Charles Tripp. "These exacted a terrible price on those whom they suspected of having joined the rebellion, leaving tens of thousands dead in their wake and seizing thousands more, many of whom were to perish in Iraqi prisons during the coming years"[9]

An estimated three million Iraqis, north and south, escaped to Iran, Turkey, and Saudi Arabia.[10] "More than 2 million Kurds fled into the snowy peaks between Iran and Turkey," said a PBS *Frontline* history. "Children died from typhoid, dehydration and dysentery. Some refugees were blown up by land mines. At one point in 1991, an estimated 2,000 Kurds were dying every day. The UN High Commissioner for Refugees called the exodus the largest in its 40-year history." The Marsh Arabs in the south, once 250,000 strong, were reduced to as little as one-tenth that number in the 1990s, either dead or displaced.[11] The total mortality resulting from the war's uprisings in 1991 was never accounted for, but it surely rose to 20,000 or more.

In a small glimpse of what would occur a dozen years later, American political leaders had not carefully anticipated the postwar dynamics in Iraq, believing (correctly) that the exercise of military power was enough to protect oil interests. Also foreshadowing the later invasion were American elites' disavowal of any responsibility for the bloody denouement of Desert Storm. The result for Iraqis was predictably catastrophic, but this did not enter into U.S. considerations. In fact, the opposite appeared to be at work: a general callousness regarding postwar Iraq, namely, through the application of sanctions that were meant to be a wartime instrument but were continued long after the war was concluded.

Inter-Bellum: War by Other Means

The period following Desert Storm continued the war by other means—sanctions, no-fly zones, and political isolation the United States and its allies employed in a morally and tactically bankrupt effort to bring down Saddam Hussein. The sanctions were intensified by military action during Desert Storm and then punctuated by frequent air attacks on Iraq. Intentionally imposed to weaken the Ba'athist regime and encourage ordinary Iraqis to revolt, they exacted a high human cost. Not only did the revolt fail; the sanctions steadily corroded society and caused high death tolls, leaving simmering unrest that later took the form of Muslim extremism.

The initial sanctions were approved in the UN Security Council within days of Saddam's occupation of Kuwait. The end of the war, chaotic as it was, should have marked the end of such severe sanctions, but they were renewed in April 1991. The sanctions effactually blocked much medicine and medical equipment, fertilizer for agriculture and farm equipment, industrial and electronics technology—virtually everything except "supplies intended strictly for medical purposes, and, in humanitarian circumstances, foodstuffs," while oil exports from Iraq were prohibited. The allowance for food and medicine provided little relief in the face of the country's impoverishment—it had little money to purchase anything; and a system was put in place that required all imports, including those from charities, to be monitored and approved by a sanctions committee. The purpose of the sanctions was supposedly to deny Saddam any possibility of rebuilding WMD capability and to exact reparations for the occupation of Kuwait. But these reasons had many others added on, some of them with no connection to the war or war-making, and were aimed quite obviously if unofficially to bring down Saddam.[12]

Even after the deprivations of the Iran-Iraq war, Iraq was a relatively modern society, with good electricity, sewage, water treatment, and health care infrastructure. One of the ironies of warfare is that the more advanced a society is, the more easily it's disabled by certain kinds of attacks. Iraq also imported something like 70 percent of its food, so the possibility—as might be the case for many traditional societies—of returning to basic self-sufficiency was not in the cards. It needed to export oil for funds to buy food and the technologies needed to rebuild its sophisticated infrastructure.

As a result, the sanctions were devastating. No oil exported meant no money to purchase wheat and other foods. And Iraq was not trying to restart from where it was in August 1990. It was trying to restart after undergoing forty-three days of intensive bombing, bombing that demolished much of its modern infrastructure. "Most means of modern life support have been destroyed or rendered tenuous," a UN undersecretary put it. "Iraq has, for some time to come, been relegated to a pre-industrial age, but with all the disabilities of post-industrial dependency on an intensive use of energy and technology."[13] What is remarkable about that disability was how intentional it was—that is, the U.S. military destroyed infrastructure not merely as a war aim but to disable Iraq after the war.

A few days after Desert Storm was launched, for example, the Defense Intelligence Agency told the military command that fresh water vulnerabilities in Iraq were great. Since water required considerable treatment to remove salt and other impurities, treatment that required chlorine or technologies would either be destroyed during Desert Storm or prohibited by sanctions. "Unless water treatment supplies are exempted from the unsanctions [sic] for humanitarian reasons, no adequate solution exists for Iraq's water purification dilemma, since no suitable alternatives, including looting supplies from Kuwait, sufficiently meet Iraqi needs," the cable reads. "Incidences of disease, including possible epidemics, will become probable. . . . The entire Iraqi water treatment system will not collapse precipitously, but its capabilities will decline steadily."[14] Water treatment plants were one of the targets of the bombing. Electric generating capacity was degraded by between 75 and 95 percent, essentially eliminating refrigeration among other uses for basic human needs and returning Iraq to the generating capacity it had in 1920. Dams, oil facilities, shipyards, and other elements of the economic and life-support systems of Iraq were also extensively damaged or destroyed.

"Some targets, especially late in the war, were bombed primarily to create postwar leverage over Iraq, not to influence the course of the conflict itself," reported Barton Gellman of the *Washington Post* four months after the war ended. "Planners now say their intent was to destroy or damage valuable facilities that Baghdad could not repair without foreign assistance." This damage, planners revealed, was done to intensify the postwar suffering in Iraq. Said one: "What we were doing with the attacks on infrastructure was to accelerate the effects of the sanctions." Another planner told Gellman, "Big picture, we want to let people know, 'Get rid of this guy and we'll be more than happy to assist in rebuilding. We're not going to tolerate Saddam Hussein or his regime. Fix that, and we'll fix your electricity.'"[15]

The results of Desert Storm and the sanctions for ordinary Iraqis became apparent very quickly. Within a few weeks of the formal war's termination, independent observers witnessed high rates of malnutrition and other health effects, particularly for small children. A study published in the *New England Journal of Medicine*, based on a household survey in Iraq, concluded that "the Gulf war and trade sanctions caused a threefold increase in mortality among Iraqi children under five years of age. We estimate that more than 46,900 children died between January and August 1991" who would not have perished without the U.S. actions.[16] Could these (plus uncounted adult casualties) be attributed directly to the war?

The high child mortality began to gain notice rather quickly, thanks in part to a number of research teams and delegations to Iraq. This began to put the Bush administration on the defensive, but the sanctions regime stayed in place and was continued without apparent regret during most of the Clinton administration. A goal of denying Saddam technology for bomb making was understandable, but the pattern of enforcing sanctions clearly showed that much more punitive motives were at work. The main tactic was delay—a long backlog of requested items were simply not acted upon, in addition to Iraq's lack of money to purchase basic necessities. As explained by Joy Gordon in her examination of the sanctions:

> The United States insisted that Iraq seek permission for each item, rather than approving categories of permitted goods, and the United States insisted as well that each item be approved on a case-by-case basis, without the use of precedent or criteria for approval . . . Because of the consensus decision-making rule, each approval required the agreement of the entire committee. Any single member of the [multinational] committee could unilaterally block the purchase of any contract for humanitarian goods by withholding its approval.[17]

As a result, the conditions of ordinary life in Iraq continued to deteriorate. The country "is being killed, far beyond food rationing," said Iraqi sculptor Mohamed Ghani at the time. "It is physical, mental, emotional and intellectual. It is the very expression of nothingness; all these people die waiting, for nothing. . . . These families waiting, these women alone with their children, their heads bowed. Passivity every day of the week. Reflection. Sadness. Examine my sculptures representing people looking at an empty box: it is ourselves, the Iraqis, we are staring at life, this vacuum, this empty box, our life under the embargo."[18]

By 1995, criticism of the sanctions was so pervasive that the UN Security Council felt compelled to alter the terms by allowing Iraq to sell a small amount of oil, the revenues of which would in part go to pay for food and medicine. The program did not produce revenues until 1997, and even then the governing committees still delayed what could get into Iraq, and the overwhelming dislocations of the sanctions persisted. Roughly $1 per capita per day was the equivalent of consumable goods imported under the Oil-for-Food program, itself administered by UN staff in Iraq. The degraded health system was in need of sizable resources, yet the committees allowing imports consistently slowed down, denied, or under-funded this need. Even after the Oil-for-Food program was well under way, the allocations were inadequate; the senior officials of the World Health Organization, UNICEF (the United Nations Children's Fund), and others agreed that the allowed sums "did not remotely meet health service needs" and that the dysfunctional infrastructure was a proximate cause of poor health as well. "Without safe water, sanitation, and electricity, diseases such as cholera, malaria," and others "would remain serious threats to public health," wrote H. C. von Sponeck, who was UN Humanitarian Coordinator for Iraq in the late 1990s. "Diarrhea and acute respiratory infections . . . constituted major and avoidable causes of child mortality."[19]

The miserly tactics of delay and obstruction practiced by the United States led two successive UN chiefs in Baghdad and other UN officials to resign in protest, an unheard-of level of dissent in the polite precincts of career diplomats.

Even by 2000, a decade after sanctions began, the situation had scarcely improved. UNICEF estimated that 500,000 children under five years of age had died as a result of the war and sanctions from malnutrition, diseases for which cures were available but medicine in Iraq was not, and poor health at birth due to prenatal effects on mothers. In fact, that was the estimate (based on a large household survey) as of 1998; an estimate about half that was the conclusion of a Columbia University researcher who calculated that the figure of a half-million deaths for small children was not reached until 2002. UNICEF also reported high rates of women dying in childbirth— nearly three times the prewar rate.[20] By the end of the 1990s, the ceilings on oil production were very nearly lifted altogether, but the damage was already done.

U.S. and British politicians and media commentators consistently blamed Saddam Hussein for mismanaging the funds he controlled, thereby being significantly responsible for the suffering, but the picture is mixed at best. The UN maintained fairly tight control over all purchases, including distribution in Iraq. Iraq's requests for supplies were backed up in a queue, awaiting approval, throughout the sanctions period. Saddam could not divert the money or goods directly from the Oil-for-Food program. And while there was some obstruction by Baghdad to protest the sanctions regime (and, separately, illicit smuggling of oil exports), actions by the regime with respect to the steady social disintegration were minor compared to the delay in New York—the long "holds" demanded by the United States, often blocking a billion dollars' worth of goods or denying altogether items like vaccines or other medicines. The hardliners on the Security Council—the United States and Britain—were, says von Sponeck, "absolutely determined not to accept the more intensive humanitarian monitoring on the part of the UN in Iraq to prevent the arrival of possible WMD-related dual-use supplies" that "would have allowed a de-linking of the military embargo from economic sanctions."[21]

Clinton administration officials would claim that Iraq's health care system was poor to begin with (not true) or simply, in the words of Madeleine Albright, the sanctions, with all their impacts, are "worth it."* The dissembling about Iraq responsibility was likely prompted by the horror the sanctions were producing. "I am resigning because the policy of economic sanctions is totally bankrupt," said Denis Halliday, assistant secretary general and lifetime UN diplomat upon leaving Baghdad in 1998. "We are in the process of destroying an entire society." Later, he told a British journalist, "I had been instructed to implement a policy that satisfies the definition of genocide: a deliberate policy that has effectively killed well over a million individuals."[22] The intention was clearly

---

* Albright claims she misspoke and regretted doing so, but her explanation (in her memoir, *Madame Secretary*) is unconvincing, as she completely blames Saddam for the conditions in Iraq when virtually every impartial observer takes exception to that view. She never disavowed the policy itself. And while she made that comment to Leslie Stahl on *60 Minutes* in 1996, her spokesman, James Rubin, frequently made erroneous assertions about the sanctions regime for years afterward. President Clinton never made a specific comment about the high mortality of children as a result of his administration of the sanctions.

visible in the U.S. wartime strategy of "accelerating" the impact of the sanctions, which provided "leverage." The concern about civilians was secondary, perhaps nonexistent. Regarding the heavy bombing on civilian infrastructure, the military scarcely distinguished between the regime and the people of Iraq. "Among the justifications offered now," reported Barton Gellman in June 1991, "is that Iraqi civilians are not blameless for Saddam's invasion of Kuwait. 'The definition of innocents gets to be a little unclear,' said a senior Air Force officer, noting that many Iraqis supported the invasion of Kuwait. 'They do live here, and ultimately the people have some control over what goes on in their country.'"[23]

Iraq's sanctions-induced misery was sometimes intensified by U.S. and British bombing, as skirmishes with Saddam's forces would often earn retaliation near major cities like Basra. Hundreds, possibly thousands, of such incidents occurred. A similar dynamic took hold in the north, where U.S. forces protected the Kurdish autonomous region. Hundreds of civilians were killed in such routine policing from the air. The ongoing drama over UN weapons inspectors looking for weapons of mass destruction, who were denied unrestricted access to all facilities and documents, led to Operation Desert Fox; this was a seventy-hour bombing campaign that targeted some suspected weapons sites (which the 2003 invasion showed were not, as claimed, parts of a WMD program) as well as the Iraqi leadership. An estimated 200 civilians were killed in the three-day bombardment.[24] The operation was carried out at the same time the U.S. House of Representatives was impeaching President Clinton for lying about his illegal sexual activities with a White House intern. Thus, the bombing of Iraq was widely viewed at the time as a political diversion. But whatever its cause, Operation Desert Fox was consistent with Clinton's policy, which was to continue tight military containment on Iraq and sustain the sanctions stranglehold.

Among the impacts of sanctions was Saddam's weakening grasp of power over the country. This was, of course, intentional, and the U.S. government publicly adopted a policy of regime change in the mid-1990s. While apparently never close to being overthrown, as U.S. planners hoped, Saddam did cede authority to local sheiks haphazardly. The 1990–2003 sanctions period reduced the amount of money Saddam could pour into his internal security apparatus, and, as a result, he invested more authority in the tribal sheiks. "He decentered responsibility for the provision of order to reinvigorated and recreated tribal networks and tribal sheiks," explained Toby Dodge; and thus Saddam "created another informal channel of power,"[25] one that would be particularly troublesome in the years after the U.S. invasion. This "decentering" had another consequence, namely, a new surge of religious devotion and activism, enabled by the lack of Saddam's authoritarian power and perhaps stirred by the deprivation occasioned by the sanctions regime. The rise of militant Islam in the aftermath of the American invasion and occupation in 2003 was not a sudden or foreign phenomenon, but one that had been simmering for years as an effect of war and society's ruination. With this decentralization and the misery produced by the sanctions, social organization became centered on the mosque. Religious devotion and ideology grew stronger in the 1990s and early 2000s, a rebuff to Saddam's secularism (although he actually launched a back-to-faith campaign in the mid-1990s). The growth of the more rigid and militant forms of Islam was becoming evident in episodes of violence against Western influences (such as television) in the late 1990s.[26] This gradual but seminal change in the authority structure was fraught with meaning for the coming decade. As was true for so many episodes of U.S. foreign policy, the unintended consequences of belligerence frequently prompt the growth of even more noxious forms of political expression, as was the case in the support of the *mujaheddin* in Afghanistan in the 1980s. In Iraq, it was first Saddam himself, and then a strategy of weakening him that gave rise to predictably militant and regressive ideologues.

The stage was set, then, for what would follow the attack on America.

9/11 AND THE WAR ON TERRORISM

Whatever the causes of al Qaeda's attack of September 11, 2001, whatever the lapses in U.S. readiness, the shocking event altered again the way that Americans would see the Middle East. While a long succession of crises had their effects, none approached 9/11 as a psychological trauma for Americans. Even the unexpected and startling—the OPEC price hikes of 1974 and 1979, the American embassy hostage crisis in Iran from 1979–81, and the attack on the U.S. marine barracks in Beirut in 1983—did not have the feel of catastrophe and danger created by the destruction of the World Trade Center and the damage to the Pentagon.

Those earlier events were and are redolent with meaning. But they could be absorbed, or were far away. The 9/11 attacks were not so easily glossed over or endured. An immediate and nihilistic threat suddenly destroyed the long-standing sense of invulnerability that Americans had enjoyed since the end of the Cold War.

President George W. Bush had been lackadaisical about terrorism before 9/11 but of course had to respond to an angry, wounded public; the attacks were also an enormous political opportunity. The right-wing news media as well as more sober journalists created a sense of panic about Muslims in our midst (a hysteria never directly prompted by President Bush, to his credit), a fear completely out of proportion to the domestic threat, which, apart from the 9/11 attackers themselves, was largely nonexistent. While most of the fear rose from the specter of being attacked from within—the oft-predicted "another 9/11" or "it's not if, but when" refrain—the dark anxieties stirred by 9/11 naturally cast a shadow over the Middle East. Who could threaten us, not only with passenger airliners but with something far more menacing, like a nuclear bomb?

While a rogue's gallery of terrorist groups soon became familiar to readers and watchers of the news media, the focus of attention—apart from the ultimate rogue and our former ally, Osama bin Laden—turned to Saddam Hussein. And why not? He was a radical Arab, already proven a despot and international criminal, and with nuclear weapons ambitions. He harbored terrorists and supported terrorism against Israel. Within hours of the 9/11 catastrophe, several key Bush advisers were planning regime change in Baghdad. The unfinished business of Desert Storm was about to be concluded.

The Culture of Vengeance

The 9/11 attacks and the immediate response in America gave new life to the nation's reversion to savage war. In what is surely the signature speech of his presidency, President Bush told Congress and the public just days later that "we are a country awakened to danger and called to defend freedom. Our grief has turned to anger and anger to resolution. Whether we bring our enemies to justice or bring justice to our enemies, justice will be done." The references to violence were attributed to the enemy, to terrorists; the ownership of justice was America's, and this was the great contest of what he termed *the war on terrorism*: "Our nation, this generation, will lift the dark threat of violence from our people and our future. We will rally the world to this cause by our efforts, by our courage. We will not tire, we will not falter and we will not fail . . . we'll meet violence with patient justice." Within the speech, he sent a signal to others: "we will pursue nations that provide aid or safe haven to terrorism. Every nation in every region now has a decision to make: Either you are with us or you are with the terrorists." Those states not with us, Bush said, would be considered hostile. He ended by repeating the black-and-white duality that not only informed this address but would mark his foreign policy. "Freedom and fear, justice and cruelty, have always been at war, and we know that God is not neutral between them."

Within three weeks, the United States was bombing targets in Afghanistan and supporting the Northern Alliance—a loose coalition of *mujaheddin* opposed to the Taliban—in its offensive to retake Kabul and control most of the country. This rapid victory appeared to have al Qaeda on the run, up into the mountains bordering Pakistan (where they remain to this day). The disruption of al Qaeda training camps and operations was one goal of U.S. planners; but the lack of a total victory, including the capture of bin Laden, left many feeling dissatisfied. Thus the Afghan operation, so promising in 2001, quickly bogged down in a frustrating inability of the U.S. military to finish off the perpetrators of the 9/11 attacks and in the Sisyphean tasks of nation building in Afghanistan itself.

However satisfying it was for Americans to witness the destruction of a regime to which they had previously paid little heed, the mood in the United States remained dark through 2001 and 2002. The shock of the attacks scarcely abated over those months. And the requirements of savage war, which few doubted was necessary, spurred a realignment in the nation's mind and habits. A yearning for vengeance was evident in many forms throughout popular and political culture, but two strains stand out: first, as mentioned, was a predictably harsh reprisal against all things Muslim and Arab American; second was an embrace of militant masculinity. The combination of these would prove to be momentous.

The racist reaction was a sensibility that America often lapses into at times of national stress. The malevolent stereotyping of outsiders drew upon centuries of European "orientalism" whose roots are very deep. Europeans had collided with armies of the Turkish sultan, Arab princes, and others from the Middle East, in epic struggles often fought in Europe to repel occupations by the Muslim invaders, occurring over several hundred years and not completely finished until the nineteenth century. Europeans were equal to the invading, conducting several incursions, some of them "crusades" or Christian jihad—in fact, the first crusade was a writ of holy war issued by Pope Urban II in 1095*—lasting for centuries and resulting in several occupations, local battles, and atrocities. This long war was most certainly a clash of civilizations (and empires), Christian and Muslim, each claiming to possess revealed truth and to be the rightful successor to Judaism, and therefore all the more ferocious in their confrontation. It has been said that this titanic contest was the source of European identity; its cultural resonances remained strong throughout the twentieth century (as in the Balkan wars of the 1990s) even as Europe had achieved, after the collapse of the Ottoman empire and the Caliphate, the most complete victory over the Arabs and Turks in a millennium. This was the moment when Iraq was created by Winston Churchill's green pen, along with the other post-1918 spoils of war. That pregnant moment was not merely the beginning of the "modern" Middle East and the superior attitudes with which Europeans judged their new vassals; rather, it was the latest chapter in this colossal, world-shaping confrontation that also shaped European beliefs about the region. Americans essentially inherited this orientalism, in blander flavors for the most part, but still made from the same stew. The Arab and Turk were long depicted in terms recognizable to Americans, so similar were these "traits" to the ways white Americans looked upon southern blacks and Mexicans through much of the twentieth century—lazy, sensuous, amoral, devious, backward, and prone to violence. Given the actual warfare that prevailed with Arabs and Turks for so many years, their essential

* Urban was responding to an urgent request from the King of Byzantium, whose Greek empire was being overrun by Seljuk Turks (a predecessor of the Osmanlı Turks, or Ottomans), who were Muslim. Among the accounts of Urban's charge at the Council of Clermont, is this: "I, or rather the Lord, beseech you as Christ's heralds . . . to persuade all people of whatever rank, foot-soldiers and knights, poor and rich, to carry aid promptly to those Christians and to destroy that vile race from the lands of our friends. . . . Christ commands it. All who die by the way, whether by land or by sea, or in battle against the pagans, shall have immediate remission of sins. This I grant them through the power of God with which I am

bellicosity was also not in doubt. In this finely woven tapestry of ethnic and religious prejudice, then, was a portrait of the savage—a dangerous and unprincipled savage, to be sure. Americans' exposure to the contemporary Arab world was often framed by political contests in which the likes of Nasser, Arafat, Assad, and Saddam Hussein were prominent, men largely portrayed in the United States as ruthless, unprincipled, and radical. When the attacks of 9/11 were shown to be the work of Arab extremists, a long cultural history was instantly mobilized.

Among the many permutations of this reaction—including some anxious months, considerable quantities of hate speech, and a scattering of violent incidents against Muslims (or those mistaken for them) in America[27]—was a powerful impulse to lay waste Afghanistan and any other place the 9/11 attackers could be associated with.

A number of newspaper and television commentators urged immediate and broad military action in the Middle East. Revenge fantasies were common in film, and paranoia struck deep via popular entertainment like the television series 24. The pervasiveness of cable television and the Internet made possible more incendiary rhetoric against Muslims in the public domain than was even conceivable during previous wars. The last major war Americans had fought was against Saddam Hussein and the attackers were mostly from neighboring Saudi Arabia—so a focus on the Persian Gulf was inevitable. And because Saddam had already been vilified for at least eleven years—depicted, for the most part, as a madman and tyrant—it was easy to include him in the post-9/11 shooting gallery of rogues.

The second impulse—a return to "manliness"—was a reaction that did not depend on the perpetrators of 9/11 but rather pulled on the cultural tropes of American settler myths. A period ensued of self-recrimination about America having become soft—that is, "feminine"—remarkably like that which seized the country during the early Cold War and the conflict in Korea. Men, somehow, had been feminized and reduced to passivity, and America's enemies had sensed this and had taken advantage of it. Drawing on Theodore Roosevelt's

---

invested. O what a disgrace if such a despised and base race, which worships demons, should conquer a people which has the faith of omnipotent God and is made glorious with the name of Christ! With what reproaches will the Lord overwhelm us if you do not aid those who, with us, profess the Christian religion!"

mind-set, these pervasive images and sentiments were voiced by a remarkably diverse range of voices in the news media—not just the old anticommunist right—and readily brought back frontier sensibilities. The Arab attackers and their like were the rampaging Indians of our push westward, and the real men of America needed to respond in kind, protecting the women and children, proselytizing our God and civilizing mission, and recommitting to violence as the redeeming exponent of the American experiment. As journalist Susan Faludi showed in her masterful, *The Terror Dream: Fear and Fantasy in Post-9/11 America*, the extent to which this fresh and nearly unquestioned surge to a new masculinity took hold of American political culture is nothing short of astonishing, but it was possibly predictable given both the residual power of the frontier myth and lingering resentment toward feminism. "We reacted to our trauma," she wrote,

> not by interrogating it but by cocooning ourselves in the celluloid chrysalis of the baby boom's childhood. In the male version of that reverie, some nameless reflex had returned us to that 1950s badlands where conquest and triumph played and replayed in an infinite loop. (For some, that replay was literal: *High Noon*, *National Review* writer Rob Long told readers, was "a movie I've been watching every few days since September 11.") From deep within that dream world, our commander in chief issued remarks like "We'll smoke him out" and "Wanted: dead or alive," our political candidates proved their double-barreled worthiness for post-9/11 office by brandishing guns on the campaign trail, our journalists cast city firefighters as tall-in-the-saddle cowboys patrolling a Wild West stage set, and our pundits proclaimed our nation's ability to vanquish 'barbarians' in a faraway land they dubbed "Indian Country."[28]

Essential to this reverie was a fixation on heroism. The 9/11 firefighters were heroes, no matter what their actual role, and this extended to virtually any American associated with the tragedy. The need for heroes was doubtlessly a reaction to the vulnerability the attacks exposed—better to exult in the men (as Faludi showed, few women got the same attention) than to cast about to blame those who let the nation's guard down or ignored bin Laden's warnings. But it did not cease with the New York Fire Department or the passengers on the fourth plane that crashed in Pennsylvania; it continued for months afterward, not only in memorializing those people but in making heroes of anyone going into harm's way to fight this new "war on terrorism." The heroic ideal is often an outgrowth of war, and war needs heroes. In this, then, every soldier sent to Afghanistan and every one sent to Iraq would be hailed as a hero. This nearly universal attribution of heroism stirs two consequences. The first is to make the war heroic, too, a sentiment that became all the more important as the Iraq War (and then the U.S. war in Afghanistan) became increasingly unpopular. Criticism of the war policy could be deflected or denounced as contempt for the men in uniform. And the second consequence is to insulate those hero "warriors" from criticism for their individual actions. Heroes are not judged by the same standards as mere mortals. A hero does what he must to protect us, and his actions are by virtue of his status as a hero above reproach, even above examination.

As a result, the reemphasis on masculinity silenced—or attempted to silence—thoughtful critics of the run-up to war or the wars themselves. Part of the "moral clarity" of the war on terrorism was to not question a militant response from the United States. Questioning, thinking about al Qaeda's motives, exploring the history of Western imperialism in the Middle East, poking at Israeli intransigence—these sorts of queries were delegitimized as passive, weak, and therefore wholly dismissible. The masculine response, the natural riposte of heroes, was to go to war; and go to war against the savage Muslim is what we did, both at home and abroad.

The Warrior Nation

The "war on terrorism" began with President George W. Bush's speech to the nation following the 9/11 attacks. This war, in effect, took two forms—internal and external war.

The first was to look for enemies within, creating a homeland security complex that parallels the national security complex created for the Cold War. This included the USA Patriot Act, providing new powers to federal law enforcement on detention, secret trials, and surveillance, among others, mainly aimed in practice at Muslims and Arab-Americans and particularly recent immigrants. This authority resulted in thousands of detentions and arrests with very few ultimately linked to anything like intention to commit acts of political violence.[29] The 9/11 Commission

Report found no evidence of domestic terror cells of Muslims or other Arabs (most Arab-Americans are Christian), and the thousands of detentions and hundreds of arrests and prosecutions since that time in the United States have uncovered no plausible plot that could do much harm. Virtually all prosecutions had targeted men who either were in very early stages of fantasy plots or were capable of harming only a few people even if they could bring off their plans. (It is worth noting that many of the most high-profile cases involved men vengeful at the U.S. killing of civilians in Afghanistan and Iraq, a finding also applicable to the more serious terrorist attacks in Madrid and London. The 2009 Fort Hood shooting also appeared to be motivated, at least in part, by the gunman's fears of deployment to Iraq.) Yet, despite this lack of a genuine homegrown threat, the attention poured into the "terrorist threat" was enormous, both from the government and from the news media. In fact, as political scientist John Mueller has shown, fears of terrorism actually rose in the five years following 9/11 despite the complete absence of any further threats domestically, a rise largely attributable to a manufactured fear: "Perhaps the most common reaction to terrorism is the costly stoking of fear and the often even more costly encouragement of overreaction by members of what might be called the 'terrorism industry,'" Mueller observed, "an entity that includes not only various entrepreneurs and bureaucrats, but also most of the media and nearly all politicians."[30]

The typing of Muslims in America as an internal threat, sympathetic or possibly supportive of foreign militants (if not al Qaeda, then Hamas, Hezbollah, the Muslim Brotherhood, etc.) was useful to the Bush administration in its political fortunes and served to cultivate an atmosphere of threat that linked the Arab monsters abroad to mortal danger in one's own neighborhood. The "long war" would require such connections, such palpable fear, to sustain the effort. So the typing of Muslims within the United States, the linkage supposedly established between them and the militants responsible for 9/11 or terrorism against Israelis, was a strong pillar of a war policy in the Middle East that would not be so popular without the sense of actual, imminent danger.

The external threat appeared at first to be relatively easy to identify: it was mainly al Qaeda's leadership hiding in the mountains bordering Afghanistan and Pakistan. Bush expanded this to include any terrorists and the states that harbored them. So while operations in Afghanistan and covert operations elsewhere attacked al Qaeda and similar networks, law enforcement agencies arrested suspected members in many countries, financial dealings were tracked and disrupted, and so on, the focus of the United States quickly turned away from this central set of tasks to attend to the unfinished business in Iraq. While insisting that the war on terrorism was the primary and historic mission of American security, U.S. war planners at the highest levels were spending increasing amounts of time and resources, by some accounts beginning in the days after 9/11, on removing Saddam Hussein from power and installing a pro-American regime. By the measure of U.S. attention—diplomatic, military planning, and intelligence allocations, for example—the external threat became identified as a state that was only marginally involved in promoting terrorism, had never attacked the United States, and was exhausted by previous wars and sanctions.

The focus on Iraq was understandable from one perspective— the United States had essentially been at war with Saddam since 1991, without a satisfying resolution—but odd in the context of anti-terrorism. The decision to seek a war appears now to be a combination of four motives (apart from the psychological speculation about Bush's peculiar relationship with his father). First and most prominent was the desire of many on the right to transform the Middle East, to jar it into recognizing that it could not continue to cultivate authoritarian regimes, acts of terrorism, anti-Israeli and anti-American politics, and the like, from which endless rounds of conflict, emigration, human rights violations, and threats to the flow of oil would result. The region "is held back by what leading Arab intellectuals call a political and economic 'freedom deficit,'" wrote Condoleezza Rice, then the national security adviser, in August 2003. "In many quarters a sense of hopelessness provides a fertile ground for ideologies of hatred that persuade people to forsake university educations, careers and families and aspire instead to blow themselves up—taking as many innocent lives with them as possible. These ingredients are a recipe for regional instability— and pose a continuing threat to America's security."[31] The contrast with North Korea is instructive: if the official and pivotal rationale for war against Iraq was to prevent the use of weapons of mass destruction, why was the despotic North Korean regime—which was much closer than Iraq to having nuclear weapons—spared the same fate? The likely answer is because North Korea is in a neighborhood that is largely on board with U.S.-led economic globalization. The Middle East—Iraq,

Syria, and Iran in particular—is not. The significance of oil is interwoven into this thinking and was at the center of the Bush White House. Before 9/11, Vice President Dick Cheney convened an Energy Task Force, whose planning was kept secret but which apparently grasped the opportunity at hand. Cheney "directed the N.S.C. staff to cooperate fully with the Energy Task Force as it considered the 'melding' of two seemingly unrelated areas of policy: 'the review of operational policies towards rogue states,' such as Iraq, and 'actions regarding the capture of new and existing oil and gas fields.'" This suggests, says a former official, "the captains of the oil industry sitting down with Cheney and laying grand, global plans."[32] The Middle East's enormous resources made its "transformation" a high priority. That this would be achieved through the use of devastating military power was a given, a fundamentalist norm of the Bush cohort. When, for example, Israel launched its powerful assault on Beirut in the summer of 2006 to weed out Hezbollah and bombed civilian neighborhoods to do so, Rice reflexively called this "the birth pangs of a new Middle East."

The second push to war—allegations that Iraq had weapons of mass destruction—was founded on weak evidence; but many reasonable analysts believed these suspicions. Bush apparently acted at least in part on the WMD case made to him by the intelligence chief; and of course Saddam had a history of seeking (or, in the case of chemical weapons, possessing and using) such weapons and appeared to be coy in denying such a program in the years and months just preceding the 2003 war. What is remarkable, however, is that the United States would initiate a major conflict on such thin evidence, data that was subject to political manipulation by Cheney and possibly other decision makers. What the WMD case offered, above all other rationales, was a veneer of international legitimacy. It was easier to justify invasion if an imminent and lethal threat was the target. The UN Security Council in particular was lobbied for its imprimatur on the war (which it withheld); seeking that approval was odd for a group of decision makers that had so ridiculed multilateralism and the UN in particular.

A third push to war—the lure of an easy triumph—also seemed to be at work, although this is more speculative. By 2002, bin Laden had escaped and was continuously able to publicize his messages. Terrorist attacks continued worldwide and some were linked to al Qaeda, including the Bali bombings of October 2002 that took more than 200 lives.

If anything, the specter of terrorism loomed larger than ever in the minds of Americans. The prospect of capturing Saddam and destroying his regime in Iraq then became, in effect, an attractive substitute for catching bin Laden and destroying al Qaeda. The U.S. military was certainly better prepared to take on the Iraq army than it was al Qaeda's elusive operatives, or at least it appeared to be. Knocking off Saddam and being hailed as liberators in Baghdad were immensely seductive attractions. There also appeared to be a bravado sentiment after the apparent triumph in Afghanistan that the United States could subdue Saddam and thereby intimidate (or even destroy) noxious regimes in Iran and Syria, and aid in the destruction of Hezbollah and Hamas as well. This would fulfill the first objective of decisively altering the political contours of the region, from the Levant to South Asia.

The fourth rationale for war centered on terrorism itself, perhaps a necessary addendum given the temper of the times. Saddam was linked to terrorists via his support of Palestinian groups, underscoring the background rationale of supporting Israel.* Remarkably, an attempt was made to connect him to the 9/11 plotters—remarkable for its flimsiness. The nuclear ambitions he had were also linked to this purported terrorist connection; that is, suggestions that the nuclear and terrorist threat were conjoined in the person of Saddam Hussein because he might give a nuclear explosive to the likes of Hamas or al Qaeda (a prospect no serious analyst ever proposed: regimes do not give away any such power to anybody). Nonetheless, the intertwining of Saddam's putative threat to the United States—itself unproven either in intention or capability—and the still-redolent specter of terrorism

---

* The assertion that Israel via its supporters in the United States was a proximate cause of the invasion of Iraq is unconvincing. There is little doubt that the fear and loathing Saddam provoked in Jews was strong and warranted. American Jews in the more conservative political organizations, the so-called Israel Lobby, were largely enthusiastic supporters of the war. Some, like the Washington Institute for Near East Policy, an Israeli-funded "think tank," had regularly proposed regime change throughout the 1990s. But it's a leap to believe that the Israel Lobby had the muscle to provoke a war on its own and equally unlikely that it was a more important interest for Bush than the control of oil. Protection of Israel, as part of the overall goal of transforming the region, was an objective, to be sure, but it was too weak to be a primary casus belli. For another, thoughtful view, see John Mersheimer and Stephen Walt, *The Israel Lobby* (Farrar, Straus and Giroux, 2008).

became a standard rhetorical point of the Bush administration and in public discourse generally. As a result, the public largely believed that Saddam was behind the 9/11 attacks.

The political foundation for taming the savage Saddam was provided in the Bush Doctrine, which was mainly a reiteration of U.S. prerogative to act first in the face of hostile intent. "I will not wait on events, while dangers gather. I will not stand by, as peril draws closer and closer," Bush proclaimed in his 2002 State of the Union address. "The United States of America will not permit the world's most dangerous regimes to threaten us with the world's most destructive weapons." The sole addition to what is standard big power policy was the notion of "preemptive war," acting well in advance of any actual threat, and the revocation of sovereignty for states harboring terrorists. The Bush Doctrine was loose and changeable, but it was certainly grand—an ambitious and encompassing assertion of American power globally, seeking to promote American notions of governance and acting to protect U.S. interests.[33]

One notable dimension of this application of American power was the calls for democratization that became a dominant theme in the administration's public discussions after Saddam's nuclear, biological, and chemical weapons threat was shown to be nonexistent. Long an aspiration of the so-called neoconservatives who were so prominent in the Bush years, this "forward strategy of freedom" was a call to actively promote political liberty, democratic governance, and market economies throughout the world, though its focus was typically the Middle East. "The advance of freedom is the calling of our time," President Bush said at a twentieth anniversary event at the National Endowment for Democracy in November 2003.

It is the calling of our country. From the Fourteen Points to the Four Freedoms, to the Speech at Westminster, America has put our power at the service of principle. We believe that liberty is the design of nature; we believe that liberty is the direction of history. We believe that human fulfillment and excellence come in the responsible exercise of liberty. And we believe that freedom—the freedom we prize—is not for us alone, it is the right and the capacity of all mankind.

Working for the spread of freedom can be hard. Yet, America has accomplished hard tasks before. Our nation is strong; we're strong of heart. And we're not alone. Freedom is finding allies in every country;

freedom finds allies in every culture. And as we meet the terror and violence of the world, we can be certain the author of freedom is not indifferent to the fate of freedom.[34]

This powerful and ambitious vision of America's "calling" was widely described as Wilsonian at the time. It was hardly the exclusive province of the right-wing neocons: a number of "liberal hawks" and others generally associated with the Democratic Party endorsed this expansion of democratic virtue.[35] It was a view of the world that had animated U.S. foreign policy for a century but again saw the Middle East in particular as the place of most troubling backwardness, one that was unfortunate for its inhabitants but also posed dangers and opportunities for Americans. It was, in a word, the frontier.

And there was no better place to apply this vision of "the spread of freedom," this ultimate taming of the wilderness through savage war, than in Iraq.

"OPERATION IRAQI FREEDOM"

By late summer 2002, the Bush administration was using the Iraqi WMD threat as a primary thrust of its policy objectives in the region. The supposed danger posed by Saddam became Topic A on the Sunday morning talk shows, the op-ed pages, and indeed the rhetoric of high administration officials, most prominently Cheney and Rice. This putative threat was the proximate and justifying cause of starting the war; the "transformation" of the Middle East was mere subtext.

By early 2003, President Bush was prepared to make the case for war:

Today, the gravest danger in the war on terror, the gravest danger facing America and the world, is outlaw regimes that seek and possess nuclear, chemical, and biological weapons. These regimes could use such weapons for blackmail, terror, and mass murder. They could also give or sell those weapons to their terrorist allies, who would use them without the least hesitation.

This threat is new; America's duty is familiar. . . . The ambitions of Hitlerism, militarism, and communism were defeated by the will of free peoples, by the strength of great alliances, and by the might of the United States of America. Now, in this century, the ideology of power and domination has appeared again, and seeks to gain the ultimate weapons of terror. Once again, this Nation and our friends are all that stand between a world at peace, and a world of chaos and constant alarm. Once again, we are called to defend the safety of our people, and the hopes of all mankind. And we accept this responsibility.

The conflation of Saddam and terrorism is notable. Earlier in this State of the Union speech, the president also spoke of preparations for homeland protection against chemical and biological weapons.* The case being made was confident and unambiguous: Saddam was hoarding vast quantities of chemical and biological weapons and 30,000 delivery munitions, and perhaps planning a WMD attack on the United States through his al Qaeda allies. ("Imagine those 19 hijackers with other weapons, and other plans—this time armed by Saddam Hussein.") There was no doubt that a war would commence soon.

While the public was somewhat ambivalent about this prospect, it was generally supportive: a Gallup survey at the onset of the war reported only 23 percent saying the war was a mistake, with 75 percent supportive. That included the "rally effect" of the public being more favorable once the military action had begun; two weeks before, the American people appeared to favor war only if the UN Security Council approved it. But support for action to remove Saddam was consistently majoritarian.[36] The public believed that Saddam Hussein was involved in the 9/11 attacks, as administration officials repeatedly hinted and which no doubt bolstered the support for the war.[37] In the run-up to the March 20 invasion, the absence of dissenting voices in the major news media and the general enthusiasm for war shown by some elite media, particularly the *New York Times* and the *Washington Post*, may

* The United States, said Bush, has "begun inoculating troops and first responders against smallpox, and are deploying the Nation's first early warning network of sensors to detect biological attack. And this year, for the first time, we are beginning to field a defense to protect this Nation against ballistic missiles. . . . I ask you tonight to add to our future security with a major research and production effort to guard our people against bio-terrorism, called Project Bioshield. The budget I send you will propose almost six billion dollars to quickly make available effective vaccines and treatments against agents like anthrax, botulinum toxin, Ebola, and plague. We must assume that our enemies would use these diseases as weapons, and we must act before the dangers are upon us." This alert could scarcely have been more alarmist in tone. By contrast, the administration was unprepared to produce flu vaccines, an actual threat.

have influenced public opinion. While there was some antiwar activity by civil society organizations, this paled in comparison to the much more sizable rallies against Desert Storm. Many of the most visible signs of antiwar sentiment were abroad, reflecting European skepticism that in fact blocked UN approval for the action. But American antiwar activity was less effective, partly due to the mixed messages in many rallies as every left-wing issue imaginable was proffered. Liberal foundations failed to support antiwar organizing.[38] A number of prominent Democrats and liberal intellectuals signed on to the war. Overall, however, the effect of 9/11 was probably responsible for this diminution of opposition.

The war was initiated, then, with very broad support of the American people, Congress, and the news media. Much of this support was based on false premises. While wars are nearly always fought on erroneous assumptions and perceptions, it is likely that this war was *knowingly* based on a set of enormous and fraudulent claims, making the horrendous consequences all the more damaging.

Cakewalk: From Invasion to "Mission Accomplished"

Controversy about military strategy began before the first shots of Operation Iraqi Freedom were fired. Not only was there a sizable debate about the WMD claims (with many arguing for more time for UN inspectors to do their work), but also about the size of the invading force. The latter became consequential for how American forces conducted the operation.

Most prominent in this debate was an open disagreement between the army chief of staff, General Eric Shinseki, and the civilian war planners, especially Defense Secretary Donald Rumsfeld. Shinseki made an almost offhand comment in a Senate hearing a month before the war in response to a question. He said the force required should be "several hundred thousand" to cope with postinvasion ethnic tensions and other occupation requirements.[39] A few days later, Paul Wolfowitz, Deputy Secretary of Defense and one of the chief architects of the war, told Congress, "There has been a good deal of comment—some of it quite outlandish—about what our postwar requirements might be in Iraq. . . . [Those] are wildly off the mark."[40]

Rumsfeld sacked the general and asserted that the force size, about 150,000, was more than adequate to the task, particularly as the Iraqis would, as Cheney vowed, welcome U.S. troops as liberators.* The Rumsfeld emphasis on a small invading force was embracing the new war doctrines of many, like the *Wall Street Journal*'s Max Boot, that small, technologically powerful forces could replace the plodding wars of attrition of yesteryear. This was an argument that had been proffered for a number of years and seemed to be plausible given the quick U.S. victory in the Kosovo campaign of 1999. It combined that with an improvised "shock and awe" or Rapid Dominance strategy developed by Harlan Ullman in which heavy bombardment, special forces operations, rapid assaults with mechanized units, and other tactics, would "create havoc" and confuse and demoralize the enemy decisively. (Among the features of the strategy was the supposition that rapid victory would reduce casualties on all sides, a conjecture that assumed that seizing Baghdad and toppling Saddam would be the end of the entire venture. "Shock and awe" suffered from a common malady of military theory: a nearly total absence of understanding the social dynamics—the will and the means to resist invaders—of the subjected peoples.) Rumsfeld also seemed to be taking aim at his rival at the State Department, Secretary Colin Powell, who as chairman of the Joint Chiefs of Staff in the early 1990s, insisted that overwhelming force should accompany U.S. military interventions, as it did in Desert Storm. Rumsfeld was so insistent on adapting these ideas to the invasion that he overruled nearly the entire uniformed war staff. Whether or not the Bush administration officials fully believed their calculations that a force perhaps one-third of adequate size would prevail, ordering a significantly greater number of troops for the invasion might have required a draft, and that would have placed the entire campaign in an

---

* This assertion about liberators tacitly invoked memory of the U.S. role in liberating Italy and France in the Second World War, of course, and was repeated often by Bush officials. It was reinforced and possibly originated by Iraqi exiles like Ahmad Chalabi and Kanan Makiya, who were relentless enablers of this push for heroic war. "People will greet the troops with sweets and flowers," Makiya told the president in January 2003 in an Oval Office meeting. (Equally striking about that encounter was Makiya and his colleagues' strong impression that Bush knew little about Iraqi society and was "unfocused on the key policy questions of the future" of Iraq.) Recounted by George Packer, *The Assassins' Gate: America in Iraq* (Farrar Straus and Giroux, 2005): 96–97.

entirely different political context, one by most reckonings that was not sustainable with the public.

The kerfuffle over the size of the invading force seemed to fade when operations commenced. U.S. and coalition forces (the British being the only other of significance) moved quickly toward Baghdad and other major cities from the south, with only one brief period of uncertainty—when so-called *fedayeen* fighters conducted some guerrilla tactics against the invading force and slowed the advance toward Baghdad. But this caused only a few days of minor consternation about the strategy. There was a pause by the invading forces to allow rest and repair. But the application of air power—1,800 aircraft flew 41,000 sorties in the first month—appeared to demolish any residual fight in the Iraqi military, including the Republican Guard—Saddam's special units—which encircled Baghdad. As commanding General Tommie Franks put it later, heavy bombers like B-52s saturated a "wide curve kill zone" stretching more than 100 miles east and west just south of Baghdad, and destroyed the Iraqis in place: "The bombardment that lasted from the night of March 25 through the morning of March 27 was one of the fiercest, and most effective, in the history of warfare."[41] Approximately two-thirds of the ordnance was precision weapons. As would occur later in the war, the air support for the rush to Baghdad was often called in by infantry when they perceived a threat. "We get a few random shots," an officer told an embedded journalist, "and we fire back with such overwhelming force that we stomp them. I call it disciplining the Hajiis."[42] As the U.S. forces moved toward the capital, the remaining Iraqi forces essentially melted into thin air—those who were not killed likely disappearing back to their towns and villages. Winning Baghdad itself took just a few days of careful assaults. Saddam took flight and was underground until his capture in December.

The relatively easy victory was not a surprise to most. Saddam had been soundly beaten in 1991 and had even fewer resources this time around. Still, it was a time of lavish self-congratulation for the administration and its supporters. Even defeating the hollowed Iraqi army occasioned accolades of "brilliant" planning and execution. "There have been major elements of military creativity in Operation Iraqi Freedom," wrote Brookings senior fellow Michael O'Hanlon. Operation Iraqi Freedom was "sheer military excellence and a devastating display of combined-arms warfare on the part of U.S. Army, Air Force, and

Navy personnel."[43] The victory occasioned much such acclaim, and more—from excoriating antiwar critics to visions of seizing Tehran and Damascus—which was understandable given the odious quality of Saddam's regime and the absence of military fight, including one with the feared chemical weapons.

What happened next was a surprise to the triumphalists and the news media, but not to many knowledgeable analysts. Indeed, even the administration had warning of the chaos to come. The dispute over Bush's assertions about weapons of mass destruction (officially acknowledged to be nonexistent in 2004) overshadowed another intelligence assessment: that of the likely condition of a post-Saddam Iraq. A major report to senior administration decision makers before the war by the National Intelligence Council, which draws on the research of several agencies, underscored as a major finding the likelihood of a "deeply divided society with significant chance that domestic groups would engage in violent conflict with each other unless an occupying force prevented them from doing so."[44] The invading and occupying force, then, needed to be large enough and with sufficient training to cope with such unrest, and this was a prominent point of prewar thinking in the government. It was ignored by the Pentagon, as was a sizable effort in the State Department to plan for a post-Saddam Iraq. What counseled that security was the sine qua non of a liberated Iraq. The thinking among the major decision makers—Bush, Cheney, Rumsfeld, Wolfowitz, and Rice—was instead that the American job was to knock off Saddam and turn the country over to the exile groups.

For a few weeks, this cavalier attitude did not have obvious consequences. There was considerable looting of Baghdad during the first weeks of occupation, which struck many as puzzling since U.S. forces were in control of the city. Seemingly a minor embarrassment at the time ("stuff happens," said Rumsfeld), it came to be seen as a signal to the Iraqi people that the United States was not prepared or willing to provide them with security. The looting affected infrastructure and the provision of services like electric power, journalist Mark Danner wrote at the time. "More important, the looting and mayhem destroyed American political authority even before it could be established; such political authority is rooted in the monopoly of legitimate violence, which the Americans, after standing by during weeks of chaos and insecurity, were never able to attain."[45] Looting was accentuated by lack of electricity, clean water, food, and general disorder. By not ensuring security at the beginning, the United States set the stage not only for insurgency but also for popular support for insurgency. At a minimum, the chaos fostered popular distaste for occupation that was not providing basic human necessities, including security from criminals, retribution, ethnic and sectarian strife, and the sizable remnants of Saddam loyalists.

The formal period of the war, from invasion to the capture of Baghdad in a mere three weeks and, in another three weeks, Bush's declaration of "mission accomplished" on the first of May, imparted not only a sense of conquest and U.S. power, but did so in the frames of reference so well grasped by the American public. The war was frequently depicted in that giddy period as "back to the days of fighting the Indians" and the new savage war, with soldiers doing Seminole war dances. "'This is like cowboys and Indians,' relayed a Marine," to a Fox News reporter, who concluded: "Indeed it is."[46] The three weeks were replete with a captivity narrative (Jessica Lynch) and increasing references to the mission as essentially Christian and possibly ordained by God. It also invoked more recent imagery: the fall of the Berlin Wall, when a statue of Saddam was toppled in what was apparently a staged event.[47] Even the more recent references, however, harkened to America's heroic role in the world. Regeneration through violence was under way.

Aftermath: The Blood Debt

The resistance to American occupation slowly simmered in the summer of 2003 and by early fall was a widespread, if disorganized, armed insurgency. In ensuing years, a metastasis of armed violence gripped Iraq. By 2010, the violence and associated disruptions—the nearly complete collapse of health care and sanitation, most prominently—took hundreds of thousands of lives—perhaps as many as a million Iraqis. The puzzle of this moral catastrophe is how and why it occurred.

First from the remnants of the old guard, then a more broadly Sunni Arab uprising that later stirred Shia reprisals, the violence and general chaos of the post-Saddam occupation had many causes and consequences. The conventional view in the United States is that the resistance to U.S. occupation was due to the loss of status of the Sunni Arabs, who as a minority in Iraq—one-fifth of the population—had enjoyed social, economic, and political dominance since Ottoman times. With the Iraqi army disbanded in May 2003 and the Ba'ath Party criminalized, the Sunnis took up the gun and the car bomb against the occupying forces as acts of revenge and in the hope of restoring their political power. (Now considered errors, these policies—dispersing the army and targeting Ba'athists—were promulgated by the civilian chief of the occupation, proconsul Paul Bremer, who has taken much of the heat for these colossal mistakes. But high-level Bush officials, including the President, were aware of the policies and possibly approved each in advance.)[48] This Sunni militancy was aggravated, and possibly caused, by the inadequate numbers of troops committed by Rumsfeld. This small force produced two major consequences. First was that the vaunted U.S. technological firepower was in effect used as a substitute for "boots on the ground." Second, and related, was that a counterinsurgency strategy requires a sizable troop presence, one that can "clear" a village of fighters and then hold it, providing security and services to the local populace in a way they understand to be stable and friendly. None of these things occurred sufficiently to avoid the debacle of 2004–2007, the worst period of violence.

The tactics used, whether with sizable forces or not, were rough. Clearing out villages and towns involved house-to-house searches that frequently violated Iraqis' social norms of privacy (especially of women and girls) and honor (especially of men). Many thousands of Iraqi men and boys were arrested in front of their families and sent to detention camps or prisons like Abu Ghraib without any evidence of wrongdoing. "Probably 99 percent of those people were guilty of absolutely nothing," a two-star army general later told Congress in 2006, "but the way we treated them, the way we abused them, turned them against the effort in Iraq forever."[49] Some 120,000 Iraqis were detained. In the house-to-house searches, if Iraqis resisted in any way, violence could readily follow. The procedure itself was violent. "You grab the man of the house. You rip him out of bed in front of his wife. You put him up against the wall," recalls an army scout posted in Baquba, the capital of Diyala province north of Baghdad. Army privates gather the other family members in one room. "Then you go into a room and you tear the room to shreds" looking for weapons. A sergeant adds that the house is turned upside down. "You've just humiliated this man in front of his entire family and terrorized his entire family and you've destroyed his home. And then you go next door and do the same thing in a hundred homes. Now, next week ten roadside bombs go off. . . . And nobody can understand why."[50]

The burgeoning resistance in the summer and fall of 2003 earned such retaliation in much of Sunni Arab Iraq, especially in Anbar province west of Baghdad, and in the capital itself. The cycle of hammering the villages and neighborhoods stirred an insurgency that was in fact many insurgencies, from very small tribal bands to confederations of fighters, some of them self-styled "jihadists," and a growing presence of foreigners associated with al Qaeda. Nationalism and revenge appeared to be from an early stage the galvanizing forces of the resistance. Bush administration officials constantly referred to the insurgents as remnants of the old regime, or terrorists. But most accounts of their sentiments pivot on resistance to occupation and national pride unaffiliated with Saddam, and on the "blood debt" of avenging a family or tribal member who had been killed. Families and tribes comprise dense kinship networks in Iraq, and an assault on one is an obligation for many to retaliate. The fact that the insurgency as a whole had no visible leadership or central command, had no obvious demands (apart from the United States leaving Iraq), and had no articulated ideology, indicated that it was decentralized, dispersed, and in many different parts. It was rising and falling as local conditions warranted, adapting quickly to U.S. tactics but growing apace as America's application of violence grew. Its shape, to the extent it could be discerned, was precisely what one would expect as a result of the U.S. strategy. A number of captured fighters would attest that their motives were defensive—they believed they were defending their families and communities against the invader. Thus the more the U.S. military used these tactics, the more insurgents it created.

Security sweeps in which atrocities like the killing of twenty-four civilians in the Anbar town of Haditha were common, but they were not the only source of enmity from Iraqis. The Haditha massacre followed a roadside bomb that killed a U.S. marine and symbolized the practice of meeting force with an overwhelming, often disproportionate response. Areas considered to be hostile were pummeled with artillery fire, just as in Vietnam, in nightly H&I (harassment and interdiction) bombardments. "We used our Paladins [howitzers] the entire time we were there," one officer wrote of his 2003–2004 tour in Anbar. "Most nights we fired H&I fires, what I call 'proactive' counterfire."[51] If American truck convoys were fired upon, or a roadside bomb was exploded or even suspected, the retaliation was potent. Roadside bombs were considered such a threat that any vehicle near the convoy, any individual on the side of the road with a cell phone or any other object that looked like it could be used to detonate a bomb, was lethally attacked. An actual explosion from the infamous IED (improvised explosives device) would prompt strafing whatever was nearby with automatic weapons. Cars in the way would be crushed, run off the road, and machine-gunned. One army specialist recalled that during training an officer asked the soldiers what they should do if a child stepped in the path of a convoy. "The answer that he gave us was 'Run him over.' He said the reason was that we shouldn't hesitate because of the way they would treat their children. . . . They don't value human life like we do and they don't share our same Western values."[52] Convoys and all kinds of military vehicles roared through Baghdad and other Iraqi cities at breakneck speeds, causing accidents and imperiling pedestrians. If traffic congestion slowed them down, they often would divert onto a sidewalk and scatter the people walking or selling goods at small kiosks. The other notorious practice centered on roadblocks, the checkpoints the U.S. military used as a net to filter out undesirables. The rules of the checkpoint were meant to use graduated force to stop Iraqi vehicles—signs, a raised hand, a raised rifle, a shouted warning, a shot in the air, and then, if the vehicle failed to stop, an attack on the car or truck. In many instances, the early signals, even if given, could be misunderstood. Warnings were in English, and soldiers escalated quickly to deadly force. Many of the most gruesome killings of civilians occurred in these vortices of miscues, confusion, and violence. An American reporter conveyed one on-the-road scene:

> Men and women watched nervously as the two soldiers went through the line of cars. And then the shooting began . . . a gunner fired bursts at a patch of long grass across the river, 200 yards away. The other Humvee's machine gun opened up, and people began running off the road. . . . I learned later that an IED had exploded down the road and the soldiers had begun shooting at passing cars.
>
> A man was killed driving in the other direction. The Army said that he had been killed by the bomb. When I came back from Baghdad a few

days later, I spoke with people who had been by the side of the road; they were certain it had been the soldiers. The day before, six people had been killed just outside Fallujah the same way. The next week the Chinook was shot down, killing sixteen soldiers headed home for R and R.[53]

This was the daily grind of U.S. operations. What Iraqis saw was an occupation force that was arresting men, demolishing buildings, and killing people in a seemingly random or indiscriminate "free fire zone" style that provided the native population with neither security nor even the bare livelihoods they had had under Saddam. The American actions, moreover, appeared to Iraqis to be mainly for the benefit of the Americans, in two ways. At the more abstract level, many came to regard the invasion and occupation as a grab of Iraqi resources or a Zionist plot. But at ground level, it seemed even clearer: the convoys were taking food and other necessities, and even luxury items, to American bases while Iraqis scraped to get by. And indeed the U.S. bases were oases of luxury and security compared with the rest of Iraq. This symbolized the broader resentment about the occupiers, which cascaded into every aspect of the occupation, from the heavily fortified Green Zone in Baghdad where Americans ran the country to the "force protection" ideology of the military in which the number one priority was to keep American soldiers and marines from being harmed. "The U.S. military's response to the insurgency has been uniformly muscular, its weapon of choice the blunt military instrument," writes Ahmed S. Hashim, a scholar at the U.S. Naval War College and a serving officer in Iraq. "This is necessary to a degree, but the existence of deep cultural misunderstandings and pervasive U.S. tendency to view peacekeeping and policing with disdain in favor of a 'robust' (force protection) approach means the missions invariably manage to enlarge the circles of alienation within the populace."[54]

Throughout 2004, the war was spinning out of control. The two battles of Fallujah, the sizable Anbar city of 300,000 mostly Sunni Arabs, was a fitting symbol of the broader conflict. An incident early in the occupation turned the citizenry sharply against the occupiers: fourteen people demonstrating peacefully were gunned down by American troops. This incident became a powder keg, and it blew the following March when SUVs carrying a Blackwater private security detail barreled into the city and came under attack, with a gruesome conclusion—four of them killed, burned, and hung from a bridge while dozens of Fallujans cheered—broadcast around the world.* The U.S. response (ordered from Washington) was swift and ferocious, using marines and plenty of air power—the AC130 gunships and Apache attack helicopters. But it could not defeat the resistance. The U.S. military ultimately negotiated a cease-fire. It was a powerful signal to the rest of Iraq. Despite the use of significant firepower, the U.S. military was unable to clean out Fallujah, and even this failed endeavor produced thousands of Iraqi casualties. At virtually the same time, a Shia uprising in Baghdad and some southern cities, mainly linked to cleric Moktada al Sadr, confronted the United States with a second front, in effect, and this one was potentially more volatile—the majority Shia, none associated with Saddam and the old regime, some linked to Iran, and many fighting what they considered to be a religious war. In November 2004, the American command saw fit to reengage Fallujah in a major battle; fortunately, by this time most civilians had fled. But the amount of fighting and sheer mayhem wrought on the city and the remaining insurgents was by all accounts terrifying. The city was repeatedly bombed, and then every house was searched three times. Millions of rounds of ammunition were expended. After several weeks, the U.S. command declared victory. "We have . . . broken the back of insurgency . . . a turning of the tide . . . the insurgents are on the run," proclaimed an American general. Others who were there were less sure. Said one colonel, "What's the impact on a ten-year-old kid when he goes back in and sees his neighborhood destroyed?"[55] Not only was an exceptional amount of air power applied, but white phosphorous—a harshly burning

---

* Private security contractors were used in very large numbers throughout the war, often to protect senior officials, convoys (also run by contractors in many cases), equipment, oil facilities, and other tasks. These armed contractors, which numbered as high as 30,000 (a number not including those merely providing unarmed services, such as drivers), came from dozens of countries. The numbers used were unprecedented in the history of American warfare. Their tasks were performed by U.S. military personnel in previous wars. They were essentially unaccountable, as indicated by a 2007 incident in which Blackwater gunmen killed seventeen Iraqi civilians and were let off unpunished by a U.S. judge. The reckless behavior, often lethal, of private security contractors was one of the major, bitter complaints of Iraqis and was never adequately addressed by American command. The April 2004 assault on Fallujah because of the killings of Blackwater employees demonstrates how closely linked the U.S. forces and private armies were.

chemical—was used in tandem with high explosives in what soldiers called "shake 'n' bake." This practice was widely discussed among Iraqis, who saw women and children affected.[56]

Despite what many recognized as a vicious cycle of violence unfolding, the military tactics did not change for nearly four years. In Tel Afar, for example, a city in the north that was often held up as a model of counterinsurgency, a soldier described their late 2005 sweeps of the city as increasingly aggressive. "We ordered residents to evacuate their homes" from a large section of Tel Afar identified as an insurgent stronghold "to camps outside the city. After that we proceeded to bomb their neighborhood for several days and nights with Spectre AC130 gunships, Apache helicopters, and tank rounds," he recalled. "We were told to search aggressively to teach the residents there a lesson—don't harbor terrorists . . . [we] generally trashed the homes we went through. My platoon found absolutely no evidence of foreign fighters, no weapons caches." So his commander sent them and the Kurdish *peshmerga* into another neighborhood and had them gather every military-age male from the entire area, and a masked Iraqi man was designated to pick out fifty men to arrest as insurgents without evidence. One of his commanding officers objected to the harsh treatment of the Iraqi civilians, but the tactics continued. "It's hard for me to believe that the Iraqis who witnessed this could possibly take seriously our version of justice and democracy."[57]

The stories from veterans and journalists of this kind of aggressiveness are legion. Even among those who did not become antiwar activists as a result of their experiences, the norms of combat, of searches and quotidian control over the populace, of detentions of Iraqis, and the other grisly duties of war are depicted as brutally degrading to all involved. "Combat distilled to its purest human form is a test of manhood," wrote Sergeant David Bellavia, one who believed in the mission. "Are you man enough? Are you tough enough? Do you have the nuts for this? Can you pull the trigger? Can you kill? Can you survive? *Yes.*" He continues: "Do we release our grip on our basic humanity to be better soldiers? Do we surrender to the insanity around us and ride its wave wherever it may take us? *Yes* . . . I am the madness."[58]

One of every five returning veterans from Iraq is suffering from post-traumatic stress disorder (PTSD), a number suggesting just how violent the war has been. Suicide rates and suicide attempts among soldiers is the highest ever recorded and has continued to rise through the course of the war. Suicide attempts were officially pegged at one thousand per month, though that is considered an undercount.[59] Suicide attempts and PTSD do not translate directly into evidence of abuse of Iraqi civilians, of course, but the correlation is suggestive. One medical specialist noted that PTSD can result from fear and seeing one's buddies blown up, and by "experiencing post-combat exposure to the consequences of combat, such as observing or handling the remains of civilians, enemy soldiers, or U.S. and allied personnel; being exposed to the sights, sounds, and smells of dying men and women; and observing refugees, devastated communities, and homes destroyed by combat."[60] The rates of PTSD are unsurprising when compared with the "problem" of soldiers not wanting to shoot their guns in combat: the army historian S. L. A. Marshall famously noted that in the Second World War only one in seven soldiers fired his rifle in combat, a number that increased to just more than half in Korea and 90–95 percent in Vietnam. Men in World War II were simply unwilling to kill even in situations where their own lives were in jeopardy, and this behavior had to be modified by the military, as it indeed has been over time with refined training techniques. "The triad of methods used to achieve this remarkable increase in killing are desensitization, conditioning, and denial defense mechanisms," explained a former officer who has studied "why Johnny can't shoot." The desensitizing is achieved through dehumanizing the enemy to a "gook" or "haji." Conditioning comes with highly realistic training. Denial involves generating contempt for the victims' humanity, the often-heard remark that the enemy does not care about human life the way we do.[61]

Camilo Mejia, a career sergeant who eventually served a prison term for refusing a redeployment to Iraq, said the harsh treatment of civilians in Iraq is "not the result of people waking up one morning as monsters, but it's part of the military culture. They train us that way. Things that would normally be considered impermissible or objectionable become the norm." Soldiers are trained to "remove the humanity from [Iraqis] to make it easier to oppress them, to brutalize them, to beat them, and in doing so, you remove the humanity from yourself because you cannot act as a human being and do all of these things."[62]

The war in Iraq differed from the conflicts in Korea and Vietnam in one key respect: the air war was less prominent in the war's carnage. While household surveys reported that many casualties resulted from "bombs," those attributions—often secondary in any case—would include artillery, mortars, and helicopter attacks, not only bombardment from U.S. warplanes. During the formal war to the taking of Baghdad, the air war was heavy, as it was again in the siege of Fallujah. But the operations of the U.S. ground troops in clearing villages of suspected Iraqi fighters was less amenable to air power; and while strikes were called and the amount of ordnance dropped was notable, the damage done by U.S. forces was mainly from those ground forces, artillery rounds, and detentions.

Most intriguing was that apart from those intense periods of air strikes in March–April 2003 and November 2004, the biggest role for air bombardment came in 2007. According to official figures the number of sorties by coalition forces was around 15,000 annually, with nearly 18,000 in 2007; but strikes with expended munitions increased by 500 percent over 2006, generally thought to be the most violent year in Iraq. How much was dropped is difficult to learn. There were relatively short periods where 100,000 pounds of munitions were used—the equivalent, as journalist Tom Engelhardt pointed out, of what the Spanish fascist forces used so infamously against the town of Guernica in the Spanish civil war. The powerful cannon rounds from aircraft like helicopters and the ground-hugging planes that provided "close air support" were likely more significant than even the 500-pound bombs that were used more sparingly. According to the air force command, during a one-day operation, for example, "F-16s and A-10 Thunderbolts not only 'dropped more than 3.5 tons of precision munitions' but also fired '1,200 rounds of 20mm and 1,100 rounds of 30mm cannon fire' in a five-square-mile area near the southern city of Najaf."[63]

The type of munitions used occasionally became controversial as well—napalm-like jellies have been used, as have tens of thousands of cluster bombs. "Every weapon available in our arsenal short of nukes is turned on Fallujah," Bellavia recalled. "The pre-assault bombardment is unrelenting. Jet after jet drops its bombs and rockets. Warthogs—the big, bruising A-10 Thunderbolt II close-support aircraft—strafe the main avenues into the city with their 30mm antitank cannon. Fallujah is smothered in bombs, shrouded in smoke. Buildings collapse. Mines detonate. Artillery roar."[64] Even outside an actual battle zone like Fallujah, the use of air power could be indiscriminate. A soldier relates how AC-130 gunships attacked an apartment building complex that clearly housed many civilians in Baghdad, "in no way a legitimate military target." He was told by command one night "they were going to put on a show for us . . . and an AC-130 mounted a sustained attack," hitting it with at least 100 rounds of 40mm explosives, with GIs watching and cheering from neighboring buildings. Another said, "we never got a true body count out of it; we never went to inspect the rubble afterwards."[65]

One of the difficulties of understanding the extent of the air war and its impacts on civilians is the lack of reporting from the areas where such action occurs. One report underscored this very lacuna when it described the consequences of the marines' Operation Steel Curtain, an attempt in late 2005 to root out Iraqi resistance fighters in western Anbar. Air strikes were prominent in the U.S. strategy. "'These people died silently, complaining to God of a guilt they did not commit,'" a local doctor told a *Washington Post* reporter at the scene. Health care workers counted ninety-seven civilians killed and thirty-eight insurgents. "'I dare any organization, committee or the American Army to deny these numbers,'" the doctor charged.[66] But the marines did deny it, in large measure, in a kind of rote ritual of blaming insurgents and claiming that the difficult missions were not producing unwanted casualties. In one notorious instance, a U.S. general denied bombing a wedding party in Ramadi in 2004, killing forty-five, by saying "Bad people have celebrations, too." Videos of the wedding backed up the victims' families' narrative of the massacre.[67] But the case came to notice because there were alternative accounts and evidence, a rare occurrence in a far-flung war.

One dimension of the Iraq War that bears strong similarities to Vietnam and Korea is the politically rickety regime the United States was supporting and the national security forces organized by both. While elections in Iraq gradually brought more legitimacy to the central government—from next to no legitimacy rooted in its origins as an American creation—the challenges of governance have been thorny. Sectarian distrust combined with suspicions of American motives, Kurdish intransigence, and Iranian, Saudi, and Syrian intrigue all make "normal politics" a chimera. In the meantime, through the first seven years of post-Saddam Iraq, a stubborn source of insecurity has been the native government armed forces, often absent in the fight against insurgents and just as often cruel exponents of one sectarian militia or another. In Korea and Vietnam, government forces were often the most mindlessly violent, and this pattern was repeated in Iraq. The promise that security in the country would be quickly and surely handed over to the Iraqis themselves has been one of the many falsehoods crippling the venture.

Once sectarian violence rose in 2005 and particularly 2006 after the February bombing of the Shia mosque and shrine in Samarra, the Iraqi armed forces were regarded as mere appendages of the Shia militias—themselves holding semi-official status from time to time—or in league with the Sunni insurgents. As early as the battles of Fallujah, when Iraqi units refused to fight and U.S. military officers believed them to be feeding intelligence to the insurgency, the reality on the ground was that no one knew who was aligned with whom. Insurgents or militia members would don uniforms of Iraqi police or army troops and then carry out horrendous crimes—murders, beheadings, sabotage, and the like. But even the official forces, particularly the 145,000 men in the Interior Ministry, were believed to be unreliable at best and possibly *genocidaires*.[68] Because the state was in the hands of the majority Shia, and the Sunnis had been provoking the sectarian strife, the organs of government were targeting Sunni men, families, neighborhoods, and towns. This, many Sunnis allege, continues. The detention camps and prisons run by these same units were the most notorious abusers of human rights. The question of how abuse and outright murder on such a scale could persist under the nose of the U.S. command was never adequately answered, but the delicacy of politics—the very survival of a plausible state—seemed as good an answer as any. Iraq needed order, even if bloody.

The sectarianism itself encouraged this behavior, as Sunni and Shia, who had generally been amicable in integrated towns and neighborhoods before the invasion, came increasingly to seize upon their religious identity as insecurity grew. Religious extremism had been noticeable in Saddam's last years, as deprivations caused by the sanctions turned needy people toward religion and Saddam's police apparatus eroded. Armed militias were socially repressive, attacking secularized women and enforcing a kind of frontier sharia, or Islamic law, which was particularly evident in the Shia south. Among the Sunni, religious militancy was also high; local mosques were often the nodes of organizing resistance, and that enhanced the power of the clergy. Unlike the Shia, which had a disciplined Friday prayer message come through the mosques from Ayatollah Sistani, Iraq's ranking Shia cleric, the Sunni clergy were more likely to respond to local conditions, including incidences of violence (from whatever source) and the imperatives of local actors.

The volatile mix of religion, sectarian killings, ongoing resistance to U.S. occupation, the presence of foreign *jihadis* loosely aligned with al Qaeda, and the chronic collapse of social services and economic sustenance all combined lethally in 2005 and 2006. The country by nearly all accounts was in a state of near chaos. Refugees and the displaced were counted in the millions. The number of deaths attributable to the war by mid-2006 stood between 400,000 and 650,000, according to two large-sample household surveys.[69] The inability of the United States and its military to provide security and services, their unleashing of deadly forces, and their own culpability in the death and casualty tolls led vast majorities of Iraqis to tell pollsters that they wanted the U.S. military out of Iraq. Hundreds of Iraqis were dying of malnutrition or lack of health care every day, or being killed by violent groups, armed forces, or criminal gangs, or in retributions and honor killings. Others in hundreds were fleeing to Jordan, Syria, and Iran.

Three unexpected changes led the violence to begin to subside by late 2007. The first was the fragmentation of the majority Shia; the stand-down of the Madhi militia in early 2007 ordered by al-Sadr, for example, was a means of controlling its own roiling factionalism, which affected national governance directly. Shia factionalism was a threat to security from the start of the state-building process and became more acute as the Sunni and Shia death squads multiplied. Governing became an exercise in controlling this factionalism, so al Sadr's retreat from militancy may have stemmed from a calculation of his own strength and from the logical view that the Shia would be the eventually winners in Iraq; also, the high levels of violence merely delayed the departure of U.S. troops and a semblance of order returning to Iraq.*

The second, related factor was the role of the foreign *jihadis*, particularly the so-called Al Qaeda in Mesopotamia led by the Jordanian

---

* Al-Sadr's calculation, if that's what it was, appeared to be paying off in late 2010, as his political party became a key player in the bargaining to form an Iraqi government and the U.S. military withdrew from a combat role by August 2010.

terrorist Abu Musab al-Zarqawi. The foreign fighters, Sunni for the most part, were overplaying their hand, killing Iraqis in often spectacular car bombings. These tactics came to be loathed by the Sunni tribal leaders (and those such as al Sadr), who gradually came to see that their own authority, as well as their security, was under assault by the chaos. Gradually the Sunni joined a loose-knit organization, the Sons of Iraq, or Awakening Councils, which formed to counter al-Qaeda in Anbar particularly. By the autumn of 2006, the Awakening Councils were cooperating with the U.S. military—which was paying each member— to drive the foreign fighters out: where the Awakening movement was strong, violence was notably reduced, and where it was not (in Diyala and Nineveh), foreign intervention remained troublesome. More than 100,000 Iraqi men joined these organizations and were paid for more than two years by the American authorities. The alliance also provided Sunni leaders with a much-needed source of strength as they became increasingly isolated by the Shias' grip on national power.

The third piece of the puzzle was the "surge" of thirty thousand extra U.S. troops announced by President Bush in January 2007. By late 2007, reported violence was down from the highs earlier that year, and this downward trend continued. The surge, which was announced with great fanfare and to considerable skepticism, was part of a new strategy adopted by General David Petraeus, who took command of the multinational force in Iraq in January 2007. Petraeus and others were convinced that population protection had too little emphasis in U.S. military practice in Iraq, and any counterinsurgency strategy had to incorporate such measures. While counterinsurgency doctrine had waxed and waned in the years of U.S. interventions in Southeast Asia and lost its traction in army thinking in the 1970s, it comprised a kind of Holy Grail for those who believed the hammering techniques of the military were clearly not working. "Frustrated with the insurgent attacks and unprepared to deal with the complexities in Iraq," reported one account, "there was 'a default to meet violence with violence on the part of some U.S. forces,' [Brigadier General John] Kelly observed, which led to civilian casualties and hardened the attitudes of many Iraqis against the Americans."[70] Petraeus, having attempted to institute these ideas while commanding the forces around Mosul just after the occupation began, sought to reverse the long-standing neglect of winning hearts and minds by writing a new manual and teaching it to officers. The new thinking, one reporter said, "draws on the hard-learned lessons from Iraq and makes the welfare and protection of civilians a bedrock of military strategy."[71] The manual made the case for population protection based on what commanders saw in Iraq for three years. "During any period of instability, people's primary interest is physical security for themselves and their families," it states. "When [U.S.] forces fail to provide security or threaten the security of civilians, the population is likely to seek security guarantees from insurgents, militias, or other armed groups. This situation can feed support for an insurgency."[72]

The Petraeus viewpoint insisted that insurgents could gain a foothold only by filling a security vacuum; they were not considered to be plausibly defending their communities, a view that reflected conventional thinking. The implementation of the manual and the new strategy, however, was an acknowledgment that the U.S. military was killing civilians excessively, so much so that the overwhelming power of the occupiers was insufficient to provide a modicum of order. This admission was almost entirely overlooked in the political debate about the surge, as if the new strategy did not matter, only the application of more force with additional troops. Whether it did work is a matter of ongoing discussion.[73] An effort has also been made to justify or explain away the annihilation doctrines obtained during the most violent periods of the occupation.[74] What is certain is that the very high mortality of the war—in the hundreds of thousands by the time the surge and the new counterinsurgency doctrine were implemented—was believed by Iraqis to be mainly the result of U.S. actions.

And those actions were driven by the errant mission, the ingrained habits, the presence of insufficient numbers of troops, and sheer confusion and fright. As Chris Hedges and Laila Al-Arian sum it up through the eyes of Iraq veteran Sergeant Ben Flanders:

> The Hobbesian world of Iraq described by Flanders is one where the ethic is kill or be killed. All nuance and distinction vanished for him. He fell, like most of the occupation troops, into a binary world of us versus them, the good and the bad, those worthy of life and those unworthy of life. The vast majority of Iraqi civilians, caught in the middle of the clash among militias, death squads, criminal gangs, foreign fighters, kidnapping rings, terrorists, and heavily armed occupation troops, were just one more impediment that, if they happened to get in the way, had to be eradicated.[75]

By mid-2004, scarcely a year after Saddam fell, the situation for Iraqis had become nearly desperate. A major household survey conducted by the UN concluded that Iraqis were "suffering from a widespread collapse in their living standards and conditions, exemplified by war-related injuries, chronic malnutrition, low life expectancy, declining health, declining literacy, and significant setbacks in women's rights."[76] From that point early in the war, the situation worsened. The resistance to U.S. forces and the Americans' actions to undermine insurgents were the main thrusts of the war's trajectory through 2004 and into 2005. Increasingly, the mayhem gushed sectarian blood, with the U.S. military unable or unwilling to provide security from this escalating violence.

From most accounts, three general themes emerge. First is the chaos the invasion and occupation created. Second is the sense of loss stemming from violence or flight or simply the absence of any sense of normalcy. Third is the grisly violence itself.

The Iraqis' fears were not only of violence—though it stalked everyday life—but of the social and political disorder the war wrought. "Leaflets and handbills," wrote an Iraqi blogger* in 2005 "have been circulated in Mosul starting from early Ramadan warning women of a terrible fate if they venture in public without the hijab. At Mosul University, several student groups handed notices to Christian students also warning them from showing up at college with their heads uncovered. As you know, Mosul is inhabited by the largest Christian community in the country, so we are talking of thousands of students here not a hundred or two. The world is more concerned [with] the Iraqi elections than the poor Iraqis themselves."[77] A mother of four in

---

* Internet Web sites sprouted up after the U.S. invasion and provide a window on Iraqi thinking. The bloggers range widely from pro- to anti-American; virtually all welcomed Saddam's demise but are leery of U.S. actions and intentions. As with all blogs, the veracity of many assertions is difficult to confirm, but the sentiments are no less valid than oral histories or other media that grew in the same period. It is worth noting that narratives of the natives of lands in which the United States wages war are extremely difficult to find in English, or at all. The Iraqi bloggers provide more than we have from Korea or Vietnam. They are, however, a thin socioeconomic slice of Iraq—literate in English, with the wherewithal to create and sustain a Web site. They tend to be young and educated, and, as one would expect, relatively cosmopolitan, and their concerns reflect that as a whole.

Baghdad told a journalist how intimidated she was by the new religious oppression imposed not only by the Shia clerics but by *salafi* Sunnis. "I resisted for a long time, but last year [2005] also started wearing the *hijab* after I was threatened by several Islamist militants in front of my house. They are terrorizing the whole neighborhood."[78]

These accounts stress the day-to-day reality of deprivation—of electricity and water, and sometimes food—in addition to physical threats, and show the families coping in such an environment. If a medical emergency strikes at night, for example, the perils of being outside could prevent anyone from leaving the house and going to a hospital. Children could not attend schools in many places for months or years at a time; parents were terrified to let their children out of the house. The aura of danger encompassed not only soldiers or insurgents, but criminal gangs who would kidnap for ransom or kill in an act of theft.

"The last few days, Baghdad has been echoing with explosions," wrote the blogger Riverbend in July 2004. "We woke up to several loud blasts a few days ago. The sound has become all too common. It's like the heat, the flies, the carcasses of buildings, the broken streets and the haphazard walls coming up out of nowhere all over the city. . . . There were clashes between armed Iraqis and the Americans on Haifa Street— a burned out hummer, some celebrating crowds, missiles from helicopters, a journalist dead, dozens of Iraqis wounded, and several others dead. It has become a part of life."[79] As the violence grew, the frustrations of ordinary Iraqis boiled over. In June 2006, from a well-known blogger, Shalash al Iraq, comes this circling despair:

We have had enough.

The fearsome nights are stifling us and we now have come to hate the Fall [of Baghdad]; we hate Liberation; we hate Sunnis; we hate Shiites; we hate turbans and sidaras [Baghdadi headgear—a reference to Adnan al-Dulaimi, a "Sunni" politician]; we hate Jihad and Jihadists, resistance and resistors; we hate concrete; we hate streets and sidewalks; we hate the Ministries; we hate Establishments; we hate news channels and news and communiqués; we hate the Parliament that has now become a venue for swearing-in ceremonies and nothing else; we hate songs; we hate commercials; we hate newspapers; we hate cars and car-depots; we hate conferences; we hate "surprise visits"; we hate neighboring countries; we hate the multinational forces; we hate the night; we hate the day; we hate Summer; we hate the sun that sends hell; we hate sleep; we hate water and electricity; we hate petrol and corruption and theft; we hate sectarianism; we hate sectarian 'allocations'; we hate Reconciliation; we hate the government of national unity; we hate committees and Commissions of Integrity, Trash, Rehabilitation and Silliness; we hate [political] parties and organizations; we hate assemblies, demonstrations, banners and chants; we hate laughter; we hate crying; we hate work; we hate study; we hate each other. And we hate ourselves. But (and this is our problem) we still love something that was called Iraq.[80]

The bitterness the war engendered has often targeted the politicians who were seen as tools of America, Iran, or one sectarian militia or another. "Our government has literally been privatized by sects and militias, and the ministries and the institutions have been subcontracted through nepotism to opportunists, stash hoarders and gangs' concierge; and Baghdad has been partitioned into boroughs for privately contracted thieves and the rest are sect-proprieties," wrote one blogger in 2006. "NO ONE WILL EVER IMAGINE HOW IT'S LIKE OVER HERE. It is tribal economies; preferential capitalism and outdated system of capital gains; 19th century civil war land-appropriations, solid privileged elitists, and Hehela style syncretism, and those are a few to mention."[81]

"[My aunt] was telling her niece from Adhamiya that she wanted to go gold shopping with her," a middle-class woman wrote of a family conversation. "'L' said, 'Sure, whenever you come over, I'll take you out. But I don't know if you'll be okay with all the corpses lying around, I've gotten used to them.' I was pretty shocked by her statement. So I asked her what she meant. 'L' is a 23 year old mother of two. She told me that next to her house it has become a dumping ground for corpses. Everyday, two or three dead bodies turn up a few steps from her gate. And they lie around for a couple of days before Iraqi security forces come and load them into the back of pick up trucks. People are too scared to report these dumpings."[82]

The loss of ordinary life was made acute by departures of family and friends. Nearly five million Iraqis—one-quarter of the population outside the relatively safe Kurdish provinces—left Iraq or were internally displaced, leaving homes and neighborhoods behind to find safety elsewhere, typically in Amman or Damascus. Many were forced to leave suddenly by deadly threats from militias and could take little with them.

The sense of loss—and actual loss—were pervasive. People left or moved to other neighborhoods or towns because of the climate of fear and the tangible, quotidian reality of a society in shambles. A photo of three boys drinking from a hose in a large run-off puddle in the street had this explanation: "The Raad brothers, and tens of thousands of children like them in this poor walled-in Shiite Muslim district, have been shaped by war, honed by poverty," wrote a blogger in "Healing Iraq." "They are witnesses to sectarian violence, Shiite militias, angry sermons echoing through mosques, Humvees gurgling through streets and pictures of religious leaders and wanted men hovering on billboards. These children may not know grammar and punctuation, but they know what to do when the bullets come, how to take cover, to hide from the kidnappers, the militants and the soldiers." The scene could be at any time in the war, but it is, notably, in late 2008. "Bloodshed and years of unrest are harsh teachers," noted one blogger, explaining the high dropout rates in school that are mainly due to the fear of going outside the home.[83]

A woman described her fear of going to a hospital to deliver her newborn at night, "because at night there were curfews and the streets were full of gangs hijacking cars and killing people. And that's aside from the random firing of soldiers—they shoot whenever they see a car coming anywhere near them."[84] She was lucky. She not only delayed her journey until morning, but there was a functioning hospital awaiting her. A year later, in 2005, doctors were scarce—they were being targeted by militias that sought to destroy the professional class—and Iraq's health care system was near collapse. Between the dissolution of the medical system and the fear of leaving homes, nonviolent mortality soared. By 2008, a major survey found that by large majorities Iraqis decried the scarcity of clean water, jobs, medical care, fuel, and security, particularly constraints on movement. These views, despite an obvious drop in violence, persisted into 2009.[85]

Those who left Iraq as refugees were the ones most threatened; in interviews, they typically described losing a family member to violence. This exodus—one of the largest post-1945 refugee movements in the world—reduced the number of targets and the actual numbers killed and hastened the sectarian segregation that eventually lowered the tolls in Baghdad. The million Iraqis in Damascus and the other million in Amman, with tens or hundreds of thousands fleeing to Cairo, Tehran, and points beyond (many to Europe) typically left with few belongings.

But they did tend to be middle-class with the wherewithal to emigrate and sustain a life in a new country. "The war that happened in Iraq was a war we hadn't lived before," an Iraqi woman in Amman told journalist Anna Badkhen in October 2008. "We have known many wars, but this one was strange to us. We didn't see killings in the other wars, but in this one we saw killings, kidnappings, dead bodies, bombings—bodies vanishing in front of you. Our morale was destroyed. We couldn't resist anymore and keep living there."[86] Jobs have been scarce for Iraqis abroad, and they sank into the gray or black economies of those countries quickly. The refugee experience tends to have common features. Families flee from fear of physical harm by the sectarian militias, who expropriate homes and kidnap family members, or worse;* they find life in Amman or Damascus difficult, even as the UN and local governments lend some help. Few seek to return. Many are likely to be permanently displaced with the mounting hardship of forced exile.

One of the older bloggers in Baghdad spoke of this aggrieved sense of loss as he sent one child after another to Amman to protect them from violence:

> I cannot imagine a father or mother hating their children. But in our miserable existence, we come very close to that.
>
> An average parent in present-day "free Iraq" spends a good portion of the day and night worrying to death over his or her children going to school, going out with their friends, being a shade late in coming home. . . . Their agony in their sleep soaking wet in their sweat during the long power cuts in the mercilessly hot summer nights of Baghdad is a dull pain of helplessness and fury in the heart.

---

* Many refugee stories mention that their homes were seized or someone they know was kidnapped for ransom. While these tactics by the militias could be "military"—cleansing a neighborhood, seeking money to support their insurgency—they could also be merely criminal. There is a history of militant political groups partially transforming into criminal gangs, as with the Protestant militias in Northern Ireland or FARC [Revolutionary Armed Forces of Colombia] in Colombia. This phenomenon has been a focal point of an intellectual debate fostered by Oxford and World Bank economist Paul Collier, in which rebel motives were counterposed as "greed v. grievance." In Iraq, as elsewhere, the significance of this trend to criminality is that criminal motives would seek a continuation of violence and instability in order to profit. One reason attributed to al Sadr's order for his militia to stand down in 2007 was that he could thereby purge the Madhi army of the criminal elements.

Most of the time you are sick with worry over their safety and well-being. The knowledge that they are in constant danger consumes you. It eats you alive.

You then realize that it is your love for them that is killing you. You begin to hate that love.[87]

The violence that so unnerved millions of Iraqis came in many forms—one reason that it was so unnerving to everyone, the U.S. forces included. It is a truism of this conflict that there are no fronts and very few set-piece battles of the kind that characterized the great wars of the nineteenth and twentieth centuries. The resistance could rise anywhere at any time. Sectarian death squads roamed Baghdad and other cities with impunity, it seemed. U.S. house-to-house searches came without warning. Violence could come from criminals, honor killings and retribution, roadblocks, convoys, errant air strikes and live bombs dropped months or years before. In the 2006 household survey conducted by Johns Hopkins researchers, the Iraq Mortality Study (IMS) that was published in the *Lancet* in October 2006, one of its findings was that most deaths (56%) were attributed to gunshot wounds, not car bombs or aerial bombardment. This suggests not only death from military actions but also from more personal or political assassinations. As one scholar noted at the height of the violence, just four assassinations per day in the seventy-five largest cities in Iraq would produce 450,000 deaths by the war's fourth anniversary—a plausible, even conservative, calculation. In another survey, which was conducted around the same time as the IMS (June 2006), fatalities from car accidents were exceptionally high. They were treated as nonviolent deaths but likely were caused in significant part by the way the U.S. military commandeered the city streets and highways.[88] And Iraqis were persistently afraid of getting caught in a crossfire if they left their homes.

To what extent the violence was attributable to U.S. actions is debatable; the IMS asked its 1,800 respondents for attribution—how did their family members die—which is less accurate than the fact of death itself. (If most people were killed away from the home, which is obvious, then the surviving members of the household may not have witnessed the death and in most cases can have only secondhand, possibly sketchy knowledge of how the death occurred.) In that survey, about one-third of all violent deaths—or 200,000—were attributed to actions of the coalition forces, and included fatalities of all Iraqis, not only civilians. (More discussion of these figures is in Chapter 10.) In other opinion surveys, a consistently high number of Iraqis blamed the American forces for most of the violence. A poll in September 2006 "found that 78 percent of Iraqis believe the U.S. military presence causes more conflict than it prevents" and that 61 percent supported "attacks on American forces." More than two-thirds favored U.S. military withdrawal. Another survey at the same time conducted by the State Department found nearly identical opinions.[89] As to withdrawal and blaming the United States for insecurity, Iraqi opinion remained constant, according to surveys, through the first five years of the war.

In 2007, a major survey commissioned by several American news organizations found that 82 percent of the respondents lacked confidence in the coalition forces to provide security. When asked how they protect themselves, large majorities responded that they avoid U.S. forces (81%) and checkpoints (66%)—by far the highest responses. And when asked what kind of violence has occurred nearby, 44 percent said "unnecessary violence against citizens by U.S. or coalition forces," with 31 percent saying the same of local militias and another 24 percent attributing civilian abuse to Iraqi security forces. (Surveys included Kurdish areas, one-fifth of the population, who were living in a relatively tranquil place.) Overall, this survey found that Iraqis blamed the U.S. forces for most of the violence (and another 9 percent blamed President Bush), by far the most significant source of violence in Iraqis' opinion. One in six respondents also said that at least one person in their household had been physically harmed in the violence, which could mean more than four million people nationwide.[90] While conditions had improved by March 2008, nearly two-thirds of Iraqis reported that they felt unsafe in their towns and that the security situation had not improved more than one year after the U.S. "surge." Over 70 percent said the U.S. presence was unwanted, and that the Americans had done a bad job in its efforts in Iraq. Half said they had plans to leave Iraq.[91]

While Iraqis as a whole were clearly pleased with Saddam's removal and initially were hopeful about their prospects politically, the attitudes about the U.S. presence and the attribution of blame for violence on the American forces was high and constant through the first five years of the war. What accounts for this disparity—the pleasure of Saddam's fall and the loathing of those that took him down? Some derives from national pride and the humiliation of a foreign power occupying the country. But the consistently high rejection of the American venture and specific blame for violence on U.S. armed forces correlates to very high casualties and abusive treatment, as with the house-to-house midnight raids, the indiscriminate detentions, and Abu Ghraib atrocities. The enormous displacement of up to five million also speaks volumes about the level of violence and the lack of confidence in the U.S. security mission. The American role, moreover, was not only a matter of direct force and misbehavior. Rather, it involved three other deadly effects—the growth of the insurgency itself in reaction to U.S. occupation (and the rough edges of that occupation), the general disorder created by the invasion and occupation, and the way the sectarian militias took advantage of that disarray and distrust without fear of U.S. competence, capacity, or willingness to suppress such murderous ways.

"We Iraqis have a nature, which is revenge" a tribal sheikh told journalist George Packer. "If my cousin kills my brother, I have to kill him. If the Americans come from thousands of miles away and dishonor our women and hurt our children, how can I spare them?"[92] The dense social networks of traditional Iraqis, who generally remain in one area and among whom first cousins can marry, become a fuse for resistance: one cousin killed or detained could explode in a dozen or two new recruits to a militant group. Religion itself is utilized as a form of social protest, intensified by competition between sects.[93] Defense of the family and community, nationalistic resistance to the Western invader, and religious fervency all get wrapped into a multidimensional conflict, spurred by the initial violence of invasion and occupation.

"I have seen many things as a doctor," said an Iraqi in al-Kindi, near Baghdad. "But what I am seeing these days is too much. I treated children with metal fragments all over their bodies because they played with unexploded bomblets that were part of cluster bombs. I saw men, women, and children with no limbs, bleeding to death because they were victims of bomb attacks."[94] Iraqi bloggers, who are even-handed in condemning violence from any source, were sharply focused on stories from checkpoints, air attacks on wedding parties and similar gatherings, and the mayhem in Fallujah. Riverbend had an especially striking entry:

> September 11 . . . he sat there, reading the paper. As he reached out for
> the cup in front of him for a sip of tea, he could vaguely hear the sound

of an airplane overhead. It was a bright, fresh day and there was much he had to do . . . but the world suddenly went black—a colossal explosion and then crushed bones under the weight of concrete and iron . . . screams rose up around him . . . men, women and children . . . shards of glass sought out tender, unprotected skin . . . he thought of his family and tried to rise, but something inside of him was broken . . . there was a rising heat and the pungent smell of burning flesh mingled sickeningly with the smoke and the dust . . . and suddenly it was blackness.

9/11/01? New York? World Trade Center?

No.

9/11/04. Falloojeh. An Iraqi home.[95]

A prominent businessman from Fallujah, watching the images of the siege of his hometown from Baghdad, "was appalled by the latest offensive, but even he, an educated moderate, spoke freely of his sympathy for the insurgents and showed few misgivings about the Islamic extremists among them," reported a British journalist, "which boasts of its campaign of kidnapping and beheadings." He believed the resistance "has largely arisen simply in opposition to the American occupation. 'If the Americans were not in this country, we wouldn't have heard of [these groups] or seen on the television what is happening now. But the pressure that the Americans brought on the Fallujan people is what made them so tough.'"[96]

Major incidents tend to draw the most ire. The Fallujah battles were one. Another was the Blackwater massacre of seventeen Iraqi civilians. Blackwater and other private security firms are viewed, correctly, as being just another aspect of a callous occupation mentality. "The bullets that tore the bodies of the innocent people came to my mind," a blogger recalled of the massacre. "I saw the wreck of a car a few days after the incident. I also remembered the tears of the old man that we met who lost his wife in the incident."[97] Checkpoint incidents were frequent and widely publicized, both a locus of U.S. violence and a place where insurgents were certain to find targets as well. The unforgettable image of a blood-splattered female toddler, whose family was shot to death by American troops at a checkpoint in Tal Afar in January 2005, was seen around the world and of course within Iraq. Such images often went with comments from U.S. soldiers and marines that, as in one incident, "we didn't know what was in that bus. . . . I'd rather see more of them dead than any of my friends. . . . Everyone understands the word 'stop,' right?"[98]

"'We all support the *muqawama sharifa*,' he said—the 'honorable resistance,' by which he meant to distinguish resistance warriors from the many armed people who attack civilians," a Sunni tribal leader told journalist Nir Rosen, describing their animus toward foreign fighters, especially al Qaeda. Another Anbar sheik and mosque leader told him why he abandoned Hit, his city. "The situation there has become disastrous. . . . They hit my son's house in an air strike and destroyed his house and killed my grandson. The people of Hit are caught between Americans on one side and al Qaeda on the other side."[99] Among the fascinating details of these accounts is a general lack of Shia-Sunni animus, as in fact the two sects lived together before the war and intermarriage was common. Sunnis are wary of Iranian influence with the returned Shia leaders, and Shia are wary of Ba'athist retribution. One can see this routinely among the bloggers, who see al-Sadr as a tool of Tehran, for example, and don't understand why the U.S. forces didn't deal with him more decisively. Sectarian violence, which came to dominate people's lives in Baghdad and other major cities by 2005, is frequently the frame used to explain the violence: Iranians versus Ba'athists, or Iranians versus al-Qaeda, with everyone else caught in the crossfire. By the end of 2006, Baghdad had largely been ethnically cleansed, with old mixed neighborhoods seized by one sectarian militia or another and American occupation forces erecting "Jersey barriers" or walls to stifle the flow of humans across these new, deadly demarcations.

In a traditional society, the treatment of women is especially sensitive, and present-day Iraq is a cacophony of competing views about how the war has generally changed the status of women. Most assert the treatment is more repressive and point to how the war has directly impacted women—for example, the constant complaint of mistreatment or dishonor by one security force or another. Among the most incendiary of charges are sexual assault, particularly rape, which tended to dominate the discourse of female bloggers. The most searing commentary centered on the crimes committed by U.S. soldiers in Al-Mahmudiyah, near Baghdad, in 2006—the case of Abeer Qassim Hamza. This fourteen-year-old girl was raped and murdered by several Americans; her mother, father, and three-year-old sister were also murdered the same night. This grisly crime was prosecuted and one soldier received a sentence of life without parole. Two other rapist-murderers received long sentences but are eligible for parole in ten and twenty years, and several others were let off without punishment for providing evidence (after some foot-dragging by the military; one of the murderers blamed the stress of war for his actions). Iraqis were outraged at the light verdicts. A number of bloggers say that while this is an especially spectacular case, the number of rapes and sexual assaults in Iraq is rampant. "Rape. The latest of American atrocities. Though it's not really the latest—it's just the one that's being publicized the most," Riverbend angrily commented after the crime was revealed. "The poor girl Abeer was neither the first to be raped by American troops, nor will she be the last. . . . We've been hearing whisperings about rapes in American-controlled prisons and during sieges of towns like Haditha and Samarra for the last three years. The naiveté of Americans who can't believe their 'heroes' are committing such atrocities is ridiculous. Who ever heard of an occupying army committing rape??? You raped the country, why not the people?"[100]

The Abu Ghraib scandal, in which a prison where Saddam detained and tortured Iraqis was being used by the U.S. military to detain and torture Iraqis, also revealed disturbing tales of sexual assault. "A female colleague of mine was arrested and taken there," a professor of political science told journalist Ruth Rosen. "When I asked her after she was released what happened at Abu Ghraib, she started crying. Ladies here are afraid and shy of talking about such subjects. They say everything is OK. Even in a very advanced society in the west it is very difficult to talk about rape." Reports of rape at Abu Ghraib did not prompt any prosecutions. "On the condition of anonymity and in great fear, some female detainees nevertheless did speak with human rights workers after being released from detention," writes Rosen. "They have described beatings, torture, and isolation. Like their male counterparts, they reserve their greatest bitterness for sexual humiliations suffered in American custody. Nearly all female detainees reported being threatened with rape. Some women were interrogated naked and subjected to derision and humiliating remarks by soldiers."[101]

The women were caught between a war system in which rape was tolerated and a social milieu in which women so dishonored were outcasts, often abused by their own families as a result of sexual crimes visited upon them. Noting the wide variety of security forces committing sexual crimes, an Amnesty International report in 2009 remarked that "most of these crimes have been committed with impunity. . . . Acts of sexual violence against women in Iraq are severely under-reported, not least because of the victims' fear of reprisal, and reported incidents are not systematically recorded." The Iraq Penal Code of 1969 that remains in force (by writ of Paul Bremer) provides only six months of jail time for honor crimes, such as a father murdering his daughter because she had been raped.[102]

The "other" sexual crime in Iraq is trafficking and prostitution. One estimate has 50,000 Iraqi girls (some as young as ten years old) and women working as prostitutes in Damascus and Syria. An Iraqi pageant queen, Myra Adel, told an American columnist that she spoke to some of the girls who had been arrested for prostitution in Syria "and they said they would rather be in prison than have to go back out there and get abused by Saudi, Kuwaiti, and other Gulf States men who still hold grudges against Iraq and find pleasure in abusing Iraqi women to make them pay for Iraq's war against these Gulf States in 1991."[103] More organized criminal syndicates operating out of Dubai, possibly the world's biggest illegal sex trafficking center, have moved thousands of women from Iraq across the region and into Europe and elsewhere.[104]

At the core of much commentary in Iraqi narratives, whether the discussion is of sexual assaults, checkpoint mayhem, house-to-house searches, or the endless spiral of murder between the Arab militias, is the plaintive cry about the absence of U.S. security. It was not only the direct abuses and bombings and firefights that so dispirited the people of Iraq; it has been the promise of the invasion undermined by its reality, a hyperpower that will not or cannot protect the people upon whom it chose to impress its power. This is the lamentation of the occupied. On an October day in 2006, a wave of violence struck Balad, a town forty miles north of Baghdad. Dozens of Sunni civilians were murdered, but no help came from the large, well-appointed U.S. army base in the same town. "People are bewildered because of the weak response by the Americans," said an Iraqi in Balad. "They used to patrol the city every day, but when the violence started, we didn't see any sign of them." A Baghdad blogger added: "Iraqis are wondering what's behind the Americans' weak response to Balad's crisis? Why haven't they intervened to stop the bloodletting?" Another resident said of the Sunni-Shia strife, "Our relations are not of months or years. It's since the beginning of time. This relationship has been destroyed in a second."[105]

"I feel like I've given the traditional words of condolences a thousand times these last few months," Riverbend wrote in July 2006. "'Baqiya bi *hayatkum . . . Akhir il ahzan . . .'* or 'May this be the last of your sorrows.' Except they are empty words because even as we say them, we know that in today's Iraq any sorrow—no matter how great—will not be the last."[106]

THE AMERICAN PUBLIC

When in February 2007 the American people were asked, for the first and only time how many Iraqis they thought had died in the war, the response was both disheartening and unsurprising: 9,890 was the median answer, a figure that was likely low by several hundred thousands. In the same survey, the respondents knew almost precisely that 3,000 American military personnel had died in Iraq; so ignorance of the Iraqi casualties did not stem from complete ignorance of the war.[107] The lack of knowledge or concern about the war's victims was an outcome of several reinforcing tendencies in American political culture: news media that only occasionally reported the costs of the war to Iraqis, the Bush administration's insistence on how the war effort was benefiting Iraq, a general avoidance of the war's consequences apart from the U.S. casualty rate, and the long-standing tendency to view the "enemy" population as a dispensable side effect of the American global mission.

In many respects the American public reacted to the Iraq War as they had to the Korean War. At first supportive of what was posed as a necessity to deal with an international threat, the war's bad turns on the battlefield drove increasing numbers of Americans from support to skepticism and opposition. The general indifference to the war's progression was also striking. Popular culture scarcely bothered with what was occurring in Iraq. There was no appreciable antiwar movement. The news media followed a pattern of intensive coverage at first, which waned over time. Movies about Iraq generally failed at the box office, particularly those critical of the war. Politicians cautiously responded to the debate about Iraq, but it was a jumbled discourse about the timing of American withdrawal, accusations about the phony intelligence used to justify invasion, and heated exchanges about who cared most about the men and women serving in the U.S. armed forces in Iraq. The people who had been "liberated" scarcely figured into this discussion at all. All of these features bore strong similarities to the situation in Korea, right down to the inconclusive ending and claims of victory or counterclaims of waste.

When Iraqis did enter the picture, they were often depicted as ingrates, unworthy of the sacrifice of thousands of American lives. When new prime minister Maliki stood up Bush during the president's visit in 2006, when an Iraqi journalist threw a shoe at Bush on a later visit, when men such as al Sadr were treated as heroes to Iraqis rather than as scourges, when Maliki called the U.S. troop withdrawal plan a victory for the Iraqi people—these were occasions to excoriate the sullen and unappreciative Arabs. Worse were opinion surveys showing large numbers—even majorities—of Iraqis approving attacks on U.S. troops as late as 2007, or the hobnobbing of Iraqi political leaders with Iran's conservative elite, or the consistently high support for U.S. withdrawal: these persistent attitudes were treated with derision or befuddlement, rather than probing to learn how such views were possible. The sacrifice of the United States was indeed enormous. More than 6,000 died, including 4,400 military; more than 32,000 were wounded by the end of combat operations in 2010. Even more suffered from permanent psychological disabilities, and $3 trillion or more would be expended on the war, reconstruction, and veterans' care, to say nothing of the 1991 war and the costs of containing Saddam until 2003. This price may have been paid for reasons other than humanitarian concern—the control of oil and a demonstration to other authoritarians in the region—but it is a high price all the same, with its many sad consequences for the thousands of families of the fallen. It would be a callous people who did not appreciate what Americans had done for them, or perhaps a people who themselves had been routinely abused and quickly forgotten, and thereby unable to sympathize with their occupiers' own tragedies.

The Uncertain Trumpet?

The American public supported the war at its outset. By 2002, in fact, a majority supported action to remove Saddam from power. This enthusiasm—asked in the context of "significant" U.S. casualties—was in part a direct result of the trauma and anger induced by the 9/11 attacks. The American people were eager to punish those who had done harm to the United States or had intentions of doing so. By the time the war was launched, the support rose to about 70 percent or more, showing the "rally-round-the-flag" effect as well as building on months of careful cultivation by the Bush administration of the WMD case against Saddam.

The public, however, had been willing to go to war with Saddam before 9/11. About 52 percent had said they would back regime change by U.S. forces in a Gallup survey nine months before the World Trade Center was brought down.[108] The events of 9/11, while intensifying emotions and attention, were not fully responsible for the support for war in Iraq. That support itself was waxing and waning in the months between August 2002—when Cheney clearly signaled the administration's intent—and April 2003. Before the final public relations push, the erstwhile majoritarian support had actually slipped to a 43–48 disadvantage in January 2003. The ensuing warnings about Saddam's nuclear and biological weapons arsenal—echoed virtually without dissent among technical experts and the news media—and the rhetoric of a "cakewalk" and the image of troops being greeted with flowers then turned the public again toward support.*

Given all the influences—9/11, long animus toward Saddam, and the alarms about nuclear, chemical, and biological weapons—the American public's backing for Operation Iraqi Freedom is unremarkable. The disagreeable Vietnam experience could be seen as a rupture in America's foreign, military entanglements: the norm was actually a consistent support for a series of interventions to protect "vital U.S. interests," and while the twenty years of war and sanctions in Iraq may have been longer and bloodier than any since Vietnam, it was in keeping with this durable tradition. Thus the base of support for war, that 52 percent in early 2001, could leap to 70 percent or more when U.S. airplanes began the assault on Baghdad.

---

* There is a striking difference between this situation, where a technical community comprised of a small number of experts relied on incomplete evidence but confidently braced the president's position, and the Cold War, in which a very large, multidisciplinary epistemic community grew to examine the U.S.-Soviet nuclear competition and served as a check on U.S. presidents who routinely overstated Soviet capabilities and intentions. Too many of the nonproliferation advocates sustain an unintentional bias by raising alarms about minor or imagined threats. These advocates (UN weapons inspection chief Hans Blix notably not among them) almost unanimously declared that Saddam had WMDs. The public, with no other information, was hostage to these views and their purveyors (who remain prominent in the discourse about Iran's nuclear development). Also noteworthy is that during the Cold War the scientists skeptical of the arms race calculated the likely human cost of nuclear war for all populations affected.

The public's enthusiasm for the venture in Iraq steadily declined very soon after Bush had declared victory on May Day. From May 2003 to January 2005, the support for the war dipped from a 72–25 margin to a slight plurality agreeing that it was a mistake, a sentiment that was nearly a majority earlier in the fall of 2004. It fluctuated around 50–50 for a year. The rise in sectarian killings in early 2006 then tipped American opinions more definitely against the enterprise: by mid-March 2006, a few weeks after the Samarra shrine was bombed and let loose a torrent of violence, the margin of the public saying the war was a mistake leaped to a 57–42 margin and has largely stayed there ever since. Even a year after the "surge" had begun and violence was clearly declining, the American public remained firmly in the "it was a mistake" camp: in April 2008, for example, the spread was 63–36. These figures are from Gallup and asked the same question—whether the war was a mistake—but other surveys reflect very similar numbers. So as the perceived costs to Americans rose, the opposition rose; when the reduction in violence in Iraq was apparent by 2008–2009, the American public still saw the U.S. involvement as a mistake.[109]

This decline occurred despite the absence of an antiwar movement of any size and reporting that was broadly uncritical in the early going. The drooping support seemed to hinge almost entirely on two factors—one was the growing number of casualties to U.S. troops, and the other was a growing body of evidence that the administration had misled the public about Iraq's purported (but nonexistent) WMD program. Some fallout from the Abu Ghraib scandal must also have had a dispiriting effect, even as top leaders tried to blame lower-ranking officers and right-wing pundits mounted a defense of torture.

The public was rarely confronted with the reality of war for ordinary Iraqis, and, as a result, it's difficult to gauge how Americans regarded this aspect of the U.S. venture. One impression can be gleaned from the reaction to the mortality studies. All became touchstones for sentiments about the war: those opposed to the war cited the high numbers in the *Lancet* articles, those who supported the war excoriated them. The news media, while reporting the second article, did not continue to probe its implications. There were other surveys and reports on mortality that received even less attention. In the end, the conservative method of Iraq Body Count, the London-based nongovernmental organization that actually counted civilian deaths as they were reported in the English language media, remained the most often cited source on the scale of the killing. None of the mortality accounts produced a discernible concern among the public.

Other instances of troubling news—the opinion polls of Iraqis cited earlier, for example, or the UN estimates of growing numbers of displaced Iraqis—failed to generate much discussion apart from those who specialized in such matters. And none of the stream of bad news from Iraq spurred a sizable social movement that demanded withdrawal, even as general public opinion was turning against the war. One Gallup survey found that while many Americans were personally upset by the war, only about one in ten of those did anything active, such as writing a congressman, to express their opinions. Where there were public outbursts of dismay, very specific violations—Bush's dishonesty, Abu Ghraib—were heralded more than any concerns about the suffering of Iraqis. Howard Dean's brief if galvanizing presidential candidacy in 2003–2004, largely based on his criticism of the war, was only tepidly popular with Democratic voters, and never focused on the war's consequences for Iraqi civilians.

While unclear as a gauge of Americans' sympathies, charities to support the war's effects on civilians in Iraq were very few and poorly funded, with little media attention. Major humanitarian relief organizations like the International Rescue Committee or Mercy Corps International were involved, particularly to help the displaced, and at times used U.S. government relief funds. But there is little evidence that Americans supported such efforts in any significant way. Compared with the outpouring of generosity by Americans for the victims of the Asian tsunami in 2004 or the Haiti earthquake in 2010, both of which had fewer overall casualties or displacement, the absence of charitable giving on behalf of Iraqis is striking. One might say that the public believed the very large amounts of money going to reconstruction and security would be enough, though the U.S. government and other agencies it supports, like the World Bank, also invested heavily in relief and reconstruction after the Asia and Haiti disasters. Foundations were largely absent as well, both in supporting relief and in advocacy or policy research; at the height of the violence, the annual meeting of the largest umbrella group, the Council on Foundations, did not have a single mention of the war on its program.[110]

The American people did demonstrate a sizable level of compassion toward the men and women who served in Iraq, however—the "heroes" in the "sandbox." One clearinghouse Web site lists 130 organizations that are aiding veterans.[111] The themes of such groups include "protecting our freedom," "deposing one tyrant at a time," a "gathering of eagles" (pro-war demonstrations), and countering war critics (particularly the ubiquitous Code Pink, an inventive and confrontational women's group). But even these sentiments seemed contrived and marginal, with public attendance low. An informal but randomized survey of yellow ribbon stickers, showing support for service personnel, on automobiles in the Northeast found them dropping from about 20 percent of vehicles (more than two-thirds on SUVs) in 2001–2003 to less than 5 percent by 2009. Even the easiest reflex to support the American venture was overwhelmed with apathy.

Reporting: WMDs, Embeds, and Arabs Killing Arabs

The performance of the major newspapers and networks in covering the run-up to the war and the war itself is now widely regarded as inadequate if not often shameful. The lack of critical reporting on the administration's WMD claims have come in for particular scorn. The pre-war episode of laxness was consequential, of course, making it easier to sell the public on the need for war, the inadequacy of the UN inspections, and the possible threats to U.S. security. Editorial and op-ed page comment followed this pattern as well: critics and skeptics were simply shut out of the debate. Many pro-war commentators, like Michael Kelly in the *Washington Post*, routinely attacked skeptics and antiwar activists as "marching with Stalinists." The panic about terrorism and the adrenaline rush of defeating the Taliban gave the editorial pages a narrow, martial bent.

What is less appreciated is that this self-censorship, or swallowing whole the administration's claims, continued to mar coverage after Saddam fell and Iraq became the grounds both of resistance to occupation and of civil war. The Bush White House and the military treated reporters who strayed off their narrative—that this was a war to democratize Iraq, and violence was perpetrated by terrorists such as Zarqawi and al Qaeda—with the proverbial cold shoulder; this chill enveloped the top news organizations as well. In late 2004, Michael Massing, the most trenchant of critics of press coverage, was able to describe this pattern, as important stories by Nir Rosen and Swedish filmmaker Urban Hamid, for example, were simply ignored by the major news media. Massing relayed a conversation in this vein with another journalist: "'At the moment, there's real sensitivity about the perceived political nature of every story coming out of Iraq. . . . Every story from Iraq is by definition an assessment as to whether things are going well or badly.' In reality, he said, the situation in Iraq was a 'catastrophe,' a view 'almost unanimously' shared by his colleagues. But, he added, 'editors are hypersensitive about not wanting to appear to be coming down on one side or the other.'"[112]

The military-led process of embedding reporters—allowing certain journalists to travel with army and marine units through Iraq—ensured predictably adulatory coverage at the outset. "The romance blossomed," wrote Sig Christenson, an embed from a San Antonio newspaper. "We were enthralled with the prospect of covering a war, the biggest story any reporter will ever get, and the troops began to like the media spotlight. A bonding began." It was a bond that inevitably led to positive coverage of the war as the action was conveyed wholly through the military's eyes. This narrative structure excluded the on-the-ground realities for the Iraqi population. When the war turned sour for America, Christenson says, the relationship turned sour, too, and the military began to bar reporters from certain stories and verbally attacked them. He quotes a three-star general saying, "Remember, these reporters were being stuffed into wall lockers in high school by the types who now run our military. They're just trying to get even."[113]

Even with more critical reporting, however, the focus was narrow: the chaos in Baghdad from car bombs and increasing Iraqi-on-Iraqi violence. Much was left out. This seemed especially true of civilian casualties. "There are a huge number of refugees from and displaced people in Iraq. Now, one refugee agency says five million people have been displaced by the war, both internally and externally. That's just a phenomenal figure, so it's hard for me to understand why that isn't one of the leading headlines we see every day," recalled a photographer who spent years covering the war. "Early on in the war, I felt that the consequence of this U.S. bombing and this invasion on Iraqi civilians was going to be missing from the dominant news narrative in the United States."[114] And it was. A typical story of an air strike on a group of Iraqis would invariably come down to a military spokesman insisting they were all insurgents and another source, such as an Arabic network like

Al-Jazeera, quoting local people claiming it was a wedding party. There was little attempt by American reporters to establish which version was correct, and the claims of the Iraqis at the scene never gained the same footing as did reports of U.S. spokesmen in the American news media.

In part, this lack of depth stemmed from the growing danger in Iraq. English-language correspondents were confined to Baghdad or the occasional run to another major city. Events elsewhere were reported—if at all—via military press release or from stringers. Only large-scale acts of violence, moreover, tended to get attention; the quotidian violence of retributions, house searches, crime, and the like went unnoticed. Most news bureaus were understaffed and had to hire interpreters, drivers, security, and so on—an immensely complex and costly endeavor. Many reporters were embedded with U.S. military units and tended to soft-pedal anything that might sound critical in order to maintain their access. The entire atmosphere worked against penetrating or comprehensive coverage. Many journalists showed immense courage and self-sacrifice in covering the war—a high number have been killed (although most of the journalists killed have been Iraqis)—but the structural constraints and political timidity among the editors back home conspired to present a picture of violence in Iraq that was, at best, partial.

In the war coverage, deadly violence was nearly always the doing of the insurgents and militias, without cause or rationality, and the rising violence in 2005–2007 was depicted as a matter of "ancient hatreds" between the two main sects: Sunni and Shia. U.S. soldiers, while sometimes portrayed as being overzealous at checkpoints, as detention guards (Abu Ghraib, mainly), and in rousting families in midnight raids, were provided ample opportunities to express their frustrations with the conditions of battle (not easily able to distinguish insurgents from civilians, for example) and their compassion for the Iraqis when things got out of hand. Few such opportunities were provided to Iraqis outside the government. The air war was rarely written about. The refugee crisis earned some reports but no sustained coverage, and the U.S. culpability for the displaced was rarely addressed.

The matter of civilian casualties rarely earned mention in an op-ed or editorial in the *New York Times* or the *Washington Post*. The major pundits in the elite media have essentially ignored the issue. The coverage of the mortality studies was uninformed—filled with errors about statistical methods, reverting to the administration's numbers if discussing it at all. Typical of this was a news story in the *Los Angeles Times* refuting the large estimate by the Johns Hopkins' scientists in October 2006, claiming that a *Times* "study" found only 50,000 fatalities, not the 650,000 the household survey had revealed. This was repeated on public radio and television. When pressed, the *Times* correspondent backtracked and said that there wasn't actually a study, but some checking in with morgues and a guess based on that. When asked whether a correction would be made, none was forthcoming, either from the *Times* or public broadcasting.[115]

Television coverage was no better. The September 11 attacks had put even more pressure on television news than on print to be patriotic and essentially to mute criticism of the war on terrorism. This was due in part to the perception of television's greater influence and the lack of time dedicated to present subtleties of world politics. Through the prelude to war and the early part of the U.S. occupation, coverage followed these tendencies as well as the long-standing habit of relying on government sources of information, a habit reinforced by the military's system of embedding journalists. "The data showed that the administration had a privileged role—and dissent was largely absent—across virtually all American news programs," noted one of the few scholarly examinations of TV news and the war. The study also concludes that "all of the American media largely shied away from showing visuals of coalition, Iraqi military, or civilian casualties. Despite advanced technologies offering reporters the chance to transmit the reality of war in real time, reporters chose instead to present a largely bloodless conflict to viewers, even when they did broadcast during firefights." Of more than 1,800 stories on six networks (NBC, ABC, CBS, CNN, Fox, and Al-Jazeera) at the war's outset, only seventy-three stories mentioned Iraqi casualties.[116] Iraq coverage dropped from 23 percent of broadcast news in early 2007 to 3 percent for networks and 1 percent for cable in 2008. The reasons were economic in part, but public apathy was reasoned to be a factor.[117]

With the decline in coverage came a decline in public interest, or perhaps the relationship was the reverse. "As news coverage of the war has diminished, so too has public interest in news about Iraq," explained a Pew Research Center report in 2008. "Iraq was the public's most closely followed news story in all but five weeks during the first half of 2007; however, it was a much less dominant story between July 2007 and February 2008." The survey found that a sharp decline in awareness of U.S. troop deaths in Iraq had occurred in only six months.[118]

The attention to the war did not merely decline; it was always a one-sided affair, with American casualties far more front-and-center than any others, and Iraqi opinion—to the extent it was reported—coming from the mouths of American-installed leaders or depicted as ethnic or sectarian grudges.[119] The war was one-sided in its coverage of the sources of violence as well. Sectarian killings earned considerable attention, but American abuses, apart from Abu Ghraib, rarely found their way onto the front page or airwaves. "When *The New Republic* ran a column by a private that recounted several instances of bad behavior by US soldiers," Michael Massing recalled, "he and the magazine were viciously attacked by conservative bloggers. Most Americans simply do not want to know too much about the acts being carried out in their name, and this serves as a powerful deterrent to editors and producers."[120] The online discussions of the war ranged widely: from the left there was an urgency to get out of Iraq, with repeated references to a Vietnam-like quagmire and less-than-honest dealings with the American public; the right-wing blogs saw Iraq as a line in the sand against a mortal civilizational challenge (Islamic militancy), while valorizing U.S. troops unreservedly. In this bifurcated dialogue, in which political predispositions lead to certain Web sites that reinforce one's opinions, a concern with ordinary Iraqis, much less actual reportage, was rare. In this, the "new media," with very few exceptions, reflected the biases of the mainstream media, but with less information and far more passion.*

---

* The "new media" in the United States added very little information to the mainstream press during the war. For all the excitement about Weblogs, YouTube, and other alternative media, the amount of fresh information from Iraq or from Washington was strikingly small. YouTube probably offered the best new entry as it is a site where independent videographers could post short pieces, many of them about Iraqis, which were otherwise largely absent from American viewing. The blogs, with a very small number of exceptions (such as Juan Cole, a scholar of the Mideast who translates the Arabic press), repackaged news items from the mainstream media with scant comment, often meant to be ironic. Alternative news sites like AlterNet were mainly analytical or focused on the politics of the war in the U.S. The right wing made more of an effort to report directly from Iraq, but by embeds who were war boosters. The Iraqi blogs were more interesting, but not widely read. As a whole, the Internet had only marginal effects on American knowledge of the war or its opinion formation, which followed patterns visible during earlier, pre-Internet conflicts.

The absence of concern, then, may have reflected to some extent an absence of in-depth treatment of the human costs of the war. Whether the major news organizations believed that the American public was not open to the grisly facts of U.S. involvement, were cowed by the administration, or sustained biases about Iraqis or the mission that impeded judgment is not easily parsed. But as the war was presented as a patriotic mission of vengeance, as reporting remained Baghdad-centric and reliant on U.S. military information, as it largely failed to engage Iraqis, and as coverage diminished over time, the human costs of the war could not be conveyed. They were rarely sought. While the public may simply not respond compassionately no matter how much coverage is offered, a topic that will be addressed in the last chapter, the near absence of any information on Iraqi casualties and displacement would in effect suppress any public concern. In this, the earlier habits of reporting in the Korean conflict were repeated, and the consequences were the same: a war-weary public tuning out the conflict and thereby easily avoiding any sense of responsibility for its carnage.

Another End of the Frontier

The number of commentators who likened George W. Bush to a cowboy probably cannot be calculated. It was an especially popular metaphor in Europe just prior to the war's onset, but in America, the image of a plain-speaking Texan who spent his spare time clearing brush from his ranch was not always an object of ridicule. It was part of a tradition. And that tradition, above all, led America to project power to war with savages, protect our women, and reap the riches of the wilderness. That this was the vivid cultural context of the war on terrorism of which the Iraq invasion was a centerpiece has been explored and elucidated by many commentators. No less a popularizer than Robert D. Kaplan explained, "The red Indian metaphor is one with which a liberal policy nomenklatura may be uncomfortable, but Army and Marine field officers have embraced it because it captures perfectly the combat challenge of the early 21st century."[121] And it captures perfectly, too, the reasons that such a gamble could be justified and, for a time, popular.

The ironic or celebratory references to Iraq as "Injun Country," as Kaplan and others called it, dwindled as the war dragged on. A kind of romance with frontier imagery briefly flourished in the late summer of 2008 during the U.S. presidential campaign when two self-styled "mavericks" were nominated on the Republican Party ticket. The ultimate hero-victim, John McCain, who was taken prisoner in North Vietnam after his twenty-third bombing run over North Vietnam ended in a barrage of antiaircraft fire, was promoting more military commitment in the region—a sentiment echoed by his running mate, who very boldly played up her frontier credentials ("The gun-toting Sarah Palin is like Annie Oakley," exulted culture critic Camille Paglia, "a brash ambassador from America's pioneer past.")[122] In nearby Afghanistan, similar imagery was deployed in 2001 and also diminished over the long American intervention. Neither conflict was turning out as it had been intended, and, as a result, the bravura of the frontier myth seemed suddenly misplaced.

In Iraq, nearly eight years of war (at this writing) had produced hundreds of thousands of Iraqi deaths, perhaps close to a million. Four million remained displaced, many of them in desperate circumstances. An estimated 750,000 war widows (some from earlier wars) included many tens of thousands unable to cope with the economic strain of raising children with no livelihoods and no husbands. "As the number of widows has swelled during six years of war, their presence on city streets begging for food or as potential recruits by insurgents has become a vexing symbol of the breakdown of Iraqi self-sufficiency,"[123] said one report. Health care systems, food distribution, clean water, viable schools—all were in shambles, or nonexistent. Vast majorities of Iraqis said in 2009 that access to clean water and electricity was wholly inadequate. The government was rated in 2009 as among the most corrupt in the world. Closer to Iran's theocratic rulers than to America in most respects, the war had doubtful results for regional stability or U.S. influence. The prime minister of Iraq hailed a U.S. announcement of a withdrawal timetable as a victory for the Iraqi people. Even the bounty of Iraq, its oil, eluded American firms, as Iraqi politicians knew they needed to avoid the appearance of handing over the industry to the Western oil giants. Instead, China and other state-owned firms won the contracts let in late 2009 and early 2010, with minor American participation; the public companies could accept lower profit margins than could Exxon Mobil et alia, although the full story of Iraqi oil remains to be written.[124]

With the human costs of the war so massive and the rewards so paltry or uncertain, it might have been an occasion for American political leaders and intellectuals to pause and reconsider the norms that led to the invasion and the methods of occupation. Instead, Iraq fell off the map of public attention almost completely. Some realism had seeped into those close to the "smoking ruin" of Iraq, including the commander, Ray Odierno. "I'm not sure we will ever see anyone declare victory in Iraq, because first off, I'm not sure we'll know for 10 years or five years," he admitted in late 2009.[125] Declaring victory was nonetheless a political parlor sport in 2009–2010 among the right-wing advocates of the invasion. "Would it have been too much for the president of the United States to have acknowledged and paid tribute to a truly remarkable recent American achievement—turning around the war in Iraq and putting that war on course to a successful outcome?" asked former Cheney aide and pundit William Kristol after Obama's first State of the Union address.[126] None of the triumphal claims mentioned the cost to the Iraqi people.

CHAPTER 8

Afghanistan

Hot Pursuit on Terrorism's Frontier

The attacks of September 11, 2001, on the World Trade Center and the Pentagon were quickly identified as the work of Osama bin Laden, the Saudi scion of wealth and privilege who was drawn to holy war by the Soviet occupation of Afghanistan two decades earlier. Bin Laden was supported by the U.S. effort to unseat the Soviets there, and indeed that resistance was the font of many Islamist insurgencies—from Algeria to Bosnia to Chechnya and elsewhere, wars waged all along the fault lines of European and Ottoman imperialism. The American involvement in Afghanistan was initially about the rollback of Soviet dominance. Remarkably, the Carter and Reagan administrations funded bin Laden and the other factions of the *mujaheddin* (mainly through Pakistan's intelligence service, ISI) to fight Soviet occupation without an apparent thought to the consequences. Despite the Iranian revolution next door and the militancy in Lebanon and the occupied territories of Palestine, U.S. political elites regarded anti-Western fervency among the Afghan fighters only through the Cold War lens. This particular errand into the wilderness left Afghanistan in ruins, ripe for the extremist Taliban to take over in 1996, and fueled the belief among jihadists that they could bring superpowers to their knees.

Bin Laden was by no means the only progenitor of such ambition, but his daring and his financial resources quickly made him an exceptional figure in this burgeoning movement. Notably, his family was

Hadrami, from the Hadramawt region of Yemen, which had a long history of trading and migration in the Indian Ocean periphery; among them were some legendary fighters against British and Dutch colonialism, and bin Laden saw himself, and was seen by others in the region, as just such a leader.[1] He was not only drawing on the recent clashes in Afghanistan, the Middle East, and elsewhere for legitimacy, but on hundreds of years of anti-imperialist lore and norms.

As a land route to India, Afghanistan was long a battleground of Western incursions into Central and South Asia, famously resisted by earlier generations of Afghan fighters; and this history braced bin Laden's worldview. It was fitting, then, that the graveyard of imperial ambitions would launch his career as a jihadist and serve as the base for his most audacious act, the 9/11 attacks.

Within days of those attacks, he would be the target of American reprisals—"wanted dead or alive," in President Bush's words—and less than a month after the twin towers fell, U.S. warplanes were bombing Taliban and al Qaeda strongholds at the outset of what has become America's longest war, Operation Enduring Freedom. The hot pursuit of bin Laden failed, and in its place came the war in Iraq and a grinding effort of low-intensity war and nation building in Afghanistan, a graveyard for the war on terrorism.

THE UNCERTAIN TRUMPET OF CAPTURING BIN LADEN

The Afghan war was meant to be accomplished with a "light footprint," a minimal ground presence of U.S. troops. Despite its popularity—90 percent of Americans approved of the action[2]—and sense of urgency, Operation Enduring Freedom (OEF) was always meant to keep U.S. casualties low (the Kosovo operation only two years before had no U.S. fatalities) and to mollify Afghan umbrage at yet another foreign incursion. The war planners, after having been rebuffed by the Taliban government to hand over bin Laden, backed the so-called Northern Alliance, one of the *mujaheddin* factions at odds with the Taliban, and initiated a bombing campaign to enhance a Northern Alliance ground offensive. Within weeks, the Taliban had dispersed and Kabul was taken. In a vivid reflection of conventional wisdom at the time, Brookings Institution scholar Michael O'Hanlon called the autumn campaign "a masterpiece of military creativity and finesse." The military leadership, he wrote in March 2002, "devised a plan for using limited but well-chosen types of American power in conjunction with the Afghan opposition to defeat the Taliban and al Qaeda. Secretary of State Colin Powell helped persuade Pakistan to sever its ties with the Taliban, work with Afghanistan's Northern Alliance, provide the bases and overflight rights needed by U.S. forces, and contribute to the general war effort." The president himself had pushed "his national security team to develop an innovative and decisive war-fighting strategy." The military campaign, O'Hanlon revealed, "deprived al Qaeda of its sanctuary within Afghanistan and left its surviving leaders running for their lives."[3]

Like the Iraq invasion, however, the ease of dispatching an odious enemy masked a far more difficult reality. Only 60,000 U.S. troops were involved, and most of the American action came from the air. Despite the victory narrative, it was widely known that bin Laden had been within grasp but escaped, due to a lack of will in the U.S. command. General Tommy Franks would not support the pleas of field commanders to dispatch 800 marines to Tora Bora, where bin Laden was trapped in late autumn; and this failure (Bush, Cheney, and Rumsfeld all had been briefed on this as well) is widely cited as the single most important mistake of the war. (In mountains near Pakistan, Tora Bora—a massive complex of caves and underground tunnels, fully equipped for war and survival—was a result of U.S. financing in the 1980s.) One knowledgeable analyst, Peter Bergen, suggested that Franks was overwhelmed with Rumsfeld's order to prepare for the invasion of Iraq at precisely the moment he should have been focused on capturing the al Qaeda leadership.[4]

The "hot pursuit" scenario, promoted like a cavalry charge to capture Pancho Villa, soon subsided as the war in Iraq loomed and the tasks in Afghanistan evolved into unglamorous and arduous nation building. Bin Laden was safely moving in the high border areas and occasionally taunting his enemies and inspiring his followers with radio and video messages. As long as Afghanistan appeared to be on a progressive trajectory toward accountable governance and protection of human rights, however, the messages seemed to carry little importance. When the center of political gravity moved west toward Iraq, the Bush administration and its loyalists depicted Operation Iraqi Freedom as the paramount front in the war on terror. Hot pursuit of bin Laden was all but forgotten. The malevolent role of al Qaeda in Mesopotamia, a terrorist affiliate in bin Laden's network, rose to prominence early in the Iraq operation and beset the nation-building efforts there throughout the U.S. occupation. So the reach of al Qaeda and its capacity to use political violence to set back American goals in the region remained disturbingly robust, even expansive. The frontier had shifted venue, but the setbacks were similar.

"Al Qaeda is a more dangerous enemy today than it has ever been before," explained former intelligence analyst Bruce Riedel in mid-2007. "Its reach has spread throughout the Muslim world, where it has developed a large cadre of operatives. . . . Osama bin Laden has mounted a successful propaganda campaign to make himself and his movement the primary symbols of Islamic resistance worldwide. His ideas now attract more followers than ever."[5] Like many analysts, Riedel had not been surprised that the 9/11 attacks were bin Laden's doing, as there were many signs that he would strike as he had previously against American targets, and indeed as he had openly forewarned. The effort to capture him, moreover, was equally limp, weakened fatally by the desire to undermine Saddam.

After the Taliban dispersed and the U.S.-backed forces took Kabul, the major powers and selected Afghan leaders forged a series of nation-building conferences, a constitution, and a peacekeeping force under the auspices of the UN and, later, NATO. The Taliban was believed to be "eviscerated" and al Qaeda broken. The "light footprint" strategy continued and gradually was exposed as inadequate. Outside Kabul, old habits of warlordism returned. Afghan security forces were very slow to develop. A "Marshall Plan" promised by President Bush was fitfully introduced, and the soon-apparent corruption of officials made security and development efforts uneven at best. Meanwhile, there was little chance of capturing bin Laden or decisively subduing his network. From 2002 until 2005, the country stumbled along in disarray, and the security situation was beset by ethnic squabbles, shifting Afghani alliances, intrigue by outside forces (most important, Pakistan), and a kind of aimlessness by the U.S. and NATO forces. This period was, as a result, marked by low levels of organized violence, in marked contrast to the escalating, bloody chaos of Iraq.

Like Iraq, the failure of the war's rationale prompted the Bush administration to substitute other goals—or to conjoin them with the counterterrorism effort—to justify the military campaign and sizable amounts of money being poured into the country. The added mission was nation building. It was nation building with two pillars: enhancing security and extending "freedom's empire," a nearly fanciful quest for the latter and a disjointed and unrealistic program for the former.

The security mission looked feasible for the first three years, as the defeat of the Taliban appeared decisive to many—the crumbling regime did not even defend Kabul—and the challenges to NATO were relatively mild. "With a senior American diplomat, R. Nicholas Burns, leading the way, they thundered around the country in Black Hawk helicopters, with little fear for their safety," noted one report about a group of NATO ministers touring Afghanistan in 2003. "They strolled quiet streets in Kandahar and sipped tea with tribal leaders. At a briefing from the United States Central Command, they were told that the Taliban were now a 'spent force.'"[6] Gradually, however, the Taliban (separate from, but cooperative with, al Qaeda) was reconstituting in the Pakistan borderlands and saw ample opportunities to win over the Afghan people in the development vacuum created by U.S. inattention. Despite a grand announcement of a Marshall Plan for Afghanistan, Bush's focus on Iraq drained the U.S. forces and yielded to disarray in the nation-building ambitions. Nearly every independent commentator sees the obsession with Iraq as the main culprit undermining the outcome in Afghanistan.

It is just as likely that the challenges in Afghanistan were insurmountable: the animus to the occupier, the inability to govern along Western models, the rootedness of political Islam—these among other factors made the prospects for nation building bleak. On the security front, for example, the anti-Soviet war had abiding effects. "The channeling of much international aid to mujahedeen groups through Pakistan reinforced the fateful link between events in Pakistan and those in Afghanistan," observed Adam Roberts, a British scholar. "The power of non-state groups and regional military chiefs, and their tendency to rely on threats and uses of force not controlled by any state, became more deeply ingrained."[7] Political authority centered in Kabul and seemingly controlled by Washington could not dislodge these years of regional autonomy and militancy. The ensuing bloodshed following the Russians' departure was generally regarded as a civil war, in effect an ethnic conflict among and between as many as five competing factions of the Pashtun majority and the Tajik minority, the former loosely aligned with the Taliban.

The civil war was intensified by the remnants of the anti-Soviet period, with various warriors—some backed by the Saudis, others by Iran, and still others by the United States and Pakistan—violently undermining efforts at political stability after the Soviet-backed regime fell in 1992. The shelling of Kabul and the creation of ever more refugees marred the "victory" over communism, with the result, in 1996, of the best-organized and supremely Islamist faction, the Taliban, coming to power to rule over a fragmented land. Their grasp on power was tenuous—at least 10 percent of the country was under the Tajik, Uzbek, and other factions comprising the Northern Alliance— and so when faced with the post-9/11 crisis, Afghanistan reverted in many respects to the warlordism and factionalism that had plagued the country for at least two decades.[8] It is worth noting that the Taliban was significantly comprised of young refugee men trained in the madrasses of the Northwest frontier and Pakistan, which continues to be a font of their movement, and with considerable support of the *ulama* of villages across Afghanistan. They were also backed—possibly created as the major force they suddenly became—by the Pakistani government led by Benazir Bhutto in a frantic gambit to control events in Afghanistan.* What was common to most of the factions, however, was identification with jihad against the West and the necessity of Islamist rule, both of which were aided and abetted by Reagan's "rollback" scheme.

* Perhaps the worst of the bad Afghan actors in this drama is Gulbuddin Hekmatyar, a *mujaheddin* leader of the anti-Soviet resistance, who was favored by the United States, Saudi Arabia, and Pakistan. A Pashtun, he attempted to bring down the first postcommunist government violently; when finally abandoned by his foreign patrons (Pakistan, disappointed with his incompetence, threw their weight to the Taliban), he went into hiding in Iran until 9/11, when he was expelled and quickly aligned with anti-U.S. jihadists. He has also turned his back on Saudi Arabia (as did most of the *mujaheddin*) by supporting Saddam Hussein in the 1991 war in the Gulf. Known for his viciousness—he deliberately massacred civilians in the siege of Kabul in the civil war—Hekmatyar reemerged in 2008–2010 as a major figure in the Afghan insurgency.

Into this hostile maelstrom, the U.S. government lunged headfirst. After it had helped to defeat the Taliban with air power, its perceived challenges were political and economic development, namely, fostering democracy and market-based economic growth. By this time, after many years of promoting these shibboleths of third world development, the strategy was rote. Find plausible political actors amenable to American sponsorship who are not too tarnished by their past deeds to form political parties and stand for election. Write a constitution, with or without substantive participation of locals. Pour money into the hands of Western contractors to construct buildings and roads, some schools and hospitals, and fund small business development. It was a strategy that "equated 'modern' with 'Western,' and assigned Western capital, political influence and knowledge an important role in promoting the modernization process," observed Astri Suhrke, a Norwegian researcher. "Modernization was seen as a package. Economic growth, political democracy, modern attitudes and Weberian rationality in state bureaucracies were all viewed as interdependent and mutually sustaining elements [which] entails a form of Western dominance that leaves the recipients little genuine choice and delivers destructive forms of development as well as positive ones."[9]

From 9/11 to Fiscal Year 2011, the American government was on track to spend $455 billion on the war and reconstruction, but the rebuilding earned only one-twentieth of that total. (The comparable figures for Iraq are $800 billion overall and $43 billion for reconstruction.) The war costs escalated through the decade, as commitment of U.S. troops increased from 10,000 in 2002 to 70,000 in 2009.[10]

Given the scale of the military enterprise and after so many years of violent turmoil, the U.S. contribution appeared puny. But the scale of development was probably less important than the difficulty or foolishness of imposing development models where they would have little traction, where corruption was rife, and where security prerogatives outweighed any reconstruction initiative. Lack of interest or fragmented tasks among the coalition were also deadening. Despite Bush's "city on a hill"-like speech at the Virginia Military Institute in April 2002 pledging the new Marshall Plan for Afghanistan, Rumsfeld just hours later signaled the administration's lack of serious interest in either major peacekeeping or reconstruction efforts. "Who's going to lead it? Who's going to pay for it?" he asked.[11] These tepid responses to

Afghanistan's needs were rendered even more ineffective by the depth of corruption in the Afghan elite. And this corruption—outright stealing of aid, rampant nepotism, manipulating development assistance for political advantage, targeting political enemies for U.S. special forces to eliminate—dealt severe blows to the reconstruction effort and security goals in a mutually reinforcing way. Ordinary Afghans could see (particularly with the help of anti-U.S. activists) the depth of corruption, the high living of the elite while they went begging or lived in peril, and the lack of development that would actually aid their lives. That such a situation would eventually work to the advantage of a resurgent Taliban was apparent.

The money that did finally arrive in Afghanistan, if not siphoned off by President Karzai and his allies, frequently aided American or other foreign contractors who were in some cases doing the work Afghans could do. Even the best intentions were skewed. "Instead of giving aid money for Afghan schools to the Ministry of Education, for example, the U.S. Agency for International Development (USAID) funds private American contractors to start literacy programs for adults," wrote Ann Jones, a veteran of Afghan reconstruction. "As a result, Afghan teachers abandon the public schools and education administrators leave the Ministry for higher paying jobs with those contractors, further undermining public education and governance."[12] In several locales, the contractors and USAID workers felt compelled to spend money faster than it could usefully be absorbed; private American firms would not get renewed contracts if their financial "burn rate" left over funds at the end of the year, leading to shoddy workmanship and other waste. Frequently, outright fraud and failed projects were the result.[13]

To a troubling extent, Afghanistan also witnessed the uneasy marriage of security and development—projects like building roads that might only marginally help the Afghans but were essential to the U.S. military. This security-development nexus has earned scrutiny from informed critics for more than a decade as distorting sustainable and bottom-up economic development.[14] The aims of the "liberal peace"— free markets, elections, human rights, property laws opening the country to foreign investment, and so on[15]—are laudable in many respects but difficult to implement from afar. In practice, and especially during armed conflict, these processes are often patched in willy-nilly with the demands of security forces. Moreover, transformations that are often

revolutionary for a country like Afghanistan, such as abruptly intro-
ducing alien concepts of governance and rights, work against stability
because distrust is sown. This is particularly so when an insistent U.S.
ambassador or commander or aid contractor arbitrarily favors one
player over another, or wastes aid, or supports corrupt leaders, or con-
ducts military operations in ways that affront, threaten, or overwhelm
do-good intentions.

The extension of "freedom," then, is chimerical: it is not entirely
wanted, it comes in often-coercive forms, it aids and abets corruption
and inequality, and it is forced by a very long war. The frontier turns
out to be a complex and resistant place. For example, one of the fundamental tenets of the liberal peace is the fair administration of justice.
For all of USAID's emphasis on the "rule of law," however, the means
of settling disputes appears to be favoring the Taliban. "The fact that
the militants have the capacity to mete out a kind of justice, and that
residents are placing their faith in it, is especially alarming," noted an
Afghan journalist working in the north, where the rebels are weaker
than in the Pashtun-dominated south. The reason that Taliban justice
in simple cases is triumphing is that the official courts are corrupt and
bring delay as well. "A recent survey by the watchdog group Integrity
Watch Afghanistan suggested that the sum of bribes paid last year
came to around one billion dollars. Half the respondents to the survey
believed the Taliban were strong because they were not corrupt."[16]

THE HUMAN ELEMENT

The failure of both security and development in Afghanistan is attributable to the social and political dynamics that were misread by U.S.
officials, an unforgivable illiteracy given how similar difficulties prevailed in Vietnam. The push-back by the population, the cancer of corruption in Afghan governance, and the attraction of an alternative had
been apparent at least since about 2004.

The Afghans' embrace of war and nation building has been equivocal
not only because of the weak and ineffective central government and
the lure of the Taliban's version of Islam. The way the war has been
conducted by the U.S. and NATO forces has contributed mightily to the
perception of uncaring or even hostile attitudes by the occupiers.

The war in Afghanistan since 2001 was never as deadly as the previous war to eject the Soviets or our war in Iraq. After the rapid dissolution of Taliban warfighting in 2001, the American military operations and those of NATO and Afghan forces were sporadic and involved relatively few troops chasing Taliban and like-minded violent groups. Even so, the military operations frequently harmed civilians, despite what appeared to be a significantly greater effort to avoid such casualties compared with U.S. campaigns in Korea, Vietnam, or Iraq. Perhaps due to the sensitivity of occupation politics—both the fact of foreign occupation and the occupier's forbearance of corruption and warlordism—the killing of civilians repeatedly raised the hackles of local populations.

The U.S. command would always aver that it was exceptionally careful, that the rules of engagement were strict, and that it deeply regretted accidents. Much was made, as in Iraq, of having lawyers in command centers providing judgments on whether certain operations—usually bombing—were legal under the Geneva Conventions, and field commanders complained that this delay would allow terrorists to get away. "The norm of non-combatant immunity had become internalized in the thinking of high-level military leaders," noted scholar Nicholas Wheeler in a thoughtful account. When civilian casualties did occur, the news media were told that despite best efforts, some bystanders would suffer. "By framing the deaths of innocents as mistakes," Wheeler continued, "the U.S. sought to avoid the deeper moral and legal questions as to whether it was attacking legitimate military targets; whether such actions satisfied the proportionality rule; and whether its ground forces were placing themselves at sufficient risk in order to mitigate the horrors of war for innocent civilians," as the air war likely caused more civilian casualties than ground operations.[17]

However, the U.S. political leadership claimed at the same time a level of national emergency that in effect sought to vitiate rules of war. The statements of Bush, Cheney, and Rumsfeld cited the 9/11 attacks as a justification for any and all military actions. It was depicted as a "supreme emergency," in the language of Just War theory, a civilization life-or-death struggle (oddly forgotten when provided its main chance at Tora Bora). By late October, it was apparent that al Qaeda, much less the Taliban, was not an existential threat to the United States, but the simultaneously numb and vengeful American public was not much interested in the finer points of the rules of war. "We did not start this war," Rumsfeld stated bluntly three weeks after the United States initiated the bombing of Afghanistan targets. "So understand, responsibility for every single casualty in this war, whether they're innocent civilians or innocent Americans, rests at the feet of the al Qaeda and the Taliban."[18] In exercising restraint by consulting lawyers, the leadership clearly saw this necessity not in moral terms or the oft-belittled norms of international law, but instrumentally: keeping civilian casualties in check, or appearing to try to do so, was a public relations imperative, particularly in regard to the publics of coalition partners and Muslim countries.

Yet the old patterns persisted. The typical story was a U.S. warplane or helicopter killing "terrorists" that turned out to be no more than civilians at a social gathering. A dispute over who was killed and why would occasionally be visible in the Western press, with villagers claiming civilians were the victims and the military spokesman insisting they were terrorists. Evidence would be brought forward, typically by eyewitnesses, and the American or NATO commanders would retreat to the safe confines of ordering an investigation into the "tragic incident." Similarly, the bombing of electricity-generating plants or dams that could scarcely affect the outcome of the quick victory over the Taliban in 2001 put civilians at risk; complaints would be discarded as enemy propaganda. Long before the Wikileaks revelations, in which 70,000 classified documents were made public, this rote avoidance of responsibility was evident; what the classified documents revealed was how extensive and pervasive this mendacity had been.* The killing of civilians was of course bad enough, but the Afghans must have felt doubly betrayed when the victims were tagged as terrorists and the occupiers would persist in misrepresenting events. The number of times this occurred, however, was far greater than most assumed before the documents were released by Wikileaks in July 2010.

* Three periodicals were granted the first publication rights and analysis by Wikileaks: *Der Spiegel* (Hamburg, Germany), the *Guardian* (London), and the *New York Times*. Because the documents were then made available immediately on the Wikileaks Web site, other news media and analysts quickly drew their own conclusions as to their significance. The American media outlets ran the initial story about the Wikileaks revelations as one of betrayal by Pakistan (because of its strong links to the Taliban) with little obvious interest in the cover-up of civilian casualties; or, they claimed that there was little new in the documents, a striking expression of indifference. The civilian abuse story in the revelations was the lead point of the *Guardian* and other foreign sources.

Afghanistan also witnessed some notorious killings by U.S. soldiers. A series of murders resulted in arrests of an entire army platoon in 2010, murders that were apparently done without provocation. In a subsequent online conversation between one of the platoon leaders and his father, the soldier declared that "there's no one in this platoon that agrees this was wrong. They all don't care . . . Everyone just wants to kill people at any cost."[19]

The depth and breadth of Afghan casualties is simply unknown. What has been documented is reliant on the counting method—deaths reported in the mainly Western and other English news media, reports from nongovernmental organizations (NGOs) and other independent observers in Kabul or in the countryside, official sources, and some morgue reports. This largely arbitrary and unsystematic approach has, not surprisingly, led to estimates that vary widely. Based on reports of the UN, Human Rights Watch, and a few others, the total for civilian deaths ranges from 15,000 to 35,000, including nonviolent, "excess" deaths, with about 9,000 directly from U.S. military action, through the first half of 2010. The number of deaths of those *not* considered civilians or official Afghan soldiers is unknown but is likely to be three to four times higher. As with Iraq and Vietnam, the U.S. military's habit of labeling large numbers of those killed as enemy terrorists—whether true or not—is significant for this estimate. So the total figures for civilian casualties must be considerably greater than even the partial counts of the UN conclude.

The growth of violence from about 2007, as the Taliban gradually recovered and reasserted itself, was mainly attributed to them. For example, in a widely publicized report in mid-2010, the UN Assistance Mission in Afghanistan (UNAMA) noted that antigovernment elements were responsible for increasing proportions of civilian deaths (72%), overall said to number 1,271 for the first six months of the year; this was itself an increase in civilian mortality. Like the other sources, however, the UNAMA data are based on what is reported to them or other agencies; what is not reported is unknown, and the documents from the Wikileaks database demonstrate that many incidents, even some with thirty to forty deaths, were not reported.[20]

The violence had its effects even on those who should have looked favorably on the U.S. mission. Village elders in the Kandahar area, one of the most contested regions of the country, told UNAMA that the

Afghan "surge" pushed by General Stanley McCrystal and approved by President Obama troubled them. They "expressed strong opposition to the impending military activity," said the report, claiming "that such operations would not protect their communities from the Taliban or improve the security environment for civilians, but rather exacerbate the already insecure conditions in their districts." They believed the operations would not improve their lot and would result in the destruction of homes and crops. "They were especially concerned about what they believe is the inability of [international forces] to distinguish between Taliban and civilians" as well as the insurgents' harmful tactics. "Elders also expressed concerns about the [forces'] lack of cultural awareness when conducting operations, the destruction of property and loss of livelihoods."[21]

Opinion surveys of Afghans show a similar and declining confidence in their security situation and their economic well-being. While about equal numbers of Afghans had positive or negative feelings about the current government (though very few wanted a return to the Taliban), support for the U.S. work in Afghanistan was declining sharply by 2009—roughly half the support it had in 2005—although there was still majoritarian support for a U.S. military presence. The ambivalence probably is related to "lesser of evils" reasoning: high numbers said that Karzai and local governments were corrupt but preferred them to other possibilities. When asked who was responsible for violence in Afghanistan, 49 percent said the Taliban or foreign jihadis, 18 percent identified the U.S. military, and another 18–20 percent blamed government or pro-government forces. A majority said they wanted U.S. forces to leave within two years even if security was not restored, perhaps because more than a third had known of civilians in their area being killed by U.S. forces.[22] Their opinions may have been swayed, too, by U.S. forces aligning themselves with some warlords and backing a corrupt state, and the poor provision of basic necessities—jobs, electricity, and water.[23] The opinions of the Afghans are similar to those of Iraqis, though the very different situations account for the variations. In Iraq, the violence was considerably greater. The animus toward Americans was one result of that, and, unlike Afghanistan, Iraq did not have a Taliban lurking in the shadows, causing mayhem and threatening to reassert its repressive rule.

Given that noxious alternative, the high and increasing distaste for the American presence may have been due to the long-standing animus to foreign troops; but the U.S. counterinsurgency strategy may also be a defining factor. While military leaders emphasized time and again the need to avoid civilian casualties (strikingly more often than in Iraq), the "light" footprint of U.S. forces on the ground meant too few troops were there to successfully carry out counterinsurgency operations; by many estimates, something like 600,000 to 800,000 troops would be required. Without these—and here the similarities to Iraq are striking—the substitution of firepower, specifically airpower, for boots-on-the-ground became routine. This was reflected in higher civilian deaths caused by air power over time; although more directives from U.S. command to protect civilians have mitigated that trend, according to the mid-2010 UNAMA report. At the same time, however, special operations squads had apparently been killing or detaining thousands of Afghans, with many mistaken identities and the consequent, often lethal, disruptions.[24]

"After an incident, it is common for Afghan families to seek out international military to ask after family members who have been detained, to seek an apology or compensation, or simply to get answers for why their family was attacked," wrote Erica Gaston, a human rights lawyer in Kabul who has tracked this issue for several years. "Most of the time, they have walked away unsatisfied. The standard response of international military to concerned Afghan civilians, or to interlocutors like myself, has been that the incident did not happen, or that no civilians were harmed."[25] Cluster bombs, checkpoints, night raids, and detentions—the same behaviors that so alienated the Iraqis—are cited as the sources of civilian distress. After nearly a decade of this—or, more precisely, three decades—the Afghans are weary of turmoil that seems to be about other countries' priorities more than their own.

THE LAST WAR OF THE WAR ON TERROR

The hot pursuit of Osama bin Laden made the U.S. involvement in Afghanistan a "good war" that had nearly universal assent in the United States at its outset. While Iraq became a far more fractious political issue, Afghanistan was untouched by criticism because the rightness of capturing bin Laden and destroying al Qaeda was so apparent. It had also been woven into the American narrative of extending freedom and democracy and thereby protecting the American homeland.* The United States, an assistant secretary of state told Congress in 2003, is helping "that country take its place among the world community of moderate democracies" and "enjoy restored liberties." A Republican leader told the same hearing that "the Afghan people are determined to take steps to ensure Afghanistan's survival as a free nation. We have faith in their determination and their commitment to freedom." And another government leader added that one of two U.S. goals included "the fostering of ideas, values and habits that will help ensure that free market democracy can emerge and endure."[26] President Bush, in a speech to the UN General Assembly in September 2004, asserted that "today the Iraqi and Afghan people are on the path to democracy and freedom." And a White House fact sheet summarizing his achievements told how he fostered the "emerging democratic Afghan government and helped improve the lives of the Afghan people, especially women and children."[27]

One remarkable aspect of the emphasis on freedom and counterterrorism as the prime objectives in Afghanistan is that it was completely bipartisan. The original Senate authorization for war passed 98–0. No dissent to the mission was voiced by prominent Democrats. While some aspects of the war on terrorism were instantly controversial— the USA Patriot Act, the war in Iraq, Guantanamo Bay detentions—the U.S. mission in Afghanistan so completely escaped such opprobrium that the Democratic candidate for president in 2008 promised to recommit America to do the job better, and then, as president, invested heavily in new military and reconstruction commitments.

Within the popular and incessant freedom narrative was, notably, a plea for women's rights. This new entry into reasons for war was an undeniable reality—the severe treatment of women and girls under

---

* "Bounty" does not seem to be part of the equation. Afghanistan has proven natural gas reserves of some significance, ranking it sixty-fifth in the world (but possibly with much more gas to be discovered), and some other mineral wealth, possibly vast reserves of lithium and others essential to manufacturing. Pipeline politics—involving natural gas from the Caspian Sea to be transported to South Asia—was and is beset by the rancid relations between the United States and Iran going back to before 9/11, and Afghanistan was and is a key consideration in that. But was any of this a proximate cause of U.S. interest and intervention? There is little known about decision making that suggests such interests were that significant, but it remains an open question.

the Taliban—and surfaced when issues of women and security were just coming to the fore with the passage of a sweeping UN Security Council Resolution in 2000 linking security to women's rights and protection.[28] Few rights activists would use this issue as a justification for war, but those inclined to war weren't so restrained. Still, an expansion of women's rights in Afghanistan would have been a triumph, however secondary to the mission, and would have fulfilled at least one aspect of the freedom agenda. In this, it added a new dimension to the war's approval, particularly among an unlikely constituency.[29]

The bipartisan political establishment was not the only war enthusiast; the news media was overwhelmingly positive about the war, as were most international security analysts, with few dissenting voices. The booming right-wing media—the Fox News talk shows, right-wing bloggers, periodicals—buttressed the broad pro-war sentiment. The "clash of civilizations" in much of the coverage and commentary framed the heroic image of the U.S. mission.

This reliably adulatory treatment of the Afghanistan venture from political leaders and the news media makes the drop in popularity in the latter years of the decade all the more notable. From the heights of 2001–2002, support for the U.S. operations plummeted to minority status in 2010 after hovering around 50–50 for three or four years prior. A CNN poll in September 2010 showed 57 percent of the American public opposed, and only 41 percent in favor. Of particular interest was a September 2009 survey asking for reasons that the U.S. military should remain in Afghanistan; nearly 90 percent articulated a counterterrorism rationale, not anything about nation building or Afghani freedom.[30]

The drop in public support likely centers on the growing number of U.S. military casualties, particularly as the conflict received renewed attention after President Obama made his major commitment to the effort. From 2004 through 2009, coalition forces' fatalities rose annually from 60 to 521, and 2010 was on track to be far deadlier. The Taliban was resurgent. Pakistan, revealed to be double dealing by supporting the Taliban, remained high on the list of U.S. aid assistance. The reconstruction efforts appeared to be stymied by corruption and incompetence. "I am angry," wrote Mideast scholar Juan Cole in 2010, "about the 1,172 US troops dead in the Afghanistan War, and all the other brave NATO and Afghan soldiers who gave their lives for a new

Afghanistan. Because they haven't gotten a new Afghanistan. They have paid the ultimate sacrifice for a ponzi scheme masquerading as a reformist government."[31]

For every advance, there seemed to be an equal or greater setback. Consider the keystone of the freedom agenda—women's rights. "Over the past three years, the rights of Afghan women have experienced steady erosion," wrote a journalist from Kabul in March 2010. "While attacks on girls' schools and targeted assassinations of Afghan women in public office are attributed to the widening influence of insurgents, there have also been setbacks in the protection and promotion of Afghan women's rights within Afghanistan's legal framework," including men's complete control over their wives and daughters, retrograde measures enabled by parliament.[32] War invariably impacts women severely, an impact overlooked in the giddy excitement of 2001. Moreover, Afghanistan remains mired near the bottom of the global economic development index. On Transparency International's 2009 ranking of public-sector corruption, Afghanistan bested only Somalia of 180 countries (Iraq was 176th).[33] An emerging consensus among American experts held that the only way out of the Afghan quagmire was power sharing with the Taliban.

The failure of Operation Enduring Freedom will take some years to parse, but the autopsies will include at least three pathologies. The first was shifting quickly from hot pursuit of al Qaeda to a nation-building task for which the Bush administration had little heart and less competence. The dogmatic devotion to the West's development preferences was a blunt instrument that likely would have failed regardless of the White House's enthusiasm. The second was coping with the active remnants of "rollback"—the Reagan Doctrine's religious warriors, weapons, and Pakistani intrigue—as well as the subsequent abandonment of the country to a violent and fractious civil war. Everything the United States faced in 2001 and afterward was poisoned by the Reagan Doctrine. And the third was the infatuation with counterinsurgency in a country where the requisite resources for such warfare were unavailable and unwanted. The many commentators who attribute failure in Afghanistan to the distractions of Iraq or to willful neglect are not wrong—these are potent molders of the outcome; but it is very possible that a much more vigorous effort militarily and economically in Afghanistan would have met the same fate.

As to the American public's caring about Afghanistan, every indication is that apart from the interest in women's rights, the prevailing sentiment bracing intervention was fear of another 9/11 launched by Osama bin Laden. The matter of civilian casualties registered virtually not at all in the public mind—no household surveys to debate, no sense of unnecessary human costs. The "good war" averted such doubts. There is always a warrant for sacrifice to expand freedom's empire, and Afghanistan, for a time, seemed to be the quintessential frontier. But the actual outcome of Operation Enduring Freedom may spell the end of this form of savage war. Counterterrorism will likely settle on the law enforcement and intelligence mechanisms that have proven vastly more successful in capturing terrorists and, by not killing innocents abroad, not creating new ones. Like so many before, this frontier—taming the wilderness through hot pursuit, righteous violence, and advancing civilization into the Muslim hinterland—is rapidly closing.

CHAPTER 9

Three Atrocities and the Rules of Engagement

All wars produce atrocities. Some are enormous and infamous for their scale and brutality. Since 1945, these monsters of war have occurred in Congo, Rwanda, Bosnia, and Darfur, scenes of genocide and widespread rape, so the scale and infamy of mass killing has not been vanquished. As noted earlier, the United States had its rendezvous with evil in its own genocide of indigenous peoples on the North American continent. The firebombing during the Second World War and the nuclear attacks in Japan, while not genocide, certainly pose troubling moral questions about mass killing. Some atrocities—the Holocaust, the Armenian genocide, the Hutu slaughter of Tutsis in Rwanda—are clearly depraved and criminal, but others seem to be given a qualified pass on moral registers.

So it is with "small" atrocities, those involving a few dozen or hundreds of innocents murdered by soldiers in wartime. These are less a matter of state policy than a consequence of circumstances, conditions in which soldiers are prompted into a killing spree that seems to be allowed or encouraged by commanding officers. In the absence of direct prompting, the permission may come from the "rules of engagement," the guidelines set by the military as to when deadly force may be used. However such incidents occur, a number of dubious assumptions are in play—namely, that civilians are dispensable objects of war, and that they are particularly dispensable when impeding the mission, when tagged with suspicions of being enemy sympathizers, or when viewed as a threat to U.S. forces. The rules of engagement being what they are, such assumptions lead to innumerable civilian casualties.

That atrocities are committed by all sides in wars is not in dispute. Atrocities committed by U.S. troops, however, provide a window through which to see how the rules of engagement routinely degrade civilian life. Atrocities also take on a public life—scrutinized by the official institutions and the news media, and eliciting responses from the American people—which is rich in revealing how America views its responsibilities toward civilians in wartime.

Three atrocities, one each from the three main wars examined, are briefly described in this chapter. They are all known by the places where they occurred—No Gun Ri in Korea, My Lai in Vietnam, and Haditha in Iraq. Each followed a pattern on the ground in the war zone and in public life. And each revealed that even in these egregious cases of murderous misconduct by U.S. men, much of official Washington and the American public cast its vote of sympathy with the soldiers, not with the civilians.

These three are selected because they were exposed to considerable publicity. There were others worth examining, too—Abu Ghraib in Iraq, or the Tiger Force killings in Vietnam, for example—but the point is not to go on about American misdeeds but to explore how misdeeds provide a deeper understanding of the treatment of civilians. Known atrocities disrupt the means by which the human consequences of war are out of view. Those means prove to be resilient even in the midst of these disruptions. Worth noting, too, is the plain fact that even the largest of these three incidents took just 400 lives, a small number compared with bombing campaigns that killed a much larger number of people and were designed to destroy civilian society to such an extent that many more would suffer for weeks or months to come. The same was true for the sanctions imposed on Iraq from 1991 to 2003. These could be considered atrocities, too, but they lack the kind of specificity and abruptness that typically shapes public discourse about atrocity. Even here, though, the impulses of rationalizing and forgetting are at work.

The killing of between 100 and 400 civilian South Koreans at No Gun Ri in late July 1950 was revealed publicly for the first time nearly a half century later when a team of reporters for the Associated Press pieced together the story with hundreds of interviews of veterans and South Koreans, along with government documents long languishing in the National Archive. The AP's interest had been piqued by a reparations claim made by No Gun Ri survivors in 1998, a claim the Defense Department summarily rejected as impossible. (Calls for an investigation by survivors actually began in 1960.) Months of searching records and interviewing survivors and soldiers of the 7th Cavalry ensued, and in September 1999 the first of several stories by the AP team was published, with considerable attention from the other news media. Secretary of Defense William Cohen ordered an investigation. In South Korea, the news was greeted with mixed emotions—anger, relief, disbelief—and stirred the creation of a Truth and Reconciliation Commission to explore the war and the repressive occupations and regimes of the country's first years after the Second World War. The AP reporters, led by veteran war correspondent Charles Hanley, followed up with other dimensions of the story and a book, *The Bridge at No Gun Ri*.

The story was indeed stunning and saddening. After being evacuated by U.S. troops from their villages nearby, 500 to 600 South Koreans were herded onto railroad tracks near the hamlet of No Gun Ri, where they suddenly were attacked by the U.S. forces. The testimony of the survivors recalls ferocious barrages over three days. After being strafed when they rested on the railroad tracks by U.S. warplanes, the civilians hid under a large, arched concrete railroad trestle; but it was open to the soldiers just a few hundred feet away. After the first barrage, survivors used dead bodies of family to protect them and their children. "It was already a living hell in there," recalls one survivor. "The entrance to the tunnel was so thick with bodies strewn everywhere, I could hardly walk without stepping on them."

> Inside, it was bedlam. Frantic villagers cried out children's names. Boys and girls screamed for their mothers and fathers. Family groups crawled to the safest spots, away from the road, shoving and pushing for space on the jam-packed sandy floor . . . some refugees were shot trying to climb back up the embankment to fetch food from abandoned bags.[1]

This went on for three days, with the barrages of gunfire, mortars, and strafing alternating with some quiet periods and assessments of the damage. The survivors claim that between 300 and 450 of their family members and neighbors were killed at No Gun Ri.

Other reporting—by the AP in addition to others—turned up more evidence, including the all-important orders to shoot and strafe civilians. Fourteen such written orders were uncovered over the years since the story first broke, finding that orders originated well up the chain of command in military and civilian leadership. For example, an order signed by Major General William B. Kean issued in July 1950 said that "all civilians seen in this area [of retreat] are to be considered as enemy and action taken accordingly." An air force colonel, Turner Rogers, issued an even more explicit description of the army's request that civilians be strafed, and "to date we have complied with the army request in this respect." (Rogers argued against the policy for public relations reasons.)[2] Some twenty or more U.S. veterans who were in that 7th Cavalry unit at No Gun Ri confirmed and described in interviews the shooting and strafing, most of them saying that they were acting under orders. (Others there deny it happened or could not clearly recall.) Some of those orders may have been oral; the log book for the 7th Cavalry went missing years ago, so the nearest U.S. record of what happened cannot be checked. But orders clearly were issued from above, confirmed in writing between the U.S. ambassador and the State Department, and by high-ranking generals. "Veterans said the heavy-weapons company commander, Capt. Melbourne C. Chandler, after speaking with superior officers by radio, had ordered machine-gunners to set up near the tunnel mouths and open fire. Chandler said, 'The hell with all those people. Let's get rid of all of them,' said Eugene Hesselman of Fort Mitchell, Ky.," one of the veterans who told AP of the massacre.[3]

It was never entirely clear why these civilians at this place were victimized. They, like many other displaced Koreans, were rousted from their homes by U.S. soldiers and accompanied or herded south. One rationale for killing civilians derived from the perception that North Korean infiltrators were among them. This perception, or excuse, was commonplace throughout the war and echoed in the reporting at the time. At No Gun Ri, no such infiltrators were present and there were no reasons to believe they were. While the rumors or fears about infiltrators quickly reached the status of an unshakable belief during the hasty retreat to the Pusan Perimeter, the cases that were confirmed could be counted on one hand. In the case of No Gun Ri, the likelihood of refugees being among the 500–600 people on the road from their villages was even more improbable. "The refugees were escorted from their villages by U.S. troops, [and] were searched by U.S. troops on the railroad tracks near No Gun Ri," wrote Charles Hanley in a recent article.[4] He pointed out, too, that reports of gunfire coming from the refugees after they were trapped under the bridge were unconfirmed, and likely were the ricochet of American soldiers' bullets in the three-day assault. But the rationale for the orders to shoot also had to do with force protection, the commitment to shield U.S. soldiers from the harm that could come from infiltrators. Another danger was the chaos of the panicky retreat by hordes of Korean civilians on the road, reacting to different instructions, sometimes contradictory, and clearly in a panic themselves. The senselessness of it all was recognized by both those who saw the incident as a regrettable consequence of war and those who were more horrified by the killings.

The initial reaction to the AP story was predictably sensational. The story ran in hundreds of newspapers around the world, on the front page of the *New York Times* and *Washington Post*, stirring editorials broadly and leading, as noted, to a Pentagon investigation. Several television networks did follow-ups. The BBC produced a particularly effective documentary, interviewing many survivors and soldiers, who retold the story much as the AP had it. The massacre was compared with My Lai, both in the telling and retelling. Unlike the My Lai revelations, however, the story's impact was muted by age: the war, a half-century before, had dulled sensitivities. Soldiers could not recall with particular clarity. Records were missing. Survivors, however scarred by the killings, had lived to see South Korea prosper. But the story was nonetheless a powerful reminder of the depredations of war and Americans' own culpability.

The story behind the story presaged the more negative reactions that appeared some months after publication. At AP, as the story gathered strength, with a sizable team of reporters engaged, interviews with dozens of veterans and dozens of South Korean survivors, and countless hours searching in the National Archive, the top editors at the venerable news agency began to get cold feet. A recent controversy at CNN, the "Operation Tailwind" scandal—in which two producers aired a report about American nerve gas use in the Vietnam War, only to be rebuffed by the government and undermined by CNN management—had chilled the fourth estate. The AP brass held up publication and nearly buried the story; one editor quit in frustration with management's foot-dragging. The consequences of going with a story that ruffles so many feathers can be severe, including the loss of access to high government sources. Finally, having done even more useful research in the fifteen months of delay, the investigative team was allowed to send the ninety-nine-paragraph article out over the worldwide Associated Press wire.

As press critic Seth Ackerman pointed out, even the first blush of publicity had its spin. The editorials in the *New York Times* and *Washington Post* followed a form that has become familiar: in the case of the *Times*, viewing No Gun Ri as an isolated incident rather than an occasion to explore the Korean War's hidden history; at the *Post*, the reversion to an obsession with dangers posed by North Korean "infiltrators" and the framing of atrocities as something committed by both sides. The AP's follow-up stories in the first few weeks were largely ignored by the major outlets.[5]

Veterans' groups and a few others objected to the story, but it stood up as written until a backlash began to form in early 2000. An active duty army officer, Robert Bateman, had uncovered evidence of a serious error in the AP story—namely, that one of the dozen 7th Cavalry men in the newswire account had not in fact been at No Gun Ri, as he had claimed. This became the basis of a broadside against the AP story by a military correspondent in *U.S. News and World Report*, published in May 2000, with a number of key journalists, such as Michael Dobbs in the *Washington Post*, following suit in questioning the entire story based on the lone fabricator.[6] The *New York Times* also gave the *U.S. News* broadside front page, above-the-fold coverage. The AP issued a correction, noting that the false testimony was one of many dozens of accounts and growing documentary evidence, but the seeds of doubt were sown. "The story was a painful one to read, first because it paints the United States, it paints the American soldier, the American army in such an unfavorable light ethically," observed Marvin Kalb, the former CBS newsman and at that time the director of a center for the news media at Harvard. "I want to believe that this is not what the United States Army did. Certainly from my own experience it's not what the United States Army did. . . . Maybe other things would come out of other journalistic efforts that would give perhaps a more balanced view of what I think happened in Korea. . . . I am puzzled about why the Associated Press should be doing this kind of investigative reporting."[7]

Kalb's misgivings touched on one of the principal reactions in the press: that the fog of war, the nature of war itself, results in "tragedy" like this one, where confusion reigns and people, perhaps innocent (perhaps not) get caught in what was in effect a cross fire. The chaos of the retreat, the poorly trained soldiers, the fear of infiltrators—these were the culprits.

By December 2000 the army's investigation was leaked and a month later it was released. It appeared to be a careful rendering of extant documents and more interviews in Korea and America. Its conclusion—widely reported and with little contrary perspective—acknowledged that civilians were killed by American soldiers at No Gun Ri. "In these circumstances, especially given the fact that many of the U.S. soldiers lacked combat-experienced officers and non-commissioned officers, some soldiers may have fired out of fear in response to a perceived enemy threat without considering the possibility that they might be firing on Korean civilians," the army's inspector general wrote. "Neither the documentary evidence nor the U.S. veterans' statements reviewed by the U.S. Review Team support a hypothesis of deliberate killing of Korean civilians."[8]

All the elements of doubt—fog of war, infiltrators, ignorance, no orders—were incorporated into the report, and this then became the dominant narrative of the episode. One of the civilian review panel's members, former congressman and war veteran Pete McCloskey, issued a dissent, and the South Korean government strongly disagreed with the low mortality implied; their investigators' calculation was 248 at a minimum, using local records. The Koreans also wanted more accountability in the line of command.

A year later, Bateman followed the army's path by publishing a lengthy book challenging the No Gun Ri account as the AP and other news organizations had depicted it. He said it was not a massacre and only three dozen or so refugees were killed, that no orders had been issued to kill civilians, and that North Korean fighters were present among those at No

Gun Ri.[9] This was essentially the army's case. It was reviewed approvingly in the military press and sometimes compared in parallel with the AP reporters' book on No Gun Ri; an example of these comparisons is a story in *Salon*, the Webzine, "What *Really* Happened at No Gun Ri?" which gave equal weight to the two accounts.[10]

Over the ensuing years, more evidence gradually turned up, most of it putting the army report in a poor light. Not only did researchers uncover more orders to shoot civilians, but historian and archivist Sahr Conway-Lanz found the letter from Ambassador Muccio to Assistant Secretary of State Dean Rusk conveying the decision at the highest command level to shoot civilians; the letter was dated days before the No Gun Ri massacre.[11] A number of other inconsistencies in the army's story became apparent, such as its claim that no air force records confirmed the strafing of civilians, when five pilots had said they had such orders and the Rogers memo confirmed the policy. The army had access to nearly all such materials and interviews but seems to have suppressed these major pieces of evidence. There were orders—many of them—to shoot civilians and there was strafing of civilians by the air force in response to an explicit policy. The military did not make these public: two glaring omissions or intentional deceit. The very high level of this policy, moreover, indicates that it was in fact *the* "rule of engagement," making implausible the proposition that such incidents were all a tragic mistake, not policy, not intentional, certainly not a crime of war.

The controversy about No Gun Ri never attained the notoriety of My Lai, and uncertainty about sources and records has muddled the affair. The large number of witnesses whose stories generally paint the same picture of a sizable and unjustified killing of civilians, and the documentary evidence of this being policy, place the episode in the realm of hazy truth. What is equally and possibly more compelling is that the AP story of No Gun Ri and the bridges destroyed a few days later nearby, killing hundreds more refugees, signals how widespread the destruction of life was in Korea, a sensibility conveyed by journalists like John Osborne and Reginald Thompson but not widely appreciated.

So a pattern emerged very much like others we are examining. A single incident of gruesome horror was discovered "by accident," in fact, voiced by the victimized civilians. Their account of what happened to them was ignored for forty years, until a reporter—a Korean

woman who worked for the AP in Seoul—began to look more carefully at a petition for redress they had mounted. This sparked the
interest of an enterprising AP editor in the New York office, and more
exploratory work was done. The depth of reporting was exceptional,
and a plausible and well-documented narrative was constructed for
public consumption. The government vowed to investigate. Some
veterans' groups in particular were outraged by the allegations. One
problem interview, a fabrication, was discovered by an army major
and was then picked up by the news media to sensationalize the
doubts as much as the original story had been trumpeted. What
ensued was a kind of delegitimizing process, undertaken not by the
right wing but by establishment opinion gatekeepers. Just as the
doubts about the AP story had been sown, the army's own investigation exonerates the military leadership and Truman administration
of any wrongdoing, and blames a less-bloody incident on the fog of
war and untrained soldiers, which prompts the president to express
"regret" but no more. Case closed.

If the AP and scholars had left it there, the No Gun Ri shootings
would have remained in the public eye as a sad but minor and confused
affair. The AP reporters, among others, did not let it rest, however, and
rebutted the criticisms by finding several unambiguous orders to kill
civilians, found more witnesses, and unraveled the tightly spun rationale of North Korean infiltrators. What remains is the testimony of the
victims, which the military's own dubious account attempted to
degrade. But whether this historical record of an intentional killing of
250 or more South Korean civilians, now rather firmly verified, has
affected the collective memory of the American public is doubtful. The
debate and discussion that should have been prompted by the victims'
petition and the AP's remarkable persistence was spoiled. Even in
South Korea, where the Truth and Reconciliation Commission has
played a vital and even therapeutic role in coming to terms with the
past, the conservative government has shut it down, the major, conservative newspapers have ignored its astonishing findings, and the
South Korean military and police have remained obstreperous.[12] Still,
the four years of work of the Commission found some 200 cases of U.S.
"atrocities" against civilians during the Korean War. But a debate did
occur there and its results will doubtlessly endure. The AP story had
that galvanizing effect, if not in America.

The killings at My Lai on March 16, 1968, have for a generation or more entered the American lexicon as a synonym for wartime atrocity committed by American soldiers. And well it should. Army Lieutenant William "Rusty" Calley took his platoon of eighteen men one morning to a village in Quang Ngai, South Vietnam's northernmost province, for a search and destroy mission in a series of hamlets collectively called Son My. The intention was to find Viet Cong, but the instructions about noncombatants were left unclear from Lieutenant Colonel Frank Barker, the commander of the special task force in the Americal Division, 11th Brigade, of which Charlie Company, and Calley's 1st Platoon, were part. When that platoon entered what the Americans called My Lai 4, they simply opened fire on anything moving. The 2nd Platoon of Charlie Company soon entered the killing spree as well. Huts were raked with automatic fire or grenades, villagers running or staggering from the onslaught were executed. Children were not spared. As the day wore on and soldiers fanned out across the few square miles, the killing became a kind of sport, along with several rapes—sometimes gang rapes—of young girls before they were shot in the head or more graphically mutilated and murdered. Most of the Americans (not everyone participated in the slaughter) thought they were following orders from Charlie Company's commander, Captain Ernest Medina, but it was apparent to everyone that these villagers had no weapons, did not resist with weapons, and thereby posed no threat. They were killed anyway. The crescendo came when a hundred were rounded up and pushed into an irrigation ditch, where, led by Calley, they were shot.

"I went to turn her over and there was a little baby with her that I had also killed," as one soldier described what happened after shooting a woman soon after entering the village. "The baby's face was half gone. My mind just went. The training came to me and I just started killing. Old men, women, children, water buffaloes, everything. We were told to leave nothing standing. We did what we were told, regardless of whether they were civilians. They was the enemy. Period. Kill."[13] By the end of the day, nearly 500 Vietnamese had been murdered.

Unlike No Gun Ri, there are unambiguous accounts of what happened. We have the confessions of many men present, and very little doubt remains about the event. That full account took some time to come out, however. A routine after-action report listed twenty-two civilians killed in crossfire with Viet Cong guerrillas, 128 of whom were reported killed—an occasion for congratulation. It took many months for the actual story of a grotesque massacre to become public, even as it was known to many U.S. officers in Vietnam. The army wanted to keep the "incident" under wraps.* A soldier who was not in Charlie Company but had heard the stories of My Lai afterward wrote letters to civilian and military leaders after he was discharged nearly a year later; virtually all but one member of Congress, Morris Udall, ignored the letter, but Udall and then a few House colleagues pressed the army to investigate. To his credit, General Westmoreland, then army chief of staff, responded by ordering an investigation. It led to Calley's being charged in September 1969, just before being discharged, and to stand trial for killing 109 Vietnamese villagers at My Lai 4.

The trial at Fort Benning, Georgia, remained in the shadows until an investigative journalist, Seymour Hersh, got a tip and began looking into the events. Hersh was blocked by the army at first, but he hunted down Calley and others of Charlie Company to get the story. Remarkably, they spoke rather openly of the event. (Paul Meadlo, one of the massacre participants, was found at his southern Indiana farm, where his mother instantly said to Hersh, "I sent them a good boy and they sent me back a murderer.")[14] Hersh peddled the story to major magazines and newspapers, none of whom would take it, and sent it out on the little-known Dispatch News Service in November 1969.[15] Calley had still not been tried. The major news media then picked up on the story, and a torrent of publicity was loosed.

The initial reaction was one of shock. The scope of the massacre and the lack of mitigating circumstances were treated in the news media with disbelief and shame. The publicity spurred by Hersh's three-part

---

* A letter was sent by a soldier to General Creighton Abrams, the commanding officer in Vietnam, detailing numerous, virtually routine incidents of mistreatment and killing of civilians. His allegations were discounted by his superiors in American Division, but an army major in headquarters was asked to investigate. His report concluded, "Although there may be isolated cases of mistreatment of civilians and POWs this by no means reflects the general attitude throughout the division. In direct refutation of this portrayal is the fact that relations between American soldiers and the Vietnamese are excellent." That report was written by Major Colin Powell. (Michael Bilton and Kevin Sim, *Four Hours in My Lai* [Viking Penguin, 1992]: 213).

account led to a furor that forced the secretary of the army, Stanley Resor, to appoint a new investigative team. There had been two investigations, one triggering the next, by the inspector general and the criminal investigations division of the army, responding to a ruckus raised by a helicopter pilot who had saved some of the civilians after witnessing what was unfolding in My Lai. The investigators had gotten much of the story from the then-scattered members of Calley's platoon, which led to Calley's being charged with multiple murders. But Resor saw the need for a higher level, independent inquiry, and appointed Lieutenant General William Peers to head it. The Nixon White House wanted to bury the story, but Westmoreland and Resor persisted. Some in Congress also wanted a whitewash. Peers was able to use much of the information already gathered, but went further. It became clear from the earlier probes that the massacre was very large— 347 by the army's reckoning. There was no enemy in the hamlets of Song My and no resistance; the sole U.S. casualty was a self-inflicted wound. What Peers also discovered was a cover-up in Calley's division that went right up to Major General Sam Koster, who had gone from the Americal Division to become superintendent of West Point. Peers found not only plenty of murderers in Charlie Company, but a long string of officers who knew of the massacre, participated in it (as Medina had), or knew it was occurring on the day.

Peers wrote a remarkable report detailing the atrocities committed in Song My and the lies the officers told to avoid deeper investigations. When it came time to release the report, however, the White House wanted a muted version made public, heavily censored, and failing to detail the massacre in the adjacent hamlet of Co Luy, taking ninety lives, which occurred on the same day and was carried out by Bravo Company. So while Peers did his job, as indeed many of the other investigators had, the public did not at first get the full story. Still, it was a jolt to hear from a senior officer that the allegations contained in Hersh's article and the earlier investigations were certainly true in all their gruesome detail. The report also provided some useful context about the attitudes prevailing in the 11th Brigade that included the guilty men. "Prior to the incident, there had developed within certain elements of the 11th Brigade a permissive attitude toward the treatment and safeguarding of noncombatants which contributed to the mistreatment of such persons during the Song My Operation," Peers wrote.

Commanders had conveyed false information, in effect, about the enemy status of Song My, leading successive officers down the chain of command to embellish the danger and the need to exterminate the residents, who were regarded as the enemy. Still, Peers noted, "In 1968, the then existing policies and directives at every level of command expressed a clear intent regarding the proper treatment and safeguarding of noncombatants, the humane handling of prisoners of war, and minimizing the destruction of private property."[16] That was a debatable point—soldiers had an hour of a lecture about the laws of war in all their predeployment training, which was an abstract rendering of those obligations interspersed with lectures about the means of survival and the ethos of the warrior; and few apparently absorbed the brief on the Geneva Conventions. Peers essentially acknowledged as much by proposing that soldiers needed better training on their responsibilities with respect to civilians and prisoners. Westmoreland had issued several directives to officers in Vietnam as early as 1965 about noncombatant fatalities, apparently responding to various reports of unnecessary civilian casualties. Such warnings were clearly not enough; the nature of the U.S. war plan, including heavy artillery and aerial bombardment, and search-and-destroy operations—both of Westmoreland's devising—was a recipe for an extraordinary mortality rate among the Vietnamese.

By the time the Peers report was issued, the Pentagon was getting 4,500 letters a day on the case. "Fifty percent continued to support Calley and the servicemen generally. Ten percent attacked the press disclosures, and a quarter was against courts-martial in the case because of the effect it would have on the morale of the troops in Vietnam."[17] Clearly, despite the horrifying details of the massacre, the public was rallying to Calley. There remained a resilient popular fiction that Charlie Company was, in the lyrics of the "Battle Hymn of Lt. Calley," a hit recording that sold one million copies in four days, merely doing its duty and returning fire. That sentiment was wrapped up with the sense of betrayal that the likes of John Kerry and many other veterans and war protestors evoked in a large minority of the American populace, that, as the song says, "While we're dying in the rice fields they were helping our defeat." The Calley trial, in fact, came to its crescendo in the spring of 1971, just a couple of months after the "Winter Soldier" hearings in Detroit at which more than 100 veterans admitted to atrocities.

The country was suddenly confronted with war crimes as never before, and most of the public was unprepared to absorb and acknowledge the moral impact of the revelations.

The sentiments instead were a mix of outrage at the war and outrage at the apparent retreat from a winning strategy. Two ideas were in play. First was the charge that such prosecutions have a dispiriting effect on the war effort; the My Lai trials led some hawks to conclude that U.S. leaders didn't have the stomach to do what was necessary to get the job done (as, apparently, Calley did). The second was that the soldiers were following orders and Calley was a scapegoat. That opinion was held not only by the super-patriots but also by war skeptics. Jonathan Schell and his brother Orville recalled in a letter to the *New York Times* that they had been in Quang Ngai just months before Calley's entry into Song My. "The 'pacification' camps became so full that army units were ordered not to 'generate' any more refugees. The army complied. But search-and-destroy operations continued," they explained. Having themselves witnessed this from the scout airplanes, they said,

> Every civilian on the ground was assumed to be enemy by the pilots by nature of living in Quang Ngai, which was largely a free-fire zone. Pilots, servicemen not unlike Calley . . . continued to carry out their orders. Village after village was destroyed from the air as a matter of de facto policy. Airstrikes on civilians became a matter of routine. It was under these circumstances of official acquiescence to the destruction of the countryside and its people that the massacre of Song My occurred. Such atrocities were and are the logical consequences of a war directed against an enemy indistinguishable from the people.[18]

Calley's trial and the lack of official culpability higher up the chain of command was evidence of structural culpability, in this view, in which Charlie Company, while hardly blameless, was a pawn of a larger atrocity—the war itself. When Calley was convicted in early spring 1971 and given a life sentence, sentiment had moved even further in his favor: 78 percent disagreed with the verdict and sentence, mainly because they thought others were involved; about the same number thought Nixon should pardon Calley (51%) or reduce his sentence (28%); and that the soldiers at My Lai were "only" following orders.[19] The polling numbers could not have been terribly surprising. Rallies for Calley, especially in the South, were commonplace. Politicians, among them Nixon, rushed to disavow the massacre as something that regrettably happens in wartime, if infrequently. The laws of war, so carefully parsed by Peers and war critics like Richard Falk, were scarcely noticeable in these swirling sentiments. In the reckoning of the left, the whole war was illegal and immoral. For conservatives, the soldiers acted to carry out the mission.

Then, as suddenly as the hot and gaseous issue of atrocity arose, it subsided. The trials of Medina and Henderson later in 1971 stirred none of the same passions as Calley's did. Nixon overwhelmed the antiwar candidate George McGovern in the 1972 election, and U.S. involvement ended soon afterward. Along the way, everyone who was charged in the case was acquitted except Calley. The men who revealed the massacre were reviled for years. Peers was punished in the army way. His superiors denied him a fourth star, and he retired. Calley was paroled after three years.

Apart from the initial soul-searching in the news media, there was little evidence of American empathy toward the Vietnamese victims. Throughout the ordeal, the focus was on the American soldiers, the U.S. command, and the American "soul." A recurring assertion of the government at the time was that My Lai was an aberration and that the system was effectively dealing with it. That it was only unusual in scale was known widely. (One of the reasons the massacre did not earn more scrutiny by journalists and officers in Vietnam at the time it occurred was because it was *not* considered aberrant.) The emphasis on "healing" in subsequent years was all about the internal rifts in the American body politic, not in coming to terms with the victims in Vietnam. To their credit, many veterans did sustain a conversation about the war's horrors and the mistreatment of the Vietnamese, including some films and novels that appeared long after the war had ended. Dealing with their demons publicly was a jarring experience for some of the American public, since the veterans' accounts—a rarity in American history—could not be cavalierly dismissed. But even many of these accounts were projected as psychological dramas of the American soldiers, with Vietnamese victims as props. "I did *Platoon* the way I lived it," said director Oliver Stone of his 1986 Vietnam film. "I did a white Infantry boy's view of the war."[20]

Coping with the My Lai exposés was dominated by shunting the whole grisly episode off to the side and permitting the public to move on or completely forget it. British scholar Oliver Kendrick convincingly details the stages of this—containing, dispersing, and abstracting culpability, all the while displacing the victims. We rarely hear the victims. None of the other atrocities in Vietnam were prosecuted and in any case, the Vietnamese were in effect silenced. The official renderings of testimony, accounts of the My Lai massacre, counting the dead, even referring to the scene of the crime were all shorn of the Vietnamese identity. Without the victims' identity, anything approximating sympathy is unlikely. And the possibilities for sympathy or empathy are further diminished if the culpability for such a grotesque crime could be dispersed (so many people involved) or abstracted ("the tragedy of war"). Despite the revelations from the "Winter Soldier" hearings at the same time, the notion that this is the way of American war, largely intentional on the ground, was intermittently alluded to but never a durable part of the My Lai narrative. Instead, a master pattern was established, which would shape the script for the Korean and Iraq wars' atrocities later on—the crime is revealed after attempts to conceal it, the press and many public figures express outrage, the military is forced to investigate, the crime is acknowledged officially, the public rallies round the troops, the victims are set off to the margins, the "tragedy" is attributed to the fog of war or misplaced zeal or the enemy's predations, an apology may be issued, and the public as a whole rejects the moral importance of the atrocity and the war, which has already become unpopular and is no longer an occasion for a learning moment.

This pattern is not wholly natural or accidental. "The memories that endure within American public culture," wrote Kendrick Oliver, "tend to be more compatible with the interests of power than those of events, like My Lai, which disrupt the identification of the nation with perpetual historical virtue, and which recommend by implication that current purposes and policies remain the subject of moral scrutiny."[21] In effect, atrocities disrupt the rather smooth surface of forgetting, or ignoring, the victims of American wars, and as a result are very much a challenge to the rightness or conduct of those wars. The efforts to contain the public relations damage, to complicate and divert the atrocity's narrative from moral consequences, are evident in all cases. Even in the case of My Lai, a most unambiguous and significant atrocity, the episode never opened a thorough examination of how the Vietnamese were victimized during the war.

An occasional remembrance does slip through. Truong Thi Le, who was thirty at the time of the massacre, had nine family members murdered by Charlie Company. She survived because she was able to hide in the rice fields with her six-year-old boy. During the massacre, "her daughter was sitting dying, holding her grandmother, who was already dead. She said to Mrs. Le: 'Mother, I think I am very badly injured, maybe I'll die, I don't think I can survive. You have survived, you had better take little brother away. Please don't stay here as the Americans will shoot you.' . . . When the troops left she carried her child home in her arms, but there was no home left. It was burned to cinders."[22] Interviewed on the thirtieth anniversary of the massacre, she tells a reporter she still works in the rice fields where she hid with her little boy. "To get there she walks 55 paces down a dirt path, to the well into which a man was thrown and shot, then 40 paces to a silkwood tree, where 15 people, two of them toddlers, were shot, and finally 70 paces to the site of a now-destroyed watchtower, where 102 villagers were assembled and slaughtered. She doesn't think about the killings all the time, she says. 'Only when I walk by here.' How often does she make that trip? 'Every day.'"[23]

IRAQ: HADITHA AND THE IRAQ MORTALITY STUDY

The war in Iraq has produced a great amount of killing. It is one of the telling aspects of this war that an enormous number of people are dying but the American political discourse does not acknowledge that the United States is significantly responsible for that outcome. In this, as noted earlier, the war is akin to the Korean War, where early disappointments and high casualties led the public to ignore the war and its consequences. The Iraq War fits the others' atrocity pattern, too, though it did not suffer the single-event atrocities that No Gun Ri and My Lai clearly were. Here then is a "small" massacre, the killing of twenty-four Iraqi civilians in the Anbar town of Haditha in November 2005, which, while an order of magnitude less than the others we've examined, still shows the pattern of cover-up, disbelief, and denial. Iraq is also the first American war in which there has been a real-time attempt to estimate the war's toll, efforts that implied a more general catastrophe that then was treated like the individual incidents of murder.

Haditha is situated along the Euphrates River in Anbar province, about 150 miles northwest of Baghdad. In late 2005, Anbar was the most restive part of Iraq, and while Haditha was outside the notorious Sunni Triangle, its hydroelectric dam and its location as a transit point of resistance fighters from Syria made the city, population 100,000, a militarily significant outpost. It was a point of tussle, sometimes violent, between U.S. marines and insurgents as the war escalated. By autumn 2005, the U.S. command committed to a major operation to clear Haditha of insurgents and sent the 3rd Battalion, 1st Marines, to do the work. But they met with virtually no resistance as they set up in an abandoned schoolhouse in early November, despite intelligence telling them they were facing a sizable contingent of Sunni Arab insurgents. On November 19, a four-vehicle patrol was hit with a roadside bomb, killing one marine. What happened next remains disputed, but what is indisputable is that twenty-four Iraqis, apparently none wielding weapons and half of them women and children, were killed by the marines as four nearby houses and a car were "cleared."

The marines say they heard small arms fire from the vicinity of the houses soon after the improvised explosive device (IED) detonated. A few of them entered each house in succession, and, using their automatic weapons and grenades, killed several women and children; in the third house, they encountered resistance from four men with weapons, they say, and killed them as well. (Later, an investigation found one gun among the Iraqi men, which had not been fired.) Around the same time, they stopped a white car—a "white car" had been listed in their intelligence brief as a possible insurgent vehicle—and removed the five men inside and killed them; the marines say they were running away, which later forensic evidence rejects. No weapons were found in the car. In all, twenty-four Iraqis were killed—nine men, including a blind seventy-six-year-old in a wheelchair, four women, and six children, ages fifteen to three.

The initial marine press release said fifteen Iraqis were killed by an insurgent IED. The day after the incident, a member of a Baghdad-based nongovernmental organization (NGO), the Hammurabi Human Rights Organization, happened to be in Haditha and took videos of the aftermath, including the mangled and bloody bodies of the victims. This they sought to share with U.S. authorities, but were turned away. So the group contacted Tim McGirk of *Time* magazine, who began asking questions of the marine command. He was told it was "al-Qaeda-like propaganda" and that he'd be aiding the enemy terrorists if he wrote about the incident. McGirk nonetheless filed a story, which generated only a little attention. But his inquiry and a demand from the Haditha City Council prompted an inquiry, which was leaked to Pennsylvania congressman John Murtha, a marine vet and longtime friend of the military. He charged that a massacre had occurred at Haditha, and then the story became front page news. "There was no firefight," said Murtha, "there was no IED that killed these innocent people. Our troops over-reacted because of the pressure on them, and they killed innocent civilians in cold blood."[24] McGirk followed with a cover story, and the *Washington Post* and other major outlets gave the killings extensive treatment. The internal report that tipped Murtha showed callousness toward Iraqi civilians and assumptions that when they were killed the insurgents were to blame. In fact, two investigations were afoot—a criminal investigation by the navy, which concluded in a 3,500-page report that murder had been committed by the Americans, and an army general's inquiry into what happened in the chain of command.

The explosive publicity in late spring 2006, just when the violence in Iraq was nearly out of control, pressured the Pentagon to take the allegations seriously, and several of the marines were charged with crimes. The new prime minister of Iraq was quick to point out that Haditha was not an isolated incident. The accounts—even those in the marines' own words—were disturbing. They cleared out the first house, they said, "Fallujah style," with grenades and without identifying who was inside. Several women and children were victims, prompting one of the killers to say, "I'm not comfortable with that."[25] The sergeant in charge acknowledged on a *60 Minutes* segment that he probably knew there were civilians in the first house they assaulted, but he proceeded all the same.

The investigation by Eldon Bargewell, the army general, was harsh on the marine chain of command and general attitudes toward civilians. The investigation's conclusions are not public, but as reported in the *Washington Post*:

"All levels of command tended to view civilian casualties, even in significant numbers, as routine and as the natural and intended result of insurgent tactics," Bargewell wrote. He condemned that approach because it could desensitize Marines to the welfare of noncombatants. "Statements made by the chain of command during interviews for this investigation, taken as a whole, suggest that Iraqi civilian lives are not as important as U.S. lives, their deaths are just the cost of doing business, and that the Marines need to get 'the job done' no matter what it takes."[26]

Despite the official opprobrium after the initial cover-up, and fairly extensive and balanced reporting in the major news media, the public exhibited either broad indifference to the killings or rallied to the marines' side. In June 2006, at the height of the publicity, 24 percent of Americans were following the case closely, according to a Pew poll, with another 31 percent following it somewhat closely. In another survey around the same time, 63 percent said that the killings of civilians were isolated incidents and about the same number said the U.S. military was doing everything it could to avoid collateral damage.[27]

This indifference was apparent even as other disturbing evidence of misconduct was surfacing. The Abu Ghraib scandal had erupted two years before and had shocked the country, but it was contained to some extent by claims of lower level responsibility, by being depicted as a bizarre and singular episode, or by being abstracted into a larger debate about torture (and, indeed, torture of terrorists), which the Bush administration insisted was not occurring.* A summary execution of three detainees ordered by *Black Hawk Down* hero Colonel Michael Steele came to light within months of Haditha, one resonating with other incidents resulting from his order to "kill all military-age men" and echoing a similar set of instructions at Haditha.[28] The rape/murders of Mahmoudiya came to light in the summer of 2006. A U.S. massacre of eleven civilians at the town of Ishaqi was revealed in a BBC report

---

* Because the crimes of Abu Ghraib involve abuse of prisoners, it's not more fully considered here. It followed a pattern similar to other atrocities, but the public never forgave the United States for this abuse—that is, opinion decried torture and specifically the kinds of humiliations meted out at Abu Ghraib. According to Gallup (June 14, 2004) "the scandal has triggered some public backlash against the conflict, but most of the decline in public support for the war seen since the official end of major combat on May 1, 2003, occurred earlier (associated with mounting U.S. casualties in the 'postwar' period)." To the war journalist Philip Gourevich, writing on the Web site TPM Café (June 2, 2008), the reaction to Abu Ghraib's notorious photos was "shuddering and turning away. . . . Dishonor was compounded by our acquiescence in it. The expose was the coverup." The lack of accountability at the top was for many observers the decisive outcome; chief among those who did not have to answer for Abu Ghraib was President Bush, who was reelected six months after the scandal broke.

shortly after Haditha's crimes were publicized. So a torrent of bad news, much of it linked to U.S. actions, swirled around the revelations about Haditha. At the same time, a defense of the marines began to appear, especially in the right-wing media; unlike earlier wars, the Internet had become a major source of daily comment on events in Iraq, and this case in particular drew the attention of bloggers. The Haditha "hoax"—a scheme by al Qaeda to fool *Time*'s McGirk—was one constant meme in this realm. Murtha, hitherto a hero of pro-military Americans, came in for a particularly nasty backlash that continued until his death in 2009. One blogger noted approvingly that "Americans aren't drinking the Kool-Aid," meaning the public was not swallowing whole the allegations of marine misconduct. Most particularly, the rally-round-the-troops sentiment formed (after the "hoax" allegation subsided) as it did in Calley's case: the marines were simply doing their jobs, according to this view, and the "rules of engagement" were faithfully followed.

Eight marines were charged in the case, none for murder, and as of mid-2010, seven of the eight were let off. The highest ranking of the accused, a lieutenant colonel charged in the cover-up, won on a technicality; five others, including Steve Tatum, one of the first to enter the houses and kill the inhabitants, were let off and granted immunity; in the words of a military official at the time of Tatum's release, he was relieved of charges "in order to continue to pursue the truth-seeking process into the Haditha incident."[29] One marine, a lieutenant who was charged with being part of the cover-up, was acquitted by a military panel. The right-wing media tried to spin this as exoneration of the "heroes" of Haditha. The remaining defendant, Sergeant Frank Wuterich, the leader of the squad that cleared the houses and the car, was, according to his defense attorney, just legally doing his job. "Everything they did that day was following their rules of engagement and to protect the lives of Marines," he said in 2006. "He's really upset that people believe that he and his Marines are even capable of intentionally killing innocent civilians."[30] But Sarah Sewell, a former deputy assistant secretary of defense and an adviser to Petraeus, noted that in a first-of-its-kind survey of troops in Iraq, "one-third of marines and one-quarter of soldiers [said] their leaders failed to tell them not to mistreat civilians. . . . The bottom line is that significant numbers of U.S. troops think and act in ways that violate their professional ethics and the laws of war."[31]

The Haditha massacre followed the pattern from the earlier wars—initial shock at the revelations, military lying and cover-up, investigations in response to the news media coverage, right-wing backlash against prosecuting or blaming soldiers, very little legal culpability achieved, and ultimate public indifference. Interestingly, the same pattern has been evident with regard to another kind of atrocity revelation: the high casualty count in the Iraq Mortality Study in October 2006. This was the effort led by Johns Hopkins School of Public Health researchers who used a household survey to estimate the number of "excess deaths" during the war. The methods of accounting for the dead in war will be discussed in the next chapter. But the political reaction to this particular survey is quite similar to the reaction to atrocities and is worth a brief review here.[32]

The Hopkins scientists, led by Gilbert Burnham, M.D., Ph.D., a former army major, and Les Roberts, Ph.D., an epidemiologist, had undertaken an earlier survey in 2004 and published the results in the *Lancet*, a well-regarded British medical journal. That survey was a cluster sample in which thirty households in each of thirty-three neighborhoods randomly selected in Iraq were surveyed, asking if anyone who lived in that household had died during the war. Comparing it to prewar mortality, also established by that same set of questions, they found that in the first eighteen months of the war, 98,000 more Iraqis had died than would have been suggested by prewar mortality trends. The results, released just before the 2004 presidential election in the United States, were discounted by their timing (appearing to be political) and by a broad misunderstanding of the method. A well-established method in epidemiology, the household survey and cluster sampling is not intuitively obvious; the accuracy of using about 1,000 interviews to estimate the deaths in a population of about 26 million, and with a broad "confidence interval" that stretches far in each direction—toward much lower or much higher estimates—confused journalists who did not understand how such surveys are done. In any case, the findings of the survey were largely ignored.

The second survey, led by Burnham, came at a time of escalating violence and was difficult to conduct for that reason. It was commissioned in October 2005, but the violence prevented it from being conducted right away. It used a larger sample—forty-seven neighborhoods, forty houses in each, both randomly selected—and used teams of Iraqi health professionals to do the interviews. This time, in the summer of 2006, the results were also startling. The researchers estimated that 650,000 "excess deaths" had occurred in Iraq—notably, inclusive of all Iraqis, not just civilians. This Iraq Mortality Study was published by MIT's Center for International Studies and appeared in the *Lancet* in early October 2006. A better-managed publicity effort yielded considerable attention, so much so that President Bush responded a day later by disparaging the method. Military leaders also responded negatively. Within days, and then lasting for several months, the right-wing reaction came. Most of it again reverted to charges of political bias—the *Lancet* editor had spoken at an antiwar rally in London, Roberts had briefly made a run for Congress as a Democrat, the release of the study three weeks before the congressional elections made it appear to be politically timed, and so on. The method again came under attack, though none of the criticisms stuck. (The science adviser to the pro-war prime minister of Britain called the method "best practice" and epidemiologists and other health professionals overwhelmingly approved the methods and their application in this case.) When bereft of plausible criticisms, some right-wing critics simply claimed that the results were made up. Despite peer reviews at the *Lancet* and a full-scale review by Johns Hopkins, both of which found the survey and analysis to be scientifically conducted and likely correct, such criticisms formed an irrepressible myth in the blogosphere. More than a year later, a new charge of political bias reignited the controversy when an insidious influence of George Soros was alleged; the *Wall Street Journal* linked the results of the survey and Soros's sponsorship (his foundation, the Open Society Institute, had made a small grant for public education long after the survey had been commissioned and designed). Soros was also an outspoken opponent of the war.[33]

Both the 2004 and 2006 surveys had estimates for those deaths likely caused by U.S. actions, though this was not the purpose of the surveys. Attributions of culpability are not as reliable as the facts of death and must be derived from causes of the fatalities—aerial bombardment, for example, which would have come from coalition planes. In fact, most of the deaths were caused by gunshot, which could come from many sources. But the intimation that the U.S. military may have been responsible for as many as 200,000 deaths was one of the triggers for outrage. Those who supported the war clearly were abashed at numbers that exceeded the death toll attributed to Saddam Hussein in his twenty-four years of tyranny. Victory could scarcely be claimed at such a price, particularly in light of polls of Iraqis that repeatedly showed they wanted America to leave and blamed the U.S. military for the violence.

The reaction to the Iraq Mortality Study followed the atrocity pattern in several ways. There was initial shock and attention to the findings. Official Washington condemned the study. The mainstream media was initially interested but then basically dropped the study as a source, reverting to a much more conservative estimate provided by Iraq Body Count, a U.K.-based NGO. The defenders of the war dismissed the findings as antiwar or even "terrorist" propaganda and insisted on the unassailable honor of the military. The American public generally seemed unmoved by the figures. The one time a survey asked Americans how many Iraqis had died in the conflict, in 2007, the average answer was just under 10,000.

In each case, with few exceptions (like Abu Ghraib), the public tended to side with the military, in part as a matter of identity—these were "our boys"—and in part as a logical consequence of seeing the military mission as a lethal undertaking in which some bystanders get hurt. That latter sentiment reflects a sense about the rules of engagement, that our young men and women are put in harm's way and must have the latitude to protect themselves, their buddies, and the mission. That was the legal defense for My Lai and Haditha. So much of the actual military doctrine pertaining to civilian losses, especially on-the-ground operations, comes down to this very basic question: when is it permissible to use deadly force against civilians?

RULES OF ENGAGEMENT

The boundaries of ethical conduct for officers and troops in combat are blurry, although two standards have remained unchanged at the poles of this terrain: civilians are to be unharmed if at all possible, and troops have an unqualified right to self-defense. Naturally, this leaves much ground for interpretation, territory that is without a definite set of rules or understandings. What has been promulgated from on high—in the four-star commands—is broad enough to allow for very loose readings, as indeed many military documents concede. What's more, even the clear injunctions about mistreating civilians are violated by officers and troops who feel pressure to be aggressive and undiscriminating.

The troubling question is, how many smaller scale No Gun Ris, My Lais, and Hadithas have there been? As one army sergeant testified before a congressional panel in 2008, "I was ordered multiple times by commissioned officers and noncommissioned officers to shoot unarmed civilians if their presence made me feel uncomfortable." And in commenting on that revelation, a lieutenant colonel who teaches at the U.S. Military Academy observed, it "jibes with reports I've received from lieutenants who returned to West Point where I taught. My former students came back and told me the same thing."[34]

The problem of protecting noncombatants seems to be fivefold. First are the contradictory signals sent from the military leadership. Second are the incentives created for officers—colonels on down to ser-geants—which in effect encourage actions that frequently lead to high civilian tolls. Third is the training and culture of the fighting men, the warrior ethos and reinforcing behaviors and attitudes that degrade the enemy. Fourth are the oft-cited difficulties of contemporary warfare in which discrimination between civilians and combatants is a constant challenge. And fifth are the permissive or indifferent attitudes of the public and its institutions toward accountability, which are thereby ineffective as a deterrent to misbehavior.

From the top, the language of rules is nearly always in line with the Geneva Conventions and frequently reiterated in strong terms. In the Vietnam War, Westmoreland sent out a dozen circulars to officers to desist from the widespread killing of civilians about which he was learn-ing from a variety of reports, and upheld rules of engagement that, in General Peers's words,

> dealt with minimizing noncombatant casualties. Noncombatants were generally described as the "hapless rice farmer and the small town in-habitant, whether at any one time [he] lives in a VC or a GVN controlled hamlet" noting that where he lives depends "to a large extent upon fac-tors and forces beyond his control." Commanders were directed to con-trol force and not use "unnecessary force leading to noncombatant battle casualties in area temporarily controlled by the VC."[35]

Peers painstakingly showed that commanding officers issued directives repeatedly down to the battalion level. But it was Westmoreland's war strategy, including the search-and-destroy techniques and the relentless use of artillery, bombing, and free fire zones, which would necessarily result in high civilian losses. Noting how the war had intensified in the previous year, Westmoreland explained in 1965 that the peasant farmer "will have to choose if he stays alive. Until now the peasant has had three alternatives: he could stay put and follow his natural instinct to stay close to the land. . . . He could move to an area under government control. Or he could join the VC. Now if he stays there are other dangers."[36] The "other dangers" were, of course, violence meted out by the U.S. military. This kind of threat was reinforced on the ground for officers as they were pressed for high body counts, a persistent demand that is widely cited as a key reason for the sustained levels of mayhem. "Officers incessantly spurred their teams on to optimize the body-count tally," noted one history of the conflict. "Sometimes monthly or weekly killing targets were laid down ex cathedra; sometimes extended leave was granted for an improved kill ratio; sometimes those who did not reach their targets were threatened with cancellation of the popular rest and recuperation breaks in Thailand, Japan, and South Korea."[37]

Supposed measures for protecting populations—requests for higher authorities to approve air attacks, for example, or leafleting a village before operations—were more honored in the breach by field officers under pressures of time or in the belief that leafletting merely aided the VC. Anything was allowable if targets were labeled as enemy, and troops began to see all civilians as enemy or enemy sympathizers. The training for officers and troops on the laws of war amounted to about one hour. Even before My Lai it was recognized internally as inadequate. "Sixty minutes of arid legal discourse, almost entirely abstracted from the real conditions of war, together with occasional exhortations to more righteous conduct handed down from on high could not really be said to amount to an ethical education," observed one scholar.[38] What overcame these meager attempts to convey the laws of war were the conditions and missions imposed on soldiers and their officers, the nature of warfare that by then should have been apparent—namely, that the "enemy" was not in uniform, but looked just like the civilians—and the trumping rule, that of self-defense. If one sees hostile intent in every village, then every village can be destroyed. That the political leadership rarely objected to this behavior, and in fact absolved many officers through legal immunity, merely encouraged more of the same.

Peers noted that in addition to extreme misconduct on the reporting of the Son My massacre, what needed urgent attention was "the provisions of the Geneva Conventions, the handling and treatment of prisoners of war, and the treatment and safeguarding of noncombatants."[39] He then essentially recommended that past poor practices be addressed mainly by training. And this the army did. Granting more time in boot camp to lectures on the protection of civilians, the treatment of detainees and prisoners, and the like was not enough, however. "Schedules for instruction in the laws of war may have been expanded," wrote Kendrick Oliver, "but the basic constitution of behavioral and attitudinal influences to which young servicemen were exposed stayed largely the same."[40] The training includes eight "mind-numbing" hours about the Uniform Code of Military Justice, in which rules of war are contained (actual rules of engagement for any conflict are classified), and the training is repeated before deployments. How deeply this new emphasis sank in remains uncertain.

The years between the Vietnam and Iraq wars brought other changes as well—most prominently, an intensification of the Cold War in the late 1970s led the military away from the kinds of counterinsurgency doctrines that had purchase during the Vietnam War. A kind of self-delusion set in about the mistakes of Vietnam, a debate alternately blaming the application of too much firepower and too little "hearts and minds" inducements. In fact, much of the worst killing happened in low-tech search-and-destroy missions. And the hearts-and-minds mission was a low percentage gambit at best, given the cultural barriers, the fundamental corruption of the Saigon regime, and the inroads made by the communists long before the United States deployed ground troops.[41] In that same period, an increasing infatuation with precision-guided munitions and other electronic wizardry, sometimes called the Revolution in Military Affairs, returned the discussion of rules of engagement to the scope of air operations.[42] In fact, the air wars in Kosovo and Desert Storm were focused on the application of air power from above 10,000 feet, but as the 2003 war in Iraq would show (as has the war in Afghanistan), it is only a part of the story and not the more consequential one: most casualties are from ground operations, close air support, or the failure of the occupiers to provide security. The old complaints from some of the military brass and their political backers about being too constrained in what they can bomb are a distraction, possibly an excuse for failure. Or, remarkably, they represent a misplaced view of the nature of a war in which increased bombing could only inflame the anti-American reactions of the population the United States has vowed to protect. The fitful learning from Vietnam, the continued focus on the Soviet Union until 1992, and the chimera of precision technologies (as if civilian deaths are only caused by errant munitions) meant that protecting civilians as an operational priority in the kinds of wars the United States would be fighting was given short shrift.

After some months of Operation Iraqi Freedom and the reports of abuse at Abu Ghraib, Fallujah, and elsewhere, the question of U.S. policy toward civilian casualties naturally arose again. The first Hopkins survey published in the *Lancet* likely helped stimulate this interest, not only because of its timing (that study, the second battle of Fallujah, and the Abu Ghraib revelations all came within six months of each other), but because it found that most of the violent deaths postinvasion were attributable to coalition forces, mainly from aerial bombardment in the first several weeks of operations.[43] Haditha and some of the other atrocities brought this burgeoning concern into sharper relief in the popular press. The defense intelligentsia was largely silent or critical of the high numbers coming from the household surveys and saw the Iraq War as far more humane than the Vietnam experience. "The U.S. military has done a better job of respecting noncombatant immunity in Iraq than is commonly thought," wrote Colin Kahl, a Georgetown University assistant professor who later was appointed to a post in the Pentagon by the Obama administration. "It also suggests that compliance has improved over time as the military has adjusted its behavior in response to real and perceived violations of the norm." Kahl rightly described the tension between annihilation doctrine and the need for restraints, but since he did not accept the mortality numbers of the empirical studies, it was easy to ascribe "conduct becoming" to the military.[44]

The rules of engagement have been nettlesome, however, not least because (as in Vietnam) local conditions apply. A lethal mixture evolved combining "intelligence" about insurgents, an ingrained practice of applying force, and loose rules of engagement. For example, apart from difficulties of discerning "hostile intent"—the cause of many killings at checkpoints and in village sweeps—the rules allow killing "status-based targets," the groups identified as enemies of the United States. A person fingered by two informants would be so targeted. But this could, and did, lead to confusion, manipulation, and additional civilian deaths.[45] Intelligence can be very dodgy even without ill-intent. Apache helicopters would often "suppress" small-arms fire by spraying a village street with cannon fire, and army lawyers in the chopper or in radio contact would approve this as legitimate even when no threat was evident. As journalists like Dahr Jamail have documented repeatedly, attacks from the air frequently have been indiscriminate, informed by vague intelligence (and therefore approved by the lawyers) but very often killing civilians. Seeing military age men at an outdoor wedding celebration, for example, in an area known for insurgent activity, can let loose a torrent of firepower.[46] For Kilo Company, the marines at Haditha, there was "intelligence" that they cited in their defense that was obviously erroneous, but there were also the permissive, conditioning attitudes of the free fire fight of Fallujah. "Officially their rules of engagement were only slightly more restrictive than those that had applied to the free hunting in Fallujah, with their tolerance for the killing of people who got in the way," explained one of the best journalistic accounts of the massacre.[47] In the perspective of the marines, their actions stemmed from self-defense; but their actions were far in excess of that right. It was commonly charged in Iraq that even two or three rounds of small-arms fire would be met with tremendous firepower from U.S. troops, with civilians among the victims.

The old habits of Vietnam also persisted. Pressures existed for high kill rates in some battalions.[48] The permission to kill all military-age men was a standing order in places like Anbar.[49] Operations like helicopter gunship strikes at times mistook gatherings of civilians for terrorist bands, attacked them, and would claim them as enemy killed. Who would contradict this assertion? Only where some survivors could reach a journalist or convince a U.S. official would an investigation ensue. So rules of engagement that were meant to protect civilians often took a back seat to local conditions, circumstances "on the ground" shaped by U.S. intelligence, tribal rivalries, disproportionate self-defense by American troops, or seeing the population itself as the enemy.

Haditha, like My Lai, prompted the military to reexamine its training.[50] As noted earlier, the new counterinsurgency manual published in late 2006 and carried into Iraq with Petraeus's command, emphasized population protection, an acknowledgment that this priority had slipped significantly in the first three and a half years of the war. The prior absence of concern was evident in a survey conducted by the military—the army's "Mental Health Advisory Team"—which reported in 2007 that "only 38 percent of marines and 47 percent of soldiers said noncombatants should be treated with dignity and respect." Similar numbers said they would report incidences of innocent civilians being killed or abused. More than a third said torture of civilians was allowable to get information; 17 percent viewed all civilians as insurgents. Two-thirds said their officers made it clear not to mistreat civilians, and even higher numbers said their training for ethical conduct was adequate.[51] These attitudes bear resemblance to attitudes reigning among officers during the Vietnam War. At Fort Benning (Calley's training venue), a survey of officer candidates in 1967 found half willing to use torture to get information, and a very large survey in 1970 found that 15 percent of officers and enlisted men did not comprehend the rules of war. A third of them gave incorrect answers to more than half of the questions about the rules of war.[52]

It is often asserted within national security circles that the military has made great strides toward ethical conduct since My Lai and the Peers Report. Of course, the vast majority of officers and troops are mindful of their obligations and do their best to uphold good conduct. But a very sizable number apparently do not. Other dynamics are in play—the strain of combat, the purported moral imperative of the mission, the firepower at their disposal, and the prevailing racial attitudes. All of these combine to threaten civilians routinely. As one veteran of the Iraq War explained, the rules of engagement and the Geneva Conventions were part of his training, but in Iraq "much of this was thrown out the window. . . . We found we were rapidly killing Iraqis in horrible ways. But we had to in order to remain safe ourselves. The war is the atrocity."[53]

CHAPTER 10

Counting

A Single Death Is a Tragedy, a Million Deaths Are a Statistic

Marla Ruzicka thought the deaths in Iraq and Afghanistan *should* be a statistic, should have at least that honor and more, and not be dismissed or ignored. She wanted an accounting. The piquant line attributed to Stalin—"a single death is a tragedy, a million deaths are a statistic"—was relevant to Iraq if the "single" was an American, but the million were not even a statistic. For in Iraq, as in Afghanistan, "we don't do body counts," was General Franks's memorable phrase. Marla wanted body counts, and she wanted to make sure the surviving members of those uncounted thousands were helped, acknowledged, and in some sense compensated, and she went to both Iraq and Afghanistan to do that. Two years after going to Iraq and changing the way some officials thought about civilian losses, she was killed by a car bomb in Baghdad.

That a lone, twenty-eight-year-old would become a widely noted tragedy and the symbol of concern for civilians in Iraq was itself telling. The absence of attention to the civilian detritus of the U.S. invasion and occupation was such that this young activist would be virtually the only one to ring the alarm. Even then, it was her death that brought more attention. "She accomplished what frankly nobody has ever accomplished," Tim Rieser, a key Senate aide, told the *Washington Post* at the time of her death. "Programs were created for Afghanistan and for Iraq to provide assistance to victims of U.S. military mistakes [because of her efforts]." She had stayed in Iraq that time a little longer, the *Post* noted, "because she believed she had found the key to establishing that the U.S. military kept records of its civilian victims, despite its official statements otherwise."[1]

The U.S. military did not reveal such records until its combat mission was finished. In July 2010 it released an unsupported statement near the end of the official mission in 2010 that 77,000 civilians and Iraqi security personnel had been killed in Iraq, a number well below every other account.[2] Then, quite unofficially, the muckraking Wikileaks released nearly 400,000 documents in October 2010 that revealed, among many sordid details, that a rough count was kept via the "after action" reports of American forces, with numbers not far off the earlier press statement. The Iraqi government's contribution to this relied on one household survey that was conducted in the middle of the war. (A former official has said privately that the government did know how many died and that the number was higher than the 2006 estimate appearing in the *Lancet*.)[3] If there is mystery surrounding these supposed lists of the dead, the more pressing question is why there should be any mystery at all. Does it not make sense for the military to keep a credible and comprehensive account of the numbers perishing in its wars?

The question does not have a ready answer. Some would say it hardly matters if the civilian dead in Iraq are 100,000 or 1,000,000 or more—that any sizable number of deaths is a travesty, particularly for a "war of choice" fought on false premises. One could say essentially the same of Vietnam. But the reasons for knowing go beyond the simple (if compelling) urge to condemn wanton destruction. Part of it, as Marla would say, is to do right by the victims. Part of it is to gauge the true costs of war for all involved, costs easily buried as distasteful news. If we don't realize the actual depth of destruction and death, no matter who is at fault, the temptation to start the next war will not be informed by the harsh consequences of the last. Coming to terms with these consequences in our relations with the affected communities is nearly impossible if we have little notion of what scars were left, and America's self-image and sense of purpose glide onward untroubled by any thought of wrongdoing or accounting for our wars. Then we wonder, as was so often asked after 9/11, "why do they hate us?" But it can also be argued persuasively that it is not the U.S. military's responsibility to do the accounting. It is their responsibility—their legal obligation—to avoid civilian casualties, to be sure, but General Franks was correct, if coarse, when saying, "We don't do body counts."

The task has instead been left to the Marla Ruzikas of the world—an increasing number, in fact. Many of them bring state-of-the-art techniques to the task of estimating casualties. Whereas in Korea and Vietnam the estimates of civilian casualties were guesswork, and not of much interest to U.S. authorities even then, the attempt to account for the dead has grown into a sizable undertaking by nongovernmental organizations (NGOs) and academics, with epidemiologists providing the most promising techniques for gathering real-time data that then yield estimates. But even this community of death accountants is wracked by controversy, some of it quite bitter. One point of agreement: those killed in wars should be accounted for, a plea that is remarkable, in fact, because they aren't.

GUESSWORK: THE CHAOS OF ESTIMATES

The Korean War presents the clearest example of guessing how many people died as a result of a major war. The range of estimates for the three-year conflict is very wide, from 770,000 to 5.5 million, including all civilians and soldiers from all sides. The civilian dead of Korea are estimated in almost exactly the same proportions—between 400,000 and three million. R. J. Rummel at the University of Hawaii has likely done more than any individual to compile the estimates, which he lists among his many publications and his Web site, "Democide." Rummel is a self-described libertarian who focuses much of his prodigious attention on the crimes of authoritarian and totalitarian states—hence the slightly odd term, *democide*—but he is serious about the magnitude and importance of the killing, including civilians. The listing of estimates and the weighting of these numbers as averages of high and low scarcely qualifies as a method, however, no matter how earnest the effort.

The low estimate for civilian mortality in the Korean War, for example, appears in a 1968 Adelphi paper, published by the Institute for Strategic Studies (ISS) in London. This paper, by ISS research associate David Wood, lists 100,000 North Korean civilian dead, an implausible number given the years of U.S. carpet bombing and the grinding ground war in the north. Wood gives no references for this estimate, moreover.[4] The figure for 3,000,000 dead used by Rummel comes from two books about Vietnam, one from the apologist Guenter Lewy and the second from Samuel Huntington, a consultant to the defense department and a celebrated professor of political science at Harvard. Rummel refers to a comment by Huntington that has no citation. Lewy references Huntington and David Rees, a historian of the Korean War, neither of whom cites a source for his estimates.[5] Apparently, John Foster Dulles also mentioned the three million figure, attributing the deaths mainly to the communists. Milton Leitenberg of the University of Maryland, with Nicole Ball, helped compile a dataset on deaths in twentieth-century wars for Robert McNamara, when the former defense secretary was president of the World Bank. In a thoughtful essay, Leitenberg reported 4.5 million Korean War dead, including 2,828,000 civilians and 1,672,000 military. His citations include Rummel, who in turn cited Lietenberg.[6] This circuitous replication of figures and citations is common.

The matter of estimating is further complicated by uncertainty about what counts as a casualty and what counts as a subject. Casualties in common parlance can mean death or injury, for example. Casualties from direct combat are one kind; casualties from indirect combat, such as soldiers killed accidentally, or, of course, noncombatants killed as "collateral damage" are additional types. "Structural" causes of death, such as death from disease or malnutrition resulting from war, are another kind. One of the largest datasets, and in effect the granddaddy of datasets, is from the Correlates of War project, based at the University of Michigan; it lists "battle deaths" for Korea at 909,000 and for Vietnam as 1,021,442. But such deaths do not include civilians, which very likely numbered more than those who were killed directly as combatants.[7] Deaths of soldiers can be counted by several means, including field reports and the "watchdog" of their families; and when field reports and censuses of the military population are orderly, these numbers can be considered reasonably accurate. Since the dozens of conflict datasets that followed the Correlates of War project were essentially variations on their methodology, the calculation of noncombatant deaths is often missing.[8]

Even for the combatant fatalities, however, the sources of the data are not uniform or rigorously comparable. Most obvious is the difficulty of estimating deaths for areas of operations to which the estimator has little or no reliable access. In the Korean War, the United States could calculate fatalities of American soldiers from field reports; the same was true for South Korean combatants, and, with less accuracy, for North Koreans on the field of battle. But what to do about North Koreans at a distance? The nature of the war, with heavy bombardment of the North over many months, makes it nearly impossible to estimate war deaths from the U.S. and South Korean standpoint. According to Rummel's database,[9] the range is from 130,000 to 520,000 military deaths among North Koreans; the U.S. Joint Chiefs of Staff estimated 214,000 (later, the Pentagon about doubled that figure). Similarly, the Chinese army suffered between 300,000 and 1.5 million fatalities, according to these kinds of estimates. At the time of the war, the Pentagon said 200,000, the Chinese almost half that number. If the estimates for the deaths of soldiers is so imprecise (estimators often apparently adopting a mid-range number), then the figures for civilians by these techniques are likely to be pure guesswork.

The war in Indochina faces similar problems of estimation. The accounts of the dead range from one million to three million in Vietnam during the direct U.S. intervention (1965–75), another 300,000 or more in the 1960–65 phase, up to 750,000 in Cambodia during the U.S. intervention, and between 50,000 and 250,000 in Laos in the 1960s and early 1970s. The total for this period, from Kennedy's election to Nixon's resignation, might be four million for those three countries. Here, even the figures for the military deaths among South Vietnamese soldiers vary widely, from 180,000 to 650,000. The North Vietnamese and Viet Cong fighters estimated to have died range from 440,000 to 1.1 million. And, as always, the least certain estimates concern civilians, up to two million in Vietnam.[10] Rummel, vigilant as ever about civilian casualties, lists estimates of 361,000 to 720,000 South Vietnamese and just 65,000 North Vietnamese (from U.S. bombing) as direct casualties of warfare. His totals for the 1960–75 period for all war dead, including soldiers, ranges from 533,000 to 1.4 million for the Viet Cong and North Vietnamese, and 400,000 to 1,033,000 for South Vietnamese, or about one million to 2.5 million for both.[11]

Once again, these ranges indicate that the derivation of the numbers remained imprecise. Guenther Lewy made one of the better attempts to use conventional means, starting with records, to account for the dead. From 1967 to 1971, he noted, civilian war casualties admitted to hospitals were recorded by South Vietnam's Ministry of Health and the U.S. Agency for International Development. From this he uses a ratio of wounded-to-dead, as reported by the army of South Vietnam, which was 2.65 "seriously wounded"—requiring hospitalization—to each fatality. By utilizing the records of hospitalization, he comes up with a total of 247,000 civilian deaths in South Vietnam for 1965–74. (An estimate based on the same or similar records by Senator Edward Kennedy's subcommittee of refugees totaled 430,000 civilian fatalities; it was based in part on reckoning that civilians got less field attention from medics than did soldiers, an assumption that Lewy criticizes.) Using the hospitalization numbers and the wounded-to-dead ratio involves several judgment calls, however. How many Vietnamese who were wounded never came to hospitals, for example, is a number that is unknowable. Another question is whether the applicability of military ratios holds for civilians. Even a slight alteration of these figures yields a very different result. Lewy does provide for a factor that few counting exercises ever do—the military's tendency to label all people killed in an operation as enemy fighters rather than civilians. He quoted a U.S. embassy cable from 1966 as asking, "How can you determine whether black-clad corpses found on the battlefield were VC or innocent civilians? [They are inevitably counted as VC]. . . . How do you learn whether anyone was inside structures and sampans destroyed by the hundreds every day by air strikes, artillery fire, and naval gunfire?"[12] Using other data, namely, the number of weapons captured compared with enemy killed in operations (a number that also ranges widely, from 3–1 to 14–1), and assuming that the U.S. estimate of enemy killed is actually one-third civilians, he prospectively added another 220,000 to the estimate for civilians killed, North and South, totaling 587,000. Total war deaths he put at 1.3 million.

Another careful historian of the war, Michael Clodfelter, said that "the Vietnamese civilian toll can only be guessed at," and proceeded to use estimates as high as 1,435,000 in the South for 1965 to 1973; he noted that there were 6.5 million refugees. He also cited the toll in Cambodia, where the U.S. air force dropped a half million tons of bombs: roughly 600,000 civilians died, he estimated, from all causes.[13] He did not provide sources. The McNamara estimate for Vietnam was 1.2 million civilians and nearly as many military on all sides (1960–75).[14]

By the 1990s, then, the advances in accounting for the dead were meager. What is apparent in the attempts to clarify numbers is that definitions and premises are as significant as the actual method of estimation—in fact, are core constituents of that method. What is a casualty? Who is a civilian? Is a death counted only if from violence? What about those from other causes that would not have occurred had there been no war? What goes into a general estimate? The guesswork could be biased by the estimator's political convictions, of course, but even setting that aside, the more basic, definitional issues in the forgoing questions can skew results profoundly. They then become part of an accepted dataset or narrative that is rarely examined. Numbers can also be inadequate substitutes for other kinds of questions. The attempt to quantify and compare complex phenomena leads to simplifications that can often be misleading—itself the subject of a ferocious debate in the social sciences—and this is no less true of war and its consequences.

NEW ATTENTION TO CIVILIANS

The determination to account for the dead became more prominent during Desert Storm and the subsequent sanctions period in Iraq. While the brevity of Desert Storm did not permit much of a discussion about civilian casualties, and the "turkey shoot" of retreating enemy troops north of Kuwait City was a primary concern about excessive use of force, the sharpest focus in that period was on the civilian victims of the U.S.-imposed sanctions regime, a war strategy that rightly should be included in Desert Storm's casualty numbers. In the early postwar period, Americans were relieved by the quickness of victory; but triumph was muted by the Kurdish humanitarian crisis and the rapid suppression of the Shia rebellion by Saddam in the south. So the effort to monitor and estimate the numbers of casualties of the war by sanctions was not noticed much for several months until those involved in it could make their compelling case. While this case—based on new epidemiological techniques discussed later—was widely accepted as fact, it stirred only minor ripples of concern and little effective change in U.S. policy.

Beginning with the Bosnia war and the genocide in Rwanda, the worldwide interest in the human cost of war rose sharply, particularly as these "new wars" targeted civilians intentionally and openly. Mary Kaldor, the British intellectual and activist, was especially prominent in arguing this latter point in the 1990s, and while some

scholars disputed the "newness" of predation on noncombatants—
one had only to look at the Balkan Wars of 1912–13 to see the similarities—the post–Cold War conflicts shocked with their ferocity and
the murderous behavior of former neighbors.[15] Legal mechanisms
like the International Criminal Court and the Bosnian war crimes tribunal rose to prosecute those who ordered such killings of civilians,
and human rights groups kept close watch on conflicts where such
atrocities occurred. The handbook *Crimes of War*, edited by journalists Roy Gutman and David Rieff, was one such notable effort and
provided readers with the juridical concepts in play, which grew into
an ongoing project. During the 1990s, too, a more robust normative
and legal basis for humanitarian intervention was developed by
Frances Deng, the UN Under Secretary General, among others, via
the concept of the "responsibility to protect," which was a framework
to protect civilians, not states, the latter being the conventional concern of international relations.[16]

During the 1990s, then, a sizable philosophical and activist complex
had grown that specifically sought to report civilian tolls and assess
culpability. That this was done unofficially, outside the "Nuremberg
principles"—the war crimes accountability and legal jeopardy that is
defined by war's victors—is all the more remarkable. Global civil society
was taking up this challenge. The news media also seemed to be paying
more attention—notably, in wars that did not involve U.S. forces. For
the most part, however, the actual counting remained guesswork.

Consider the Bosnia war, fraught with ugly ethnic killing on a scale
not seen in Europe since 1945, killing that prompted the Bosnian Muslims, the most victimized group by all reckonings, to make repeated
and desperate appeals to the international community to intervene.
Possibly as a result of that victimization and urgency, their nascent
government tended to use maximum estimates of deaths, finally figur-
ing 200,000–250,000 from 1991 to 1995, a range widely cited to this
day. Since then, a considerable effort to count the dead was made, however, using records of various kinds, and the account for all war dead
(Bosnian Muslims, Serbs, and Croats), soldiers and civilians, settled at
97,000–102,000. The lower number was generated in "The Bosnian
Book of the Dead" by the Research and Documentation Center (RDC)
in Sarajevo more than a decade after the war, involving an apparently
exhaustive search for records. The higher figure, similarly researched,

came from the International Criminal Tribunal for the Former Yugo-slavia.[17] The totals counted those directly killed by warfare, not the larger numbers who died due to war's effects on health, sanitation, and the like—the total "excess deaths." The Tribunal also relied on records, though extensively cross checked with residency and other standard census-like data, over a period of time long after the war had ended. The directors of the efforts believed they had the correct number to within 10 percent.

This kind of direct counting is more accurate than others that use one source of unknown credibility—such as news media accounts—and was carried out carefully in a nonviolent period in which there was good access to multiple sources. These projects did not include nonviolent deaths, however, which cannot be readily estimated from the kinds of records they utilized. So the total mortality for the Bosnia war, including fighters and nonviolent excess deaths, could have breached 200,000.

BRINGING SCIENCE TO THE TASK

Occurring out of the public spotlight during this period was the development of epidemiological measures that could fill in some of the key gaps of the counting and estimation methods, such as they were. It was a coincidence, perhaps, that the heightening concern in some quarters with civilian war-related vulnerability was answered with much more precise and "real-time" techniques of calculation. By 2003, that new scientific capability dovetailed with the notion that states have a moral duty to account for the victims of war, a view that had a relatively high profile in civil society, especially among human rights groups, some journalists, and a growing number of scholars. Compared with the outset of the Korean War or the Vietnam War, this level of attention was infinitely greater, not least because of the communications revolution and the growth of global civil society, the nonprofit, nongovernmental organizations that often serve as watchdogs of conflicts. That fresh attention to war's impacts on civilians was boosted markedly when the Johns Hopkins scientists published their first estimate in the Lancet in late October 2004, nineteen months after the invasion of Iraq. It drew on "population-based" methods used in epidemiology—in this case in which households are surveyed and household members asked questions directly about who has died during a war.

One of the principal researchers of the Iraq War mortality studies, Les Roberts, had done such surveys before, notably in the Congo. But the survey techniques had been applied to war conditions even before that, also in Iraq. In 1991, the study team looking at the effects of the sanctions had conducted a household survey to determine the change in infant mortality rates as a consequence of the war (which they found to have increased 300 percent).[18] This effort was repeated later during the 1990s and continued to find high mortality and other effects of the sanctions. So the method had a considerable amount of field testing and extensive analysis by a large number of medical professionals, epidemiologists, and statisticians.

Population-based surveys and statistical calculations were applied retrospectively as well. In the mid-1990s, American and Vietnamese demographers used data from a Vietnam Life History Survey, a household survey conducted in 1991 in four districts, to calculate war mortality based on probabilities of life expectancies drawn from questions about the deaths of parents and siblings of the respondents. It is a clever piece of sleuthing, but it does rely on many assumptions that could be erroneous, particularly recall bias going back so many years. They calculated about 800,000 deaths (1965–75) of Vietnamese over fifteen years of age, or 900,000 including children (estimated from a different calculation).[19] The problem of "survivor bias"—when there are no survivors from a family to interview—could be particularly acute in Vietnam. More important, the selection of sampled areas was likely to produce underestimates for the nation as a whole: two of the four places were in the North, and the numbers reported here may have been representative of military casualties (for conscripted men fighting elsewhere). But these sampled areas could not accurately reflect civilian casualties overall, which were much greater in the South (and, in the North, casualties were much higher closer to Haiphong or Hanoi than in the sampled areas). Still, the attempt to pull out useful data from a survey and calculate according to certain carefully wrought assumptions was different from the earlier estimations for Indochina.

The household survey technique was then applied in Iraq after the 2003 invasion. The approach taken by Roberts was simple if dangerous: randomly select a certain number of clusters, or neighborhoods, throughout the country. Make sure that this selection reflects certain general attributes of the society as a whole—geographically, urban/rural, ethnic, and sectarian. Select randomly a point in the neighborhood to begin asking the questions of heads of households, and select randomly another twenty-nine houses from that point. The questions, asked by Iraqi health care workers (mainly physicians), were few in number: Has anyone who was living in this household died since January 2002? If so, had that person been a continuous resident for at least three months prior to death? When did he or she die? How did the person die? If a violent death, who was responsible? Do you have a death certificate? By asking these questions as they did, the surveyors were able to establish a prewar mortality rate (from January 1, 2002 to March 20, 2003) that matched well the mortality rates the Central Intelligence Agency (CIA) had established for Iraq and the surrounding countries. By using that prewar mortality rate (about 5.5 per thousand per year) and the mortality rate since the war began, the scientists could estimate the "excess deaths"—the difference between mortality prewar and postinvasion—or those generally attributable to the war. It made no distinction between civilians and combatants. Their numbers yielded a result of 98,000 "excess deaths" in the first seventeen months of the war, or 0.4 percent of the Iraqi population, from violent and nonviolent causes, a wholly plausible number given how deadly the invasion phase was and how violence had been increasing as the insurgency rose in 2004.

The survey was repeated in 2006, with a larger number of clusters and a larger number of households in each cluster, to narrow the "confidence interval," or the range of possible results. This confidence interval is akin to the margin of error used in polling, though it is represented like a bell curve by a very narrow and high range in the middle and much lower possibilities as the graph moves out across the full range, higher or lower. In statistics, with a suitable number of households and a suitably robust randomization, the researcher will achieve a 95 percent confidence level in this range and the midpoint estimate—where the curve is at its peak. But more households and more clusters would reduce the confidence interval, which had been a common source of misunderstanding by journalists in particular when the 2004 survey was published. (The important error made by many in the news media was the supposition that there was an equal chance that the actual result could be anywhere within the confidence interval. One blogger ranted that it was akin to throwing darts at a dartboard. It plainly is not. It is vastly more likely that the correct number is near the mid-range point, or "point estimate.")[20]

The 2006 survey was conducted by Gilbert Burnham, a medical doctor and public health Ph.D. at the Hopkins Bloomberg School of Public Health who alternated between teaching, research, and operating clinics in Afghanistan, East Africa, and elsewhere. A less partisan and more earnest scientist would be rare, and Burnham, a former military officer, set about the business of gathering the new data and bringing in top statisticians to analyze the results. And the results were startling: the point estimate of excess mortality was 655,000 in the first forty months of the invasion, a shocking number that was greeted with some derision by journalists and a few others, but was endorsed (as to method) by epidemiologists. Still, the negative media storm engineered by the small number of critics led Johns Hopkins to conduct a thorough scientific review, which found nothing amiss in the methods or procedures that would affect the results.[21] Other professional reviews agreed.[22]

In 2008, partial results of another household survey were published in the *New England Journal of Medicine*.[23] It had been conducted by the Iraq Ministry of Health (MoH) at nearly the identical period as the second Hopkins survey. This Iraq Family Health Survey Study was a much broader gauge of conditions in Iraq than mortality alone—a long survey that took an hour or more to conduct—and visited many more clusters (1086 versus 40) and households (10,860 versus 1850) than the Hopkins team did in 2006. Its conclusion was that 151,000 violent deaths occurred in that period. However, excess deaths, calculated from their statistical appendix, totaled 400,000 or more. This survey had one major advantage over the Hopkins survey in that the surveyors visited many more clusters, thereby getting a broader gauge of the country. One of the drawbacks to cluster sampling is that killing can be quite high in some neighborhoods, higher than the national average, and correspondingly low in other neighborhoods. If the random selection of neighborhoods catches too many of a high or low mortality, then the estimate for a nationwide number will not be accurate. Apparently, such "heterogeneity" is more of a problem with cities. This design effect can be compensated for by adding clusters and making mathematical adjustments. By sampling in many more clusters, the Ministry of Health could reduce the chances that the heterogeneous nature of violence would yield errors.

The Iraqi survey had three problems that the Hopkins study did not, however. A long questionnaire of the kind they administered, querying about many different topics, is known to produce lower numbers of mortality; the questions about household members who had died were not asked until dozens of other questions had been asked, with the entire survey taking an hour or more to complete.[24] Second, the authors acknowledged that they could not visit a tenth of the selected clusters because those areas were too dangerous. Instead, they used a "proxy"— data from the Iraq Body Count, which, as explained later, has its own serious limitations, and its researchers acknowledge that their estimates are an undercount by at least a factor of two. Third, the Ministry of Health at that time was in the hands of the militant Shia cleric Moktada al-Sadr, and respondents would likely be aware of that and skew their responses accordingly. The respondents might have avoided answering the mortality question honestly, fearing that if it was known that a family member was killed violently it might mean they were fighters or soldiers from another faction. Equally or more likely, they would attribute a death to nonviolent causes, which appears strikingly in the statistical index of the Web-based publication (and, strangely, not discussed in the *New England Journal of Medicine* article or by the editors).[25] For example, the number of deaths by auto accidents rose by four times from the preinvasion rate; had this single figure been included in the violent death category, the overall estimate would have risen to 196,000. What we know about road deaths in this period strongly suggests they were part of the war, not just accidents. A category of nonviolent death called "unintentional injuries" doubled during the war and equaled 43 percent of those deaths attributed to violence. And there was an extraordinary number of "don't know" responses concerning the cause of death, equivalent to 53 percent of the number attributed to the war's violence.[26] The Hopkins survey had none of these drawbacks.

It's also worth noting that this Ministry of Health estimate faced none of the scrutiny that the *Lancet* articles withstood; generally, the MoH estimate was reported in contrast to the Hopkins survey— that is, as "only" one-quarter the number of violent deaths that Burnham et al. had estimated, with no reference at all to the total excess deaths readily calculable from their results. The MoH analysis maintained, moreover, that violent deaths remained constant from 2004 through June 2006, which by all other accounts was obviously untrue—violence was rising sharply in that period. The MoH analysis also claimed that most of the killing was taking place in Baghdad; the Multi-National Force (MNF) statistics (which recorded reports of attacks to MNF soldiers) for that period had Baghdad at only about 25 percent of attacks, which is virtually the same proportion of excess deaths calculated in the 2006 Johns Hopkins study. Killing in Anbar, Mosul, Tal Afar, and Diyala was, after all, very high.

All population studies—such as these household surveys—contend with these data-gathering difficulties and other possible sources of inaccuracy. Recall bias is frequently cited, although the fact of death is vivid and likely accurate for these relatively short periods. Survivor bias is another hazard: if a selected household is empty, its inhabitants may have been killed or have fled because of death or fear of violence and thus never become part of the estimate. The massive displacement of Iraqis—20 percent of the population—and the lack of a recent census made the surveyors' problems more acute, a kind of survivor's bias on a grand scale. Survivor's bias and recall bias tend to reduce the reports of mortality, lowering number estimates. Another challenge to population studies is the prewar mortality rate—it must be accurate, or the death rate attributed to the war period will be off. This is a frequently voiced criticism whenever such surveys are published, and so it was in Iraq. But both Hopkins studies found the same prewar mortality rate, and it was consistent with other surrounding countries. (The MoH estimate was even lower.) Another general difficulty of this method is the accuracy of estimating a total number of deaths from a sample, although repeated testing of the method in situations where other forms of estimates were available have shown that such calculations from household surveys are reasonably robust. Other criticisms popped up over time*—and a review of the scientific literature

* One example of a persistent critique that missed the mark but had a technical patina was the charge that the 2006 Hopkins survey suffered from "main street bias"—that an excessive number of households were sampled on main streets where most violence occurs, skewing overall results upward (Neil F. Johnson et al., "Bias in Epidemiological Studies of Mortality," *Journal of Peace Research* 45:5, 2008). Burnham responded that they were completely mistaken about the

demonstrates serious and respectful groping for accuracy and integrity—but the household survey appears to have proven itself as the most plausible way to estimate war deaths in "real time."

One other fascinating effort using sibling survival data was published in 2009 by Ziad Obermeyer and colleagues at the University of Washington; it used a large dataset produced by the World Health Organization in 2003 to estimate war deaths in thirteen countries, including Bosnia and Vietnam. The randomized samples were large—4,092 households for Vietnam, 1,028 for Bosnia—and conducted in peacetime, avoiding some of the problems of cluster surveys taken during conflict. Their estimations, also requiring complex assumptions for missing data or correlations, found 176,000 violent fatalities in the Bosnia war (not total "excess deaths"), and 3.8 million in Vietnam.[27] The latter is nearly what the Vietnamese government calculates and is quite a bit higher than other estimates. Even this is conceivably an undercount. "The study only includes violent deaths," wrote Richard Garfield, a Columbia University professor and leading expert. "In the poorest countries, where most conflicts now occur, a rise in deaths from infectious diseases often dwarfs the number of violent deaths during a conflict. For all these reasons, Obermeyer and colleagues' study is likely to underestimate the importance of conflict as a cause of death."[28] This sibling method has come in for some other criticisms, but as a tool to gain some insights on long-ago conflicts, it is remarkably helpful.

---

selection criteria in the Hopkins study, and that main streets were not privileged. But the paper also misunderstood the nature of violence in Iraq. If the violence along main streets put those households at higher risk, then the female proportion of total mortality (by most accounts, about 10%) should have been much higher than reported since women remain near the household more than men, to cite one obvious error in their thinking. It also bought into the common misperception that events like car bombs or bombs in markets were major sources of mortality, which they were not. The main sources of violence—gunshots at roadblocks, house-to-house searches, and sectarian and revenge killings, as well as aerial bombardment—would not discriminate according to people living on "main streets." A 2007 review by the World Health Organization dismissed the "main street bias" conjecture. Science blogger Tim Lambert, who ran an ongoing and highly enlightening discussion on the *Lancet* papers on his site, Deltoid, after dissecting the "main street bias" paper, concluded that "the only way Johnson et al. were able to make 'main street bias' a significant source of bias was by making several absurd assumptions about the sampling and the behaviour of Iraqis." Lambert is skilled in statistics and attracts others like him. See http://scienceblogs.com/deltoid/2006/12/main_street_bias_paper.php; accessed April 10, 2010.

Oddly enough, despite these advances in accounting for the dead, the principal source cited for Iraqi casualties was not the epidemiological studies but an NGO in London that literally counted the civilian dead. While prospectively the optimal method, for Iraq it had its drawbacks, and serious drawbacks they are. Iraq Body Count (IBC) was founded by academics and activists concerned about the lack of attention to civilian casualties and set out to record every civilian death by violence, mainly by using news media reports appearing in English. Their fastidious approach to this is evident from their well-used Web site. It has become the most frequently cited mortality statistic in the news media. It is part of a laudable trend in estimating, reflected in the Correlates of War project and similar efforts such as one kept by two Norwegian institutes, to bring some standardization to the numbers available—that is, defining what will be counted, what constitutes a source of data, attempting to cross check among sources, and so on. The Bosnia count cited earlier is one of the most complete of this kind for a single conflict. Iraq Body Count was taking on the considerably more daunting task of counting from afar during wartime.

As a result, the IBC effort faces considerable barriers. Unlike the active surveillance of the household surveys, it is passive surveillance, relying on others to collect or report data. And in this case, the surveillance mechanism—the news media—is highly imperfect. Collecting mortality data is not a reporter's primary interest. Killings of significance—spectacular car bombings, for example—tended to gain attention, whereas the quotidian incidences of targeted shootings did not. More important, the news media were concentrated in Baghdad, with some reporting from major cities like Basra and Kirkuk. But the killings in other sizable cities (there are eighty cities with populations of 20,000 or more) could go unreported; many places were too dangerous for reporters, and the resources of news organizations were stretched. As a result, great swaths of Iraq were opaque. Dexter Filkins of the *New York Times*, one of the longest serving American reporters during the war, said during the height of the violence that "98% of Iraq, and even most of Baghdad, has now become 'off-limits' for Western journalists."[29] As noted, U.S. military reports indicated that most of the attacks on U.S. forces were taking place outside Baghdad. Yet the news media was concentrated in, and significantly confined to, the capital.

Another difficulty with counting from news media reports is that the surveillance instrument—the number and dispersion of reporters—changes over time. The English-language news organizations were not only concentrated heavily in Baghdad, but they were also changing in numbers of reporters at work and what they were focused on. In the first half of 2007 alone, for example, while violence remained very high and the interest in the "surge" was beginning, the news devoted to Iraq in American news dropped from 25 percent to 10 percent of the "news hole" in five media sectors, a broad gauge; coverage of events in Iraq specifically fell by nearly 40 percent.[30] If the "eyes and ears" of this counting method are constantly changing, the output can change not as a result of the levels of violence changing but from alterations in the capacity to record that violence. Iraq Body Count changed its method at the end of 2007, following the peak years of violence, from requiring two English-language reports of each death to one such report, a dramatic revision in method. They were also reliant on others' definitions of "civilians"—often the security forces, who would tend to report a fatality as an insurgent: "Excluded from IBC are those . . . reported as initiating deadly violence or being active members of a military or paramilitary organization," says the methods section on its Web site. But who is the source of such an identification? It was often the coalition forces, which frequently overstated the number of "insurgents" killed in their operations. IBC's definition of death by direct violence also, like the Ministry of Health survey, excluded deaths by car accidents and similar injuries, which, as noted, reached into the tens of thousands or more and were very likely to be a result of war.

Too much during wartime is overlooked in a society stressed to the breaking point. As described by Gerald Burke, a former major in the Massachuetts state police and a senior adviser in Iraq, "we don't have a good handle" on the violence: "I suspect the [killed in action] is drastically underreported," he explained after two tours of Iraq. "Bodies were immediately put on the back of a pickup truck, wrapped in sheets, and not taken to a morgue, not taken to a police station, but taken back to the family . . . [which] would prepare the body for burial, and within a few hours at most, the body would be in the ground." Part of this process was based on tradition, part on fear: "I think a lot of people mistrust the police, first, and get a sense of futility. Why bother telling the police, because they're not going to investigate it anyway. So they don't even report the murders and deaths to the police."[31] So the counting method in the midst of war, when record-keeping is dodgy and reporters are scrambling, is highly incomplete.

The bottom line is that one does not know what is being missed. This gap has been documented in other cases, like the civil war in Guatemala, where at best 10 percent of violent deaths were reported during the worst periods.[32] Morgue records are scarcely better, since many victims are buried immediately by relatives, with only a fraction going to a morgue or even dying in a hospital. Death certificates may be issued to the bereaved by a local doctor but not recorded anywhere else; the information flows in such circumstances are notoriously unreliable, and the health care system itself—those doctors and others who would issue death certificates and then collate and send the data to the Ministry of Health—was under intensive attacks. Yet counting methods rely on this fragile and fragmented system, and no other data are provided. (A more reliable metric than morgue counts is graveyard counts, which among Shia at the enormous cemetery in Najaf were reported to be at least twice the prewar average through the first four and a half years of the war.[33] No systematic survey of graveyards was conducted, however, to help gauge overall mortality.)

As a result, this technique of totaling up the dead is incapable of accounting for the deaths that were *not* being recorded, whether by the English-language news media or the chaotic health care system. It's not surprising, then, that IBC recorded only about 40,000 civilian deaths by violence in mid-2006, around the same time that the household surveys were calculating all violent deaths at three to ten times more. IBC's count rose to over 100,000 only in 2010.

However, the shaky scientific grounds of the Iraq Body Count never dissuaded the news media from using it as the Rosetta Stone of violence in Iraq. The Iraq Index compiled by the Brookings Institution and widely cited in the press essentially uses the IBC and similar methods to compile data. When the Wikileaks documents were dissected in October 2010, the news media found the military's mortality reporting to be roughly congruent with these other passive surveillance totals.* But, of course, the soldiers' "method" suffered the same flaws as IBC and like-minded efforts: they were partial, disorganized, and could never calculate what was being missed. An award-winning Iraqi journalist, Sahar Issa, said that Iraqis "laugh" at such numbers "because they know that [the number is low]," she told an interviewer in late 2010. "Iraqis know that they have lost hundreds of thousands."[34] A number of media critics, notably Media Lens, a London-based organization, and the scientific community recognize the shortcomings of counting methods. Yet this remains as the idée fixe in popular discourse of the war.[35]

The most authoritative review of all the mortality estimates—passive and active—appeared in the professional journal *Conflict and Health* in 2008, and concluded that population-based surveys are superior (for the reasons discussed here); also, "of the population-based studies, the Roberts and Burnham studies provided the most rigorous methodology as their primary outcome was mortality. Their methodology is similar to the consensus methods of the SMART initiative, a series of methodological recommendations for conducting research in humanitarian emergencies." The passive reporting, these seven experts agree, suffers from under-reporting and inability to capture indirect deaths, and thereby called into question the estimates of IBC, the Brookings index, the UN office in Baghdad, and other such efforts. "The utility of such collection data serves strictly as a 'sentinel case' alert that should prompt further population-based cluster sampling before such findings are widely disseminated or quoted as fact."[36]

As to how casualty figures are used in popular discourse, remarkably little attention is paid to related evidence. For example, the enormous

* Every major media outlet in the U.S. made this mistake of seeing the Wikileaks documents as a verification of the lowest counts. Indeed, the coverage of the Wikileaks revelations focused more on the personality of the founder and other details—e.g., Iran's involvement, or abuse of detainees—than on the mortality issue, which was referred to in a relatively casual manner. Some used the occasion to denounce higher estimates, such as those in the 2006 *Lancet* article, as the *Washington Post* did in an editorial (October 26, 2010). But most simply ignored any penetrating discussion of mortality and claimed that nothing new was revealed. Yet an analysis of the mortality recorded in Wikileaks documents showed that IBC had missed at least two-thirds of those violent deaths, so that even with the partial and "passive surveillance" of U.S. military personnel, the death by violence numbers in Iraq would exceed 330,000. (See http://cumc.columbia.edu/dept/sph/popfam/fm/)

number of refugees and internally displaced persons is a canary-in-the-coal-mine of high violence and death. It is regularly reported that between 3.5 and 4 million Iraqis were at any given time displaced by the war after 2003, reflecting official figures from the UN High Commissioner on Refugees. This represents up to 14 percent of the total population, and 17 percent of the population outside the Kurdish provinces—a very large number. What does it mean? In other recent conflicts, a ratio of displaced to dead can be estimated, and the range is between 3:1 and 10:1. Interviews with refugees, moreover, indicate that their departure from Iraq was motivated by fear of violence—many had already lost a family member—and their very slow repatriation also indicates this gripping fear. (These huge numbers of displaced indicate that "survivor bias" in the household surveys was significantly large.)[37] Another indicator is the number of widows. While these estimates are imprecise, the Iraqi government put the number of war widows from all conflicts at 750,000 or more.[38] This includes widows from the Iran-Iraq war (1980–88), in which perhaps 250,000 Iraqis died, though not all married men. We also have polls of Iraqis—the conventional opinion polls cited earlier. One conducted by several Western news organizations in early 2007 found that one in six Iraqis reported that someone in their household had been physically harmed by the war, or the equivalent of 3.7 million in the non-Kurdish provinces; using that metric, a plausible 5:1 ratio of wounded to killed would yield more than 700,000 fatalities.[39]

These kinds of correlations were never pursued during the war, and with the perfervid challenges to the Hopkins studies (which in fact were not the highest estimates),[40] journalists tended to default to the safest numbers, those of Iraq Body Count (or the similarly derived numbers published by the UN office in Baghdad). It was a perplexing lacuna in the coverage. Few if any of the major news organizations explained the different methods of accounting for the dead, the inadequacy of using press reports, or the complexities and potential of household surveys. In fact, very little analysis of Iraqi deaths occurred at all, apart from the frequent observation that Shia and Sunni militias were killing each other.

Analysis of the deaths appeared to be a taboo topic, in part because the number was so difficult to grasp in its magnitude and in part because of confusion about how many people were dying and who was responsible. But this habit of ignoring or downplaying the numbers killed in the war reinforced the tendency of the American people to ignore war's victims. By obscuring, minimizing, or deflecting this topic, the news media, government officials, and prominent intellectuals were in effect giving the public permission not to pay attention. And not pay attention is what they have done. The vast gap in the discourse does not, however, wholly explain the avoidance of responsibility.

The small community that has tried to devise better methods of real-time calculations of war fatalities is split between those who think media-based counting is enough, and those who seek to utilize the household survey methods that are more robust, however difficult the circumstances of collecting data on the ground during armed conflict. The population-based surveys logically appear to be more accurate. Those practitioners, mainly epidemiologists, are refining and experimenting with the methods, as they should. The use of "triangulation"—building historically valid correlations between refugees and mortality, and between wounded and fatalities, among other possibilities—can serve as an essential comparison, too. Once a conflict is over, then the use of actual records—census, medical, property, and others where good records are indeed kept—can be used to provide more dimension to the survey results. For knowing what the scale of killing is during wartime, however, the household surveys, where possible, are clearly superior.

Marla Ruzicki was not a social scientist and her outlook would have kept her clear of the acrimonious debate that has sometimes surrounded the issue of war mortality. What she did know, however, was that the civilians caught in war or targeted by the combatants needed to be noted, their deaths dignified by the institutions that perpetuate violence and by society as a whole. The most basic form of that conveyance of dignity would be acknowledgment of the tragic fact of death itself.

CHAPTER 11
The Epistemology of War

Fatalities of civilians in American wars have not been part of public debate. All three of the major conflicts since 1945 exhibited similar characteristics of public engagement: initial caution about involvement, "rally-round-the-flag" enthusiasm once a commitment to combat was made in Washington, growing disillusionment with the war effort as U.S. casualties mounted and achieving war aims proved elusive, and then unshakable opposition to the war among a solid majority until the war was over for U.S. troops. Because of the way each war began there are variations on this theme, but all soon followed these contours more or less uniformly.

Each war became unpopular and increasingly seen as unnecessary, so it's worth asking if, and in what ways, Americans were apathetic or indifferent about the U.S. role in those interventions. As discussed earlier, the Korean War and the Iraq War of this last decade both seemed to lose salience as political concerns: for the Korean intervention, the public tuned out after the Truman-MacArthur imbroglio passed, and for the final two years of the three-year war, public interest seemed remarkably low. For Iraq, the quick revelation that Saddam Hussein did not possess nuclear, biological, or chemical weapons; the unusually perplexing nature of the insurgency; and the increasing chaos inside the country left the public cool to the tasks of war-making. The enormous protest movement against involvement in Indochina made that period look different, but even then the antiwar fervor was subsiding after Nixon won a landslide reelection and the U.S. troops were being withdrawn, (even though the war had three years to run).

To some extent, one can gauge the American public's mood about wars from opinion polling, political debates and elections, and the trappings of popular culture, but those indicators measure the public's attitude toward U.S. policy more than anything else. Indifference is a harder quality to grasp. For all the cynicism and irony that has imbued what's fashionable in American society, it remains difficult for Americans to claim indifference toward a U.S. war. Interest and attention may be more fragmented than careless: the surfeit of entertainment options and the decline of the traditional news media allow Americans to turn away easily nowadays, and political debate is fragmented and aggravated by the cable TV "talking heads" and the equivalent on the Internet. But indifference was equally evident in the early 1950s when the communications universe was very different.

Whatever the ups and downs of public enthusiasm for a U.S. war, the abhorrence of American casualties in war has never been in doubt. One cannot say the same for the other victims of war, the enemy soldiers or the populations of civilians in the war zone. And this is one of the central puzzles of the matter of civilian casualties in American wars. Simply put, there is little evidence that the American public cares what happens to the people who live where our interventions are conducted. And the question is, why? Why are Americans indifferent to this suffering, the truly massive suffering that is significantly a consequence of military actions they approved? And what are the consequences of this vast carelessness?

MEASURING INDIFFERENCE

Without very extensive surveys among Americans, the ways to gauge indifference and its nature are difficult and imprecise. It goes without saying that the lack of survey data on this question is itself a symptom.

Some useful surveys exist, however. Consider public opinion in the United States about the Iraq War, which began in 2003. Even though Americans saw the situation in Iraq as unstable, they wanted U.S. troops removed. Most would interpret the U.S. presence as stabilizing, so the public's favoring of withdrawal indicated a strong preference for the safety of U.S. troops over the safety of Iraqi society. In 2009, for example, by large majorities, the public said the situation would worsen as security was turned over to the Iraqis. At about the same time, Americans averred that the war was not worth the costs to the United States, even as the outcome as of 2009 looked like the violence had subsided and some normalcy might be within Iraq's grasp. So while the "United States is . . . making significant progress toward restoring civil order in Iraq" and even though turning over the responsibilities for keeping order to Iraqis would result in more instability and violence, the U.S. troops should nonetheless be withdrawn. A CNN poll in mid-2009 asked, "If there is a significant increase in the number of attacks on Iraqi citizens by insurgents after the U.S. withdraws its troops from Iraqi cities, do you think the U.S. should or should not send combat troops back into those cities?" The answer was overwhelming: 63 percent said we should not, 35 percent said we should.

Another such question was posed eight times over seventeen months beginning in January 2007 by the *Washington Post* and ABC News: "Do you think the United States should keep its military forces in Iraq until civil order is restored there, even if that means continued U.S. military casualties; OR, do you think the United States should withdraw its military forces from Iraq in order to avoid further U.S. military casualties, even if that means civil order is not restored there?" Here the responses were more equivocal, with slightly declining support for keeping troops in Iraq; the average for the eight surveys was 42 percent in favor of keeping troops there, and 55 percent favoring withdrawal.[1]

Support for withdrawing U.S. troops could have much more to do with wanting to protect "our boys" than with any particular attitude about Iraqis. It could also reflect distaste for the false reasons for intervention. During the run-up to Operation Desert Storm, Americans were equivocal about the wisdom of sending troops to the Gulf; once the war was being conducted successfully (in terms of driving Iraqi occupiers out of Kuwait), the support for the effort rose dramatically, from about half to 80 percent.[2] Success and low casualties made the cause popular even though the direct threat to America was low compared with the depiction of the threat in 2003. American casualties and achievement of war aims tend to be the key variables of popularity, not the local impact. In that vein, too, the support for continuing U.S. military action in the surveys cited in the last paragraphs (roughly 35–42 overall) does not necessarily represent concern about Iraqis; nore likely, such sentiment reflects a desire to "finish the job" of ng terrorists, redeeming the U.S. mission, and similar rationales. As noted earlier, news media coverage of Operation Iraqi Freedom dropped dramatically over time, in part due to the exceptional costs of sustaining reporters and providing security in such difficult circumstances. (It was also a period of sharp decline for newspapers in particular.) In late 2008, a report noted that "Iraq accounted for 18 percent of . . . prominent news coverage in the first nine months of 2007, but only 9 percent in the following three months, and 3 percent so far this year." Public interest seemed to parallel that, with more than half of Americans showing keen interest in the war early on, a number declining to 30 percent by mid-2007. Hundreds of reporters had been embedded with the U.S. military in 2003–2004, a number that had declined to a handful by 2007.[3] The declining interest and coverage may have been due to a number of factors, but it's likely that apathy or indifference about the war and its local population has been part of that mix.

Notably, a CBS News poll in July 2009 found that a plurality of Americans thought Iraqis were resentful rather than grateful about the U.S. invasion and occupation (44–38 percent, with 11 percent "unsure").[4] This sentiment, coupled with the strong desire to exit Iraq quickly regardless of the consequences, may be the clearest indicators of unease and possible indifference toward Iraqis. These opinions reflect the absence of stated concern among elites: few major politicians, if any, expressed compassion for the Iraqis' suffering; no major religious figures came forward with calls to help the victims of violence and neglect; editorials about Iraq in major newspapers rarely mentioned civilian casualties, refugee issues, impoverishment of widows, and similar issues. A LexisNexis search of the New York Times, for example, found that "Iraqi deaths" yielded seventy-five stories, many about court cases against U.S. soldiers, or from columnist Bob Herbert, from March 2003 to April 2010. A cross reference to "American public" yielded one reference to a statement given by the head of Blackwater, the private security firm with many contracts in Iraq. The editorials and op-eds of the Times—less than 200 mention "Iraqi" and "casualties" in the same column—rarely take up the culpability or scale of civilian mortality from the war. Compassion and sustained interest in Iraqi casualties was simply absent from elite discourse, and the inescapable inference is that indifference was present instead.

The Vietnam War period was less straightforward, since the mention of civilian suffering was more frequent, especially among war protestors but also among some of the most important reporters, like Jonathan Schell and Neil Sheehan. But the polling of the time revealed little empathy for the Vietnamese, as discussed in Chapter 5, and the ready abandonment of Indochina indicated that anticommunist concerns were exhausted; the South Vietnamese would just have to fend for themselves. By the mid-1970s, no one was still calling for a bloodbath, as Reagan had, but neither was there evident and widespread appreciation for the scale of suffering—death, disease, impoverishment, and dislocation—brought to South Vietnam by the U.S. intervention. What dominated discourse was that the war was simply a "mistake." The atrocities and bombing of the North also rang few alarms about the human cost of the war to Vietnamese. The scale of mayhem in Cambodia, significantly caused by U.S. intervention, does not register in American culture or politics at all.

The Korean War, as discussed, was "the forgotten war," not least because of American indifference; however, the forgetfulness is typically framed as overlooking American soldiers' sacrifices rather than the Koreans' casualties. If indifference greeted the U.S. troops, it goes without saying that the Koreans' plight was even lower—if even discernible—on the scale of concern. Like that of later wars, the Korean War period was thin on cultural representations of the victim populations. The novels and films of those periods focused either on the stories of battle from the American perspective or on the home front and the effect of war losses on individuals and families. As noted earlier, there were precious few films during the Korean War at all; most of the best Vietnam War films were made after the war ended; the few films about the Iraq War have generally been box office failures. Whatever the war or period, the people of the war zones were essentially invisible. Documentaries like *Hearts and Minds* were the rare exception.

This encompassing indifference is fascinating with regard to depictions of American soldiers in these three wars during and after combat. Korean War vets were "forgotten"; Vietnam War vets were subjects of fierce rhetorical broadsides—with a few antiwar leaders decrying the solders' willingness to carry out the war and many others rallying to their defense (even someone like Calley); and Iraq veterans being subject to virtually no criticism and embraced as heroes. The soldier becomes the emotional barometer of war sentiment. The promiscuous making of heroes—namely, *any* American remotely associated with resisting threats from Muslims—is a post-9/11 phenomenon, and in Iraq it became a diversion from the failures of the war soon after the invasion in 2003. So the indifference to, or even blaming of, the veterans in Korea and Vietnam was transformed into exalting every soldier as a hero and broadly adopted in political and popular culture, just as Iraqis who resisted were transformed into terrorists. On the one side are heroes, and on the other are terrorists. Since ordinary Iraqis consistently rejected the U.S. intervention and wanted the United States to leave the country (there were no such polls in Korea and Vietnam), it was easy to implicate Iraqi civilians as, if not enemies, at least not worthy of our attention and certainly not our compassion. The U.S. military was there to protect us, not them.

EXPLAINING INDIFFERENCE

While indifference to civilian deaths in our wars is reasonably clear, what's harder to get at are the reasons for this indifference. The subject rarely comes up—either the fact of uncaring attitudes or what explains them—and, as a result, there have been few attempts to discuss anything related to it.

It is worth noting that the military has likely considered the matter of civilian deaths more than any other institution or set of thinkers. Their attention appears to follow three stages, though it is far from an organized discourse. The worries about public reaction to civilian casualties, particularly in situations where U.S. troops might have behaved recklessly, have been apparent on a number of occasions and some of these were discussed earlier. This concern may explain the first stage of military attention: rote reaction of military spokesmen to minimize or outright deny that any such recklessness has occurred. Flat denial of culpability, experience suggests, will result in the public's not holding anyone accountable for killing civilians. A second stage of this, if needed, is stonewalling, either through making information difficult to access or vowing to investigate incidents, usually without legal consequences. The third stage is a more aggressive public stance of questioning the motives of the journalists or others who revealed the incident, a tactic readily joined by the war's supporters, rendering justice (as with My Lai, among others) haphazard or vitiated.

When a 2007 video of a U.S. Apache helicopter gunship opening fire on Iraqi civilians and two Reuters journalists, killing twelve, was released in spring 2010, the Pentagon's reaction was to verbally attack and threaten the small organization, Wikileaks, that obtained and released the video. The tape showed a group of unthreatening men walking across a square; permission was quickly granted to gun them down, then to shoot and kill other men who came to take away the wounded or dead. Two children in a van were severely wounded by the helicopter barrage, and the U.S. helicopter gunmen were jocular about the incident. A short flurry of attention ensued, much of it generated by journalists' organizations. What was particularly poignant about the revelations, and a point overlooked in the brief attention to it, was that the army lied about the incident at the time, and, after Reuters demanded an investigation, simply reported that the gunmen were acting in accordance with their rules of engagement. The matter would have been forgotten had the video not found its way to the Internet. Even then, the Secretary of Defense claimed that "these people can put out whatever they want and are never held accountable for it."[5] The incident overall demonstrated the public relations tactics routinely used by the military and civilian leadership, the easy acceptance in the news media of this frame for seeing the incident, and the apparent lack of concern for the casualties of war.* The management of the war news by the U.S. government essentially challenges in these three ways any account that "collateral damage" has occurred and thereby drains the victims' accounts of the emotional impact that might then register among the American public as something like concern. (Individual

---

* The flap demonstrated yet again how such troubling incidents are handled by the most prominent communications channels. The *New York Times* followed the release with a story about the trauma visited upon U.S. military personnel as a result of such incidents (April 7, 2010), and *Washington Post* longtime columnist David Ignatius described the Wikileak video as "counter-embedding," which he defined, "to embed with the insurgents and report what the war looked like from their side," which is "dangerous" (May 2, 2010). Even the comic Stephen Colbert took an uncharacteristically serious swipe at the editor of Wikileaks. However, two of the soldiers involved in the incident on the ground apologized to the Iraqi people for their role in the occupation (BBC, April 23, 2010).

cases of killing civilians are often handled by quietly paying a small amount in compensation, such as $2,000, to the family.)

The indifference of the public is only partly due to the stratagems of the authorities, however, and one can reasonably contend that the machinations of officials could not consistently succeed if other factors were not in play. The three we consider are racism, the frontier myth, and psychological aversion.

The Role of Racism

Because of the long history of racism in America, its powerful political effects over the whole of American history, and its insinuation into U.S. expansion, its plausibility as the base of indifference is apparent. The populations of the first two wars were Asian and the population of the third was Arab. Both have been the central objects of "orientalist" prejudice in Europe and America. The roots of American globalism— "freedom's empire," in Laura Doyle's conception—were based in part on a supposition of white superiority and destiny that was scarcely questioned from the earliest days of the European settlements. Even the anti-imperialists of the late nineteenth and early twentieth centuries adhered to notions of white supremacy. As noted throughout this volume, the constant references to "gooks" and "hajis" place racist attitudes very prominently in explaining insensitivities about killing large numbers of natives, whether hostile or not. The indifference of the public would follow these same lines.

Racism was central to every modern empire. We are particularly familiar with this strain of politics in the British Empire—brought to us today through English literature like Paul Scott's *The Jewel in the Crown* or the comic novels of William Boyd, among many others—and the French experience in North Africa, particularly Algeria. Orientalism both as a colonial ideology and as the West's academic lens through which to study the global south was a European (mainly British and French) invention.[6] The racism of the West European colonial powers involved both *essentialism*—attributions of personal and group characteristics based on race—and attitudes of the *superiority* of Europe in which the characteristics of Europeans (posited as rationality, industriousness, Christian piety, sexual restraint, etc.) were held to be obviously suited to ruling over others who did not possess such qualities. Both essentialism and superiority tended to combine into racism that denigrated the "oriental" in particular. As Edward Said put it in his seminal 1978 treatment of the subject, in Western media the Arab

> appears as an oversexed degenerate, capable, it is true, of cleverly devious intrigues, but essentially sadistic, treacherous, low. . . . In newsreels and or newsphotos, the Arab is always shown in large numbers. No individuality, no personal characteristics or experiences. Most of the pictures represent mass rage and misery, or irrational (hence hopelessly eccentric) gestures. Lurking behind all of these images is the menace of *jihad*. Consequence: a fear that the Muslims (or Arabs) will take over the world.[7]

The attitudes toward Muslims have been deeply ingrained in the European mind since the early second millennium C.E., punctuated and buttressed by the Ottoman military triumphs in Southeast Europe, especially the Balkans, and the seven-century Muslim ascendancy in Spain. This confrontation, which of course included many European incursions into the Levant, Egypt, and elsewhere in Muslim North Africa and Western Asia, gripped Europe right into the late nineteenth century. The "Turk" (readily applied more broadly to all Muslims of the region) was invariably depicted in the most devilish terms, and the need to not merely resist Ottoman encroachments but to dominate and even destroy the Muslim states was virtually a given of European consciousness for hundreds of years. These attitudes thread through much of church history, emerging notions of sovereignty, and European culture and self-image, and to some degree were handed on to Americans.

Orientalism is not merely the depiction of the Muslim or the sense of threat. Said and other critics of orientalism centrally argue that the "study" of the Orient is not only racially framed but is a form of domination itself—in effect, the control of information and ways of understanding the region and people. In the most recent manifestation of this—mainly American—it takes the form of "scientism," social science in particular, which privileges expertise above the European literary tradition, for example, which was the mode of early orientalist musings. We "know" the Arab through academic analysis—area studies, historiography, international relations, comparative politics and sociology, and so on—and through such "discourses" constitute the representation of, say, Iraqis in the American news media and in policy discussions. (Journalism tends to skim off the top of the same types and frames of knowledge.) An entire set of understandings about a place can be built on such expertise. Every war is dependent to some extent on this type of knowledge, the lens of Western understandings, methods, and prejudices. Whether game theory for Vietnam or weapons-proliferation expertise for Iraq, the narrow constructions of technical knowledge applied to targeted countries produced immensely destructive results; one could say they were destructive precisely because they were divorced from historical or sociological treatments. However, the original sin is the ready assumption and acceptance of superficial stereotypes about the people and cultures these sciences are meant to interpret or remedy. The prescriptions and effects of war, it was and is presumed, can be represented in charts as numerical relationships because that is what "science" is meant to be. But the voices of the Koreans, Vietnamese, and Iraqis themselves are not heard, or, when occasionally breaking through (as with semiannual polls in Iraq) are discounted as disgruntled or ignorant. Orientalism contributes to this by serving to legitimate American expertise of that kind, treating a variegated people as a unitary type that needs our "help" to modernize. As Said presciently concluded his discussion of orientalist dogma, "the Orient is at bottom either something to be feared (the Yellow Peril, the Mongol Hordes, the brown dominions) or controlled (by pacification, research and development, outright occupation whenever possible)."[8]

The critique of orientalism is important because it shows that mere racism is not the only sensibility at work. Rather, it's the structure of how we generate knowledge, the modes of seeing, that conditions our perceptions about things like the human costs of war. That is, one might or might not subscribe to the idea that racism is a powerful feeling that lowers caring about target populations. The debate about orientalism alerts us to the very representation of those populations: at various times, we have "known" that they do not care as much about human life as we do, that they have no appreciation for freedom or democracy (or, indeed, act violently because they "hate our freedoms," as President Bush insisted), or are underdeveloped or prone to violence or are beholden to backward traditions or subscribe to a violent religion or embrace strong leaders or are sympathetic with the Maoists or the Soviets or al Qaeda—"knowledge" that contributes to whatever natural inclinations exist for racism and can justify the terrible swift sword of American action. Orientalism and its kin provide a veneer of scientific veracity to U.S. violence, both in the initiation of violence and in enabling us to regard its consequences as the responsibility of the Koreans, Vietnamese, and Iraqis.

Racism itself remains a vexing social syndrome in America. Its expression is far less virulent than in the past, of course, but its history as a prime molder of American perspectives on domestic and global affairs is undeniable. Needless to say, racism is common across time and space and has infected all empires in their treatment of foreign subjects. It was common to the Soviet Union, for example, even as Soviet communists excoriated the West's racism and did not acknowledge any racial or ethnic dimension to their own policies. The Russians were first-among-equals, and the denial of ethnicity or outright discrimination toward Muslim Caucasians, for example, was a long-standing practice[9] (one that blew back on Moscow in the post-Soviet uprisings), as was the better known ill-treatment of Jews. The Japanese empire in Asia in the first half of the twentieth century was imbued with racist attitudes, often violent in expression, and the Chinese have demonstrated theirs in Muslim hinterlands. The exact expressions of racial attitudes are not always identical, of course, but they appear like clockwork as a means of domination of minorities and political mobilization of dominant groups. In the United States, racism is typically discussed as white discrimination against blacks, but it appeared in virulent forms in the nineteenth century against the Chinese, leading to no less than complete bans on immigration of Chinese workers. Attitudes of racial prejudice remain surprisingly strong in America, despite obvious advances, and Americans clearly perceive that racism remains a problem.[10]

That a philosophy of racial superiority has been part-and-parcel of American globalism is most apparent in the beginnings of that modern era, the war in the Philippines especially. Theodore Roosevelt, speaking at Arlington National Cemetery in 1902—at a moment when his administration was attempting to declare the Philippines war a victory and the insurgency as "banditry"—described the war as "the triumph of civilization over forces which stand for the black chaos of savagery and barbarism."[11] Like the variegated expressions of racism in other empires, the U.S. experience was not uniform or static. As historian Paul Kramer argued persuasively, the relationship between American empire and racial dominance was specific to place and time, a "racial remaking of empire and the imperial remaking of race," a two-way dynamism affecting the racial dimensions of the encounter between America and the colonized.[12] The nature of U.S. racism toward the native populations of the Philippines, Korea, Vietnam, and Iraq were not necessarily the same during the time of U.S. wars: in the Philippines, it was evidently an attitude of the "white man's burden"; in Korea and Vietnam, an enabling adjunct to an ongoing epic struggle against Asian communism; and in Iraq, a more personal sense of threat from Islamic militancy, although rooted in the centuries-old "clash of civilizations." It can be argued that the military and political strategies reflected and reinforced those attitudes—"racial extermination" in the Philippines, massive military mobilizations with China looming large in Korea and Vietnam, and confused, scattershot, and counterproductive violence in Iraq. But the likeness of racial antipathies in all the wars is also striking and important. One salient similarity were American attitudes toward local governance, for example, in which Washington was highly manipulative not least because American elites regarded the natives as incapable of self-governance. This persistent attitude, which led to much more bloodshed than might otherwise have been, was based both on ideas of political modernization that were embedded in a form of Western superiority, and a calculation that only strong leaders could tame the "black chaos of savagery."

However racism manifested, did racial attitudes—negative attitudes toward Asians and Arabs—account for the indifference to casualties among those groups that we see in the U.S. wars in Korea, Vietnam, and Iraq? Racism today in America has been convincingly described as "passive" and is expressed as racial apathy with respect to the plight of African Americans—a set of mental constructs that would describe indifference toward foreign populations as well. One analyst argued that prejudice does not always manifest as aggressiveness or overtly hostile attitudes, but as "expressions of apathy or withdrawal. The individual protects himself from a difficult or demanding world and salvages his self-respect by retreating within his own shell." In that vein, another observer noted that "violating the norm of 'human hearted-ness' can result from fear and threat, or jealousy and envy; it can range from intense hatred to simple indifference and an absence of human sympathy." This indifference toward racial minorities in America is attributed either to ignorance of racial inequality or to "delegitimizing" the racial inequality narrative because those minorities are culturally deficient and deserve their status.[13]

Some scholars have described how broad indifference to violence against racial minorities is "socially authorized," and, in fact, that "productions of societal indifference are related to the occurrence of violence"—that is, the lack of caring is "produced" in order to allow violence to proceed unimpeded.[14] Such a social ordering is in part geospatial, on the margins of society (e.g., shantytowns on the edge of the metropolis), out in the hinterlands (e.g., mining towns in South Africa), or in faraway places of the global south. Violence can be more easily allowed or even initiated in such places where there are no eyes for "normal" society to see. This is literal distancing that reinforces or permits mental and moral distancing from acts of instrumental violence by the state that are often rooted in racial domination.

Of course, we are distant from many injustices in the world—massive poverty, displacement, and disease—many of which have roots in racial discrimination. Since racism is so much a part of the American story, it is difficult to exclude any major episode of American history (such as war) from being entangled with racially based senti-ments. It is also worth asking if blaming indifference on racism isn't a kind of tautology.

More important for what's being explored here is the counterexam-ple of the Cold War. The "twilight struggle" of the twentieth century, after all, was with an ideology born in Europe and manifested most menacingly by a white nation with strong Christian roots—Marxist Russia. This was *the* grand contest of global hegemony of the last cen-tury, and the indifference toward the consequences of this contest can-not be explained purely or even primarily on the basis of racism. The Bolsheviks and their progeny (here and abroad) were certainly thought to be savages, and it was the march of Marxism-Leninism that gener-ated the fears that fueled wars in East and Southeast Asia, and proxy wars in the Middle East, Africa, and Latin America. But the original communist nation was white and Christian (fallen, an apostate, no less), and the sources for the colossal clash of the two superpowers was the contest for the wilderness, its bounty, and its moral treasury. It was not about race.

The Frontier Myth and Societal Indifference

The frontier myth has been at work in all of the wars in American history. As explored in Chapter 2, the frontier provided a mobilizing set of understandings and principles for American expansion. The commanding idea of the errand to the wilderness justified the European-American genocide of indigenous tribes and, when the continent was "settled," was a recurring gloss for global intervention. The expression of this errand in continental and global expansion was and is the taming of the wilderness and the subduing, even annihilation, of the savages who are native to the wilderness. In this, then, we find the "savage wars of peace" and other ideological patinas that have been remarkably durable over four centuries.

That this set of ideas, myths, and self-identity has been at work, providing the lens through which Americans can regard their history and mission, is not much in dispute. The question here is how this persistent ideology affects Americans' thinking about the consequences of the "errand." If racism is a necessary but not wholly sufficient explanation for the American public's indifference to the chaos wrought by American military interventions in Korea, Indochina, and the Persian Gulf, does the broader, uniquely American episteme of the frontier provide a more complete understanding?

It can in two different ways. First is its breadth compared with racism, but also its particularity—that is, the frontier myth imparts some specificity as to what is "wilderness" and what is "savage." It is broader because racial difference is not strictly necessary to define "savage," as noted regarding the Russians and the Cold War, and the Germans and the Second World War. Although there were ample attempts to characterize Russians and Germans in those periods as different from Americans, this was more a depiction of the savagery of communists and Nazis rather than an ethnic or racial assertion. (Notably, a very sizable proportion of Americans are of German ancestry.) The Soviets were often depicted as a subset of the Asian horde, but this was far less germane than the communism and the implications of savagery, which was amply reinforced by Stalin's brutality. The frontier myth's particularity enters as a quality of how and where the United States chooses to dominate militarily. The entry into the Second World War, even the Cold War, were not pursued exclusively by the United States, of course; force of circumstances dictated much of the U.S. reaction to Hitler and Stalin. But the U.S. interventions in the Philippines, Korea, Vietnam, Iraq, and Afghanistan, as well as countless smaller conflicts in Latin America, were largely powered by our own sense of mission. So an element of choice is central to these wars and is predicated, as shown in earlier chapters, on the frontier sensibilities sustained after the closing of the continental frontier, not on racism per se.

The frontier myth provides another difference from other explanations like the sibling notion of American "exceptionalism," which is born of the same Puritan experience, the belief in a special destiny. That difference is the central role of violence. Exceptionalism and imperialism are frames through which we can understand the attitudes of superiority—racial as well as moral—and the U.S. hegemonic impulse, the imperium without colonies. But neither notion provides a self-referential explanation for the particular uses of violence. In most of the discussions of American imperialism, such as it is, violence is purely instrumental, a means to an end. In the official or conventional accounts of American involvement in the world, violence is typically regarded as a necessity utilized with restraint. But even in the more critical accounts, the organized violence of the U.S. military is an instrument of power projection and a manifestation of racism. These explanations for violence are insufficient, however, and fail to connect American public attitudes with what is occurring in the war zones.

Richard Slotkin's cardinal notion of *regeneration through violence* more adequately completes the picture. The expansion across the continent of European settlers was enabled by violence, and it was depicted in two ways that are revealing. First is that the violence of the frontier was almost always defensive, a reaction to Indian savagery. This is crucial in linking the propaganda of frontier violence with the psychology of violence, which will be explored later. The wars of the global era— the Spanish-American War, the two world wars, and the wars in Korea, Vietnam, Iraq, and Afghanistan—were and are depicted as defensive violence. The other key dimension of frontier violence is this notion of regeneration, that violence itself refreshes the mission, the identity, the moral worth of its practitioner. It is energizing, an act of rebirth. The regeneration for Puritans was profoundly spiritual, of course; for later Americans it was a more secular faith in the natural rightness of Anglo-Saxon liberty, civilizational superiority, and the will to overcome European decadence and class conflict. Violence was not merely necessary for conquest and control, but was purifying, mobilizing, and redemptive—all of which prompt repetition. And there is an American uniqueness in it. "What is distinctively 'American' is not necessarily the amount or kind of violence that characterizes our history," wrote Slotkin, "but the mythic significance we have assigned to the kinds of violence we have actually experienced, the forms of symbolic violence we imagine or invent, and the political uses to which we put that symbolism."[15]

If war's violence nourishes a nation's soul, then the victims of that violence will not turn a hair on the head of the American body politic. In detailed studies of American attitudes, reactive violence has been found to be considered justified and consistent with a coherent moral system, as well as positively correlated with the embrace of "frontier values."[16] The very fundamental norm of nation building and national survival as enabled by violence against savages and indeed as protection from savages is enormously consequential for how the deaths of savages will be viewed. Again, it's not merely reaction to threats or defensiveness, however, but the cleansing and rejuvenating quality of righteous violence that will vitiate empathy for the victims.

Does this apply to all applications of military force? The wars in Korea and Vietnam were most obviously fought in the Cold War context. China was a 100-year aspiration for Americans, a national project that envisioned East Asia as the ultimate wilderness. So the "loss" of China to the communists in 1949 was more than a Cold War setback: it was the disruption of the most verdant frontier fantasy of the late nineteenth and early twentieth centuries. In the calculus of anticommunism, the "loss" was emasculating because no attempt to save China (with American men) was undertaken. As a result, the communists' invasion of South Korea just a year later prompted both reactive violence and the chance to redeem the loss of China. Regeneration through violence would be a reward for this, the need to replenish the sense of mission in East Asia, a mission that was different from (while largely consistent with) that of global anticommunism. With regard to the

Vietnam War, the strategy of containment of communism was more firmly set by the early 1960s, and the sting from the loss of China had faded some. But the war was still framed as reactive—the communists attempting to take over all of Indochina—and as an errand to subdue savages, essentially the same communist savages to whom we lost China and battled in Korea. If the idea of the wilderness and its bounty was less compelling, Vietnam as a symbolic, global contest between communism and liberty, enslavement and freedom, was no less potent.

In Iraq, the urge to regeneration was all the more apparent. The trauma of the 9/11 attacks had challenged many tenets of the American self-concept. The consequent, reactive violence was first aimed at Afghanistan, but the escape of bin Laden and the ouster of the Taliban (mainly the work of the Northern Alliance) were at best instrumental in putting al Qaeda on the run, and thereby unsatisfying. Targeting Iraq as unfinished business, possibly with a direct link to the 9/11 atrocities, was meant in effect to more fully regenerate American will and dominance after a period of softness (multilateralism, treaty making, peacekeeping, and the like). Little new prompting to see Arabs as savages was necessary after four decades or more of excoriating the Arab nationalists (Nasser, Asad, Saddam) and Islamists (Hezbollah, Hamas). And there, in Iraq, the promise of bounty was as tangible as could be.

In all three major wars, as well as the hot pursuit of bin Laden in Afghanistan, the necessary conditions of regarding the native populations as savage in some pervasive sense (communist or Arab/Islamic), and the wars as both reactive and as an errand to the world's tamable hinterlands, were altogether present. The violence was central to a moral system that also pitted survival against danger, even enslavement. (The hysterical alarms about an eventual Muslim takeover of Europe and the United States that had to be stopped in Iraq echo very closely earlier "Red" scares—both of communists and Indians.) The hope of vanquishing the communists and the Arab terrorists was more than mere defense or imperialism; it was a morality play in which the protagonist is triumphant physically (safe, secure, prosperous) and renewed morally through the completeness of the triumph.

The native populations, then, whether friend or foe, are bit players in this drama and scarcely of concern: the applied violence is not about them, in the American view, but about us—our ability and willingness to stop or reverse communism or Islamic fundamentalism, the costs of doing so (U.S. blood and treasure), the lessons we will teach the rest of the cowering world, and our own sense of self-worth. If large numbers of civilians die, that is a moral debit on the ledger of the North Koreans and Chinese, the North Vietnamese, and the Muslim jihadists, since the United States is reacting to their provocations. Those civilians, moreover, have proven to be either outright enemies, sympathetic to the bad guys, unreliable and ungrateful, or uncivilized in some fundamental sense—in all cases unworthy of empathy.

The focus on how Americans feel about these populations and their fates leads to a psychological explanation, which is largely absent from the historical and political analyses that refer broadly to jingoism, exceptionalism, and the like. To Slotkin's credit, he explored the interaction between the European colonists and the indigenous tribes at some length and painted a complex picture of how the pioneer, often a hunter-warrior, came to know and appreciate the Indians but still seek their demise. Empathy does not enter much, if at all, in this inexorable tale of European-American expansion across North America. But the need for explanations that interrogate the mentality of the settlers, what became the people of the United States, is apparent.

Psyche and Thanatos

Our immediate world, that of our daily lives, is filled with dangers and threats that require us to mentally construct defenses to allow us to function, that seek to mitigate the terror of death and meaninglessness. Social psychologists have explored this intimate aspect of human existence with considerable care, and while a number of explanations abound, they apparently agree that defense or coping mechanisms are at work to protect us from challenges to our self-esteem and fears regarding our own mortality. Prominent among these mechanisms are obedience and conformity to the prevailing social and cultural norms of our "in-group," with an attendant worldview that is held by that group, a group that can in many respects extend to the nation. While culturally determined to some important degree, the holding of a worldview that reflects and reinforces the norms of social organization is common to all peoples.

We tend to believe that the world is orderly, that actions are consequential and knowable, and that things happen for a reason. When bad things happen to others (disease, natural disaster, social or economic dislocation, violence) we tend to react in ways that use that worldview—that the world is essentially "just"—to make judgments about the misfortune. Altruism or a simple desire to help the victim is sometimes in play, though typically it is active for those we have some personal connection to, and in very small numbers. Far more often, however, the acts that produce victims are upsetting to our belief in a "just world," and our reactions to those incidents attempt to protect us from the implications—that is, that the world is perhaps unjust, threatening, and random.

This is the basis of Just World Theory and similar hypotheses, developed mainly by psychologist Melvin Lerner and several colleagues beginning in the 1960s, and verified and refined in hundreds of experiments by many scientists since then. The theory has several dimensions, but relevant here are the ways people in our society react to misfortune of others. Among those are denial or withdrawal. We simply do not want to witness suffering and therefore naturally seek to avoid it. Lerner told the story, for example, of a pediatrician who would avoid children who were not curable, apparently a common reaction even among these caregivers, so she could maintain her belief that all children could be saved. "All it requires is an intelligent selection of the information to which one is exposed," he wrote. "And it has the added advantage of requiring no direct distortion of reality."[17] A second defense is redefinition of the event, particularly a new interpretation of the outcome. If we see virtue in an outcome that objectively would suggest otherwise—for example, that the poor are happy because they know the simple pleasures, or that the Haitian earthquake will enable them to reconstruct their country in a more sustainable way—that serves to mitigate the horror of the outcome we're witnessing.

Three other reactions are significant. First is a reinterpretation of the cause of the misfortune, namely, blaming the victim. This has been shown time and again to be a dominant interpretation of observers of rape cases and AIDS victims, but it also applies much more broadly. In this view, if we live in a just world and someone is terribly hungry, homeless, infected, or buffeted by violence, it must be that victim's fault. This derogation of the victim has been experimentally verified with remarkable consistency. Related is the reinterpretation of the character of the victim, "people who, by virtue of some act they committed or would be likely to commit, or some personal quality, are assigned to an inferior position. They are judged to merit 'punishment.'"[18] Last is a sense of "ultimate justice," that eventually the injustice will be corrected and therefore need not trouble us.

These reactions tend to be all the stronger when the event more directly challenges the observers' sense of safety or their just worldview. "Observers' fluctuating and seemingly inconsistent responses to victims may be a function of the degree to which they perceive a threat to their own physical integrity and a threat to their fundamental beliefs about justice,"[19] which helps account for generous donations to an Indian Ocean tsunami relief fund (an event that challenges almost no one in the United States) but little heed for victims in Afghanistan. There may be a calculation of feasibility (whether rational or affective) in compassion: a number of studies suggest that the capacity for active assistance diminishes dramatically as numbers of victims grow larger; indeed, the optimal number for action is one.[20] But this observation is drawn from situations that were unthreatening to the observer. Victim derogation, or blaming the victim, or avoidance was found in studies of individuals observing other individuals, not large numbers, so compassion is contingent on the victims not disrupting the worldview of the observers.

Having greater information about the event does not change the dynamic of indifference, even anger, toward the victims. A frequent charge against the press is that the absence in news media of imagery of victims and suffering, a near-absence that was certainly noticeable during the Iraq War of the last decade, accounts for a lack of compassion. But the experimental data suggest the opposite. In one experiment, for example, an appeal for help with a picture of a needy child prompted greater avoidance from passersby than a less salient appeal.[21] So, contrary to expectations, the news media's inattention to civilian casualties may not be as relevant a cause of public indifference as one might suspect, assuming *some* information about casualties is being conveyed (though it may still say a lot about the preferences of editors and reporters).[22] This dimension is worth more investigation, however, since the signaling in an experiment is reduced to a very simple transaction, whereas the news media's reporting on a war is a far more complex communication. To use again the example of the Haitian earthquake—would Americans react more compassionately (which is to say, would *more* Americans behave compassionately) to Iraqi civilian casualties if the information and images were as plentiful as they were in the aftermath of the earthquake, with as many opportunities for charitable giving? We don't know for sure the answer to that question.

The psychological distancing, what Robert J. Lifton called (in a different context) "psychic numbing," is intensified if the innocent victims are from another group, but the effect of racism or other out-group identity is not wholly necessary for distancing, blaming, avoidance, and the like to occur. "People can see targets of injustice as belonging to a different world than their own; thus, for example, individuals can separate their own just world from the unjust or random world of innocent suffering," observed two academics surveying the experimental evidence. "Targets of injustice are seen as so unlike oneself as to inhabit a different world that is governed by different rules (or has few rules at all)."[23]

One of the findings of research on victim derogation focuses on the presence of a perpetrator and its effect on the observer. "When a person behaves in a certain way towards another person, we assume that these actions are in part responses to verbal or nonverbal behaviors of this other individual," wrote Ronnie Janoff-Bulman, a leading theorist. "In the case of victimizations involving the malicious intent of another individual, this premise of social interaction results in increased victim-blaming. Non-victims believe that the victim must have done something to bring about his or her victimization . . . [causing] the perpetrator to act in such a terrible, harmful way."[24] Victims of more impersonal fates—natural disasters, to be sure, but also those of "anonymous" human agency—will earn less opprobrium from observers. So when identifiable perpetrators are involved, the victim is more likely to be blamed, and this blaming itself strengthens the observer's belief in a just world.[25]

These powerful psychological constructs prospectively demonstrate how large majorities of the American public as well as the political and information elite could ignore the scale of mayhem that occurred in American wars in Korea, Vietnam, and Iraq. In the majority's view, the United States intervenes in these countries in a righteous cause. Relatively soon, the wars go badly. Large numbers of U.S. soldiers are killed and maimed. Along the way, the news media report that large numbers of "enemy" are also dying, actually in far greater numbers than Americans are. The fact that enormous numbers of civilians are victims is not prominent in the reporting, but is not hidden. Concern for these civilian casualties is almost entirely absent from public discourse. (It's worth noting in this regard that a large portion of the civilian victims are those we are meant to protect—South Koreans, South Vietnamese, and Iraqis. Only in Korea were more "enemy" than "allied" civilians killed.) These innocent victims—and we know there are many victims—are avoided by psychological distancing, avoided as if they do not exist.

Even more, they are sometimes blamed. Victim derogation in these wars is not the emotion that rises to the top of public discourse, but it is noticeable in some of the language used. It was common during the most violent years in Iraq, 2004–2008, to hear commentators insist that the Iraqis stand up for themselves, or to blame violence on the Iraqi sectarian divisions, when neither of these factors existed before the U.S. invasion. The loyalty of the civilian populations in South Korea and South Vietnam was constantly questioned, as if devotion to the United States and its mission were paramount. Recall, too, General Westmoreland's infamous assertion that Asians don't value life as much as we do. In Iraq, the large numbers of deaths reported in the 2006 *Lancet* article prompted Christopher Hitchens to cheer the demise of "the sort of people who have been blowing up mosques, beheading captives on video, detonating rush-hour car bombs, destroying pipelines, murdering aid workers, bombing the headquarters of the United Nations, and inciting ethnic and sectarian warfare."[26] John Bolton, an assistant secretary of state and U.N. ambassador during much of the Iraq war, told journalist Nir Rosen that the millions of Iraqi refugees and displaced have "absolutely nothing to do with our overthrow of Saddam. Our obligation was to give them new institutions and provide security. We have fulfilled that obligation. I don't think we have an obligation to compensate for the hardships of war."[27] Bolton's statement contains three elements of Just World Theory. There is a reinterpretation of the event and outcome (we brought justice to Iraq), derogation of the victim (the war has nothing to do with their misery, so something is wrong with them and their claims to the contrary), and the belief in "ultimate justice" (a common assertion now, which is to claim "victory" with no reference to the reasons for invading or the human costs).

While blaming the victim is ever present, if subtle, the far more frequent reaction is indifference and neglect. The automatic reference to

the lowest numbers of possible casualties, the absence of media attention to innocent victims of U.S. actions, the sharp reaction to accusations of atrocities or harsh treatment of civilians or the high mortality
numbers from household surveys, the redefining of civilians as terrorists, the derogation of Iraqi or Vietnamese or Korean politics and
culture as inherently violent or incompetent (and a similar attribution
to Islam in Iraq)—all of these attitudes are primarily explicable as psychological distancing from the horror of innocent victimization.

This also goes far to explain why the public tuned out of the war
(Korea and Iraq particularly) at an early stage, showing less interest
and support. It was not merely that the wars were in many respects
failures in terms of policy objectives, but that the public simply turned
away from the gruesome spectacle of the war generally. Of particular
interest in this regard is how the public also turned away from U.S.
veterans: for all the valorization of these "heroes" in the news media
and popular culture, especially in the last decade, those who came back
with injuries, post-traumatic stress disorder, or tales of violence were
often shunned or worse. Each of these wars stirred in the public the
five responses to vicitimization described by Lerner—avoidance, redefining the outcome, blaming the victim, redefining the character of the
victim, and the prospect of ultimate justice—and provide us with the
psychological constructs we need to explain the remarkably consistent
behavior of the public and elites over many decades and many wars. By
circling back to integrate the earlier explanations of racism and the
frontier thesis with these insights into mind and behavior, we have a
more complete account of Americans' vast indifference.

The Fortress of Indifference

The belief in a just world is rooted in a cultural, social, and political
schema that creates those expectations about justice. "Society provides
an ordered, nonrandom set of social arrangements," wrote one social
psychologist, "which will embody a stock of accumulated explanations
and justifications for existing social arrangements, and of solutions
for common problems." This social order is learned in childhood and
constantly reinforced.[28] It is not only reinforced; it is innately conservative in that this schema tends to be unchanging, not adaptive. Citing

Jean Piaget, Janoff-Bulman explained that we "are particularly good at remembering schema-consistent information" and that people "interpret information—both new information and information from memory—in ways that are consistent with their schema . . . our schemas guide our perceptions, memories, and inferences."[29] The schemas are central to understanding how indifference to suffering manifests: what, exactly, is being ruptured, and how? Social psychologists tend to pose only general, even abstract qualities to this social structure—orderliness, predictability, fairness—which are, notably, characteristic of a stable society. The actual manifestations of "just world" thinking are culturally determined. Apart from stability, however, what cultural forms that shape the schema of social perception are relevant?

Correlating beliefs in a just world with beliefs in American "values" is an essential addendum to understanding indifference. The frontier thesis is complementary in several ways. It is a foundation of American culture and has been from the beginning, and it powerfully shapes the attitudes and behavior of Americans from childhood. In its sheer explanatory power for the "American experience," it really has no rivals. It is an account of the entire scope of European immigration, expansion, and subjugation of the indigenous tribes, class conflict, and, finally, American globalism. In that last phase, the interventions in Korea, Indochina, and Iraq were promoted by political leaders as extensions of the frontier, in effect, in which we would bring democratic values to these particular wildernesses and subdue (or civilize) the savages. As missions in concordance with the American construct of a just world—a world in which the United States and its values are morally and racially superior—the wars earned high support at their outset as defenses of the American ideal. When the savages turned out to be difficult to subdue, when they rejected our civilizing impulse, and when the costs of the enterprise became weighty, the popularity of each war declined. But what also occurred was an application of force breathtaking in its ferocity, with casualties that such force invariably yield; and this, too, must have turned the American public away, distancing itself from the carnage and resenting the victims' lack of appreciation for our heroic sacrifices. Their resistance brought on their high human toll. And they defeated U.S. designs; had they played the role of the Apache or Cherokee or Sioux, resistant but finally subdued, the "just world" would have been sustained. But the Koreans, Vietnamese, and Iraqis didn't thoroughly follow that script.* And so their woeful losses of lives, livelihoods, and homes did challenge the American sense of a just world, and total indifference to their losses ensued. That this pattern has been repeated (five times, including the Philippines and Afghanistan) at the "macro" level of the wars and at the "micro" level of atrocities is strongly indicative.

While the notion of the "savage" and belief in a just world do not necessarily involve racial prejudice, in these wars they did. Racial difference influences—intensifies—victim derogation and avoidance. Does this extend to wars abroad? Two psychologists conducted a series of experiments with Americans regarding attitudes toward the fate of Iraqis and Afghans compared with Americans during the wars of the last decade. They did so by measuring whether increments in lives lost or saved of an "outgroup" (Iraqis and Afghans) would affect the level of caring and whether it varied significantly from the same increments of an "ingroup" (Americans). Their results "showed an ethnocentric indifference to magnitude in that participants were relatively indifferent to the magnitude of lives lost or saved for the outgroup compared to the ingroup," and that "participants showed a strong ethnocentric valuation of lives, and, in particular, more indifference to the number of lives lost or saved for the outgroup."[30] Not surprisingly, the less one identifies with victims, the more indifference or hostility will be evident.

The combination of these three explanations—the frontier myth, racism or ethnocentrism, and Just World Theory—forms a structure, an architecture of indifference, accounting for the silence and the animus the American public displays toward the civilian victims of U.S.

---

* An interesting question arises in how indifference rose with respect to the indigenous tribes in America if their demise fit with "just world" beliefs of the European-American settlers; for the white indifference toward Native Americans could not be more apparent. They resisted, but were defeated, and entire nations were victims. This, however, was the *intention* of frontier ideas—the Indians would be not merely defeated and subdued but annihilated: they were meant to be victims, *guilty* victims. Hence their demise was consistent with—that is, did not disrupt—"just world" constructs. Here, I suggest, indifference rose as a consequence of conquest and dehumanization rather than as a rupture of a belief in a just world. As the degraded status of American Indians persisted through the twentieth century, however, they were increasingly perceived as innocent victims, and this then stirred the indifference and hostility that Just World Theory posits. A feeling of shame cannot be discounted, either, which can also prompt withdrawal.

wars. It is a sturdy, forbidding structure, a fortress that protects its denizens from the chaos outside. Whether this differs substantially from structures of indifference erected by the colonial powers in their heyday is difficult to say with confidence; certainly, major similarities would be likely, especially racial attitudes and dehumanization of the colonized people. But however common, the phenomenon remains potent and troubling. It is troubling for moral reasons, most obviously, and potent in its self-nourishing quality, both of which have consequences of the most profound kind.

THE CONSEQUENCES OF INDIFFERENCE

The way the wars were fought and the American public's lack of concern about what happened to civilians in that fighting have two kinds of broad consequences—how it has affected the people in the war zones, and how it has affected American war policies and practices. While the wars we've explored obviously had severe and abiding consequences for the native populations, the broader consequences—for animus toward the United States and for regional and global peace—are not so easy to discern. Because there were important differences in the origins and outcomes of the wars, it's not easy to draw general lessons from them. The Korean War ended in a stalemate, with repressive regimes on both sides for many years, and, after some three decades, a liberalization in the South while the North became ever more difficult and dictatorial. Vietnam won a victory over the United States, in effect, and has gradually improved diplomatic ties with the West, including France and the United States. It remains an authoritarian state, however, with scant freedom of speech. Iraq's fate is at this writing unknown, likely to be careening for some years between a fitfully functioning democracy beleaguered by ethnic and sectarian low-intensity conflict, to something more authoritarian, possibly religiously so. Afghanistan's future looks very much like Iraq's. Under these circumstances, it is next to impossible to describe how the people of these countries view the wars that were fought and the reactions, indifferent or otherwise, of the American public.

Certainly, anti-Americanism has rocked South Korean politics for years, particularly once the authoritarianism eased in the late 1980s. It sparked very sizable protests, but the proximate causes tended to be about misbehavior by U.S. soldiers stationed there. U.S. support for repressive, right-wing governments has been a long-standing grievance that predates the war, and the Truth and Reconciliation Commission stirred up more painful memories of mistreatment. South Korean attitudes toward America are complex, tempered by the protection the U.S. military has provided and the prosperity that its ties to the United States has fostered. North Korea maintains a state-imposed narrative that draws from the war very specifically; indeed, it based its legitimacy to some degree on that savage pounding from the air. A sixty-plus-year history cannot be crystallized easily, but it's reasonable to say that the "forgotten war" and the forgotten people of the war zone play a role in simmering resentments, however benign their broader effects might be.[31]

Vietnam's triumph in its long war to expel foreigners doubtlessly colors its memory of the war, though, like all states, it uses the war to shore up legitimacy and to valorize the role of the Communist Party in the country's liberation. Long-term effects of U.S. use of Agent Orange and the twenty years of isolation before normalization of ties in 1995 are not readily forgotten. Like China, however, its pragmatic leadership has come to recognize that lingering animosities cannot be allowed to become an impediment to economic trade and growth; and thus after some postwar years of difficulty—wars in the region, the boat people escaping Vietnam, and other turmoil—a modus vivendi with the United States has been established. The bifurcated nature of the conflict and the authoritarianism of the regime do not lend themselves to clear answers about the abiding effects of the war or attitudes toward Americans.

The full consequences of the war in Iraq remain an open prospect. Notable anti-American feeling rose in Muslim countries during the first six years of the conflict,[32] and the terrorist bombings or attempted attacks in Europe and America were all linked to violence of the Iraq war—that is, the attackers in Madrid, London, and Fort Hood regarded the U.S.-instigated violence against the Iraqi people as a reason to counterattack. The consistently high numbers of Iraqis expressing opposition to U.S. troops, cited earlier, braces the view that Muslims in particular have reacted very sharply to the high casualties in Iraq and American indifference. "The Iraq conflict has become the *cause celebre* for jihadists, breeding a deep resentment of US involvement in the Muslim world and cultivating supporters for the global jihadist movement," noted a major 2006 U.S. intelligence assessment; while scholars of terrorism clearly see jihadist recruiting based significantly on anger—"sacred rage"—at U.S. actions in Iraq and Afghanistan toward Muslim noncombatants in particular.[33] There is, in fact, little doubt that the wars have stirred enormous hostility to the United States among Arabs and Muslims more broadly. Whether those negative feelings are durable is not known. But the near-term consequences—the strengthening of the appeal of al Qaeda and similar groups, in particular—are enough to be worrisome.

While abroad the effects of civilian casualties and the indifference of the American public is very difficult to gauge, the impact in the United States is clearer. The assertion cited earlier that the U.S. military is constrained with regard to civilians because they would be chastised by American public opinion is simply not supported by the evidence.[34] In fact, the exact opposite is at work. The American public's indifference toward the fate of the civilians in U.S. war zones provides an implicit license to war planners and field officers to do whatever they must to win. While this license is not reflected in official U.S. policy, which would be a violation of international law, it does provide considerable room for maneuver when circumstances in the field are violent or threatening to American troops. Officers do what they "need" to do to accomplish a mission—call in air strikes, harass with long-range artillery fire, "clear" villages, and so on—knowing that only the most egregious instances of civilian abuse will earn opprobrium from their superiors, if that. The American public, far from the battlefield, essentially out of touch and uncaring, does not provide a check on this too-frequent behavior. Only rarely is Congress's interest sparked, either—late in the Vietnam War, for example, when Senator Edward Kennedy held hearings, or during the Iraq war, when two House renegades, Dennis Kucinich and Ron Paul, held a hearing on the Johns Hopkins Iraq Mortality Study. The Executive, including the military, virtually never engage the issue except to deny that civilians are being killed in large numbers, with the notable (and laudable) exception of General David Petraeus's new counterinsurgency doctrine, itself coming on the heels of the mortality study and the brief media kerfuffle it stirred. Petraeus's guiding principle seems to be that high civilian casualties tend to be counterproductive, however, not that the American people might have moral qualms. Attention to civilian safety in Afghanistan by the U.S. military seemed to be more apparent after 2006, but the full extent of civilian casualties there is, of course, unknown, and the public does not show any more visible concern than it has in previous wars.

The U.S. military now operates with the self-contradictory impulses of its traditional doctrines of annihilation of the enemy—which can and typically does include enemy civilians, often in the way or a key to "morale"—and the more recent emphasis on restraint in the smaller wars against outmatched foes. This paradox is taken seriously by military planners, trainers, and responsible officers, but the public is essentially clueless and, if anything, less restrained than the professional military. In each of the major wars since 1945, when things started going badly there was a sizable chorus of public opinion chanting for more violence, not less, for letting loose the political and legal constraints on the generals to get the job done. As ever, the ordinary people living in those war zones were not mentioned.

THE EPISTEMOLOGY OF WAR

The dead of war have something to tell us. The way that wars are fought leaves a signature, a pattern of destruction on the societies where they occur. The war makers on all sides tend to mirror this pattern, but their impact varies: those with a certain kind of hammer—say, fighter-bombers or long-range artillery—will see the nail of warfare differently from those who possess only punji sticks or IEDs. Those who are defending their homeland will use the tools of war differently from those who are invading, and the war itself will shape the tactics and the numbers who will take up arms. The deaths of many of your villagers affect your sensibilities about the conflict differently from the death of a neighbor fighting in an army far away; it will alter your perceptions about safety and who is protecting you, with whom to share your sense of insecurity and need to react, how to align your life to attempt to ensure that an attack does not happen again. Fight or flee: just as the numbers of displaced paint a portrait of the conflict, so too will the numbers of dead and how they died. This is what General William Tecumseh Sherman called the "epistemology of war."

Knowing how and why civilians die in wars tells us a great deal about the conduct of war from either side. The death of large numbers of civilians at the hands of the U.S. military, no matter how unintentional, stirs a reaction that will affect the contours of the war to come. (It works both ways: the high toll of innocents wrought by al Qaeda in Iraq turned the Sunni rebellion into an ally of the occupiers.) And reading the topography of death of civilians *and* combatants provides a view of its moral landscape: why is there fighting, why this kind of killing in this place, and why is death visited upon these particular people? If death has no meaning for a warrior, if it's just a number to be compiled or, worse, if distorted or hidden or forgotten, then the knowledge is lost or distorted as well.

The ways we know about the war dead are equally one-dimensional on the home front. The epistemology of war in Washington pivots on success, an elusive concept in itself. We know a war is worthwhile if success is its result. And success in the post-1945 American wars has hinged on regimes—the regimes the U.S. policy makers are trying to prop up, or the regimes they are trying to bring down. The formula for this calculation includes the costs of war, namely, the costs in American blood and treasure to save Rhee or Diem, or to bring down Saddam, or to prop up Karzai, but this state-centric calculus never includes the blood of those who lived there. For Washington, the topography of death is an American setting, a national portrait of the faces of the soldiers and marines who made the ultimate sacrifice. This knowledge is Ptolemaic: everything we know is what we see through our eyes and can thereby rationalize.

A *system* of knowledge has evolved that permits this very partial perspective. It is not intentional, for the most part, but the result of four centuries of national expansion that would have been impossible were its consequences for the natives a guiding moral concern. The fate of the natives is effectively excluded from the discourse of war. It may be considered many years later, as it has with Native Americans (though without restitution), but the system of knowledge in war time disallows, in effect, a serious and sustained effort—a politically consequential effort—to regard the human costs. It is impermissible not only because it muddies war aims and war's conduct, or because it's contentious, but because it challenges fundamentally Americans' self-regard, our mission, our place as the city on a hill.

The epistemology of war as practiced braces the demiurge of continuously making war with impunity to extend the American frontier. If there are no moral consequences (for even the American dead are valorized, have died a "good death"), there is no reason to think anew about those errands to the wilderness. And so more errands are commenced. Even if the global frontier is closing—perhaps *because* that frontier is closing—the national need to intervene, to sustain or recapture American economic prerogatives, and to build "freedom's empire" remains a powerful, self-nourishing impulse. To do so requires near-complete disavowal of the effort's human toll.

Whether this impulse can be vitiated is impossible to predict. The global frontier is closing, to be sure, but the animating ideas of the frontier myth will reach a slower demise. That decline would be usefully aided by a Copernican revolution in war's epistemology, an ability to know the universe of war's causes and consequences more fully and from many angles, viewpoints that are honored as much as our own. It may be that the turning away from carnage is too ingrained in human nature to provide us with new perspectives. Until we try, we won't know.

ACKNOWLEDGMENTS

I thank those who made timely suggestions or contributions that proved valuable, which especially includes Nichole Argo and Nick Bromell. My editor at Oxford University Press, Dave McBride, was unusually attentive and constructively demanding. Thanks to my agent, Robin Straus, who has been both encouraging and realistic. Dick Samuels at MIT has been particularly supportive. Thanks also to Sanam Naraghi Anderlini, Anna Badkhen, Susan Brynteson, Gilbert Burnham, Richard Healey, Jennifer Leaning, Ken Oye, and Yaddo. To the memory of my late friend and teacher, Howard Zinn, I pay special homage.

To my family, Nike and Coco, goes my appreciation for tolerating the hours I was squirreled away, inattentive, or grouchy. And to my late parents, who made my life possible in countless ways.

NOTES

CHAPTER 2

1. Laura Doyle, *Freedom's Empire: Race and the Rise of the Novel in Atlantic Modernity, 1640–1940* (Duke University Press, 2008): 3.
2. *Gunfighter Nation: The Myth of the Frontier in Twentieth Century America* (University of Oklahoma Press, 1998): 10. Originally published by Atheneum Press, 1992.
3. Ibid., 12.
4. Ibid., 14. See also Perry Miller, *Errand into the Wilderness* (Harvard University Press, 1956).
5. Peter Bulkeley, "The Gospel-Covenant," in A. Heimert and A. Delbanco, eds., *The Puritans in America: A Narrative Anthology* (Harvard University Press, 1985): 120; cited by Deborah L. Madsen, *American Exceptionalism* (Edinburgh University Press, 1998): 19–20.
6. Quoted by Madsen, 33.
7. Sacvan Bercovitch, *American Jeremiad* (University of Wisconsin Press, 1980): 6.
8. James David Drake, *King Philip's War: Civil War in New England, 1675–1676* (University of Massachusetts Press, 1999): 2–4. Casualty figures range much higher in other accounts.
9. Quotation of Roger Williams, Drake, *King Philip's War*, 109; "sufficient light . . .," Richard Slotkin, *Regeneration through Violence: The Mythology of the American Frontier, 1600–1860,* (Wesleyan University Press, 1973): 76, quoting a Puritan account of their massacre of Pequots.
10. Madsen, 37–38.
11. Roger G. Kennedy, *Mr. Jefferson's Lost Cause: Land, Farmers, Slavery, and the Louisiana Purchase* (Oxford University Press, 2003).
12. Cited in Howard Zinn, *A People's History of the United States* (Harper & Row, 1980): 147–49. The officer writing in his diaries was Ethan Allen Hitchcock.
13. Quoted in Mark E. Neely, Jr., *The Civil War and the Limits of Destruction* (Harvard University Press, 2007): 9
14. Paul Foos, *A Short, Offhand, Killing Affair* (University of North Carolina Press, 2002): 113.
15. Robert Walter Johannsen, *To the Halls of the Montezumas: The Mexican War in the American Imagination* (Oxford University Press, 1985): 311.
16. Mark S. Schantz, *Awaiting the Heavenly Country: The Civil War and America's Culture of Death* (Cornell University Press, 2008): 1.
17. Drew Gilpin Faust, *This Republic of Suffering: Death and the American Civil War* (Knopf, 2008): 33.
18. Mark E. Neely, Jr., "Was the Civil War Total War?" *Civil War History*, vol. 50, no. 4 (2004): 447. Sherman quotation, 446.

19. Russell F. Weigley, *The American Way of War: A History of United States Military Strategy and Policy* (Indiana University Press, 1977): chap. 7.
20. Faust, 46.
21. Schantz, 4.
22. Quoted by Slotkin, *The Fatal Environment: The Myth of the Frontier in the Age of Industrialization, 1800–1890* (University of Oklahoma Press, 1998): 303. Originally published by Atheneum Press, 1985.
23. This argument is made in Franny Nudelman, *John Brown's Body: Slavery, Violence and the Culture of War* (University of North Carolina Press, 2004).
24. Patrick J. Kelly, "The Election of 1896 and the Restructuring of Civil War Memory," in the very useful volume edited by Alice Fahs and Joan Waugh, *The Memory of the Civil War in American Culture* (University of North Carolina Press, 2004).
25. Department of Interior Census Office, *Report on Population of the United States at the Eleventh Census, 1890*, http://www2.census.gov/prod2/decennial/documents/1890a_v1–01.pdf.
26. Guillaume Vandenbroucke, "The U.S. Westward Expansion," IEPR Working Paper 06.59, Institute of Economic Policy Research, University of Southern California, December 2006.
27. Dee Brown, *Bury My Heart at Wounded Knee: An Indian History of the American West* (Macmillan, 2007): xxiii.
28. David E. Stannard, *American Holocaust: The Conquest of the New World* (Oxford University Press, 1993). The mortality numbers for indigenous peoples are varied, to say the least. Most large-scale killing, famines, and epidemics occurred in Mexico and Peru, apparently. Stannard calculates the total for the Americas at 100 million. In what is now the United States, conservative estimates range from 150,000 to 500,000 by violence, and 4 million by the diseases brought to the continent by Europeans and Africans. See Russell Thornton, *American Indian Holocaust and Survival: A Population History since 1492* (University of Oklahoma Press, 1990).
29. James Rankin Young et al., *History of Our War with Spain* (W. J. Holland, 1898): iii–iv.
30. For a good treatment of the decision for war, see Richard F. Hamilton, *President McKinley, War, and Empire: President McKinley and the Coming of War, 1898* (Transaction Publishers, 2006): esp. chap. 4.
31. *Record, 56* Cong., I Sess., 704–12.
32. Quoted in Slotkin, *Gunfighter Nation*, 113.
33. Quoted in Howard Zinn, *The Twentieth Century: A People's History* (Harper Perennial, 1998): 25.
34. Andrew Bacevich, "What Happened at Bud Dajo: A Forgotten Massacre—and Its Lessons," *Boston Globe*, March 12, 2006.
35. Samuel Clemens, "Comments on the Moro Massacre," included in the anthology edited by Howard Zinn and Anthony Arnove, *Voices of a People's History of the United States* (Seven Stories Press, 2004): 250.
36. John M. Gates, "War-Related Deaths in the Philippines, 1898–1902," *Pacific Historical Review*, vol. 53, no. 3 (August 1984): 367–378.
37. Stuart Creighton Miller, *Benevolent Assimilation: The American Conquest of the Philippines, 1899–1903* (Yale University Press, 1984): 253.
38. See the extended and excellent discussion of this in Paul Alexander Kramer, *The Blood of Government: Race, Empire, the United States, and the Philippines* (University of North Carolina Press, 2006); and Eric T. L. Love, *Race over Empire: Racism and U.S. Imperialism, 1865–1900* (University of North Carolina Press, 2004).

39. William Appleman Williams, *The Tragedy of American Diplomacy*, excerpted in Henry W. Berger, ed., *A William Appleman Williams Reader* (Ivan R. Dee, 1992): 125.

40. David S. Foglesong. *America's Secret War against Bolshevism: U.S. Intervention in the Russian Civil War, 1917–1920* (University of North Carolina Press, 1995).

41. See David Cole, *Enemy Aliens: Double Standards and Constitutional Freedoms in the War on Terrorism* (New Press, 2003): esp. 116–24.

CHAPTER 3

1. David Lundberg, "The American Literature of War: The Civil War, World War I, and World War II," *American Quarterly*, vol. 36, no. 3 (1984): 383.

2. For a good treatment of air power in the Great War, see Tami Davis Biddle, *Rhetoric and Reality in Air Warfare: The Evolution of British and American Ideas about Strategic Bombing, 1914–1945* (Princeton University Press, 2004).

3. W. G. Sebald, *On the Natural History of Destruction*, translated by Anthea Bell (Random House, 2004): 26–27.

4. Sherwood Ross, "How The United States Reversed Its Policy on Bombing Civilians," *Humanist*, July–August 2005: 14–22.

5. LeMay, quoted in Robert Pape, *Bombing to Win: Air Power and Coercion in War* (Cornell University Press, 1995): 92; McNamara, from the documentary film, *Fog of War*; Dower, quoted by Howard French, "100,000 People Perished, But Who Remembers?" *New York Times*, March 14, 2002.

6. Thomas R. Searle, "'It Made a Lot of Sense to Kill Skilled Workers': The Fire-bombing of Tokyo in March 1945," *Journal of Military History*, vol. 66, no. 1 (January, 2002): 104.

7. Michael S. Sherry, *The Rise of American Airpower: The Creation of Armageddon* (Yale University Press, 1987): 324.

8. Quoted in Kai Bird and Martin J. Sherwin, *American Prometheus: The Triumph and Tragedy of J. Robert Oppenheimer* (Knopf, 2005): 317.

CHAPTER 4

1. David Halberstam, *The Coldest Winter: America and the Korean War* (Hyperion, 2007): 632.

2. Richard Slotkin, *Gunfighter Nation: The Myth of the Frontier in Twentieth Century America* (University of Oklahoma Press, 1998): 91. Originally published by Atheneum Press, 1992.

3. Quoted in Regin Schmidt, *Red Scare: FBI and the Origins of Anticommunism in the United States* (Museum Tusculanum Press, University of Copenhagen, 2000): 239.

4. Ellen Schrecker, *The Age of McCarthyism: A Brief History with Documents* (St. Martin's Press, 1994), http://www.english.illinois.edu/maps/mccarthy/mccarthy.htm.

5. James Burnham, *The Web of Subversion: Underground Networks in the U.S. Government* (Americanist Library, 1954): 204.

6. Quoted by Patrick N. Allitt, "Catholic Anti-Communism," InsideCatholic.com, April 4, 2009, http://insidecatholic.com/Joomla/index.php?option=com_content&task=view&id=5744&Itemid=100

7. Quoted by Thomas Doherty, *Cold War, Cool Medium: Television, McCarthyism, and American Culture* (Columbia University Press, 2003): 8.

8. From his Lincoln Day speech in Wheeling, West Virginia, February 9, 1950, http://historymatters.gmu.edu/d/6456.

9. Jeff Woods, *Black Struggle, Red Scare: Segregation and Anti-Communism in the South, 1948–68* (LSU Press, 2004): 85.

10. Gerald Horne, *Black and Red: W.E.B. Du Bois and the Afro-American Response to the Cold War, 1944–63* (SUNY Press, 1986): 202.

11. K. A. Cuordileone, "'Politics in an Age of Anxiety': Cold War Political Culture and the Crisis in American Masculinity, 1949–1960," *Journal of American History*, vol. 87, no. 2 (September 2000): 516.

12. Ibid.

13. David Caute, *Great Fear: The Anti-Communist Purge under Truman and Eisenhower* (Simon & Schuster, 1978): 26

14. Nelson Polsby, "Towards an Explanation for McCarthyism," *Political Studies*, vol. 8, no. 3 (October 1960): 250–71; Michael Paul Rogin, *Intellectuals and McCarthy: The Radical Specter* (MIT Press, 1967); Earl Latham, *The Meaning of McCarthyism* (Heath, 1965). For an excellent review of this literature, see Thomas C. Reeves, "McCarthyism: Interpretations since Hofstadter," *Wisconsin Magazine of History*, vol. 60, no. 1 (Autumn 1976).

15. Quoted in Sergei N. Goncharov, John Wilson Lewis, and Litai Xue, *Uncertain Partners: Stalin, Mao, and the Korean War* (Stanford University Press, 1995): 7.

16. Steven I. Levine "A New Look at American Mediation in the Chinese Civil War: The Marshall Mission and Manchuria," *Diplomatic History*, vol. 3, no. 4 (October 1979): 349–76.

17. Harry S. Truman, *Memoirs: Years of Trial and Hope* (Doubleday, 1956): 89–90.

18. Odd Arne Westad, *Decisive Encounters: The Chinese Civil War, 1946–49* (Stanford University Press, 2003): 7.

19. *Papers of Robert Taft*, edited by Clarence E. Wunderlin, Jr. (Kent State University Press, 2006): 124–25.

20. Address to Midwest Council of Young Republican, May 9, 1950; quoted in Robert Griffith, *The Politics of Fear: Joseph R. McCarthy and the Senate* (University of Massachusetts Press, 1987): 89.

21. Lloyd E. Eastman, "Who Lost China? Chiang Kai-shek Testifies," *China Quarterly*, vol. 88 (December 1981): 658.

22. Quoted by Richard Madsen, *China and the American Dream: A Moral Inquiry* (University of California Press, 1995): 30.

23. Michael H. Hogan, *A Cross of Iron: Harry S. Truman and the Origins of the National Security State, 1945–1954* (Cambridge University Press, 1998).

24. George F. Kennan, *Memoirs, 1925–1950* (Little, Brown, 1967): 364.

25. László Borhi, "Rollback, Liberation, Containment, or Inaction? U.S. Policy and Eastern Europe in the 1950s," *Journal of Cold War Studies*, vol. 1, no. 3 (Fall 1999): 70; Peter Grose, *Operation Rollback: America's Secret War behind the Iron Curtain* (Boston: Houghton Mifflin, 2000); see also Gregory Mitrovich, *Undermining the Kremlin: America's Strategy to Subvert the Soviet Bloc, 1947–1956* (Cornell University Press, 2000).

26. Bruce Cumings, *The Origins of the Korean War* (Princeton University Press, 1991), Vol. 2, 165.

27. Ibid., 31.

28. Ibid., 30.

29. William Appleman Williams, *The Tragedy of American Diplomacy* (W.W. Norton, 1988), originally published 1959 by World Publishing Co.; Gabriel Kolko, *The Roots of American Foreign Policy: An Analysis of Power and Purpose* (Beacon Press, 1969); Gabriel Kolko and Joyce Kolko, *The Limits of Power: The World and United States Foreign Policy 1945–1954* (Harper & Row, 1972); Richard J. Barnet and Ronald E. Müller, *Global Reach: The Power of the Multinational Corporations* (Simon & Schuster, 1974); Richard J. Barnet and John Cavanagh, *Global Dreams: Imperial Corporations and the New World Order* (Simon & Schuster, 1995), among others.

30. Adrian R. Lewis, *The American Culture of War: The History of U.S. Military Force from World War II to Operation Iraqi Freedom* (Routledge, 2007): 90.
31. Bruce Cumings, *Origins of the Korean War*, Vol. 1 (Princeton University Press, 1980): xxvi.
32. Quoted in William Stueck, *Rethinking the Korean War: A New Diplomatic and Strategic History* (Princeton University Press, 2002): 37
33. "Points Requiring Presidential Decision," June 25, 1950 memo, Truman Library collection.
34. Memorandum of conversation, June 25, 1950, by Philip C. Jessup, Truman Library collection.
35. Thomas J. Christensen, "Windows and War: Trend Analysis and Beijing's Use of Force," in Alastair I. Johnston and Robert S. Ross, eds., *New Directions in the Study of China's Foreign Policy* (Stanford University Press, 2006): 57
36. Kennan, *Memoirs*, 489.
37. Declassified cables, MacArthur to Joint Chiefs, September 28, 1950; Marshall to MacArthur, September 29, 1950; MacArthur to Marshall, September 30, 1950, all from the Truman Library collection.
38. Cumings, *Origins of the Korean War*, Vol. 2, 748.
39. Stueck, 113.
40. Halberstam, 592.
41. Halberstam, 593.
42. Rosemary Foot, *The Wrong War: American Policy and the Dimensions of the Korean Conflict, 1950–53* (Cornell University Press, 1985): 174–76.
43. Roger Dingman, "Atomic Diplomacy during the Korean War," *International Security*, vol. 13, no. 3 (Winter 1988–1989): 74.
44. Cumings, Vol. 2, 750.
45. Sahr Conway-Lanz, *Collateral Damage: Americans, Non-Combatant Immunity, and Atrocities after World War II* (Routledge, 2006): 138.
46. Foot, 184.
47. Richard H. Immerman, *John Foster Dulles: Piety, Pragmatism, and Power in US Foreign Policy* (Rowman and Littlefield, 1998): 69ff.
48. Cumings, Vol. 2, 749.
49. The restraint from using atomic weapons is summarized by Dingman: "If at times [American statesmen] were concerned about public demands for atomic action, far more often their choices were shaped by professional and bureaucratic imperatives in the Pentagon. In July 1950, General Vandenberg's desire for action was crucial in bringing about B-29 deployments; six months later, his caution, General LeMay's desire to protect the integrity of the SAC striking force, and General Collins' skepticism about the utility of bombing alone, all worked against nuclear action of any kind. It also seems clear that military professionals' understanding of the psychology of nuclear deterrence and their reluctance to weaken it through precipitate action grew during the Korean conflict. Finally, Pentagon parochialism, as manifested in the service-chieftains' quarrels over shares of weapons to be deployed overseas from December 1950 through July 1953, also constrained civilian leaders' ability to use nuclear weapons in managing the Korean conflict." 90.
50. Cumings, Vol. 1, xix.
51. Lewis, 144. See also Andrew White's helpful Web site, "Death Tolls for the Major Wars and Atrocities of the Twentieth Century," http://users.erols.com/mwhite28/warstat2.htm#Ko; and Anne Leland and Mari-Jana "M-J" Oboroceanu, "American War and Military Operations Casualties: Lists and Statistics" (Congressional Research Service, February 26, 2010).
52. Rhee's intention to "march north" was well known and a goal he harbored throughout the 1950s. See Yong-pyo Hong, *State Security and Regime Security:*

    President Syngman Rhee and the Insecurity Dilemma in South Korea, 1953–60 (Palgrave Macmillan, 1999): 25 ff.

53. Hak-Kyu Sohn, *Authoritarianism and Opposition in South Korea* (Taylor & Francis, 1989): 15.

54. Cumings, Vol. 2, 186.

55. Cumings, Vol. 2, 189.

56. Do Khiem and Kim Sung-soo, "Crimes, Concealment and South Korea's Truth and Reconciliation Commission," *Japan Times*, August 1, 2008. Hausman's role, which was quite extensive before and during the war, is detailed by Dong-Choon Kim, "The War against the 'Enemy Within': Hidden Massacres in the Early Stages of the Korean War," Truth and Reconciliation Commission of Korea, April 23, 2008. Dong-Choon Kim is a professor at Song Kong Hoe University, South Korea, and a member of the Commission, http://www.jinsil. go.kr/English/Information/notice/read.asp?num=146&pageno=22&stype=&sv al=&data_years=2009&;data_month=.

57. Dong-Choon Kim, "Beneath the Tip of the Iceberg: Problems in Historical Clarification of the Korean War," *Korea Journal*, Autumn 2002: 66.

58. Hugh Dean, *The Korean War, 1945–53* (China Books, 1999): 60.

59. Dong-Choon Kim: "Beneath the Tip of the Iceberg," 69–70.

60. Walter Sullivan, *New York Times*, March 6, 1950; quoted by Cumings, Vol. 2, 289.

61. The estimates have ranged far higher. In the Chejodu massacre alone, 60,000–80,000 civilians were killed. Bruce Cumings, paper presented at the 50th Anniversary Conference of the April 3, 1948 Chejudo Rebellion, Tokyo, March 14, 1998, http://www.iacenter.org/Koreafiles/ktc-cumings.htm, accessed October 8, 2010; "Ghosts of Cheju."*Newsweek*. June 19, 2000, http://www. newsweek.com/2000/06/18/ghosts-of-cheju.html, accessed October 8, 2010; Noam Chomsky, *Deterring Democracy* (Hill and Wang, 1991), cited by Jon Halliday and Bruce Cumings, *Korea: the Unknown War* (Viking, Pantheon, 1988): 358, http://www.naturalthinker.net/trl/texts/Chomsky,%20Noam/Chomsky,_ Noam_-_Deterring_Democracy.pdf, accessed October 8, 2010.

62. Dong-Choon Kim, "Beneath the Tip of the Iceberg," citing Nichols's own work.

63. Charles J. Hanley and Jae-Soon Chang, "Summer of Terror: At Least 100,000 Said Executed by Korean Ally of US in 1950," Japan Focus, Associated Press wire story, July 28, 2008.

64. "New Evidence of Korean War Killings," BBC report, April 21, 2000. Some of these may have been part of the Bodo League massacre, and some were already political prisoners; one report has the prisoners executed en masse before the war broke out.

65. Lee Chae Hoon, "Revisiting the Satanic Period of the Bodo Massacre," Truth and Reconciliation Commission of Korea (TRCK), June 10, 2008, http://www. jinsil.go.kr/English/Information/notice/read.asp?num=185.

66. Dong-Choon Kim, "Forgotten War, Forgotten Massacres: The Korean War (1950–1953) as Licensed Mass Killings," *Journal of Genocide Research*, vol. 6, no. 4 (December 2004): 523–44.

67. Dong-Choon Kim, "Beneath the Tip of the Iceberg."

68. Ibid.

69. Hanley and Chang, July 23, 2008; based on a declassified document written by the approving officer, http://www.jinsil.go.kr/English/Information/notice/read. asp?num=205&pageno=18&;stype=.

70. "Massacres of Prisoners in the Busan and Gyeongnam Regions," Truth and Reconciliation Commission of Korea, March 31, 2009, http://www.jinsil.go.kr/ English/Information/notice/read.asp?num=350&pageno=1&stype= title&sval=busan&data_years=2009&;data_month=.

71. Hanley and Chang.
72. Cumings, Vol. 2, 702. He is quoting an internal North Korean assessment, so it could be biased, of course; but as he points out, it seems unlikely that the report writer would fabricate an intelligence report intended for internal use only. Of the 29,000, 21,000 were prisoners, which is consistent with other ROK atrocities.
73. John Osborne, "The Ugly War," *Time*, August 21, 1950, http://www.time.com/time/magazine/article/0,9171,812987–1,00.html.
74. Dong-Choon Kim, "Beneath the Tip of the Iceberg.,"
75. Conway-Lanz, 86.
76. Walter G. Hermes, *United States Army in the Korean War: Truce Tent and Fighting Front* (Center of Military History, United States Army, 1992): 322, http://www.history.army.mil/books/korea/truce/ch14.htm.
77. Quoted by Cumings, Vol. 2, 753.
78. Quoted in Robert Pape, *Bombing to Win: Air Power and Coercion in War* (Cornell University Press, 1996): 145. Pape is among the skeptics who does not believe much damage was done during the conventional bombing and that nuclear coercion worked in Korea.
79. Marilyn Young, "Bombing Civilians: An American Tradition," History News Network, George Mason University, http://hnn.us/articles/67717.html.
80. Conway-Lanz, 106–7.
81. Foot, 177–78.
82. Cumings, Vol. 2, 755.
83. M. L. Docktrill, "The Foreign Office, Anglo-American Relations and the Korean Truce Negotiations July 1951–July 1953," in James Cotton and Ian Neary, eds., *The Korean War in History* (Manchester University Press, 1989): 102.
84. Pape, 160.
85. Foot, 189 ff.
86. Lewis, 143.
87. Docktrill, 101.
88. Conway-Lanz, 93.
89. "The U.S. Air Force Bombing Incidents in Uiryeong-Verified on December 30, 2008," Truth and Reconciliation Commission of Korea, April 3, 2009, http://www.jinsil.go.kr/English/Information/notice/read.asp?num=353&pageno=1&stype=title&sval=air%20force&data_years=2009&;data_month=.
90. "Commission Urges S. Korea to Negotiate with U.S. Gov't for Restitution and Initiate Memorial Project," *Hankyoreh*, May 8, 2008, http://www.jinsil.go.kr/English/Information/notice/read.asp?num=233&pageno=1&stype=title&sval=bombing&data_years=2009&;data_month=.
91. Jae-Soon Chang, "In Korea's 'Crying' Cave, 100s Die in Attack," Associated Press, April 8, 2009.
92. Choe Sang-hun, "South Korea Says U.S. Killed Hundreds of Civilians," *New York Times*, August 3, 2008.
93. Charles J. Hanley, "Korean War Pilot: 'We're Not Lily-white,'" Associated Press, August 4, 2008.
94. James A. Toner, "American Society and the American Way of War: Korea and Beyond," *Parameters*, March 1981, 83. Toner was quoting British journalist René Cutforth, *Korean Reporter* (Allen Wingate, 1952).
95. Suh Ji-moon, "The Korean War in the Lives and Thoughts of Several Major Korean Writers," in Philip West, Chi-mun Sŏ, and Ji-Moon Suh, *Remembering the "Forgotten War": The Korean War through Literature and Art* (M. E. Sharpe, 2001): 102.
96. Conway-Lanz, 113.
97. Quoted by Cumings, Vol. 2, 705.

98. Truth and Reconciliation Commission, Republic of Korea, *Report on the Activities of the Past Three Years* (December 2008): 30, http://www.jinsil.go.kr/ English/Information/notice/read.asp?num=315&pageno=1&stype=title&sval= Report&data_years=2009&;data_month=.
99. Charles W. Hanley and Sang-Hun Choe, "Ex-GIs Tell AP of Korea Killings," Associated Press, September 30, 1999, http://www.washingtonpost.com/ wp-srv/aponline/19990930/aponline065913_000.htm.
100. Conway-Lanz, 98. Conway-Lanz discovered this letter, a key piece of evidence in the controversy following Hanley's reporting.
101. Conway-Lanz, 99.
102. Osborne.
103. Reginald Thompson, *Cry Korea: The Korean War: A Reporter's Notebook* (Reportage Press, 2009): 71. Originally published in 1951. This is doubtlessly the best eyewitness account of the war, and was recognized as such in Britain. Thompson wrote for the *Daily Telegraph*.
104. Ibid., 173.
105. Lewis, 96.
106. Malcolm Nuir, Jr., "Air and Sea Power in Korea," in B. A. Elleman and S. C. M. Paine, eds., *Naval Blockades and Seapower: Strategies and Sounter-Strategies, 1805–2005* (Taylor & Francis, 2006): 149.
107. Osborne.
108. Thompson, 55.
109. Quoted by David McCann, "Our Forgotten War: The Korean War in Korean and American Popular Culture," in Philip West, Steven I. Levine, and Jackie Hiltz, eds., *America's Wars in Asia: A Cultural Approach to History and Memory* (M. E. Sharpe, 1997): 81.
110. John R. Mueller, "Trends in Popular Support for the Wars in Korea and Vietnam," *American Political Science Review*, vol. 65, no. 2 (June 1971): 360.
111. Oli R. Holsti, *Public Opinion and American Foreign Policy* (University of Michigan Press, 2004): 26.
112. Edward A. Suchman, Rose K. Goldsen, and Robin M. Williams, Jr., "Attitudes toward the Korean War," *Public Opinion Quarterly*, vol. 17, no. 2 (Summer, 1953): 171–84.
113. William Jorden, "Eyewitness Report: B-29 Armadas Rain Death on 60,000 Reds," *Los Angeles Times*, August 17, 1950.
114. I. F. Stone, *The Hidden History of the Korean War* (Monthly Review Press, 1952): 257–58.
115. Steven Casey, *Selling the Korean War: Propaganda, Politics, and Public Opinion in the United States, 1950–53* (Oxford University Press, 2008): 45.
116. "Stranded Enemy Soldiers Merge with Refugee Crowds in Korea," *New York Times*, September 30, 1950.
117. George Barrett, "Village Massacre Stirs South Korea," *New York Times*, April 11, 1951.
118. "Koreans Watch U.N. Murder Trial as Test of Curb on Unruly Behavior," *New York Times*, August 21, 1951.
119. I. F. Stone, 256
120. "Civilians in Korea Face Grim Winter," *New York Times*, October 21, 1951.
121. Casey, 58.
122. Quoted by Nancy E. Bernhard, *U.S. Television News and Cold War Propaganda, 1947–1960* (Cambridge University Press, 1999): 107.
123. Casey, 313.
124. "General Terms Korea Toll among Civilians 'Horrible,'" *New York Times*, May 6, 1951.
125. "Korean War Casualties Set at 4 Million," *Washington Post*, June 30, 1951.

126. "No Wanton Bombing," *Washington Post*, August 6, 1952.
127. William S. White, "Taft Opposes Troops for Europe," *New York Times*, January 6, 1951.
128. Conway-Lanz, 91.
129. Conway-Lanz, 157. He has the best discussion of this remarkably unexamined topic.
130. Stanley Sandler, *The Korean War: No Victors, No Vanquished* (University Press of Kentucky, 1999): 108.
131. McCann, 79–80.
132. Bruce Cumings, *War and Television* (Verso, 1994): 149, 146.
133. Richard Slotkin, *Gunfighter Nation: The Myth of the Frontier in Twentieth Century America* (University of Oklahoma Press, 1998): 352. Originally published by Atheneum Press, 1992.
134. Nadia Kim, "The Migration of White Racism to South Korea," paper presented at the annual meeting of the American Sociological Association, Boston, Mass., July 31, 2008. See also McCann.
135. From a letter to the *New York Times*, July 16, 1950, quoted by Cumings, Vol. 2, 695.
136. Cumings, Vol. 2, 696.

CHAPTER 5

1. NSC 124/2, quoted in the *Pentagon Papers*, Gravel Edition, Vol. 1, ch. 2 (Beacon Press, 1971): 89.
2. Quoted in Robert Mann, *Grand Delusion: America's Descent into Vietnam* (Basic Books, 2002): 115.
3. David L. Anderson, *Trapped by Success: The Eisenhower Administration and Vietnam, 1953–1961* (Columbia University Press, 1991): 19.
4. A very good treatment of this is Michael Rogin, "Kiss Me Deadly: Communism, Motherhood, and Cold War Movies," *Representations*, No. 6 (Spring, 1984): 1–36.
5. *Pentagon Papers*, 190.
6. *Pentagon Papers*, Vol. 1, 367.
7. *Pentagon Papers*, Vol. 1, 76–77.
8. Norman Mailer, "Superman Comes to the Supermarket," *Esquire*, November 1960, http://www.esquire.com/features/superman-supermarket, accessed July 1, 2009.
9. Quoted by Kai Bird, *The Color of Truth: McGeorge Bundy and William Bundy: Brothers in Arms* (Simon and Schuster, 1998): 202.
10. Lawrence Freedman, *Kennedy's Wars: Berlin, Cuba, Laos and Vietnam* (Oxford University Press, 2000): 147.
11. Bird, 208–10.
12. Quoted by Bird, 222.
13. *Pentagon Papers*, Vol. 2, 19.
14. *Pentagon Papers*, Vol. 2, 141.
15. Quoted by Bird, 250.
16. *Pentagon Papers*, Vol. 3, 356.
17. *Pentagon Papers*, Vol. 3, 391.
18. Neil Sheehan, *A Bright Shining Lie: John Paul Vann and America in Vietnam* (Vintage Books, 1989): 308.
19. Lewis, 255.
20. *Pentagon Papers*, Vol. 4, 60; emphasis in original.
21. *Pentagon Papers*, Vol. 4, 56; emphasis in original.
22. *Pentagon Papers*, Vol. 4, 39.

23. *Pentagon Papers*, Vol. 4, 83.
24. Lewis, 249.
25. Jeffrey Kimball, *Nixon's Vietnam War* (University Press of Kansas, 1998): 135–36.
26. Ibid., 195.
27. Quoted in Lewis, 290.
28. Stanley Karnow, *Vietnam: A History*, 2nd ed. (Viking Penguin, 1991): 616.
29. Kimball, 365.
30. Sheehan, 533.
31. Quoted by James William Gibson, *The Perfect War: Technowar in Vietnam* (Atlantic Monthly Press, 1986, 2000): 137.
32. Jonathan Schell, *The Real War* (Pantheon, 1987): 203–4.
33. Gibson, 136.
34. Deborah Nelson, *The War Behind Me: Vietnam Veterans Confront the Truth about U.S. War Crimes* (Basic Books: 2008): 127–29.
35. Quoted by Gibson, 142.
36. Quoted by Lewis, 259.
37. Lewis M. Simmons, "Free Fire Zones," *Crimes of War*, http://www.crimesofwar. org/thebook/free-fire-zones.html.
38. Karnow, 482.
39. Arthur Everett and others, *Calley* (Dell, 1971), quoted in John Clark Pratt, ed., *Vietnam Voices: Perspectives on the War Years* (University of Georgia Press, 1984, 1999): 358.
40. Sheehan, 689.
41. Nick Turse, "The Vietnam War Crimes You Never Heard Of," http://hnn.us/ articles/1802.html. Kerrey's incident remains controversial, as he claims that they were shooting into a group of what they thought were Viet Cong.
42. Sheehan, 690.
43. Quoted in Nelson, 74–78.
44. Saburo Kugai, "The Balang An Massacre," in Richard A. Falk, Gabriel Kolko, and Robert Jay Lifton, eds., *Crimes of War* (Vintage, 1971): 391.
45. Bong MacDoran, interviewed by Christian G. Appy, *Patriots: The Vietnam War Remembered from All Sides* (Viking, 2003): 524.
46. Quoted by Lewis, 260.
47. Quoted by Nelson, 89–90. The original article appeared in the June 19, 1972, edition of *Newsweek*.
48. Quoted in Douglas Valentine, *The Phoenix Program* (iUniverse.com, 2000): 216.
49. R. W. Komer, "Impact of Pacification on Insurgency in South Vietnam," paper presented at the annual meeting of the American Political Science Association, Los Angeles, CA, September 8–12, 1970.
50. While they were typically called "refugees," these were actually "internally displaced" as most of them had not crossed borders. There were 2.6 million new refugees registered between 1965 and 1968 in the South. See "Humanitarian Problems in South Vietnam and Cambodia: Two Years after the Cease-Fire," A Study Mission Report, Subcommittee to Investigate Problems Connected with Refugees and Escapees, Committee on the Judiciary, U.S. Senate, January 27, 1975: 4. An estimate for whole war is five million in the South; see Frances Fitzgerald, *Fire in the Lake: The Vietnamese and the Americans in Vietnam* (Atlantic-Little, Brown, 1972): 427.
51. Quoted by Valentine, 218. For a defense of the pacification program, and Phoenix, see Richard A. Hunt, *Pacification: The American Struggle for Vietnam's Hearts and Minds* (Westview Press, 1995).
52. Mark Moyar and Harry G. Summers, Jr., *Phoenix and the Birds of Prey: Counterinsurgency and Counterterrorism in Vietnam* (University of Nebraska Press, 2007): 203.

53. Fitzgerald, 431.

54. Sheehan, 625.

55. Fred Turner, *Echoes of Combat: Trauma, Memory, and the Vietnam War* (University of Minnesota Press, 1996): 29. Turner is drawing from the survey of veterans done in the late 1970s: Arthur Egendorf, Charles Kadushin, Robert S. Laufer, George Rothbart, and Lee Sloan, *Legacies of Vietnam: Comparative Adjustment of Veterans and Their Peers* (U.S. Government Printing Office, 1981). The data on observing abuse includes non-U.S. troops, but 78 percent of the observed acts of abuse were committed by Americans.

56. Sheehan, 618–19.

57. Seymour Hersh relays the story of a protestor on a hunger strike to call attention to the destruction of 130,000 acres of croplands in March 1966; see "Chemical Warfare in Vietnam," in Falk et al., *Crimes of War.*

58. Cecil B. Currey, "Residual Dioxin in Viet Nam," *Viet Nam Generation*, vol. 4, no. 3–4 (November 1992), http://www2.iath.virginia.edu/sixties/HTML_docs/Texts/Scholarly/Currey_Dioxin.html. The figures are for 1987.

59. Tom Fawthrop, "Vietnam's War against Agent Orange," BBC News, June 14, 2004, http://news.bbc.co.uk/2/hi/health/3798581.stm, accessed December 5, 2010.

60. Sheehan, 620–21.

61. Phan Xuan Sinh, interviewed by Appy, *Patriots*, 26.

62. Harrison Salisbury, "A Visitor to Hanoi Inspects Damage Laid to U.S. Raids," *New York Times*, December 25, 1966, 1ff.

63. Harrison Salisbury, "U.S. Raids Batter Two Towns," *New York Times*, December 27, 1966, 1ff.

64. Harrison Salisbury, "Hanoi during an Air Alert," *New York Times*, December 28, 1966, 1ff.

65. Harrison Salisbury, "Bomb Controversy: View from the Ground," *New York Times*, January 13, 1967, 1ff.

66. Karnow, 504.

67. *Pentagon Papers*, Vol. 4, 153.

68. Pape, 179.

69. Pape, 190, 193.

70. *Pentagon Papers*, Vol. 4, ch. 1, 134. The "summer study" was conducted by Jason, the group of prominent scientists that advise the secretary of defense.

71. Shaun Malarney, "The Realities and Consequences of War in a North Vietnamese Commune," in M. Young and R. Buzzanco, eds., *A Companion to the Vietnam War* (Wiley-Blackwell, 2002).

72. Richard Gott, "Precision Bombing, Not Very Precise," in Falk et al., eds., 399. Originally published in the *Manchester Guardian Weekly*, February 28, 1970.

73. Tran Luong, interviewed by Appy, 520.

74. Tin Bui, Judy Stowe, and Do Van, *Following Ho Chi Minh: The Memoirs of a North Vietnamese Colonel*, translated by Judy Stowe and Do Van (University of Hawaii Press, 1999): 71.

75. Tran Luong, 521.

76. Bernard B. Fall, *Viet-Nam Witness, 1953–66* (Praeger, 1966): 299.

77. Lewis, 292; a useful review of estimates, with its own demographic calculation, can be found in Charles Hirschman, Samuel Preston, and Vu Manh Loi, "Vietnamese Casualties during the American War: A New Estimate," *Population and Development Review*, vol. 21, no. 4 (December, 1995): 783–812; the most recent attempt to estimate mortality via household survey is Ziad Obermeyer, Christopher J. L. Murray, and Emmanuela Gakidou, "Fifty Years of Violent War Deaths from Vietnam to Bosnia: Analysis of Data from the World Health Survey Programme," *British Medical Journal* (2008), bmj.com. This is the highest estimate.

78. John Duffett, ed., *Against the Crime of Silence: Proceedings* (Simon & Schuster, 1970).
79. Quoted in Todd Gitlin, *The Sixties: Years of Hope and Days of Rage* (Bantam, 1987): 178, 184.
80. Lawrence W. Lichty, "Comments on the Influence of Television on Public Opinion," in Peter Braestrup, ed., *Vietnam as History: Ten Years after the Paris Peace Accords* (Woodrow Wilson International Center for Scholars, 1984): 158; cited by William M. Hammond, "The Press in Vietnam as Agent of Defeat: A Critical Examination," *Reviews in American History*, vol. 17, no. 2. (June 1989): 315.
81. Michael Mandelbaum, "Vietnam: The Television War," *Daedalus*, vol. 111, no. 4 (Fall 1982): 160.
82. Slotkin, *Gunfighter Nation*, 520–33.
83. Raymond M. Scurfield, *Healing Journeys: Study Abroad with Vietnam Veterans: Vol. 2, A Vietnam Trilogy* (Algora, 2006): 75, 77.
84. John E. Mueller, "Trends in Popular Support for the Wars in Korea and Vietnam," *American Political Science Review*, vol. 65, no. 2 (June 1971): 358–75.
85. John E. Mueller, *War, Presidents and Public Opinion* (John Wiley, 1973): 129–30.
86. E. M. Schreiber, "Anti-War Demonstrations and American Public Opinion on the War in Vietnam," *British Journal of Sociology*, vol. 27, no. 2 (June 1976): 225–36.
87. Howard Schuman, "Sources of Antiwar Sentiment in America," *American Journal of Sociology*, vol. 78, no. 3 (November 1972): 519.
88. Godfrey Hodgson, *America in Our Time: From World War II to Nixon, What Happened and Why* (Vintage, 1976): 392, 393.
89. Schuman, 521, 524.
90. Cited by Mark Lorell and Charles Kelley, Jr., *Casualties, Public Opinion, and Presidential Decision Making during the Vietnam War* (RAND, 1985): 27.
91. Hodgson, 391.
92. Schuman, 519.
93. On this, see, among others, Herbert Shapiro, "The Vietnam War and the American Civil Rights Movement," in Walter L. Hixon, ed. *The Vietnam Antiwar Movement* (Garland, 2000), originally published in the *Journal of Ethnic Studies*, vol. 16, no. 4 (1989) Shapiro shows that black leaders were opposed to the war from an early stage.
94. See the useful discussion of this in Christopher Waldrep and Michael A. Bellesiles, *Documenting American Violence: A Sourcebook* (Oxford University Press, 2006).
95. Todd Gitlin, *The Sixties: Years of Hope, Days of Rage* (Bantam Books, 1987): 316.
96. Quoted by Andrew Hunt, *The Turning: A History of Vietnam Veterans against the War* (NYU Press, 2001): 51.
97. Gerald Nicosia, *Home to War: A History of the Vietnam Veterans' Movement* (Carroll & Graf, 2004): 120ff.
98. "Days of Protest," *News Hour* (PBS), April 28, 2000, http://www.pbs.org/newshour/bb/asia/vietnam/protests.html, accessed August 31, 2009. The speaker was Joseph R. Barnes.
99. Robert J. Lifton, *Home from the War—Vietnam Veterans: Neither Victims nor Executioners* (Simon & Schuster, 1973): 145.
100. Nick Bromell, *Tomorrow Never Knows: Rock and Psychedelics in the 1960s* (University of Chicago Press, 2000): 153–54.
101. Quoted by Gitlin, 415.

CHAPTER 6

1. Harold Schechter and Jonna G. Semeiks, "Leatherstocking in 'Nam: *Rambo, Platoon*, and the American Frontier Myth," *Journal of Popular Culture*, vol. 24, no. 4 (Spring, 1991): 17–25; quotation, 17.

2. Robert C. Tucker, "Reagan's Foreign Policy," *Foreign Affairs*, vol. 68, no. 1 (January 1989): 15. Emphasis added.
3. Quoted by James M. Scott, *Deciding to Intervene: The Reagan Doctrine and American Foreign Policy* (Duke University Press, 1996): 22.
4. Greg Grandin, *Empire's Workshop: Latin America, the United States, and the Rise of the New Imperialism* (Macmillan, 2006): 116.
5. Scott, 188.
6. Michael McFaul, "Rethinking the 'Reagan Doctrine' in Angola," *International Security*, vol. 14, no. 3 (Winter 1989–1990): 106–7.
7. Victoria Brittain, "Jonas Savimbi," *Guardian*, February 25, 2002, http://www. guardian.co.uk/Archive/Article/0,4273,4362364,00.html, accessed October 4, 2009.
8. Inge Tvedten, *Angola: Struggle for Peace and Reconstruction* (Westview Press, 1997): 110ff.
9. Scott, 82.
10. Eugene R. Wittkopf, *Faces of Internationalism: Public Opinion and American Foreign Policy* (Duke University Press, 1990): 119, 74.
11. Scott, 11.

CHAPTER 7

1. Phebe Marr, *The Modern History of Iraq* (Westview Press, 2004): 23.
2. Toby Dodge, *Inventing Iraq: The Failure of Nation Building and a History Denied* (Columbia University Press, 2003): 61ff.
3. Ibid., 31.
4. Bruce W. Jentleson, *With Friends Like These: Reagan, Bush, and Saddam, 1982–1990* (W.W. Norton, 1994): 94ff.
5. Adrian Lewis, *The American Culture of War*, 341
6. Lewis, 342; and GlobalSecurity.org, http://www.globalsecurity.org/military/ ops/desert_storm.htm, accessed October 29, 2009, says 109,800 missions; the Department of Defense claims 116,000, http://www.defenselink.mil/news/ newsarticle.aspx?id=45404, accessed October 29, 2009.
7. Dilip Hiro, *From Desert Shield to Desert Storm: The Second Gulf War* (iUniverse, 2003): 387.
8. Lewis, 343.
9. Charles Tripp, *A History of Iraq*, 2nd ed. (Cambridge University Press, 2002): 256.
10. All but 100,000 returned to Iraq. See Human Rights Watch, *Endless Torment: The 1991 Uprising in Iraq and Its Aftermath*, June 1992, http://www.hrw.org/ legacy/reports/1992/Iraq926.htm, accessed November 3, 2009.
11. Dave Johns, "The Crimes of Saddam Hussein," Frontline/World, http://www. pbs.org/frontlineworld/stories/iraq501/events_uprising.html, accessed November 3, 2009.
12. Geoffrey Leslie Simons, *The Scourging of Iraq: Sanctions, Law, and Natural Justice* (Palgrave Macmillan, 1998): 35ff.
13. Under Secretary General Martti Ahtisaari, UN document S/22366, 20/3/91, paragraph 8, quoted in Anglican Observer Office at the UN et al., "Iraq Sanctions: Humanitarian Implications and Options for the Future," http:// www.globalpolicy.org/component/content/article/170/41947.html#3, accessed November 12, 2009.
14. "Iraq Water Treatment Vulnerabilities," January 22, 1991, http://www.gulflink. osd.mil/declassdocs/dia/19950901/950901_511rept_91.html. For a further explanation and other supporting documents, see Thomas J. Nagy, *The Secret behind the Sanctions: How the U.S. Intentionally Destroyed Iraq's Water Supply*, September 2001, http://www.progressive.org/mag/nagy0901.html.

15. Barton Gellman, "Allied Air War Struck Broadly in Iraq," *Washington Post*, June 23, 1991, A1ff.
16. A. Ascherio, R. Chase, T. Cote, G. Dehaes, E. Hoskins, J. Laaouej, M. Passey, S. Qaderi, S. Shuqaidef, M.C. Smith, et al., "Effect of the Gulf War on Infant and Child Mortality in Iraq," *New England Journal of Medicine*, vol. 327 (September 24, 1992): 931–36, http://content.nejm.org/cgi/content/abstra ct/327/13/931?ijkey=d9b24694aae44fadf9ebfdfb68c715610a341c1b&keyt ype2=tf_ipsecsha, accessed November 12, 2009.
17. Joy Gordon, *Invisible War: the United States and the Iraq Sanctions* (Harvard University Press, 2010):61.
18. Quoted by Reem Bahdi, "Iraq, Sanctions, and Security: A Critique," *Duke Journal of Gender Law & Policy*, vol. 9 (Summer 2002): 240–41, http://www.law.duke. edu/shell/cite.pl?9+Duke+J.+Gender+L.+&+Pol'y+237#B8, accessed November 13, 2009.
19. H. C. von Sponeck, *A Different Kind of War: The UN Sanctions Regime in Iraq* (Berghahn Books, 2006): 45.
20. "Iraq Surveys Show 'Humanitarian Emergency,'" UNICEF Information News Brief, August 12, 1999, http://www.unicef.org/newsline/99pr29.htm. See also Biswat Sen, "Iraq Watching Brief: Overview Report," UNICEF/World Bank, July 2003, http://www.unicef.org/evaldatabase/files/Iraq_2003_Watching_ Briefs.pdf. Estimates by the Columbia University researcher, Richard Garfield, were cited in "The Debate over Sanctions," *Frontline* (n.d.), http://www.pbs. org/frontlineworld/stories/iraq/sanctions.html, accessed November 13, 2009.
21. Von Sponeck, 161.
22. John Pilger, "Squeezed to Death," *Guardian*, March 4, 2000, http:// www.guardian.co.uk/theguardian/2000/mar/04/weekend7.weekend9.
23. Gellman. A1.
24. See Von Sponeck, chap. 3, for discussion of the bombing effects.
25. Dodge, 162–63.
26. Ahmed S. Hashim, *Insurgency and Counter-Insurgency in Iraq* (Hurst, 2006): 27ff. See also David Siddharth Patel, "Studies of Iraq in the 1990s—contrasting known and unknown unknowns," Paper presented at the Annual Meeting of the Middle East Studies Association, San Diego, CA, November 21, 2011; http://mymesa.arizona.edu/meeting_program_session.php?sid=7dce90ebdbc4 11cc59f1ca3865961b0d (abstract), accessed November 26, 2010.
27. The rise in hate speech and nonviolent hate crimes against Muslims and Arabs (most of the Arab-American population is Christian) did rise very significantly after 9/11 and continued for a year or more. It was rightly alarming to those groups in America. The actual number of violent crimes was relatively low, however. Still, the sense of intimidation, blaming, and so on, that Muslims and other Arabs felt in the United States was significant. See John Tirman, ed., *The Maze of Fear: Security and Migration after 9/11* (New Press, 2004), especially chapter by Cainkar.
28. Susan Faludi, *The Terror Dream: Fear and Fantasy in Post-9/11 America* (Henry Holt, 2007): 4–5. Faludi draws very substantially on the framework provided by Slotkin.
29. See David Cole, "The Priority of Morality: The Emergency Constitution's Blind Spot," *Yale Law Journal* vol. 113, no. 8 (May 2004): 1753–8000.
30. John Mueller, *Overblown: How Politicians and the Terrorism Industry Inflate National Security Threats, and Why We Believe Them* (Free Press, 2006): 33.
31. Condoleezza Rice, "Transforming the Middle East," *Washington Post*, August 7, 2003.

32. Jane Mayer, "Contact Sport: What Did the Vice President Do for Halliburton?" *New Yorker*, February 16, 2004, http://www.newyorker.com/archive/2004/02 /16/040216fa_fact?printable=true, accessed January 30, 2010.

33. On these points, see Jacob Weisberg, *The Bush Tragedy* (Random House, 2008); Graham T. Allison, *Nuclear Terrorism: The Ultimate Preventable Catastrophe* (Macmillan, 2004): 126ff; Robert Jervis, "Understanding the Bush Doctrine," *Political Science Quarterly*, vol. 118, no. 3 (Fall 2003): 365–88.

34. "Remarks by the President at the 20th Anniversary of the National Endowment for Democracy," November 6, 2003, http://georgewbush-whitehouse.archives. gov/news/releases/2003/11/20031106–2.html.

35. See, for example, Tamara Cofman Wittes, "Arab Democracy, American Ambivalence: Will Bush's Rhetoric about Transforming the Middle East Be Matched by American Deeds?" *Weekly Standard*, vol. 9, no. 23 (February 23, 2004), http:// www.brookings.edu/views/articles/fellows/wittes20040223.pdf; Wittes, then at the Brookings Institution, became a deputy assistant secretary of state for the Middle East in the Obama administration.

36. Gallup survey can be found at http://www.gallup.com/poll/1633/Iraq.aspx#1. The earlier survey was on March 16 in *USA Today*, http://www.usatoday.com/ news/world/iraq/2003–03–16-poll-iraq_x.htm. It was also conducted by Gallup. ABC News/Washington Post Poll in early March 2003 showed roughly similar opinions, with support jumping from 59 percent to 72 percent once the war began. The support for removing Saddam from power stayed consistent between 56 percent and 65 percent over the six months prior to the war, according to Peter Hart's surveys for NBC and the *Wall Street Journal*. For results see http://www.pollingreport.com/iraq16.htm, all accessed December 5, 2009.

37. CBS News polls in September 2002 and April 2003 both showed similar results: 52 percent to 53 percent believing Saddam "was personally involved" in the attacks, with only 32 percent to 33 percent not believing that. For results see http://www.pollingreport.com/iraq.htm.

38. One of the small peculiarities of the period is that the major foundations continued to focus on nuclear weapons issues, a largely inadvertent reflection of Bush administration priorities. The liberal donors had played a key role in stirring antiwar activity during the wars in Indochina and the antinuclear sentiment of the early 1980s, but the Iraq situation earned no such interest; perhaps the post-9/11 angst and ambivalence about the politics of the region made it too controversial to warrant any significant funding to oppose war, an odd stance for what are self-described "peace donors." For the earlier history, see my book, *Making the Money Sing: Private Wealth and Public Power in the Search for Peace* (Rowman and Littlefield, 2000).

39. Hearing before the Committee on Armed Services, United States Senate, on the Posture of the United States Army First Session, 108th Congress, February 25, 2003 (record version), http://armed-services.senate.gov/statemnt/2003/ February/Shinseki.pdf

40. Quoted by Thomas E. Ricks, *Fiasco: The American Military Adventure in Iraq* (Penguin, 2006): 97. Ricks covers this ground very adeptly: see chap. 6.

41. Franks, quoted in Lewis, *The American Culture of War*: 431.

42. Evan Wright, *Generation Kill: Devil Dogs, Iceman, Captain America and the New Face of American War* (Berkeley Caliber: 2004): 179.

43. Michael O'Hanlon, "Was the Strategy Brilliant?" Brookings Daily War Report, Brookings Institution, April 9, 2003.

44. Quoted by Paul R. Pillar, "The Right Stuff," *National Interest*, September/ October 2007: 6. Pillar was a senior U.S. intelligence analyst at the time and

worked on the prewar assessments. Top military leaders were aware of the likelihood of problems in post-Saddam Iraq at least from a half-decade earlier. "In 1997, the U.S. Central Command exercise 'Desert Crossing' demonstrated that many postwar stabilization tasks would fall to the military. The other branches of the U.S. government lacked sufficient capability to do such work on the scale required in Iraq. Despite these results, CENTCOM [U.S. Central Command of the U.S. military] accepted the assumption that the State Department would administer postwar Iraq. The military never explained to [President Bush] the magnitude of the challenges inherent in stabilizing postwar Iraq." Lieutenant Colonel Paul Yingling, "A Failure in Generalship," *Armed Forces Journal*, May 2007; http://www.armedforcesjournal. com/2007/05/2635198, accessed December 4, 2010.

45. Mark Danner, "Iraq: The New War," *New York Review of Books*, vol. 50, no. 14 (September 25, 2003): http://www.nybooks.com/articles/archives/2003/ sep/25/iraq-the-new-war.

46. "back to the days . . ." (Robert Kaplan of the New America Foundation) quoted by Faludi, 5; Fox report: "Reporter's Notebook: Cowboys and Indians" (no date), http://www.foxnews.com/story/0,2933,189147,00.html, accessed December 17, 2009.

47. The evidence that toppling the statue was a staged event that occurred while much of Baghdad was gripped by fighting is presented well (as is the Jessica Lynch story) in Frank Rich, *The Greatest Story Ever Sold: The Decline and Fall of Truth from 9/11 to Katrina* (Penguin, 2006): 82–87. It bears repeating that Lynch did not concoct the story that the army promoted and has always honored the soldiers who were wounded and killed in the episode.

48. Edmund L. Andrews, "Envoy's Letter Counters Bush on Dismantling of Iraq Army," *New York Times*, September 4, 2007, http://www.nytimes. com/2007/09/04/washington/04bremer.html, accessed December 21, 2009.

49. Quoted by Chris Hedges and Laila Al-Arian, *Collateral Damage: America's War against Iraqi Civilians* (Nation Books, 2008): 79. The speaker was Major General John Batiste (Ret.), Senate hearing, September 26, 2006.

50. Quoted by Hedges and Al-Arian, 5–54.

51. Quoted by Ricks, 234.

52. Quoted by Hedges and Al-Arian, 13.

53. Patrick Graham, "Beyond Fallujah: A Year with the Iraqi Resistance," *Harper's*, June 2004, http://www.harpers.org/archive/2004/06/0080071, accessed February 2, 2010.

54. Ahmed S. Hashim, *Insurgency and Counter-Insurgency in Iraq* (Hurst, 2006): 325.

55. Quoted by Ricks, 405.

56. Jamie Wilson, "U.S. Admits Using White Phosphorous in Falluja," *Guardian*, November 16, 2005, www.guardian.co.uk/world/2005/nov/16/iraq.usa, accessed December 28, 2009.

57. Scott Ewing, Iraq Veterans against the War "Winter Soldier" investigation, March 16, 2008, http://www.ivaw.org/wintersoldier/testimony/racism-and-war-dehumanization-enemy-part-1/scott-ewing/video.

58. David Bellavia, with John R. Bruning, *House to House: A Soldier's Memoir* (Free Press, 2007): 112–13.

59. Lisa Chedekel and Matthew Kauffman, "Army Sees Record Number of Suicides in Iraq," *Hartford Courant*, May 30, 2008, http://www.courant.com/news/ nation-world/hc-soldiersuicides0530.artmay30,0,1889387.story, accessed January 10, 2010. The figure does not include veterans who have left the armed forces and have attempted suicide. On attempts, also see Bob Brewin, "Suicides of Iraq Veterans Could Top Combat Deaths," Government Executive.com, May

6, 2008, http://www.govexec.com/dailyfed/0508/050608bb1.htm, accessed January 10, 2010.

60. Matthew J. Friedman, "Posttraumatic Stress Disorder among Military Returnees from Afghanistan and Iraq," *American Journal of Psychiatry*, vol. 163, no. 4 (April 2006): 587.

61. Dave Grossman, *On Killing: The Psychological Cost of Learning to Kill in War and Society* (Little, Brown, 1995, 1996): 251 ff.

62. Winter Soldier investigation, http://www.ivaw.org/wintersoldier/testimony/ Racism+and+War%3A+the+Dehumanization+of+the+Enemy%3A+Part+1, accessed January 2, 2010.

63. Nick Turse, "The Secret Air War in Iraq," *Nation*, May 24, 2007, http://www .thenation.com/doc/20070611/turse, accessed January 12, 2010. Figures for total sorties and tonnage from Anthony H. Cordesman, "U.S. Airpower in Iraq and Afghanistan, 2004–2007," Center for Strategic and International Studies, December 13, 2007, http://csis.org/files/media/csis/pubs/071213_oif-oef_ airpower.pdf, accessed January 2, 2010.

64. Bellavia, 74.

65. Winter Soldier investigation, http://www.ivaw.org/wintersoldier/testimony/ rules-engagement-part-1/clifton-hicks-steven-casey/video.

66. Ellen Knickmeyer, "U.S. Airstrikes Take Toll on Civilians," *Washington Post*, December 24, 2005, http://www.washingtonpost.com/wp-dyn/content/ article/2005/12/23/AR2005122301471.html, accessed January 2, 2010.

67. "Iraq Wedding-Party Video Backs Survivors' Claims," Fox News, May 24, 2004, http://www.foxnews.com/story/0,2933,120721,00.html, accessed January 3, 2010.

68. Dexter Filkins, "In Shadows, Armed Groups Propel Iraq toward Chaos," *New York Times*, May 24, 2006: 1ff.

69. The surveys were conducted, respectively, by the Ministry of Health, Iraq, and published in 2008 by the *New England Journal of Medicine*, and by a team of doctors and epidemiologists at the Johns Hopkins School of Public Health, and published in the *Lancet* in October 2006. These surveys, among other accounts of mortality, are taken up in detail in later chapters.

70. Michael R. Gordon and Bernard E. Trainor, *Cobra II: The Inside Story of the Invasion and Occupation of Iraq* (Random House, 2007): 494.

71. Michael R. Gordon, "Military Hones a New Strategy on Insurgency," *New York Times*, October 5, 2006, http://www.nytimes.com/2006/10/05/ washington/05doctrine.html, accessed July 2, 2009.

72. U.S. Army, *Counterinsurgency* (December 15, 2006) document number FM 3–24/MCWP 3-33.5: 3–11, http://www.fas.org/irp/doddir/army/fm3-24.pdf, accessed June 24, 2009.

73. An excellent summary is Jon R. Lindsay, "Does the 'Surge' Explain Iraq's Improved Security?" Audits of Conventional Wisdom, MIT Center for International Studies, August 2008, http://web.mit.edu/cis/pdf/Audit_09_08_lindsay. pdf, accessed January 17, 2010.

74. See, for an example of a persistent apologist, Colin Kahl, "In the Crossfire or the Crosshairs? Norms, Civilian Casualties, and U.S. conduct in Iraq," *International Security*, vol. 32, no. 1 (Summer 2007): 7–46. Kahl became a deputy assistant secretary of defense in the Obama administration.

75. Hedges and Al-Arian, xvi.

76. Ahmed S. Hashim, *Insurgency and Counter-Insurgency in Iraq* (Hurst, 2006): 297. This was drawn from the *Iraq Living Conditions Survey 2004*; for a summary, see http://www.fafo.no/ais/middeast/iraq/imira/Tabulation%20reports/ english%20atlas.pdf, accessed January 9, 2010.

77. "A Family in Baghdad," January 28, 2005, http://afamilyinbaghdad.blogspot. com/2005_01_23_archive.html, accessed January 6, 2010.

78. Quoted by Nadje Sadig Al-Ali, *Iraqi Women: Untold Stories from 1948 to the Present* (Zed Books, 2007): 241.

79. Riverbend, "Baghdad Burning," September 15, 2004, http://riverbendblog. blogspot.com/, accessed October 11, 2009.

80. Shalash al Iraq, translated by Abu Khaleel from Arabic, June 23, 2006, http:// glimpseofiraq.blogspot.com/, accessed December 23, 2009.

81. Al-Tarrar, "Baghdad Connect," July 25, 2006, http://baghdad-connect.blogspot. com/2006_07_01_archive.html, accessed January 2, 2010.

82. Fatima, "Thoughts from Baghdad," November 19, 2006, http:// thoughtsfrombaghdad.blogspot.com/search?updated-min=2006–01–01T00% 3A00%3A00–05%3A00&updated-max=2007–01–01T00%3A00%3A00–05% 3A00&max-results=50, accessed January 22, 2010.

83. "Healing Iraq," October 20, 2008, http://healingiraq.blogspot.com/, accessed January 21, 2010.

84. Quoted by Al-Ali, 225.

85. "Iraq Poll March 2008," conducted by D3 Systems for ABS, BBC, and other news organizations, http://news.bbc.co.uk/2/shared/bsp/hi/pdfs/14_03_ 08iraqpollmarch2008.pdf, accessed January 3, 2010. See especially pp. 6–8. Again, these figures include the Kurdish provinces. A bare plurality still described the U.S. invasion as a mistake. For the 2009 poll by the same organizations, see http://abcnews.go.com/images/PollingUnit/1087a1IraqWhe reThingsStand.pdf, accessed January 25, 2010.

86. Interview with Anna Badkhen, October 2008, film transcript, commissioned by the MIT Center for International Studies.

87. Abu Khaleel, "Glimpse of Iraq," July 20, 2006, http://glimpseofiraq.blogspot. com, accessed January 11, 2010.

88. Iraq Mortality Study: Gilbert Burnham et al., "The Human Cost of the War in Iraq," October 2006, MIT Center for International Studies, http://mit.edu/ humancostiraq/reports/human-cost-war-101106.pdf, accessed November 24, 2009. The *Lancet* version is less complete. The second survey is that done by the Iraqi Ministry of Health in cooperation with the UN World Health Organization, Iraq office: Amir H. Alkhuzai et al., "Violence-Related Mortality in Iraq, 2002 to 2006," *New England Journal of Medicine*, vol. 358, no. 5 (January 31, 2008): 484–493, http://www.nejm.org/doi/full/10.1056/ NEJMsa0707782.

89. David Alexander, "Most Iraqis Favor Withdrawal of U.S. Forces Soon: Poll," *Washington Post*, September 27, 2006, http://www.washingtonpost.com/ wp-yn/content/article/2006/09/27/AR2006092701561.html, accessed, October 5, 2006; this was from a poll conducted by the Program on Interna- tional Policy Attitudes at the University of Maryland, http://www. worldpublicopinion.org/pipa/articles/brmiddleeastnafricara/250.php. The State Department survey, which was not made public, was described in Amit R. Paley, "Most Iraqis Favor Immediate U.S. Pullout, Polls Show," *Washing- ton Post*, September 27, 2006, http://www.washingtonpost.com/wp-dyn/ content/article/2006/09/26/AR2006092601721.html, accessed October 5, 2006.

90. Susan Page, "Democracy Support Sinks," *USA Today*, March 19, 2007; poll results at http://www.usatoday.com/news/graphics/iraqpoll_pdf/iraq_poll.pdf, accessed January 23, 2010. Virtually nothing concerning attitudes about violence was included in the news stories about the poll. The numbers remained relatively constant through much of 2007: see "US Surge Has Failed—Iraqi Poll," BBC

News, September 10, 2007, http://news.bbc.co.uk/2/hi/middle_east/6983841.
stm, accessed January 23, 2010.

91. "Poll Suggests Iraqis 'Optimistic,'" BBC News, March 17, 2008, http://news.bbc.
co.uk/2/shared/bsp/hi/pdfs/14_03_08iraqpollmarch2008.pdf, accessed
January 23, 2010.

92. George Packer, *The Assassin's Gate: America in Iraq* (Farrar Straus and Giroux,
2005): 308.

93. Nichole Argo, "Transnational Violence in the Persian Gulf," MIT Center
for International Studies, Workshop Report, April 20–21, 2007, http://web.
mit.edu/cis/pdf/pg1_0406_report.pdf, accessed January 20, 2010.

94. Quoted by Al-Ali, 235.

95. Riverbend, September 15, 2004, http://riverbendblog.blogspot.com/, accessed
January 5, 2010.

96. Rory McCarthy, "The View from the Red Zone," *Guardian*, January 29, 2005,
http://www.guardian.co.uk/world/2005/jan/29/iraq.rorymccarthy1,accessed
December 28, 2009.

97. Quoted by Michael Massing, "As Iraqis See It," *New York Review of Books*,
January 17, 2008, 18.

98. James Meek, "One Boy's War . . . Bathed in Blood of His Family," *Guardian*,
April 6, 2003, http://www.guardian.co.uk/world/2003/apr/06/iraq16,
accessed December 28, 2009. One of the more remarkable gaps in Americans'
understanding of the war, the checkpoint mayhem, finally got traction in the
news media when an Italian security agent was killed. PBS *News Hour*
introduced its piece on this person's death thus: "In the wake of the friendly
fire shooting of an Italian security agent in Iraq Friday, checkpoints and
their security are coming under scrutiny," http://www.pbs.org/news
hour/bb/middle_east/jan-june05/checkpoint_3-7.html, accessed January
7, 2010.

99. Nir Rosen, "The Flight from Iraq," *New York Times Magazine*, May 13, 2007,
http://www.nytimes.com/2007/05/13/magazine/13refugees-t.html, accessed
April 15, 2008.

100. Riverbend, July 11, 2006, http://riverbendblog.blogspot.com/2006_07_01_
riverbendblog_archive.html#115264752348608248, accessed January
5, 2010.

101. Ruth Rosen, "The Hidden War on Women in Iraq," Tom Dispatch, July 13, 2006,
http://www.tomdispatch.com/post/101034/, accessed December 1, 2009.

102. Amnesty International, http://www.amnesty.org/en/library/asset/
MDE14/005/2009/en/e6cda898-fa16–4944-af74-f3efc0cf6a4d/
mde140052009en.pdf.

103. Suki Falconberg, "Ms. Iraq Comments on the Prostitution of Iraqi Women and
Girls," *American Chronicle*, August 14, 2008, http://www.americanchronicle.
com/articles/view/71470, accessed January 25, 2010.

104. "Sex Traffickers Target Women in War-torn Iraq," IRIN News, October 26,
2006, http://www.irinnews.org/report.aspx?reportid=61903, accessed January
24, 2010.

105. First Balad resident: "Quotes of the Day," *Time*, October 17, 2006, http://www.
time.com/time/quotes/0,26174,1547015,00.html, accessed January 31, 2010.
Baghdad blogger: Imad Khadduri, "Free Iraq," October 20, 2006, http://
abutamam.blogspot.com/2006_10_01_archive.html, accessed January 4, 2010.
Second Balad resident: quoted by Ellen Kickmayer, "In Balad, Age-Old Ties Were
Destroyed in a Second," *Washington Post*, October 23, 2006, http://www.
washingtonpost.com/wp-dyn/content/article/2006/10/22/
AR2006102201071.html, accessed January 31, 2010.

106. Quoted in Al-Ali, 235.
107. AP/Ipsos Poll, "Military/Civilian Deaths in Iraq Study," February 12–15, 2007, http://surveys.ap.org/data/Ipsos/national/2007–02–16%20AP%20Iraq-soldiers%20topline.pdf, accessed December 7, 2010.
108. Douglas C. Foyle, "Leading the Public to War? The Influence of American Public Opinion on the Bush Administration's Decision to Go to War in Iraq," *International Journal of Public Opinion Research*, no. 3 (2004): 273–74.
109. Figures can be found on the Gallup Web site under the heading "Iraq," http://www.gallup.com/poll/1633/Iraq.aspx#1, accessed January 29, 2010. For other polls, see the handy compendium, "Public Opinion and the War in Iraq," American Enterprise Institute, July 24, 2008, http://www.aei.org/docLib/200701121_roody2.pdf, accessed January 29, 2010.
110. Peter Panepento, "Foundations Have 'Lost Their Way' in Debate over Iraq War," *Chronicle of Philanthropy*, April 18, 2007, http://philanthropy.com/blogPost/Foundations-Have-Lost-Thei/9348/, accessed January 29, 2010.
111. "Support Our Troops," http://troopssupport.com/, accessed February 6, 2010.
112. Michael Massing, "Iraq, the Press and the Election," *New York Review of Books*, vol. 51, no. 20 (December 16, 2004), reposted on http://www.tomdispatch.com/post/2020/, accessed December 5, 2010.
113. Sig Christenson, "Truth and Trust: In Iraq War Coverage, They've Become Casualties," *Neiman Reports*, Summer 2005, http://www.nieman.harvard.edu/reportsitem.aspx?id=101084, accessed February 1, 2010.
114. Kael Alford, "Telling Untold Stories of What Happened in Iraq," *Neiman Reports*, Winter 2009, http://www.nieman.harvard.edu/reportsitem.aspx?id=101986, accessed February 6, 2010.
115. Personal communication between the author and Borzoi Daragahi, LA Times bureau chief in Iraq, October 15, 2006. The author wrote to Ray Suarez of PBS's *News Hour with Jim Lehrer*, and WBUR-FM's Robin Young, the host of *Here and Now*, where Borzoi's claim to having conducted a study was aired. Neither Suarez nor Young responded.
116. Sean Aday, "Embedding the Truth: A Cross-Cultural Analysis of Objectivity and Television Coverage of the Iraq War," paper presented at the annual meeting of the International Communication Association, New Orleans, La., May 27, 2004: 8, 15, 24, http://www.allacademic.com/meta/p.113064_index.html, accessed January 21, 2010.
117. Sherry Ricchiardi, "Whatever Happened to Iraq?" *American Journalism Review*, June/July 2008, http://www.ajr.org/Article.asp?id=4515, accessed January 2, 2010.
118. "Awareness of Iraq War Fatalities Plummets," Pew Research Center for the People and the Press, March 12, 2008, http://people-press.org/report/401/awareness-of-iraq-war-fatalities-plummets, accessed January 2, 2010.
119. A simple Google search of "casualties, Iraq" will show that sixteen of the top twenty links focus on U.S. casualties, not Iraqis.
120. Michael Massing, "Iraq: The Hidden Human Costs," *New York Review of Books*, vol. 54, no. 20 (December 20, 2007), http://www.nybooks.com/articles/20906, accessed June 1, 2009.
121. Robert D. Kaplan, "Indian Country," *Wall Street Journal*, September 25, 2004, http://www.opinionjournal.com/extra/?id=110005673. For other analysis of the frontier imagery and attitudes used, see, for example, Karen Dodwell, "From the Center: The Cowboy Myth, George W. Bush, and the War with Iraq," *Americana: The Journal of American Popular Culture*, March 2004, http://www.americanpopularculture.com/archive/politics/cowboy_myth.htm; Barry Stephenson, "Swaggering Savagery and the New Frontier," *Journal of Religion*

and Popular Culture, vol.16 (Summer 2007), http://www.usask.ca/relst/jrpc/
art16-swaggering.html; Stephen W. Silliman, "The 'Old West' in the Middle
East: U.S. Military Metaphors in Real and Imagined Indian Country," *American
Anthropologist*, vol. 110, no. 2 (June 2008): 237–47, http://people.hofstra.edu/
daniel_m_varisco/sillimanaa.pdf; Jamie Wilson, "Former Powell Aide Attacks
'Cowboy' Bush," *Guardian*, October 21, 2005, http://www.guardian.co.uk/
world/2005/oct/21/usa.dickcheney; John Brown, "'Our Indian Wars Are Not
Over Yet': Ten Ways to Interpret the War on Terror as a Frontier Conflict,"
TomDispatch, January 19, 2006, http://www.tomdispatch.com/post/50043/;
David J. Morris, "Playing Cowboys and Indians in Iraq," *Salon*, November 12,
2004, online at http://dir.salon.com/story/opinion/feature/2004/11/12/
fallujah/index.html, all accessed January 30–31, 2010. See also Kaplan's longer
treatments of his *Wall Street Journal* article, Robert Kaplan, *Imperial Grunts: The
American Military on the Ground* (Random House, 2005); and "Imperial Grunts"
Atlantic, October 2005.

122. Camille Paglia, "Fresh Blood for the Vampire," *Salon*, September 10, 2008,
http://www.salon.com/opinion/paglia/2008/09/10/palin/, accessed September
3, 2009. On these themes, see my essay, "The Future of the American Frontier,"
American Scholar, Winter 2009, http://www.theamericanscholar.org/the-future-
of-the-american-frontier/.

123. Timothy Williams, "Iraq's War Widows Face Dire Need with Little Aid," *New
York Times*, February 22, 2009, http://www.nytimes.com/2009/02/23/world/
middleeast/23widows.html?_r=1&scp=1&sq=iraq%20widows&st=cse, accessed
February 2, 2010. At the time that the Johns Hopkins mortality study was
released in 2006, I briefed a group of academics in Cambridge, most of whom
were incredulous at the high numbers. One retorted, "Where are all the
widows?"

124. Michael Schwartz, "The Iraqi Oil Conundrum Energy and Power in the Middle
East," Tomdispatch, February 2, 2010, http://www.tomdispatch.com/
archive/175199/, accessed February 3, 2010.

125. Michael Mount, "Odierno: May Not Be Possible to Declare Victory in Iraq,"
CNN.com, October 1, 2009, http://www.cnn.com/2009/US/10/01/us.iraq.
odierno/index.html, accessed February 3, 2010.

126. William Kristol, "What Obama Can't Bring Himself to Say—We Won in Iraq,"
Washington Post, January 27, 2010, http://voices.washingtonpost.com/
postpartisan/2010/01/what_obama_cant_bring_himself.html; see also Jeff
Jacoby, "Bush's 'Folly' Is Ending in Victory," *Boston Globe*, March 25, 2009,
http://www.boston.com/bostonglobe/editorial_opinion/oped/articles/
2009/03/25/bushs_folly_is_ending_in_victory/; a declaration by right-wing
American bloggers that the war is over and the United States is victorious,
November 22, 2008, e.g., http://gatewaypundit.firstthings.com/
2008/11/happy-victory-in-iraq-day-november-22-2008/; and "Victory in
Iraq," *New York Sun*, July 18, 2008, http://www.nysun.com/editorials/
victory-in-iraq/82194/, all accessed February 4, 2010.

CHAPTER 8

1. Enseng Ho, *The Graves of Tarim: Genealogy and Mobility across the Indian Ocean*
(University of California Press, 2006).

2. Gallup survey, November 8–11, 2001, http://www.pollingreport.com/afghan.
htm, last accessed August 29, 2010.

3. Michael E. O'Hanlon, "A Flawed Masterpiece," *Foreign Affairs*, March/April 2002,
http://www.foreignaffairs.com/articles/58022/michael-e-ohanlon/
a-flawed-masterpiece, accessed August 25, 2010.

4. Peter Bergen, "The Battle for Tora Bora," *New Republic*, December 22, 2009, http://www.tnr.com/print/article/the-battle-tora-bora, accessed August 20, 2010. See also "Tora Bora Revisited: How We Failed to Get Bin Laden and Why It Matters Today," Report of the U.S. Senate Committee on Foreign Relations, November 30, 2009, http://foreign.senate.gov/imo/media/doc/Tora_Bora_Report.pdf, accessed August 23, 2010; and Mary Anne Weaver, "Lost at Tora Bora," *New York Times Magazine*, September 11, 2005, http://www.nytimes.com/2005/09/11/magazine/11TORABORA.html?_r=2& pagewanted=1, last accessed August 28, 2010.

5. Bruce Riedel, "Al Qaeda Strikes Back," *Foreign Affairs*, May/June 2007, http://www.foreignaffairs.com/articles/62608/bruce-riedel/al-qaeda-strikes-back, last accessed August 27, 2010.

6. David Rohde and David Sanger, "How a 'Good War' in Afghanistan Went Bad," *New York Times*, August 12, 2007, www.nytimes.com/2007/08/12/. . ./12afghan.html, last accessed September 1, 2010.

7. Adam Roberts, "Doctrine and Reality in Afghanistan," *Survival*, vol. 51, no. 1 (February–March 2009): 30.

8. Martin Ewans, *Afghanistan: A Short History of Its People and Politics* (Harper-Collins, 2002); Angelo Rasanayagam, *Afghanistan: A Modern History* (I. B. Tauris, 2005): esp. chap. 14.

9. Astri Suhrke, "Reconstruction as Modernisation: The 'Post-conflict' Project in Afghanistan," *Third World Quarterly*, vol. 28, no. 7 (2007): 1293.

10. Amy Belasco, "The Costs of Iraq, Afghanistan, and Other Global War on Terror Operations since 9/11" (Congressional Research Service, July 16, 2010), http://www.fas.org/sgp/crs/natsec/RL33110.pdf, accessed September 3, 2010.

11. James Dao, "Bush Sets Role for U.S. in Afghan Rebuilding," *New York Times*, April 18, 2002, http://www.nytimes.com/2002/04/18/international/18PREX.html, accessed October 11, 2010.

12. Ann Jones, "The Afghan Scam," TomDispatch.com, January 11, 2009, http://www.tomdispatch.com/post/175019/ann_jones_the_afghan_reconstruction_boondoggle, accessed August 12, 2010. Jones was an aid worker in Afghanistan from 2002 to 2006.

13. Ben Arnody, "Afghanistan War: USAID Spends Too Much, Too Fast, to Win Hearts and Minds," *Christian Science Monitor*, July 28, 2010, http://www.csmonitor.com/World/Asia-South-Central/2010/0728/Afghanistan-war-USAID-spends-too-much-too-fast-to-win-hearts-and-minds, accessed August 21, 2010.

14. See, for example, Mark R. Duffield, *Global Governance and the New Wars: The Merging of Development and Security* (Palgrave Macmillan, 2001); Fiona Terry, *Condemned to Repeat? The Paradox of Humanitarian Action* (Cornell University Press, 2002); and Nicholas J. Wheeler, *Saving Strangers: Humanitarian Intervention in International Society* (Oxford University Press, 2003).

15. The "liberal peace" is predicated on the theory of liberal internationalism, specifically that democratic and liberal values in human rights, self-determination, free markets, and so on, are a path to a democratic or liberal peace. These ideas were most compellingly argued by the American scholar Michael Doyle; see his articles, "Kant, Liberal Legacies, and Foreign Affairs," *Philosophy and Public Affairs*, vol. 12, no. 3 (1983): 205–35; Michael W. Doyle, "Kant, Liberal Legacies, and Foreign Affairs, part 2," *Philosophy and Public Affairs*, vol. 12, no. 4 (1983): 322–53; and "Liberalism and World Politics," *American Political Science Review*, vol. 80, no. 4 (December 1986): 1151–69.

16. Qayum Babak, "Taleban Justice 'Fairer' than State Courts," ARR Issue 369, August 17, 2010, http://iwpr.net/report-news/taleban-justice-%E2%80%9Cfairer%E2%80%9D-state-courts, accessed August 31, 2010.

17. Nicholas J. Wheeler, "Dying for 'Enduring Freedom': Accepting Responsibility for Civilian Casualties in the War against Terrorism," *International Security*, vol. 16 (2002): 211, 212.
18. State Department briefing, October 29, 2001, cited by Wheeler, ibid., 217.
19. "Status Update," *Harper's Magazine*, December 2010: 22–23.
20. "Afghan War Diaries, 2004–2010," http://wikileaks.org/wiki/Afghan_War_Diary,_2004–2010, last accessed September 7, 2010. The introduction to the data notes that "the reports cover most units from the US Army with the exception of most US Special Forces' activities. The reports do not generally cover top secret operations or European and other ISAF Forces operations."
21. UNAMA Human Rights, "Afghanistan Mid Year Report 2010: Protection of Civilians in Armed Conflict," (August 2010): 16.
22. "Afghan People Are 'Losing Confidence,'" BBC, February 9, 2009, http://news.bbc.co.uk/2/hi/south_asia/7872353.stm, accessed August 14, 2010. If anything, Afghan opinion worsened for the U.S. mission in 2010: see the Reuters report, Adrian Croft, "NATO Not Winning Hearts and Minds: Poll," July 17, 2010, http://www.reuters.com/article/idUSTRE66G0D820100717, accessed September 6, 2010.
23. Seth G. Jones, "The Rise of Afghanistan's Insurgency: State Failure and Jihad," *International Security*, vol. 32, no. 4 (Spring 2008): 7–40. The lack of security in many places, even when knowing a bombing was caused by the Taliban, would rebound against the U.S. military for being in places where civilians could be harmed. See Habiburrahman Ibrahimi, "Taleban Attacks Inflame Anti-Western Feeling," ARR Issue 364, June 17, 2010, http://iwpr.net/report-news/taleban-attacks-inflame-anti-western-feeling, last accessed September 2, 2010.
24. This also came from the Wikileaks documents. See, for example, Pratap Chatterjee, "Secret Killers: Covert Assassins Charged with Hunting Down and Killing Afghans," Tomdispatch.com, August 29, 2010, http://www.alternet.org/story/148012, accessed August 30, 2010.
25. Erica Gaston, "What's Missing from the Wikileak Afghanistan Logs," HuffingtonPost.com, July 26, 2010, http://www.huffingtonpost.com/erica-gaston/whats-missing-from-the-wi_b_660043.html, last accessed August 31, 2010.
26. The first speaker quoted was assistant secretary, Bureau of South Asian Affairs, Department of State, Christina B. Rocca, "Afghanistan: Democratization and Human Rights on the Eve of the Constitutional Loya Jirga," Joint Hearing before the Subcommittee on the Middle East and Central Asia and the Subcommittee on International Terrorism, Nonproliferation and Human rights of the Committee on International Relations House of Representatives, 108th Congress, First Session, November 19, 2003, 16. The second speaker was the subcommittee chairwoman, Ileana Ros-Lehtinen, 4. The third speaker was vice president of the National Endowment for Democracy, Barbara Haig (daughter of Alexander Haig), 38.
27. "The Bush Record," http://georgewbush-whitehouse.archives.gov/infocus/bushrecord/factsheets/freedomagenda.html, accessed September 6, 2010.
28. Sanam Naraghi Anderlini, *Women Building Peace: What They Do, Why It Matters* (Lynne Riener, 2007).
29. The women's rights agenda of the Bush war did engender a fairly lively debate, however, as critics of the war quickly saw this as a public relations gambit and several prominent women figures—Eleanor Smeal, Jane Smiley, and others—very publicly were thankful for what Bush was doing for Afghan women. See Jane Smiley, "Women's Crusadec," *New York Times Magazine*, December 2, 2001, http://www.nytimes.com/2001/12/02/magazine/02GAZE.html, accessed September 7, 2010; and a rejoinder by Laura Flanders, "Beyond the Burqa: The Rights Women Need in Afghanistan Are Basic Human Rights," December 12, 2001, www.workingforchange.com, last accessed September 7, 2010.

30. The CNN survey reflected ongoing sentiment from earlier in 2010. Other polling results tended to show similar levels of opposition, depending on how the question was asked. The second poll was a New York Times/CBS poll in which some answers were volunteered; the reconstruction effort was not directly asked about. Both polls are found at http://www.pollingreport.com/afghan.htm, accessed August 27, 2010.

31. Juan Cole, "Collapse of Kabul Bank Points to Fatal Corruption of Karzai Government," September 3, 2010, http://www.juancole.com/2010/09/collapse-of-kabul-bank-points-to-terminal-corruption-of-karzai-government.html, accessed September 4, 2010.

32. Aunohita Mojumdar, "Afghanistan-Women's Rights Movement Slowly Taking Shape in Kabul," Eurasianet.org, March 7, 2010, http://www.eurasianet.org/departments/civilsociety/articles/eav030810a.shtml, accessed September 6, 2010. A field study of women's rights in Afghanistan, especially the rural areas, showed in effect no improvement: Neamatollah Nojumi, Dyan E. Mazurana, and Elizabeth Stites, *After the Taliban: Life and Security in Rural Afghanistan* (Rowman and Littlefield, 2009), chap. 5.

33. "Corruption Perceptions Index, 2009," Transparency International, http://www.transparency.org/policy_research/surveys_indices/cpi/2009/cpi_2009_table, accessed September 8, 2–10.

CHAPTER 9

1. Charles Hanley, Sang-Hun Choe, and Martha Mendoza, *The Bridge at No Gun Ri: A Hidden Nightmare from the Korean War* (Henry Holt, 2002): 129.

2. Ibid., photocopies of the memos are reproduced between pages 110 and 111.

3. Sang Hun Choe and Charles J. Hanley, "Ex-GIs Tell AP of Korea Killings," *Washington Post*, September 30, 1999, http://www.washingtonpost.com/wp-srv/aponline/19990930/aponline065913_000.htm, accessed February 28, 2010.

4. Charles J. Hanley, "No Gun Ri: Official Narrative and Inconvenient Truths," *Critical Asian Studies* vol. 42, issue 4 (December 2010): 589–622. A study by a team of military officials in July–August 1950, in trying to discern why the North Koreans were able to advance so quickly, found reports of infiltrators "unconfirmed," and located the problem with large gaps in the U.S. lines.

5. Seth Ackerman, "Digging Too Deep at No Gun Ri," *FAIR*, September–October 2000, http://www.fair.org/index.php?page=1043, accessed February 19, 2010.

6. Joseph Galloway, "Doubts about a Korean Massacre," *US News and World Report*, May 14, 2000, http://www.usnews.com/usnews/culture/articles/000522/archive_016967.htm, accessed February 26, 2010; Michael Dobbs, who had used the fabricator, Edward Daily, far more extensively than the AP had in a *Washington Post Magazine* story in February 2000, was among the more prominent journalists ready to question the entire story once Daily was exposed. See "War and Remembrance: Truth and Other Casualties of No Gun Ri," *Washington Post*, May 21, 2000, B1.

7. Terence Smith, interview with Marvin Kalb, *News Hour with Jim Lehrer*, May 2000, http://www.pbs.org/newshour/media/nogunri/kalb.html, accessed March 1, 2010.

8. Department of the Army Inspector General, *No Gun Ri Review*, January 2001, Executive Summary: 15, http://www.army.mil/nogunri/BookCoverJan01Summary.pdf, accessed March 1, 2010.

9. Robert L. Bateman, *No Gun Ri* (Stackpole, 2002).

10. Emphasis added. See Judith Greer, "What Really Happened at No Gun Ri? An Army Major Says the Associated Press' Pulitzer-winning Story of American Soldiers Massacring Korean Civilians Is Grossly Exaggerated and Dishonest,"

Salon, June 3, 2002, http://dir.salon.com/story/books/feature/2002/06/03/nogunri/, accessed March 1, 2010. Note the subhead and how it frames the article.

11. Ibid., 98–99.
12. Dong-Choon Kim and Mark Selden, "South Korea's Embattled Truth and Reconciliation Commission," *Asia-Pacific Journal*, March 1, 2010, http://japanfocus.org/-Kim-Dong_choon/3313, accessed March 2, 2010.
13. Quoted by Michael Bilton and Kevin Sim, *Four Hours in My Lai* (Viking Penguin, 1992): 130.
14. Seymour Hersh, interviewed by Brooke Gladstone, *On the Media*, WNYC Radio, August 15, 2008, http://www.onthemedia.org/transcripts/2008/08/15/03, accessed March 5, 2010.
15. Seymour M. Hersh, "Lieutenant Accused of Murdering 109 Civilians," *St. Louis Post-Dispatch*, November 13, 1969, the first of three articles on the massacre, reproduced at http://www.pierretristam.com/Bobst/library/wf-200.htm, accessed March 6, 2010. Hersh's subsequent account of the cover-up can be found in his book, *My Lai 4: A Report on the Massacre and Its Aftermath* (Random House, 1970).
16. United States Department of the Army, *Report of the Department of the Army Review of the Preliminary Investigations into the My Lai Incident* (March 14, 1970): 12–1, 12–7.
17. Bilton and Sim: 305.
18. "Slaughter in Songmy," *New York Times*, November 26, 1969, quoted by Noam Chomsky, *At War with Asia* (AK Press, 2004): 225–26.
19. Louis Harris poll for the White House, April 1971, at "My Lai Courts-Martial," http://www.law.umkc.edu/faculty/projects/ftrials/mylai/Survey Results.html.
20. Charles L. P. Silet, ed., *Oliver Stone: Interviews* (University of Mississippi Press, 2001): 76. This interview, from *Playboy* in 1988, is interesting not least because the interviewer, journalist Marc Cooper, asks Stone, "The Vietnamese lost perhaps 2,000,000 of their people, but they are barely mentioned in *Platoon*. Do you think this sort of self-absorption is what gets us into places like Vietnam?" Stone recounts how difficult it was to get financing for the movie, which won the Best Picture Oscar in 1987, and notes in response to Cooper's questioning that Hollywood would never make a movie about the war from the Vietnamese point of view. Cooper, a freelance journalist at the time, has mainly been associated with the *Village Voice* and the *Nation*.
21. Kendrick Oliver, *The My Lai Massacre in American History and Memory* (Manchester University Press, 2006): 233.
22. Bilton and Sim, 158. They have a few other stories from survivors.
23. Tim Larimer, "Echoes of My Lai," *Time*, March 16, 1998, http://www.time.com/time/magazine/1998/int/980316/vietnam.html, accessed March 21, 2010.
24. Dana Millbank, "No Retreat, No Retraction, No Comment from Marines," *Washington Post*, June 8, 2006, http://www.washingtonpost.com/wp-dyn/content/article/2006/06/07/AR2006060701967.html, accessed March 24, 2010. Murtha was lamenting the stress that U.S. troops were under and that this was regrettable evidence of that stress, but he was vilified all the same.
25. "Frontline: Rules of Engagement," WGBH-TV, February 19, 2008, http://www.pbs.org/wgbh/pages/frontline/haditha/, last accessed on March 24, 2010.
26. Josh White, "Report on Haditha Condemns Marines," *Washington Post*, April 21, 2007, http://www.washingtonpost.com/wp-dyn/content/article/2007/04/20/AR2007042002308_pf.html, accessed March 24, 2010.

27. Pew poll, Peace Research Center for the People and the Press, June 20, 2006, http://people-press.org/report/278/iraq-views-improve-small-bounce-for-bush; another survey, an Associated Press poll, can be found in *USA Today*, June 9, 2006, http://www.usatoday.com/news/washington/2006-06-09-iraq-poll_x.htm, last accessed March 23, 2010.

28. Robert F. Worth, "Sergeant Tells of Plot to Kill Iraqi Detainees," *New York Times*, July 28, 2006, http://www.nytimes.com/2006/07/28/world/middleeast/28abuse.html?pagewanted=print, accessed March 23, 2010.

29. http://www.washingtonpost.com/wp-dyn/content/article/2008/03/28/AR2008032801923.html.

30. http://www.washingtonpost.com/wp-dyn/content/article/2006/06/10/AR2006061001129_pf.html.

31. Sarah Sewell, "Ethics on the Battlefield," SFGate.com, July 1, 2007, http://articles.sfgate.com/2007-07-01/opinion/17252759_1_ethical-civilians-marines/, accessed May 31, 2010.

32. As noted in the introduction, I was involved with the second survey the Hopkins researchers conducted, in effect commissioning the survey from funds in the Persian Gulf Initiative project I manage at the MIT Center for International Studies. I helped with the public education effort and, six months after the survey was commissioned, was able to raise additional money for the survey for the publicity effort.

33. The *Journal*'s contribution was "The *Lancet*'s Political Hit," an editorial that appeared on January 9, 2008. It drew from an error-filled and sensationalistic treatment of the Iraq Mortality Study in a Capitol Hill insider's weekly, *National Journal*. The *Wall Street Journal* and *National Journal* made much of the Open Society Institute's support, even though I had carefully explained that Soros and OSI had nothing to do with the commissioning of the study, the method, or the results. The principal article is Neil Munro and Carl Cannon, "Data Bomb," *National Journal*, January 4, 2008: 12–22, http://news.nationaljournal.com/articles/databomb/index.htm. For a rebuttal, see the letters from Roberts and Burnham, http://online.wsj.com/article/SB120027535200287505.html, as well as my detailed exposure of dozens of errors in their article at http://www.johntirman.com.

34. "Iraq Vets Recount Concerns over Rules of Engagement," PBS *News Hour*, May 21, 2008, http://www.pbs.org/newhour/bb/military/jan-jun08/witnesses_05–21.html, accessed March 23, 2010.

35. United States Department of the Army, *Report of the Army Review of the Preliminary Investigations into the My Lai Incident*, vol. 1: Chapter 9, page 8. Hereafter, Peers.

36. Bilton and Sim, 35.

37. Bernd Greiner, *War without Fronts: The USA in Vietnam* (Bodley Head, 2009): 105. See also Bilton and Sim, 38ff.

38. Oliver, 421.

39. Peers, vol. 1, Chapter 12, page 8.

40. Oliver, 246–47.

41. Angel Rabasa, Lesley Anne Warner, Peter Chalk, Ivan Khilko, and Paraag Shukla, *Money in the Bank: Lessons Learned from Past Counterinsurgency (COIN) Operations* (RAND Corporation, 2007). The study was prepared for the Office of the Secretary of Defense.

42. Edward N. Luttwak, "From Vietnam to Desert Fox: Civil-Military Relations in Modern Democracies," *Survival*, vol. 41, no. 1 (Spring 1999): 99–112.

43. Les Roberts, Riyadh Lafta, Richard Garfield, Jamal Khudhairi, and Gilbert Burnham, "Mortality before and after the 2003 invasion of Iraq: Cluster Sample

Survey," *Lancet*, published online, October 29, 2004, http://image.thelancet.
com/extras/04art10342web.pdf, last accessed March 19, 2010. Aerial bombardment was more prominent in the "formal" part of the war, the first six to seven
weeks, when very significant bombing occurred. Since then, aerial bombardment
would more likely mean artillery, helicopter gunships, and "close air support" of
ground operations. The primary cause of death as measured by the second
Hopkins survey was gunshot wounds.

44. Colin H. Kahl, "In the Crossfire or the Crosshairs? Norms, Civilian Casualties,
and U.S. Conduct in Iraq," *International Security*, vol. 32, no. 1 (Summer
2007): 7–46.

45. For a good case study of this, see Raffi Khatchadourian, "The Kill Company," *New
Yorker*, July 6 & 13, 2009, 41ff.

46. See his excellent dispatches, http://dahrjamailiraq.com/, and his collection,
Beyond the Green Zone: Dispatches from an Unembedded Journalist in Occupied Iraq
(Haymarket, 2008).

47. William Langewiesche, "Rules of Engagement," *Vanity Fair*, November 2006,
http://www.vanityfair.com/politics/features/2006/11/haditha200611, last
accessed November 1, 2009.

48. Khatchadourian; Aaron Glantz, ed., *Winter Soldier, Iraq and Afghanistan:
Eyewitness Accounts of the Occupations* (Haymarket, 2008).

49. Associated Press, "Accused Troops: We Were under Orders to kill," MSNBC, July
21, 2006, http://www.msnbc.msn.com/id/13974639/, accessed October 14,
2010. One reason for the news media's daftness on this is that the embeds rarely
saw the more troubling behavior. A soldier "explained one reason why establishment media reporting about the occupation in the U.S. has been largely sanitized.
'Anytime we had embedded reporters, our actions changed drastically,' he
explained. 'We did everything by the books, and were very low key.'" Dahr Jamail,
"Rules of Engagement 'Thrown Out the Window,'" Inter-Press Service, March 15,
2008, http://ipsnews.net/news.asp?idnews=41605, accessed October 14, 2010.

50. Frontline, interview with General James Conway, commandant of the marine
corps, http://www.pbs.org/wgbh/pages/frontline/haditha/themes/haditha.
html, last accessed March 30, 2010.

51. Mental Health Advisory Team, Operation Iraqi Freedom, *Final Report* (Office of
the Surgeon, Multinational Force-Iraq, and Office of the Surgeon General, U.S.
Army Medical Command, November 2006), http://www.armymedicine.army.
mil/reports/mhat/mhat_iv/MHAT_IV_Report_17NOV06.pdf, accessed March
30, 2010; quotation is from an editorial on the report, "Eroding Battlefield
Ethics," *New York Times*, May 28, 2007, http://www.nytimes.com/2007/05/28/
opinion/28iht-ediraq.1.5895623.html, accessed March 23, 2010.

52. Fort Benning, cited by Greiner, 100; large survey, cited by Oliver, 242.

53. Jamail.

CHAPTER 10

1. Ellen Knickmeyer, "Victims' Champion Is Killed in Iraq," *Washington Post*, April 18,
2005, http://www.washingtonpost.com/wp-dyn/articles/A61492-2005Apr17.
html, accessed April 2, 2010. A particularly moving tribute to her by journalist
Philip Robertson was published in *Salon*, http://www.salon.com/news/feature/
2005/04/18/marla/index.html. Her work continues in the NGO she founded,
Campaign for Innocent Victims in Conflict (CIVIC): www.civicworldwide.org.

2. Associated Press, "U.S. Military Tallies Deaths of Iraqi Civilians and Forces," *New
York Times*, October 15, 2010, A8. The numbers were actually for 2004 through
August 2008. No sources were provided; the announcement appeared without
fanfare on the Central Command Web site.

3. Personal communication, November 2006. The speaker had to remain anonymous.
4. David Wood, "Conflict in the Twentieth Century," *Adelphi Series*, vol. 8, no. 48 (1968): 27. ISS has since been renamed the International Institute for Strategic Studies.
5. The first Huntington citation, directly from Rummel, is found in the interesting discussion edited by Richard M. Pfeffer, *No More Vietnams? The War and Future of American Foreign Policy* (Harper & Row, 1968): 39. The second Huntington reference (Lewy), also unsourced, is from "Democracy Fights a Limited War: Korea, 1950–53," in Merrill D. Peterson and Leonard W. Levy, eds., *Major Crises in American History: Documentary Problems*, Vol. II (Harcourt, Brace, and World, 1962): 538. In both cases, Huntington claimed that two to three million Korean civilians were killed or died as a result of the war. Lewy, who sought to demonstrate that Korean mayhem was worse than Vietnam's, and therefore defended the latter as less objectionable, also cited David Rees, *Korea: The Limited War* (St. Martin's Press, 1964); Rees noted, "the total number of civilian Koreans dead has never been accurately calculated" (441).
6. Milton Leitenberg, "Deaths in Wars and Conflicts in the 20th Century," Cornell University Peace Studies Program, Occasional Paper #29 (3rd ed., 2006): 77.
7. COW Inter-State War Data, 1816–1997, http://www.correlatesofwar.org/, accessed last on April 9, 2010.
8. Leitenberg makes this point. For an explanation of the extant data sets, see Kristine Eck, "A Beginner's Guide to Conflict Data: Finding and Using the Right Dataset," UCDP Paper No. 1, Uppsala Conflict Data Project, December 2005, http://www.pcr.uu.se/publications/UCDP_pub/UCDP_paper1.pdf, accessed April 10, 2010.
9. Rummel's Web site and the relevant statistics are found at http://www.hawaii.edu/powerkills/MURDER.HTM.
10. See Matthew White's remarkable Web site, "Twentieth Century Atlas," for a compilation of figures of all wars of that century, http://users.erols.com/mwhite28/warstat2.htm.
11. http://www.hawaii.edu/powerkills/SOD.TAB6.1A.GIF.
12. Quoted in Guenther Lewy, *America in Vietnam* (Oxford University Press, 1978): 443. His calculations are contained in his Appendix I, 442–53.
13. Michael Clodfelter, *Vietnam in Military Statistics: A History of the Indochina Wars, 1772–1991* (MacFarland, 1995). For numbers cited on Vietnam, 257ff.; on Cambodia, 278.
14. This is the Ball and Leitenberg estimate. Robert S. McNamara, "The Post-Cold War World: Implications for Military Expenditure in Developing Countries," in *Proceedings of the World Bank Annual Conference on Development Economics* (World Bank, 1991): 95–126.
15. Mary Kaldor, *New and Old Wars: Organized Violence in a Global Era* (Stanford University Press, 1999). For a critical examination of Kaldor, see Stathis N. Kalyvas, "'New' and 'Old' Civil Wars: A Valid Distinction?" *World Politics*, vol. 54, no. 1 (October 2001): 99–118; and Mats Berdal. (2003). "How 'New' are 'New Wars'? Global Economic Change and the Study of Civil War," *Global Governance*, vol. 9, no. 4 (October–December 2003): 477–502. Part of this discourse has to do with processes of globalization and their contribution to civil wars. The attention to mass killing of civilians, however, was a feature of this discussion and was relatively new compared with war studies of earlier decades.
16. See, for example, Francis Deng, "The Guiding Principles on Internal Displacement and the Development of International Norms," and Kenneth W. Abbott, "Privately Generated Soft Law in International Governance: Comment on Francis M. Deng," in Thomas J. Biersteker, Peter J. Spiro, Chandra Lekha Sriram,

and Veronica I. Raffo, eds., *International Law and International Relations: Bridging Theory and Practice* (Routledge, 2006).

17. Nidzara Ahmetasevic, "Justice Report: Bosnia's Book of the Dead," Balkan Investigative Reporting Network, June 21, 2007, http://birn.eu.com/en/88/10/3377, accessed April 15, 2010, among other news reports. In the words of the RDC's major donor, the Norwegian foreign ministry, "In their laborious work, employees at the RDC have gone through 31,445 photos, registered 363 mass graves, listened through 8,000 statements, read 6,000 newspaper articles, and gathered 3,500 hours of video material. This material constitutes the evidence which they build their facts on. Further, they have mapped each individual's death cause, ethnicity, sex, if they were soldiers or civilians, place of living, place they were killed, etc. The profile of each individual victim is published in an electronic database, and information and statistics about the victims of the war can easily be found." Norwegian Embassy, Sarajevo, http://www.norveska.ba/ARKIV/Ongoing_Projects/6CFD9857_BDFA_402B_8CF2_45E9803E08B5/, accessed April 16, 2010. The International Criminal Tribunal for the Former Yugoslavia study can be found in Ewa Tabeau, and Jakub Bijak, "War-related Deaths in the 1992–1995 Armed Conflicts in Bosnia and Herzegovina: A Critique of Previous Estimates and Recent Results," *European Journal of Population*, vol. 21 (2005): 187–215.

18. Alberto Ascherio et al., "Effect of the Gulf War on Infant and Child Mortality in Iraq," *New England Journal of Medicine*, vol. 327, no. 13 (Special Issue, September 24, 1992): 931–36. It had a large number of clusters—247, with 25–30 households visited in each.

19. Charles Hirschman, Samuel Preston, and Vu Manh Loi, "Vietnamese Casualties during the American War: A New Estimate," *Population and Development Review*, vol. 21, no. 4 (December, 1995): 783–812.

20. For a very helpful primer on this subject, see Francesco Checchi and Les Roberts, *Interpreting and Using Mortality Data in Humanitarian Emergencies: A Primer for Non-epidemiologists*, Network Paper No. 52 (September 2005), published by the Humanitarian Practice Network at the Overseas Development Institute, London.

21. A review by Johns Hopkins University was undertaken in part because of the controversy the study stirred. Burnham was disciplined because the interview sheets used by the Iraqi surveyors contained some names of interviewees, which is not allowed according to the research protocol being used. He was suspended from the privilege of being the principal investigator on Hopkins research projects, which shows how seriously Hopkins investigated the survey. The review determined that nothing else was amiss in the conduct of the research, and that results had been available to other researchers since April 2007. See "Review Completed of 2006 Iraq Mortality Study," Johns Hopkins Bloomberg School of Public Health, Press Release, February 23, 2009, http://www.jhsph.edu/publichealthnews/press_releases/2009/iraq_review.html, accessed December 5, 2010.

22. See, for example, Christine Tapp et al (see note 36); "Mortality Estimates for Iraq," Report of an Ad Hoc Experts Group Meeting, World Health Organization, Geneva, May 10–11, 2007; and Heba Fatma Morayef, "The Politics and Limitations of Counting the Dead: A Review of Two Mortality Studies on Iraq," *Depaul Journal of Health Care Law*, vol. 11, issue 3 (Summer 2008): 413–429.

23. Iraq Family Health Survey Study Group, "Violence-related Mortality in Iraq from 2002 to 2006," *New England Journal of Medicine*, vol. 358 (2008): 484–93.

24. The questionnaire is available on the Web site of the World Health Organization, http://www.emro.who.int/iraq/pdf/ifhs_household_questionnaire.pdf, last accessed April 25, 2010.

25. One of the peculiarities of the *New England Journal of Medicine* article presentation is that death by injury is included in a table in the article, but death by violence is never defined, leading to the impression that death by auto accident, for example, might have been included. But the statistical index (cited below) is clear on causes, to the extent described herein, in which road accidents and the other categories discussed are "non-violent deaths."

26. "Supplementary Appendix," E-Table 3, online at http://content.nejm.org/cgi/data/NEJMsa0707782/DC1/1, accessed last on April 15, 2010. The questionnaire used is no longer available, but my own recall is that it was approximately eighty-five questions in length. As for the al Sadr connection, it is also worth quoting the appendix: "Each week, checked and completed clusters in the South/Centre were sent to the Federal Ministry of Health in Baghdad for further checking and editing."

27. Ziad Obermeyer, Christopher J. L. Murray, and Emmanuela Gakidou, "Fifty Years of Violent War Deaths from Vietnam to Bosnia: Analysis of Data from the World Health Survey Programme," 1482–486; published online June 19, 2008.

28. Richard Garfield, "Measuring Deaths from Conflicts," *British Medical Journal*, vol. 336 (2008) was an editorial in the same issue in which Obermeyer et al. appeared. Garfield was one of the researchers on the 2004 survey of Iraq mortality published in the *Lancet*.

29. Quoted in *Editor & Publisher* (September 16, 2006), www.editorandpublisher.com/eandp/news/article_display.jsp?vnu_content_id=1003122985, accessed October 4, 2006.

30. Pew Research Center, "Iraq News Coverage Drops Off in 2nd Quarter," August 2007, http://www.journalism.org/node/7071, accessed May 31, 2010.

31. Quoted by Charles Ferguson, *No End in Sight: Iraq's Descent into Chaos* (Public Affairs, 2008): 361. Colloquialisms in the spelling of Burke's speech were corrected.

32. Patrick Ball, Paul Kobrak, and Herbert F. Spirer, *State Violence in Guatemala, 1960–1996: A Quantitative Reflection* (American Association for the Advancement of Science, 2005), http://shr.aaas.org/guatemala/ciidh/qr/english/en_qr.pdf.

33. Jay Price and Qasim Zein, "As Violence Falls in Iraq, Cemetery Workers Feel the Pinch," McClathey News Service, October 16, 2007, http://www.mcclatchydc.com/2007/10/16/20530/as-violence-falls-in-iraq-cemetery.html, accessed May 5, 2010. Since the Najaf cemetery takes corpses from Iran, too, a doubling of their daily "intake" would indicate more than a doubling of excess mortality in Iraq. This would of course not include Sunnis and Kurds. Coffin makers were reported to have a similar spike in demand during the war.

34. Sahar Issa, interviewed by Paul Jay, TheRealNews.com, October 28, 2010, http://therealnews.com/t2/index.php?option=com_content&task=view&id=31&Itemid=74&jumival=5789, accessed December 6, 2010. She said that one million dead is plausible.

35. It is also used uncritically by a remarkable number of academics in the social sciences; see, for example, Peter Andreas and Kelly M. Greenhill, *Sex, Drugs, and Body Counts: The Politics of Numbers in Global Crime and Conflict* (Cornell University Press, 2010), especially the chapter by Greenhill and Lara Nettlefield.

36. Christine Tapp, Frederick M. Burkle, Jr., Kumanan Wilson, Tim Takaro, Gordon H. Guyatt, Hani Amad, and Edward J. Mills, "Iraq War Mortality Estimates: A Systematic Review," *Conflict and Health*, vol. 2, no. 1 (March 7, 2008): 9–10, http://www.conflictandhealth.com/content/pdf/1752-1505-2-1.pdf, last accessed on June 4, 2010. The group reviewed thirteen studies of mortality in Iraq; it is the single best review of the methods as well.

37. There is an increasing number of refugee accounts from the war in the public domain. Brian De Palma's film, *Redacted*, has on its DVD version a number of interviews with refugees in Jordan. See also Deborah Amos, *Eclipse of the Sunnis* (PublicAffairs, 2010), and her interview on NPR's *Fresh Air*, March 10, 2010, http://www.npr.org/templates/player/mediaPlayer.html?action=1&t=1&islist=false&id=124492426&m=124529968, accessed April 28, 2010. Assuming the displaced were traveling as family units of six, that means that about 600,000 or more families were in motion. If half of those lost a family member to violence, which interviews indicate is a plausible assumption, that would translate into 300,000 dead that might not be recorded by the household surveys due to survivor bias.

38. Timothy Williams, "Iraq's War Widows Face Dire Need with Little Aid," *New York Times*, February 22, 2009, http://www.nytimes.com/2009/02/23/world/middleeast/23widows.html?_r=1&scp=1&sq=iraq%20widows&st=cse, last accessed March 17, 2010.

39. Tom Nagorski, "Iraq: Where Things Stand," ABC News, March 19, 2007, http://abcnews.go.com/International/story?id=2962206&page=2, last accessed April 19, 2010. Among soldiers in U.S. wars, the ratio is often narrower—roughly 3:1 for both Korea and Vietnam. For civilians, the dynamics are different; they are not targeted directly as often as soldiers are, but, on the other hand, they do not receive the same rapid medical attention that American soldiers do.

40. A business polling firm in the U.K.—Opinion Business Research—conducted a large household survey that found 1.2 million dead as of September 2007; they revised it downward to 1,033,000 later. Generally, the sampling methods used were considered to be far less rigorous than the other household surveys. ORB Newsroom, http://www.opinion.co.uk/Newsroom_details.aspx?NewsId=120, last accessed April 19, 2010.

CHAPTER 11

1. These polls are collected on the very useful site, PollingReport.com, http://www.pollingreport.com/iraq.htm, last accessed May 6, 2010.

2. American Enterprise Institute, "Public Opinion on the War with Iraq," July 24, 2008, 126–27, http://www.aei.org/docLib/200701121_roody2.pdf, last accessed May 7, 2010.

3. Richard Perez-Pena, "The War Endures, but Where's the Media?" *New York Times*, March 24, 2008, C-1. The figures were from survey research done by the Pew Research Center. The decline in news coverage impacts the mortality counts that rely on such coverage for their data.

4. PollingReport.com, last accessed May 6, 2010.

5. Julian E. Barnes, "Gates Criticizes Leaks Group for War Video," *Los Angeles Times*, April 13, 2010, http://www.latimes.com/news/nationworld/nation/wire/sc-dc-gates-video14-20100413,0,4550653.story, last accessed May 10, 2010. The Wikileaks site for the 2007 video is http://www.collateralmurder.com/, which has other resources regarding the incident. The U.S. military called it "a threat to its operations"; see Norman Cohen and Brian Stelter, "Iraq Video Brings Notice to a Web Site," *New York Times*, April 7, 2010, http://www.nytimes.com/2010/04/07/world/07wikileaks.html, last accessed May 9, 2010.

6. See the clear and handy treatment by John M. MacKenzie, *Orientalism: History, Theory, and the Arts* (Manchester University Press, 1995);

7. Edward W. Said, *Orientalism* (Vintage, 1979): 278–79.

8. Ibid., 301.

9. Eric Weitz, "Racial Politics without the Concept of Race: Reevaluating Soviet Ethnic and National Purges," *Slavic Review*, vol. 61, no. 1 (Spring 2002): 1–29.
10. See the several polls listed at PollingReport.com: http://www.pollingreport.com/race.htm, accessed May 9, 2010.
11. Paul Alexander Kramer, *The Blood of Government: Race, Empire, the United States, and the Philippines* (University of North Carolina Press, 2006) 156.
12. Ibid., 3.
13. See the thoughtful essay by Tyrone Forman, "Color Blind Racism and Racial Indifference," in Maria Krysan and Amanda E. Lewis, eds., *The Changing Terrain of Race and Ethnicity* (Russell Sage Foundation, 2006): 50–52. He quotes the first analyst in that paragraph, Daniel Katz, "The Functional Approach to the Study of Attitudes," *Public Opinion Quarterly*, vol. 24, no. 2 (1960): 163–204; and the second observer, Thomas Pettigrew, "Prejudice," in Stephen Thernstrom, Ann Orlov, and Oscar Hanlin, eds., *Dimensions of Ethnicity: Prejudice* (Harvard University Press, 1980).
14. Kara Naomi Granzow, "Racism, Violence and the Politics of Societal Indifference in Edmonton, Alberta," doctoral dissertation (University of Alberta, 2010): 16.
15. *Gunfighter Nation: The Myth of the Frontier in Twentieth Century America* (University of Oklahoma Press, 1998): 13. Originally published by Atheneum Press, 1992.
16. William Ascher, "The Moralism of Attitudes Supporting Intergroup Violence," *Political Psychology*, vol. 7, no. 3 (September 1986): 403–25; James Shields and Leonard Weinberg, "Reactive Violence and the American Frontier: A Contemporary Evaluation," *Western Political Quarterly*, vol. 29, no. 1 (March 1976): 86–101.
17. Melvin J. Lerner, *The Belief in a Just World: A Fundamental Delusion* (Plenum Press, 1980): 20.
18. Ibid., 21.
19. Gilad Hirschberger, "Terror Management and Attributions of Blame to Innocent Victims: Reconciling Compassionate and Defensive Responses," *Journal of Personality and Social Psychology*, vol. 91, no. 5 (2006): 833.
20. This work is nicely summarized in Paul Slovic, "If I Look at the Mass I Will Never Act": Psychic Numbing and Genocide," *Judgment and Decision Making*, vol. 2, no. 2 (April 2007): 79–95, http://www.sas.upenn.edu/~baron/journal/7303a/jdm7303a.htm, last accessed May 22, 2010.
21. S. Mark Pancer, "Salience of Appeal and Avoidance of Helping Situations," *Canadian Journal of Behavioural Science*, vol. 20, no. 2 (1988): 130–37. A lengthy literature also describes how new information correcting erroneous beliefs tends not to change those beliefs, especially those that are embedded in political ideology, and indeed new, corrective information may actually lead to stronger attachment to the erroneous belief. This finding fits well with Just World Theory. See Brendan Nyhan and Jason Reifler, "When Corrections Fail: The Persistence of Political Misperceptions," *Political Behavior*, vol. 32, no. 2 (2010): 303–330.
22. On this, see the thoughtful essays by Julian Petley, "War without Death: Responses to Distant Suffering," *Journal for Crime, Conflict and the Media*, vol. 1, no. 1 (2003) 72–85; and Hugh Gusterson, "Nuclear War, the Gulf War and the Disappearing Body," *Journal of Urban and Cultural Studies*, vol. 2, no.1 (1991): 45–55.
23. Laurent Bègue and Carolyn L. Hafer, "Experimental Research on Just-World Theory: Problems, Developments, and Future Challenges," *Psychological Bulletin*, vol. 131, no. 1 (2005): 146.
24. Ronnie Janoff-Bulman, *Shattered Assumptions: Towards a New Psychology of Trauma* (Free Press, 1992): 152.
25. Barbara Reichle, Angela Schneider, and Leo Montada, "How Do Observers of Victimization Preserve Their Belief in a Just World Cognitively or Actionally?" in

Leo Montada and Melvin Lerner, eds., *Responses to Victimizations and Belief in a Just World* (Springer, 1998).

26. Christopher Hitchens, "The Lancet's Slant," *Salon*, October 26, 2006, http://www.slate.com/id/2151607/, last accessed April 21, 2010. Hitchens's most sober analysis of Iraq was rarely convincing, but for him to cheer high numbers of deaths because the "murderers" would have taken more lives is a category mistake of the most obvious and embarrassing kind; the "murderers" would not have been afoot had the United States not invaded as it had and subsequently failed to provide security, as international law requires.

27. Nir Rosen, "The Flight from Iraq," *New York Times Magazine*, May 13, 2007, http://www.nytimes.com/2007/05/13/magazine/13refugees-t.html?pagewanted=1&_r=1, last accessed May 12, 2010.

28. Nicholas Emler, "What Do Children Care about Injustice? The Influence of Culture and Cognitive Development," in Riël Vermunt and Herman Steensma, eds., *Social Justice in Human Relations, Volume 1: Societal and Psychological Origins of Justice* (Plenum Press, 1991): 145.

29. Janoff-Bulman, 30.

30. Felicia Pratto and Demis E. Glasford, "Ethnocentrism and the Value of a Human Life," *Journal of Personality and Social Psychology*, vol. 95, no. 6 (2008): 1418.

31. David I. Steinberg, ed., *Korean Attitudes toward the United States: Changing Dynamics* (M.E. Sharpe, 2005), is an excellent survey of the many issues in play.

32. See the series of surveys at www.worldopinion.org, especially "Negative Attitudes toward the United States in the Muslim World: Do They Matter?" May 17, 2007.

33. Office of the Director of National Intelligence, "Declassified Key Judgments of the National Intelligence Estimate. Trends in Global Terrorism: Implications for the United States," April 2006, http://www.dni.gov/press_releases/Declassified_NIE_Key_Judgments.pdf, accessed May 28, 2010. On the link to terrorism, see Marc Sageman, *Understanding Terror Networks* (Penn Press, 2004), among many other works.

34. Colin H. Kahl, "How We Fight," *Foreign Affairs*, vol. 85, no. 6 (November–December, 2006): 83–101.

INDEX

Bateman, Robert, 291–292
Bay of Pigs invasion, 135
Bergen, Peter, 270
Bellavia, David, 235, 237
Berlin crisis (1961), 136–137
Beveridge, Albert, 43
Bhutto, Benazir, 273
Bin Laden, Osama, 187, 212–213, 216, 220–221, 268–271, 281, 285, 353,
Bird, Kai, 136
Bigart, Homer, 116, 171
Bodo League, 96–98
Boone, Daniel, 21, 26
Bordieu, Pierre, 15
Bosnia war, 322–324, 330
"The Bosnian Book of the Dead," 323
Bolton, John, 358
Bradley, Omar, 85
Brown, Dee, 36
Bryan, William Jennings, 39, 46–47
Bulkeley, Peter, 22
Buckley, Kevin, 157
Buckley, William F., 76
Bundy, McGeorge, 124, 136–137, 139–140, 142
Burke, Gerald, 332
Burnham, Gilbert, 307, 327–329, 334
Burnham, James, 64, 75–76
Burns, Nicholas R., 272
Bush Doctrine, 222
Bush, George H.W., 198–200, 203, 207
Bush, George W., 11, 193, 212–213, 217–224, 226, 228–229, 241, 249, 256, 258–259, 265, 269–272, 274, 277, 282, 305, 308, 346

Calley, William
   Americans' opinion of, 299–300, 306, 342
   "Battle Hymn of Lt. Calley," 298
   role at My Lai, 155, 295
   trial of, 296–300
Casablanca conference (1943), 52
Cambodia, U.S. war in, 124, 147–150, 177, 183, 320–321, 341
Castro, Fidel, 135, 182
casualties, military, killed-in-action
   in Iraq, U.S. (Operation Iraqi Freedom), 255–256
   in Korea, 92
   in Vietnam, U.S., 171
   in Vietnam, Vietnamese, 167, 318–320
casualties, civilian, see mortality and specific wars
casualty aversion, 12, 123
Catholic Church, 51, 62, 93
CBS News, 146, 263, 340
Census Bureau, 38
Central Intelligence Agency (CIA), 93, 128–129, 131–132, 135, 139–140, 143, 146, 183–185, 326
Chamberlain, Neville, 51
Chandler, Melbourne C., 289
Chang, Jae-Soon, 96
Charlie Company, 295–297, 299, 302
Cheney, Dick, 203n, 220, 223, 226, 228, 257, 267, 270, 277
China
   as American "imaginary," 72
   Chinese Communist Party, 70–72

civil war in, 5, 70–71, 85, 92,
Christian missionaries in, 72
involvement in Korean War, 81, 85–86, 91, 114, 120
Japanese war occupation of, 52, 70
China Lobby, 77, 83, 88
Chomsky, Noam, 15, 171
Christensen, Thomas, 85
Church, Benjamin, 24, 26
civilians in wartime
   and American attitudes about, 18–19, 337–362
   and legal aspects of, 8–9, 310
   and news media's treatment of, 7, 90, 106, 115, 261–263, 278n, 291, 334n
   and U.S. policy towards, 8, 11, 52–56, 89, 99, 101–102, 103, 107, 154, 162, 164, 236, 242, 289, 309–315
   and wartime deaths of, see specific wars
Clark, Mark, 90, 100
Clodfelter, Michael, 321
contras, 183, 187–190
Conway-Lanz, Sahr, 99, 293
Correlates of War project, 319, 331
Churchill, Winston, 52, 70, 214
Civil War (American) 4, 17–18, 23, 31, 33, 35, 41, 92
Clinton administration, 207, 209
Clinton, Bill, 209n, 210
Cohen, William, 288
Cold War, 4, 67, 89, 110, 112, 127–128, 133, 190, 199, 217, 257n, 312, 349–351
   and Korean War, 59, 79, 82, 84, 86, 114, 117, 119–120, 122
   and Vietnam War, 137, 140, 180
Confederacy, Confederates, 32, 36
counterculture, 168, 170, 172, 177, 184
counterinsurgency, 18, 125, 135, 138–140, 143, 158, 160, 235, 241–242, 281, 284, 312, 314
Crockett, Davey, 21, 28, 28n, 168
Cuba, 39–42, 46–47, 129, 135–137, 168, 182, 187–188
Cumings, Bruce, 77–78, 94, 101, 119–120
Custer, George Armstrong, 21, 36

Daejeong prison, 96
Danner, Mark, 228
Davis, Peter, 161, 167
Dees, Martin, 62
Defense Department (Pentagon), 84, 89, 154, 179, 211, 228, 268, 288, 290, 298, 304, 319, 320, 343, 373n
democide, 318
Democratic Party, 175, 223
   and the Democratic National Convention (1968), 172
Democratic People's Republic of North Korea (DPRK). See North Korea
Deng, Francis, 323
Detroit Area Survey, 178n
Detroit Free Press, 178n
Diem, Ngo Dinh, 130–132, 136–140, 366
Dispatch News Service, 296
Doolittle, Jimmy, raids, 54, 73n
Dower, John, 54
Doyle, Laura, 20, 344

Dulles, John Foster, 76, 90, 110, 125–127, 130–131, 319
Dodge, Toby, 211

Eisenhower, Dwight D., 57, 59, 76, 82, 89–90, 125–132, 135–136, 147
Ellsberg, Daniel, 131n, 136
errand to the wilderness, 13, 22, 27, 45, 73, 181, 191, 268, 350
estimating war mortality
 for the Bosnia war, 323–324, 330
 using census records, 319, 324, 336
 controversies over, 313, 329, 335
 for Desert Storm, 201, 325,
 by guesswork, 318, 320, 322–323
 by household surveys, 10, 207–208, 243, 248, 263, 307, 325, 327, 330, 336
 for the Iraq War (2003–), 207, 248, 307–308, 320, 326
 for the Korean War, 92, 99, 117, 318–320
 by morgue reports, 263, 279, 333
 using news media reports, 331–332
 as ratio of displaced, 335
 as ratio of wounded, 321, 335
 for the Vietnam War, 167–168, 171, 318–321
 and U.S. military records, 317

Faisal, King of Iraq, 195
Fall, Bernard, 167
Fallujah, 14, 233–234, 237–239, 250–251, 304, 313–314
Faludi, Susan, 216
Faust, Drew Gilpin, 32
Filkins, Dexter, 331
Fire bombing
 Dresden, 53
 Hamburg, 52
 Tokyo, 54
Foos, Paul, 30
Formosa (Taiwan), Formosa Straits, 84–85
Forrestal, Michael, 139
Foucault, Michel, 15
Franklin, Benjamin, 25
Franks, Tommy, 227, 270, 316–317
Freedman, Lawrence, 135
Frontier myth, 19–49
 and China, 39, 120
 and indifference to war victims, 13–14, 20–21, 48, 344, 350–351, 361
 and Iraq, 266
 and Korea, 120, 122, 172
 and Vietnam, 168

Galbraith, J. K., 55
Garfield, Richard, 330
Gaston, Erica, 281
Gellman, Barton, 206, 210
Geneva Conventions, 8, 11
Ghani, Mohammad, 207
Gitlin, Todd, 177
Gorbachev, Mikhail, 190, 199
The Green Berets, 173
Gourevich, Philip, 305n
grant-making foundations, indifference to war, 225, 259, 383n–384n

Grenada, U.S. invasion of, 182
Grutzner, Charles, 115
Guatemala, 128, 183, 187
Guomindang, 70–72

Haditha massacre
 accounts of, 304
 American opinion about, 305–306
 investigation of, 303–306
 prosecutions of marines for, 306,
Hadrami, 269
Haitian earthquake, 7, 259, 356–357
Halberstam, David, 60, 87, 139, 171,
Halliday, Denis, 209
Hanley, Charles J., 96, 105–106, 288, 290
Hashim, Ahmed, 233
Hausman, James, 94–95, 98,
Hayden, Tom, 164
Hearts and Minds, 161, 167, 341,
Hekmatyar, Gulbuddin, 273n
Hersey, John, 88
heroes, heroism, 8, 21, 24, 30, 33, 36, 57, 119, 124, 133–134, 173, 181, 216–217, 253, 256, 359, 306, 342, 359
Hersh, Seymour, 155, 296
Hesselman, Eugene, 289
Hiro, Dilip, 201
Hiss, Alger, 63, 66n, 69, 72
Hitchens, Christopher, 358
Hitler, Adolf, 51–52, 56, 351
Ho Chi Minh, 125, 128, 131, 160, 164
Hodge, John, 84, 93–94
Hodgson, Godfrey, 174–175
Hoover, J. Edgar, 48, 61–62
House Un-American Activities Committee (HUAC), 62–64, 68–69
Huntington, Samuel, 159n, 319
Hussein, Saddam
 and 2003 invasion, 192,
 and Desert Storm, 200–202
 Reagan's support of, 184
 and terrorism, 212, 215, 221, 224,
 and WMD issue, 198, 205, 220, 222–224, 257, 337

Ignatius, David, 343
Indian Removal Act, 26
Indians (Native Americans), 17, 20, 22–25, 27, 35–37, 61, 350, 354, 360–361
indifference to war victims
 consequences of, 4, 362–365
 explanations for, 6, 12, 14, 19, 338, 342, 348–350, 356, 359, 361
 lack of cultural representations of victims as, 341, 357
 news media as indicator of, 12, 255, 305, 340
 and political discourse, 255, 302
 surveys of Americans showing, 305, 338–340
International Criminal Tribunal for Former Yugoslavia, 324
Iran-Iraq War, 197, 205, 335
Iran-*contra* scandal, 189–190
Iran, revolution in, 183–185, 197–198
Iraq
 European role in, 194–195, 214